The Pandemic Reader
Pedagogies of Social (In)justice in the Time of COVID-19

Edited by
Mako Fitts Ward, Arizona State University
Jennifer A. Sandlin, Arizona State University
Michelle McGibbney Vlahoulis, Arizona State University
Christine L. Holman, Arizona State University

D0760170

This book is part of the *Critical Pedagogies* Series
Series Editor: Shirley R. Steinberg

We dedicate this collection to the millions of lives lost to COVID-19 and to those fighting this virus on the front lines. We also dedicate this work to the lives lost at the hands of state-sanctioned racial violence and to the vanguard of social justice movements agitating for the protection of our civil liberties and the universal right to breathe.

ISBN 978-1-64504-118-4 (Paperback)
ISBN 978-1-64504-119-1 (Hardback)
ISBN 978-1-64504-120-7 (E-Book)

Library of Congress Control Number: 2020948522

Printed on acid-free paper

Table of Contents

Foreword:
From Pedagogies of Unrest to
Pedagogies of Commitment

by David Omotoso Stovall

The current moment of COVID-19 (SARS-CoV-2) has many of us in what feels to be a perpetual state of exhaustion. Given the calamity of millions infected, to the millions who have transitioned to the ancestral realm, very few of us are old enough to know what it is to live through a global health pandemic. What we do know, however, is that stress, anxiety, loneliness, helplessness, and continued precarity are magnified as state-sanctioned violence is waged on those who have historically had the least. Sometimes I feel as if there are no words left to say. I have to be honest with myself in stating that there is a lot going on. As strongmen dictators and imitators of dictators in democratic governments contest elections and punish their citizenry through poisoning, extradition, violent police suppression, and false distractions of fear, I write this to you from a country where many people wrongly thought that this could never happen on its shores. The world warned the U.S. government, but a country led by an overly tanned orange buffoon did not listen and leaned too mightily on the false notion of American exceptionalism. Where we are reminded of the sheer absurdity of the moment, it has also let us in on the secret that it has always been this way. The only difference is that many of us just decided to ignore it. The pandemic of COVID, however, in its sheer devastation and upending of the "comforts" of life under late-stage capitalism, disallows for such ignorance.

It is in these uncertain days that we must come to grips with the fact that we are in the midst of three pandemics. One is a relatively new health concern, while the others (White supremacy and capitalism) are the pre-existing conditions. Where COVID is considered new in the annals of history, the pandemics of White supremacy and capitalism are not. Their totalizing power has laid bare what Black, Indigenous, and other people of color have told the world for centuries: *White supremacy and capitalism cannot be wished away.* Ignoring the issue actually makes it worse. From disparities in housing, health care, food security, education, and employment, the world has come to grips with the fact that there are those who have historically been denied, isolated, and contained. Going "back to normal" is problematic because it was never good for many of us *before* COVID.

Despite the severity of the times, I am pleased that the same grouping of people has determined that the terms and conditions of the day are unacceptable. They have decided to break the racial contract between oppressor and oppressed, to the point that the world is witnessing the largest movement for racial justice in the history of the planet. Similar to their ancestors, women and young people remain at the forefront of this movement, alerting the world that late-stage capitalism is unsustainable. As the wealthy continue to hoard, poach, and pilfer from those who are suffering, the gap between the wealthy and poor widens to the point where fewer than 100 billionaires have more wealth than half of the planet. Given the staggering reality of the aforementioned point, the current iteration of justice movements embraces a group of people that have called for the abolition of the things that continue to kill and contain them. Their work has brought attention to the reality that the Black body is criminalized before it is considered human. Taking a page from Black radical feminist Saidiya Hartman, they are taking to the streets as the bodies of Black women are thought of as the naturalized site of gratuitous punishment. They are forcing the world to come to grips with what they know in their daily existence. For the rest of the world, there is nowhere to run. When we sit in this reality and come to grips with its intensity and depth, we have to make a decision: will we side with the oppressor or join in the struggle of the oppressed?

Thankfully, the chapters in this edited volume are intentional in their understanding of White supremacy as an international phenomenon that uses the same rules (White racial extremist terror against Black, Indigenous, and people of color in the name of White superiority, draconian policies, state-sanctioned violence at the hands of the police, xenophobic behavior towards immigrant populations, etc.) under a different set of conditions. They have also taken it upon themselves to identify late-stage capitalism as the pandemic that claims lives in the attempt to save itself. As the poor are exploited and alienated to the point of death as "essential workers," market-based solutions reveal their futility when no one is able to work. When schools enter the global marketplace, capitalism in the form of competition guarantees the winners and losers before the game is played. Again, none of this is sustainable.

At the same time, I am thankful for the editors taking a chance on me to offer some opening words. It's something I take seriously as I have become more used to being un-invited to participate. Like the nascent movements on the streets in cities throughout the globe, I understand the pages before you as a series of meditations that are intended to ignite your capacity to think, talk, and act. The essays remind us that in this moment of unrest, there is a small window to move on our freedom dreams. These words dare to alert us to the fact that reform has never been enough. Even though coming to grips with what we must do often feels like a herculean task, it becomes a lot simpler if we are willing to take the first steps. Struggle in this moment means we must claim our humanity and personhood in the face of extreme repression. The work ahead will be hard, but it remains necessary. Now is the time to call on the abolitionist hidden inside all of us as we join the struggle to eliminate all things that continue to dehumanize, isolate, and marginalize. In our commitment to build something better, we cannot be fearful of what White supremacy has in store for us. We are battle-tested. Our ancestors have prepared us for this. We must take this moment of reckoning to build permanent revolutions because this world cannot wait.

Chicago, Illinois
September 14, 2020

Preface

It was the first of April 2020 and we were weeks into the statewide stay-at-home order. Our university transitioned all in-person classes to remote instruction online. While this disruption in learning was triggered by a 'novel' coronavirus outbreak, there was nothing new about online instruction for us, as seasoned educators who value the intersection of technology and learning to democratize access to higher education. In the midst of this moment where university faculty around the world acclimated to new modes of student engagement, we were thinking ahead and preparing for what felt like the inevitable use of remote learning for our annual summer bridge program for incoming first-year college students. The program is an opportunity for students who have selected majors across our school to get the typical classroom experience and encounter ideas that travel across our transdisciplinary fields, including critical race studies, gender and sexuality studies, Black and African diaspora studies, and social justice studies. Jenny and Mako welcomed Chris and Michelle to our teaching cohort and in our first planning meeting, we discussed ways to transform the curriculum in the event we would have to teach online. As we reflected on how to hold the climate of the health pandemic, we realized that we had to center COVID-19 as a frame for students to register themes of class inequality, racial disparities, access to health systems, and the precarity of labor. Our conversation was generative and we quickly realized that our planning efforts were bigger than the curricular design of a summer program.

The idea for this collection of essays was inspired by our commitment, as educators, to use the (virtual) 'classroom' as a site of placemaking that responds to the immediacy of the moment. As education scholar Lenny Sánchez notes, the "placemaking framework," which locates "the process of creating and maintaining the places we inhabit," can be used to contemplate "how the academic parameters of classrooms and schools become contested sites for the construction of knowledge and identity"[1]. In the midst of teaching prep and securing a publisher for this volume, the George Floyd murder occurred, galvanizing thousands around the world to take to the streets in protest. This was the second high-profile police killing in the U.S. during the pandemic lockdown. Yet, public clamor and media attention to Floyd's death overshadowed the March 13, 2020 death of Breonna Taylor. As we were addressing the impacts of the health pandemic, the global reach of the Black Lives Matter (BLM) movement expanded. What was clear to us, as feminist educators, was the gender discrepancy in the attention to the killing of a Black male over that of a Black female and how the BLM's intersectional message was unduly activated and, unfortunately, promoted this conflict[2].

The Pandemic Reader is an offering of critical perspectives on the sweeping injustices intensified by COVID-19 and the resurgence of racialized state violence. It offers context, data, viewpoints, and solutions to collectively teach, learn, and thrive. It takes up the abolitionist teaching methodology which centers "vulnerability, healing, joy, and community" to amplify intersectional racial justice strategies across learning spaces[3]. This collection is a pedagogical intervention to locate how individuals and communities propel us forward through the multiple pandemics of 2020 and beyond.

---

1 Sánchez, L. (2011). Building on young children's cultural histories through placemaking in the classroom. Contemporary issue in early childhood, 12(4), p. 333. Retrieved from https://doi.org/10.2304/ciec.2011.12.4.332

2 https://www.brookings.edu/blog/how-we-rise/2020/09/25/breonna-taylor-police-brutality-and-the-importance-of-sayhername/

3 https://abolitionistteachingnetwork.org/guide

Acknowledgments

The editors would like to thank the contributors for offering urgent perspectives and responding to the political and socio-ecological crises precipitated by the COVID-19 pandemic. The editing process was a truly collaborative one that included a team of amazing graduate research assistants—Amber Acosta-Green, David Jonathon Jaulus, and Hannah Grabowski. We are grateful for their generative ideation in the early stages of the book process and assistance in identifying news sources, creating the teaching resources chapter, and indexing. We would also like to thank Jorge Lucero for capturing the spirit of this collection with his brilliant cover art, and Shirley Steinberg and Michel Lokhorst at DIO Press for believing in this project and helping shepherd it through to completion.

The editors would like to thank Nathan Martin for his leadership in undergraduate student engagement and for bringing us together to co-teach in the Early Start program. We are grateful for research development support from across Arizona State University, including the Social Science Division of The College of Liberal Arts and Sciences, and the School of Social Transformation and its Summer Fellows Program.

Introduction: Ecologies of Erasure, Crisis Politics, and Investments in Hope

by Mako Fitts Ward, Jennifer A. Sandlin, Michelle McGibbney Vlahoulis & Christine L. Holman

I'm exhausted. I can't breathe. What can I do? This is the sequence of responses that we find ourselves drawing on, repeating with every question of "How are you?" and every reaction to the news of COVID-19's grasp on our social world with increasing infection rates, deaths, and morally bankrupt responses by world leaders. As educators and thought leaders, we are navigating a rapidly changing socio-political landscape. The function of education systems is challenged by a breakdown in political and economic infrastructures due to crises in leadership and the diminishing capacity for human survival. As of August 18, 2020, the Centers for Disease Control and Prevention (CDC) reported that hospitalization rates in the U.S. for American Indians, African Americans, and Latinx communities are, on average, 4.8 times the rate ratios compared to Whites, and African Americans are twice as likely to die than Whites[1]. While this points to the salience of race and ethnicity as "risk factors for other underlying conditions" such as "socioeconomic status, access to health care,"[2] and increased occupational exposure as frontline and essential workers, these social facts have little impact on policy change as they exist within a zeitgeist where racialized rhetorics of patriotism and nationalism reflect an abiding, institutionally ingrained White supremacist cultural politic.

Avery Gordon uses haunting as a heuristic to emphasize how violent historical occurrences affect individual and communal trauma, offering us a way to comprehend the moment. She weaves social facts with historical fiction to accentuate the constructive nature of time and how what we perceive as 'the past,' and therefore gone or displaced, is actually quite present. "Ghostly matters" are manifestations of what must be rendered visible and framed within a contemporary context[3]. The project of mapping the evolutionary nature of COVID-19 runs alongside a similar mapping of its disparate impacts, which, not surprisingly, are traced along a congruent ghostly trajectory that haunts scholars of critical race, labor, gender, and sexuality studies.

COVID-19 is the official name designated by the World Health Organization (WHO) to classify the disease caused by SARS-CoV-2, the novel coronavirus that scientists believed originated in animals and spread to humans after an initial outbreak in December 2019 in Wuhan, China. This is one of seven known coronaviruses, respiratory tract infections that occur in a range of illnesses from the common cold to severe acute respiratory syndrome or SARS. Viruses are adaptive; they reproduce, morph, and evolve with every new infection. The novel coronavirus has also been the cause of four influenza pandemics over the last century in 1918 (H1N1 virus), 1957-58 (H2N2 virus), 1968 (H3N2 virus), and 2009 (H1N1pdm09 virus)[4]. Throughout January 2020, cases of a "mysterious pneumonia" were reported in Wuhan and, by virtue of rapid human travel, cases quickly spread worldwide[5]. The WHO declared COVID-19 a pandemic in March 2020, and as of September 14, 2020, they report almost 29 million confirmed infections and over 920,000 deaths[6].

A retrospective, or as Jean Baudrillard surmised, a necrospective (or a retrospective of death), of past pandemics reveals the lack of systemic engagement with addressing the social determinants of health, or "the conditions in which people are born, grow, live, work and age" that are "shaped by the distribution of money, power and resources at global, national and local levels"[7]. This includes socioeconomics, as well as limited access to healthcare, education, environment, housing stability, food, job security, and social support networks. The resulting economic downturn caused by COVID-19 requires government intervention to prevent, on the macro level, a collapse in the global economy and, on mezzo and micro levels, the devastating hardships on the world's most vulnerable individuals, communities, and localized systems of care. In 2014, U.S. federal agencies collaborated with the WHO, World Organisation for Animal Health (OIE), the Food and Agriculture Organization (FAO) of the United Nations, and 30 countries to establish the Global Health Security Agenda, preventative measures, and rapid responses to "biological threats of international concern"[8]. Health experts warned that without acknowledging the impacts of "poverty, inequality, and social determinants of health" on "the transmission of infectious diseases," local and global health systems responses will only further "unequal burdens of morbidity and mortality"[9]. Yet, the compounding politics of right-wing nationalism and anti-Black racism, evidenced in the wake of the racially-motivated police killings in the U.S. of George Floyd and Breonna Taylor and the social uprising that ensued, preserves the conditions to sustain these disparate impacts with little hope for structural change.

The Pandemic Reader invites readers to consider how the COVID-19 pandemic has radically altered every facet of social life. From education and communication to structures of government, health systems, social and recreational services, the justice system, and the global economy, educators were forced to consider new ways of teaching and learning in the midst of survival. Drawing on the public writing of scholars, journalists, health professionals, public intellectuals, and activists, the essays in this collection explore the transformations and consequences of pandemics, along with evidence-based responses, critical analysis, and sociohistorical framing, all necessary tools for situating the disparate impacts and contributing to public debates.

Part 1, "Grammars of Negation: Who Counts? Who is Erased?" begins with what Elise A. Mitchell calls American grammars of negation. This concept functions as a grounding principle for the book to guide readers toward an understanding of American (in)justice and the social forces that impede justice and the basic right to survive for BIPOC (Black, Indigenous and People of Color) lives. As Mitchell's essay suggests,

> The American grammar was designed to negate and alienate Black people. It was meant to kill us...So, our mourning and movements err to the extreme and bring excess to bear in plain sight—vacillating between loud and flamboyant and silent and modest, constantly contesting, taunting, and exceeding the American grammar. In the words of Audre Lorde, we "integrate death into living, neither ignoring it nor giving in to it" to chart a path through the dark at the crossroads of death"[10].

Part 2, "The Pandemic of Racism: Exposing the Racial Contract," offers perspectives that frame the racial and ethnic impact discrepancies as part of what George Lipsitz calls a "possessive investment in whiteness," or the assets leveraged consciously and unconsciously by White Americans by way of structural advantages, social networks of support, psychological entitlement, and the transfer of intergenerational wealth[11]. Part 3, "Investments in Coronavirus Capitalism," applies Naomi Klein's groundbreaking concept of disaster capitalism—"the ways in which crises have been systematically exploited over the last half-century to further a radical pro-corporate agenda"[12]—to consider how governments and markets respond to the pandemic.

Parts 4, "The Politics of Exposure and Protection," and 5, "The Politics of Space," explore the levels of precarity for essential workers with respect to conditions of labor, consumption, and habitation. Zuleyka Zevallos's essay describes the "moral panic" conditions that draw upon racial discourses of fear to render "poor people, migrants, refugees and Aboriginal people" as both vulnerable and deviant, which justify heightened surveillance as a legitimate pandemic response[13]. Part 6, "Ecologies of Justice," takes a holistic approach to understanding what J. T. Roane and Justin Hosbey describe as "the ecologies of living—the spaces that sustain and reproduce normative forms of biological and social existence" that engender "ongoing injury, gratuitous harm, and premature death"[14]. The "overlapping social, economic, and ecological vulnerabilities"[15] are examined in Part 6 through an intersectional lens to reimagine pandemic responses that acknowledge the multiple injuries of COVID-19, structural racism, anti-Blackness, and climate devastation.

Part 7, "Crises in Leadership: (Confronting) Nationalism and Populism," explores the politicization of COVID-19 through the competing responses by governments and the political elite. Francis Fukuyama's essay provides the baseline conditions for effective pandemic responses, which are "state capacity, social trust, and leadership,"[16] and in the absence of these, individuals and communities continue to suffer. Part 8, "Narratives of Resilience," offers strategies, on multiple levels, to endure personal isolation, familial chaos, structural breakdown, and social upheaval. As John Patrick Leary's essay reminds us, resilience discourse is a slippery slope and we have to remain vigilant in our desire to support individuals and communities while also recognizing and ultimately upending the chronic conditions that sustain social disparities and the unequal distribution of loss. In Part 9, the last section of the book, Amber Acosta-Green and David Jonathon Jaulus provide teaching tools and resources to adopt this collection of essays across teaching and learning spaces.

The world-systems response to COVID-19 conjures the universality of sufferation that haunts the collective consciousness, a reminder of the living legacies of structural oppression. *The Pandemic Reader* offers critical frames for understanding the dynamics of power at the root of societal responses to the virus and its impacts. It also offers unique perspectives on the human will to not only survive but to transform through possibilities for equitable social transformation. This is a moment where we must consider, as Paul Gilroy beautifully articulates, a "transcendental commitment to an alternative order" that remakes "the broken world we have inherited"[17].

Notes

1   https://www.cdc.gov/coronavirus/2019-ncov/covid-data/investigations-discovery/hospitalization-death-by-race-ethnicity.html
2   https://www.cdc.gov/coronavirus/2019-ncov/covid-data/investigations-discovery/hospitalization-death-by-race-ethnicity.html
3   Avery Gordon (2008). *Ghostly Matters: Haunting and the Sociological Imagination*. Minneapolis: University of Minnesota Press.
4   https://www.cdc.gov/flu/pandemic-resources/basics/past-pandemics.html
5   https://www.yalemedicine.org/stories/2019-novel-coronavirus/
6   Ibid.
7   https://www.who.int/social_determinants/sdh_definition/en/

8   https://www.ncbi.nlm.nih.gov/pmc/articles/PMC4170985/#B3
9   Ibid, 263.
10 Mitchell, Chapter 2, this volume
11 George Lipsitz (2006). *The Possessive Investment in Whiteness: How White People Profit from Identity Politics, Revised and Expanded Edition.* Philadelphia: Temple University Press.
12 https://theintercept.com/2017/01/24/get-ready-for-the-first-shocks-of-trumps-disaster-capitalism/
13 https://theintercept.com/2017/01/24/get-ready-for-the-first-shocks-of-trumps-disaster-capitalism/
14 https://crdh.rrchnm.org/essays/v02-05-mapping-black-ecologies/#fn:1
15 Ibid.
16 Francis Fukuyama, Chapter 45, this volume
17 Paul Gilroy (2005). Could You Be Loved? Bob Marley, Anti-Politics and Universal Sufferation. *Critical Quarterly, 47*(1-2), 18.

Part One

Grammars of Negation: Who Counts? Who is Erased?

1.1

'If Bitterness Were a Whetstone'—On Grief, History, and COVID-19

by Elise A. Mitchell

Originally published in *Black Perspectives*, APRIL 23, 2020

"Somedays, if bitterness were a whetstone, I could be sharp as grief."
— Audre Lorde, *The Cancer Journals*[1]

The COVID-19 numbers are grim. We have all seen the numbers. First, there were the number of cases, the number of tests versus the number of people who have tested positive, and the number of hospitalizations versus the declining number of hospital beds. Then came the projected death count—animated by its exponentiating curves[2], climactic peaks, and the prospective plunge. There was that skyrocketing graph of the sharp rise of unemployment[3], the inverse of the market crash. While these numbers circulated without faces or names, some began to see that a disproportionate number of the people those numbers represented were Black[4]. Though the United States fails to generate numbers with any integrity, the numbers we have reveal that Black people are dying of COVID-19 at a disproportionately high rate[5]. Were it not for social distancing, Black people would be mourning and marching[6]—resisting—the streets, as we have for some 500 years on behalf of our dead and for our survival[7].

The numeracy of COVID-19—the reductive quantification of Black life and death[8]—recalls the morbid mathematics of slavery and the slave trade[9]. From the earliest days of the slave trade, Europeans recognized that trafficking humans across the Atlantic posed a public health threat that could jeopardize their fledgling settlements[10]. When the first smallpox outbreak struck the Americas in the 1500s, Spanish friars in the Caribbean wrote back to Castile requesting enslaved Africans, warning that they would have to take precautions to ensure that the captive Africans did not foment outbreaks. For nearly 400 years thereafter, captive Africans struggled to survive both contagious diseases and Euro-American public health practices aboard slave ships and in the Americas. European and Euro-American medical interventions on slave ships and in the Americas were not for the benefit of the enslaved, rather they were designed to mitigate mortality[11] and compel enslaved women to reproduce[12] to maximize enslavers' wealth and profits.[13] The Western rationalism that engendered slavery-era ciphers to value, quantify,[14] and commodify[15] Black people (both living and dead) anticipated the formulae for modern medical triage that imperil Black people's lives under the guise of objective criteria[16]. This history is always with us.

COVID-19 is the latest chapter in the long and violent history of race and public health in the Americas[17]. The Center for Disease Control's COVID-19 mitigation strategies evade race and class in ways that conceal the boundaries of the "public" it purports to protect[18]. In the era of the slave trade, colonial officials and slave trading companies collaborated to develop sanitary protocols that would protect "public health" and ensure that "contagious diseases [were] not communicated to the residents"[19]. In this context, European definitions of the "public" and the "residents" were flexible and rarely explicit about who was included or excluded. Nonetheless, these public health policies consistently exploited enslaved and free people of African descent on the margins of the categories, sacrificing their lives first in pursuit of mitigation. This history repeated itself, with smallpox epidemics[20], yellow fever epidemics[21], the 1918 flu pandemic[22], the ongoing HIV/AIDS pandemic[23], and now, the COVID-19 pandemic.[24]

The American grammars of Black mortality conceived in the era of slavery also persist—"ditto"[25] became the "null value"[26], "negro" the reductive "black body", "Venus"[27] and "nigger" the "N.H.I." ("no humans involved")[28]—"refuse"[29] begot the unclaimed corpse in the morgue, a freezer truck[30], a vacant hospital room[31], or a "temporary mass internment"[32] cemetery[33]. This wholesale negation of Black life occurs on multiple registers every day; now, it is exponentiating at an unfathomable rate while we are kept apart. This American grammar was designed to negate and alienate Black people[34]. It was meant to kill us. It defines Blackness as a "scene of negation" and pervades all of American culture. So, our mourning and movements err to the extreme and bring excess to bear in plain sight—vacillating between loud and flamboyant and silent and modest, constantly contesting, taunting, and exceeding the American grammar. In the words of Audre Lorde, we "integrate death into living, neither ignoring it nor giving in to it"[35] to chart a path through the dark at the crossroads of death[36].

The American grammar will never guide us through the dark. Thus, the emerging mainstream digital funeral culture is insufficient for our spiritual, social, and political needs, which exceed and elide dominant Western notions of "closure"[37]. Video conferencing, with all of its potential for connection, has already been appropriated as a tool for surveillance, racism, and sexual harassment[38]. Moreover, it does not allow us to see and touch one another, to dance, eat, and drink with the dead. It does not create the soundscape of cries, laughter, screams, and booming or somber music. It does not yield space for passionate remarks and equally passionate interruptions, for strayed kin to show up late and lurk in the eves, for forgiveness, for kisses and hugs, for fistfights, for play, for the divine, or connection at the wake, the funeral, or the repass. The digital funeral culture we are fed to us does not allow us to walk our dead through the streets while calling out their names—performing both a litany and a liturgy for survival—demanding that we are seen and heard[39].

Black mourning has always been political[40]. Our mortuary practices, both public and private, fuse Vincent Brown's "mortuary politics"[41] and Christina Sharpe's "wake work"[42]. Writing about slavery, Brown explains, "People have derived profound social meaning from the beliefs and practices associated with death, and they have employed those meanings—charged with cosmic importance—in struggles towards particular ends. I call such activity *mortuary politics*, employing a capacious general definition of politics as concerted action toward specific goals." Historically, when colonial, imperial[43], or state officials permitted epidemics of disease and violence to besiege and alienate enslaved people, the enslaved "engaged the dead" to commemorate them, to avenge them, to galvanize their communities to political protest, revolt, and revolution; harness spiritual and ancestral power; affirm social ties; assert geopolitical claims; and "recover a sense of their common humanity." The dead continue to occupy the foreground in Black praxes of survival, healing, resistance, and prophetic discourses about redress. Thus, Sharpe ushers us to "the wake." She theorizes "the wake," in all its connotations, to understand "how slavery's violences emerge within the contemporary conditions of spatial, legal, psychic, material, and other dimensions of Black non/being as well as in Black modes of resistance." She offers "wake work" as a way to "attend to physical, social, and figurative death and also to the largeness that is Black life" in the face of pervasive precariousness—"to imagine new ways to live [...] in slavery's after-lives, to survive," and to "imagine otherwise from what we know now."

To survive and heal, our new methods of mourning will have to match our political needs. Perhaps a song played during a car caravan becomes recessional for the departed, and the caravan the demonstration for the survivors[44], and the prophetic procession towards the future we desire. Perhaps, the chalk drawings and graffiti become the prayer[45], the eulogy, the battle cry, the incantation, or the echo. Perhaps the strike becomes the speech to heed and moves the crowd to boycott in place of applause. Perhaps our doctors attend[46] to the people the state refuses[47]. Perhaps our digital tools require new uses, mediums, methods, and political ends to strengthen emerging coalitions and avoid obsolescence under the pressure of increased economic disparities, physical distance, and state and corporate surveillance[48]. Perhaps the end of the pandemic is yoked to incarceration's demise[49]. Perhaps mutual aid[50] is the pivot away from the cruelest capitalism and the prophetic pilot program for a world we can't imagine yet[51]. Perhaps the archive is what we make it when we convene[52] to create[53], curate[54], and circulate information about how the pandemic and state responses impact Black communities[55]. Perhaps, history repeats.

In the belly of a world that devours Black lives[56], Black people have rallied time[57] and again[58], to commemorate the dead, to heal one another, to seek reprieve and redress, to bend the world or die trying, or just survive in it[59]. History repeats. The work has already begun[60].

1.2

Coronavirus is Pushing People Into Poverty—But Temporary Basic Income Can Stop This

by Eduardo Ortiz-Juarez

Originally published in *The Conversation*, AUGUST 5, 2020

The rapid spread of COVID-19 across developing countries has led to a devastating loss of life and livelihood[61]. The pandemic is having immediate economic effects[62] and long-lasting consequences on development[63]. This is because developing economies are less able to handle shocks than advanced ones.

Around 80% of workers in developing countries are engaged in tasks that are unlikely to be performed from home,[64] meaning lockdowns are preventing them from working. And 70% of workers make a living in informal markets[65], with the majority not being covered by any form of social protection. COVID-19 containment measures are leaving a large number of people without any income.

Global poverty has fallen over the past three decades, but many of those lifted out of it have remained vulnerable. They sit just above the poverty line, but are ineligible for existing anti-poverty cash assistance. In a previous article[66], my co-authors and I argued that this could lead to an increase in global poverty for the first time since the 1990s, with tens of millions falling back below the poverty line. Such a situation, I believe, calls for drastic action.

Extraordinary Measures

In a recent working paper for the United Nations Development Programme[67], my co-author George Gray Molina and I argue that unconditional emergency assistance—what we call temporary basic income (TBI)—is an urgent, fair, and feasible way of stopping people falling into poverty or further impoverishment as a result of the pandemic.

Looking at pre-crisis data that covers 97% of the developing world's population, we've estimated what the cost would be of providing TBI to all people currently either below the poverty line or vulnerable to falling under it. This equates to 2.78 billion people across the world's 132 developing countries.

We investigated three ways of delivering TBI:

1. Top-ups on existing incomes among poor and near-poor people, up to a minimum level that is at least 70% above the poverty line in that region of the world.

2. Lump sum transfers equivalent to half the income enjoyed by the typical citizen.

3. Lump sum transfers that are uniform regardless of the country where people live. Under this system, the amount we simulated was US$5.50 (£4.30) a day per person, which is the typical level of the poverty line among upper middle-income countries.

Which option is best will depend on the situation. For instance, the first will only work in countries where registry systems have accurate information on what people earn. In countries where such systems are absent or weak, flat amounts according to general living standards (as in option two) or poverty lines (option three) might be better.

The total cost amounts to between US$200 billion and US$465 billion per month, depending on the policy choice. This is equivalent to between 0.27% and 0.63% of developing countries' combined monthly GDP.

It's a relatively moderate cost to cover such a profound shock and protect people from poverty. And providing TBI could have other positive effects as well: unconditional cash transfers can lead to people spending more money on their diet[68] and can potentially improve health outcomes[69] and school attendance[70]. They can also protect people's assets and allow them to diversify their livelihoods[71].

Will We Actually See This Happen?

TBI isn't a radical idea. Forms of basic income are being rolled out under different names and with different funding levels around the world. Tuvalu has a fully-fledged temporary universal basic income[72], and Spain has brought forward a minimum income scheme for low-earning households in response to the pandemic[73].

But our proposed scheme would be much larger—and would aim to reach as many excluded people as possible within the next six to 12 months. There are at least three obstacles to this.

The first one is administrative. Reaching eligible people who are currently invisible to official records and payment systems will require some work—they will need to be digitally registered before they can receive any assistance. Some people are beyond the traditional reach of the state because they lack formal documentation or live in informal settlements, which are more common in developing countries.

In these cases, alternative solutions—such as partnering with local social networks that have greater proximity to poor and vulnerable people[74]—may be needed to find everyone eligible. The cost of adding each new person is not insignificant, but pales in comparison to the direct and indirect benefits of providing those people with TBI.

The second obstacle is obvious: funding. Given the temporary nature of the challenge, funding TBI by additional taxation could be politically difficult. Other ways of covering the costs are instead worth exploring.

For example, funds could be raised by repurposing nonessential spending, including wasteful expenditures and energy subsidies (which usually tend to benefit the better off)[75]. Alternatively, debt repayments could be paused for a period. Developing countries are expected to make debt payments of US$3.1 trillion this year[76]. A comprehensive repayment freeze for 12 months, if possible, would fund 16 months of TBI under the top-up option, 12 months under option two and up to six months under option three. Also, as emergency cash transfers are often steered towards immediate essential consumption[77], part of the money will be recaptured by indirect taxation such as VAT and sales taxes, thus providing a degree of self-funding[78].

The third obstacle is trust. Governments will need to be trusted not to re-direct whatever they raise towards other purposes, nor to allow temporary mea-sures to last any longer than agreed. They will need broad (possibly cross-party) support to launch these schemes, and they will need to make sure that those that don't benefit from them still see the schemes as credible[79]. These are all political challenges that need to be addressed on a country-by-country basis.

TBI schemes are not expected to reverse country-wide economic down-turns, nor substitute for comprehensive social protection systems. They can, however, mitigate the worst immediate effects of a crisis that has been mag-nified by deep-rooted structural inequalities and injustices that haven't been decisively addressed in the past.

1.3

What the Coronavirus Proved About Homelessness

by Yasmeen Serhan

Originally published in *The Atlantic* JULY 18, 2020

Britain's efforts to house thousands of people amid the pandemic prove that even the most intractable problems are solvable—with enough political will.

When the coronavirus forced countries into lockdown and confined people to their homes, governments had to confront an urgent question: How do stay-at-home orders apply to those without a home?

For Britain, the answer was simple: "Bring everyone in"[80]. Within days of imposing its national lockdown on March 23[81], the British government told local authorities to shelter any person in need of accommodation. It was an extraordinary task—one requiring millions of pounds, not to mention the ef-forts of huge numbers of officials and charities. But it worked. Thousands of unhoused people were placed in vacant hotel rooms, student dormitories, and other forms of temporary housing[82]. A goal the government had given itself years to accomplish was achieved much more quickly[83].

For all the existing vulnerabilities the coronavirus has exposed within sup-ply chains[84], health-care systems[85], and the global economy[86], it has also re-vealed how easily seemingly intractable problems can be fixed—with enough political will. Although the coronavirus hasn't solved Britain's homelessness problem outright, it has proved what many within the housing and charity sectors have known to be true for years: that with enough funding and prioriti-zation, governments can bring people off the streets. The question is no longer whether or how Britain's homelessness crisis can be resolved, but whether the country's leaders will still be willing to expend the resources and political capi-tal necessary to do so once the pandemic has passed.

Britain isn't the only country that has utilized the sudden abundance of empty hotels to house its unsheltered population during the pandemic—Australia[87], France[88], and parts of the United States have done the same[89]—but it has arguably done so with the most success. In England alone, nearly 15,000 people[90], including more than 90 percent of "rough sleepers," as those who live on the streets are known, have been given some form of temporary accommo-dation in which to isolate during the pandemic[91]. (Issues related to housing and homelessness are the responsibility of regional governments; similar efforts were made in Northern Ireland[92], Scotland[93], and Wales[94].)

Unhoused people rarely have the luxury of separating themselves from others. Conventional services available to them prior to the pandemic, such as overnight shelters, are communal and cramped, making the prospects of self-isolation all but impossible. By providing them with their own rooms, Britain managed to avoid the kind of large-scale outbreaks[95] seen in unshel-tered populations[96] elsewhere[97]. According to the U.K.'s Office of National Statistics, at least 16 unhoused people have died of COVID-19 in England and Wales[98], a figure the charity Crisis said "could have been much worse" had au-thorities not intervened[99]. Though a majority of unhoused people in Britain are relatively young, they are more likely than the rest of the population to suffer from underlying medical conditions that put them at higher risk of illness.[100] People suffering from chronic homelessness have an average life expectancy decades shorter than that of the general population[101], and are more likely to be vulnerable to COVID-19 as well.

This "Everyone In" campaign has done more than simply put a roof over people's heads. For many, it also provided access to vital services, including immigration advisers and charity workers. Lucy Abraham, the CEO of the London-based charity Glass Door, told me that the assistance required is often as simple as opening a bank account or replacing a lost ID—steps that could help a person secure a job and, ultimately, a path off the streets. But such help can only go so far when those seeking it don't have a fixed place to call home. "It's much harder to help people when they're on the street," Louise Casey, the former head of the government's Rough Sleepers Unit, who has been leading Britain's efforts to house rough sleepers during the pandemic, told me. "If they've had three square meals a day and a decent night's sleep and they are feeling in a better place, you can say ... 'Let's get your bureaucracy sorted.'"

While Britain's success in shielding its unhoused population from the worst of the pandemic is to be lauded, it also raises a question: Why did it take a pandemic for this to happen? In the past decade, homelessness in the country has increased by 141 percent[102]—a crisis fueled by a nationwide housing shortage, rising rents, and local budget cuts spurred by years of austerity[103]. If more investment was the solution, what stopped the government from taking action sooner?

When I put this question to Suzanne Fitzpatrick, a professor of housing and social policy at Heriot-Watt University in Edinburgh, and an expert on global homelessness, she told me the "housing first" model—which rests on the notion that the best and most cost-effective way to solve chronic homelessness is to give people homes first, and then help them find their footing—is already widely accepted, having been used in other places, such as Finland, which last year all but eradicated rough sleeping in its capital, Helsinki[104]. "For the great majority of the homeless population, what they want and what they need is their own self-contained accommodation and ordinary neighborhoods with the support that they require to sustain that accommodation," Fitzpatrick said. "And that's what all the evidence of housing first tells us works best."

The "Everyone In" program has proved this as well. Lorraine Tabone, the founder of a community group called Lola's Homeless, which serves rough sleepers in the East London borough of Newham, told me that the pandemic presented a "golden opportunity" for unhoused people in her community, which has the highest rate of homelessness in the country[105]. When I first met Tabone in early February, dozens of the people she and her volunteers worked with could be found sleeping in an old shopping center. Since the lockdown was imposed, the shopping center has closed, and many of its former inhabitants have been moved into hotels[106]. Tabone said that of the more than 200 unhoused people in Newham who were sheltered through "Everyone In," a handful have moved on to other temporary accommodations. Some have even found jobs. "There are some good stories coming out of it," Tabone said. "It just shows how they can end homelessness overnight...With money, things can be done."

But solutions like the housing-first model aren't cheap, requiring the types of investment that the British government has only recently shown itself willing to spend. Finland, for example, spent about €300 million, or about $343 million, over a decade to create 3,500 new homes and hire 300 support workers[107]. In the long term, though, studies have shown that this type of spending results in savings, particularly when it comes to emergency health care, social services, and the criminal justice system. While the cost of ending homelessness is high, the cost of letting it continue it is significantly higher[108].

Though Britain's recent spending splurge offers a raft of emergency measures that address the issue[109], including a temporary ban on evictions[110] and an additional £105 million ($132 million) in funding to keep those who have been housed during the pandemic off the streets[111], it's unclear how long that kind of funding will last, or who will have access to it. One concern facing local authorities and charities right now is whether this money will be accessible to those who are ineligible for state benefits—a group that includes possibly thousands of undocumented migrants, European nationals who are not permanent residents, and people with pending immigration cases[112]. While the government's push to house people at the start of lockdown initially disregarded whether those being housed were eligible for public funds, charities such as Crisis and Glass Door have expressed concern that restrictions could apply to future funding[113].

Andrew Fraser, who chronicled his four years spent rough sleeping in a book called *Invisible*, told me that while the government's efforts have been life-changing for many people, they mean little if the threat of being put back on the streets remains. "The cruelest thing you can do to a homeless person is take them off the streets and tell them they're safe and then return them to it," he said. "That will push a lot of people over the edge."

When I asked Casey about whether future support would extend to those ineligible for public funds, she said there were no plans to restrict anyone from keeping their temporary accommodation during the pandemic, irrespective of immigration status. "We don't think we should be messing around with people's lives just because our own system of immigration or benefits doesn't accommodate that," she said, adding that no one wants to see a return to the status quo. "Everybody I talk to does not want to go back to mass rough sleeping in the U.K. … The responsibility for that lies not just with government, but with all the charities and local governments, to make sure we don't go back. And we don't have to. We've got enough money not to."

For now. But the homeless epidemic existed long before the viral one came around, and it will take more than a one-time influx of cash to solve it in the long term. Local authorities have warned that as many as half a million house-holds could be at risk of homelessness once the full economic impact of the coronavirus is realized[114]. When that challenge comes to pass, no one will be able to claim that it is an intractable problem that will take years to solve. The solution is already here.

1.4

Survivance Through Digital Storytelling: How Indigenous[115] Girls Used a Virtual Camp to Explore the COVID-19 Pandemic[116]

by Jessica A. Solyom, Sharon Henderson Singer, Kai Kline, Lydia McInnes, & Mary L. Smith[117]

Research on Indigenous girls in computer science and STEM, although informative and growing, has primarily focused on the American Indian and Alaska Native context. Less discussed in the literature are the experiences of Native Hawaiian girls in STEM. This oversight deserves immediate attention as Native Hawaiian girls are the least likely of many of their peers to complete a STEM degree. Of the total STEM degrees awarded for in the 2016-2017 school year, Pacific Islander girls earned 0.2% of them. Native Hawaiian students earned 0.3% of the total degrees awarded at the Associates level, 0.2% of total Bachelor's degrees, 0.2% of total Master's degrees, and 0.1% of PhDs (National Center for Education Statistics, 2019)[118].

Lack of access to supportive mentors and culturally responsive teaching as well as limited access to advanced computing courses have been reported as systemic reasons for low representation in STEM. In order to improve enrollment and achievement in the field, scholars have recommended incorporating a culturally relevant approach to science education[119,120]. The remainder of this chapter examines how the authors of this chapter designed a culturally responsive computing curriculum to explore computer science and STEM for Native Hawaiian girls during the spring 2020 COVID-19 epidemic.

While we originally proposed to introduce participants to computer science thinking through place-based learning that sought to explore environmental and community challenges, given the state of the world—with schools shut down, mandatory quarantines, and stay-at-home orders in some states as a result of the global COVID-19 pandemic, and the social unrest related to police brutality—we recognized the need to offer participants a virtual opportunity to share their own stories, and those of their community, of how they are managing to survive such tumultuous times while also ensuring their health and safety. Thus, we shifted from offering an in-person learning experience to a virtual one.

The camp's goal was to introduce prospective high school students (ages 13 to 17) to technology as a form of digital communication and storytelling. The curriculum was designed to introduce them to basic project management skills as well as collaborative work environments. Through discussions with Hawaiian kumus (respected teachers and scholars), participants engaged in discussions related to the goals of cultural, individual, and collective storytelling and focused on how technology can change, shape, or help to tell/share a story. Camp projects and activities explored diverse techniques, platforms, and approaches associated with storytelling, including digital storyboarding (through storyboard.com), mural (mural.com), and other platforms. Lastly, participants were challenged to create a final project that illustrated a community or individual story of survivance[121] during COVID-19. The program allowed girls from Oceania, including Hawai'i and Saipan, and Indigenous girls from tribal communities in the southwestern United States to engage in culturally responsive virtual discussions and activities that blended Indigenous knowledge systems with technology discussions and video creation. Students' final projects were designed to feature their understandings of community cultural storytelling as a way of passing down historical and cultural knowledge of events, and as acts of cultural survival in the face of community adversity. In addition to the activities, students were connected with informal mentors, Native Hawaiian cultural practitioners. With these mentors, they were able to "talk story" and learn about past large-scale events that affected their community. These mentors also shared how their communities survived and passed down tales of those events to future generations. We additionally challenged the girls to create videos of what survivance during the COVID-19 pandemic looks like for them, their families, and their communities. The resulting videos allowed us to discuss the importance of herstory in storytelling and the responsibility of sharing community narratives as Indigenous young women.

Why Was This Camp Created?

The COVID-19 pandemic is disproportionately affecting Black, Latino, and Indigenous communities. This pandemic has ushered in a rise of additional concerns related to health, education, and economic outcomes for BIPOC communities who already face challenges due to systemic inequities, historical trauma, and limited access to recovery resources. As COVID-19 began to spread rapidly in the spring, schools responded by closing their doors and quickly shifting from in-person instruction to remote learning. This shift was understandable, given the context, but accentuated existing inequities for BIPOC students, including access to technology and Wi-Fi, and satisfactory support for social, emotional, behavior, and physical health—including perceived self-efficacy in online environments. The pandemic has highlighted what many low-income and people of color already know: our communities are filled with mothers, fathers, aunts, uncles, and family who work in fields classified as 'essential.' This means family members are less likely to be available to assist their students in virtual and remote learning environments, which contributes to heightened education inequities.

Residents of rural and American Indian reservation areas face additional challenges in accessing resources necessary to prevent COVID-19, including limited access to nutritious food, water, and PPE supplies. It is important to note that about half of Native Americans live on reservations, mainly in the West, Midwest, and South. Of these citizens, many may live in small homes where the virus can easily spread through families. Moreover, some houses and communities lack electricity and running water, so washing hands and accessing online resources and information is more challenging. Another common concern for rural and urban-based Latinx and Indigenous peoples is food insecurity. Some communities exist within food deserts where fresh fruit and vegetables are unavailable, and nutrient-deficient junk food is cheap and abundant.

Thus, we expected our students to face a plethora of challenges during this time. Despite these challenges, participants in the camp expressed appreciation for receiving access to mentors who could help them learn, help them reflect on how the global pandemic changed their world, and offer insight into strategies for surviving during the pandemic while remaining connected to their community. Participants' final projects reflected their concerns for their community. For example, one student created a video that detailed how, despite COVID-19 limiting the ability of her immediate and extended family to gather together and engage in traditional meals, celebrations, and events, she and her family found ways to (re)purpose technology to connect via video chat and socially distanced practices. Others talked about new ways to express love and affection with ohana (family) that shifted from traditional practices involving physical closeness to other non-verbal and creative methods that allowed family members to feel close while ensuring health safety. Specifically, students documented shifting away from hugging, kissing on the cheeks, and giving "honi"—the pressing of noses and foreheads together, inhaling and exhaling at the same time (which symbolizes the exchange of "ha")—which could cause virus transmission. Instead, students recommended giving elbow bumps and blowing kisses. They felt that these techniques and other safety practices should be taught to ensure the safety of tutu (grandparents), keiki (children), elders, and those who may be more susceptible to the virus while maintaining the spirit of love and connectedness across space.

Notable Observations

The analysis of data related to this camp is not yet complete; however, a few notable observations have emerged. First, our observations suggest that the strategies of resilience the camp offered responded to some of the girls' educational concerns and provided strategies for them to manage the pandemic. The virtual camp allowed girls to navigate the persistence of precarity exacerbated by COVID-19 by allowing students to connect with fellow youth across large distances and share their stories, challenges, and accomplishments during this time with each other. Our curriculum provided activities designed to emphasize youths' personal asset-building, reflection of their computing experiences and intersecting identities, and connectedness with their peers and communities.

Few STEM programs have incorporated Indigenous Knowledge Systems (IKS)—including a focus on language, land, and culture—and Indigenous-specific research methodologies to establish an intersectional project. Thus, this culturally relevant Indigenous STEM curriculum for Native Hawaiian and Pacific Islander girls was innovative in its focus on blending discussions of technology and STEM with conversations about girls' survival during a global pandemic. While our initial goal was to expose girls to computer science principles, given the nature of the reason for having to cancel the in-person camp (COVID-19) and our knowledge that some youth in the program had limited access to technology and Wi-Fi, we shifted our focus to examining how technology can be used, (re)purposed, and executed to amplify the voices of girls of color as they shape their own (her)stories and futures through digital storytelling.

Of course, attendance was not perfect, and not all participants attended every session. We began with 11 participants and concluded with six girls who attended over 80% of the sessions. Reasons for attrition varied from family members contracting the virus, other family obligations, work responsibilities, and/or other academic responsibilities (e.g., needing to attend summer school). For some girls, the pressure to meet the financial responsibilities of supporting their family conflicted with the camp. We expected and understood this. When the number of participants dropped to just a handful some weeks, we persisted and took the opportunity to provide one on one mentorship and discussion opportunities to explore how participants were feeling and what was going on in their world. During these weeks, girls were encouraged to reflect on positive outcomes for the summer. Some spoke of learning a new skill or hobby. For instance, two participants bonded when one girl in the southwest US revealed she was learning to skateboard and another girl in Hawaii, a seasoned skateboarder, offered tips on how to do it. Another participant expressed how the camp allowed her to experiment with new digital video platforms as she "tested out" a storytelling format she had seen on YouTube and blended it with her own version of community cultural storytelling. Thus, the camp provided a needed reprieve for some participants while spurring them to innovate existing storytelling formats and introduced others to technical programs they had never used before.

Moving Forward

Programs that target BIPOC students can help increase the workforce and provide an essential benefit for women who get to explore and learn how to develop and share their voices, ideas, perceptions, experiences, and expertise in spaces they have been historically excluded from, including virtual and computer science spaces. One aspect that inspired participation in this virtual environment was the use of dyads. Pairing students to discuss daily questions related to the curriculum appeared to help remove their hesitation to use their individual voices and share their perspectives in a group setting. This allowed them to develop stronger interpersonal bonds in a virtual platform and allowed us to better capture the benefits of cohort learning. This became evident as participants began to engage in conversations beyond the day's curriculum and share tips from how to learn to skateboard to how to create graphics for a new video project.

This observation aligns with research that has found BIPOC students benefit from cohort experiences. Cohorts are believed to counter the sense of independence, individualism, and competitiveness that characterize Western classroom settings and may promote values that align with BIPOC communities, including generosity, sharing, harmony, and group-oriented learning environments[122,123]. Thus, we used the cohort model to help reduce feelings of isolation and lack of belonging by providing a group-based learning context that emphasizes mutual learning and support. We believe that were we not facing a global pandemic that directly affected some families and led to student attrition, this group-based learning approach would have increased the persistence of participants. We recommend considering a cohort approach and promoting group-based learning opportunities to inspire BIPOC girls in

STEM. Such approaches are not only supported by the scholarly literature as conducive to improving learning outcomes, but they also allow students to develop their leadership skills in a group setting and prepare them to work successfully in teams. Engaging in successful teamwork has been highlighted as a necessary skill in STEM and one that our participants excelled in.

In conclusion, we admit that educating is never an easy task, especially in our current social, political, and economic moment. However, if we are to emerge from this crisis stronger, we need to start recognizing and serving the needs of underrepresented students in STEM. Incorporating IKS into culturally responsive frameworks, as our program did, while promoting group-based and discussion-based learning, is an important first step. Further exploration and implementation of these techniques are needed to better understand and address the needs of underrepresented students. Continuing with culturally relevant curriculum development and empirical research into the implementation of these curriculums are additional measures that can be taken in the immediate to begin the necessary process of recognizing and better serving BIPOC students.

1.5

From Exotic To 'Dirty': How the Pandemic Has Re-Colonised Leicester

by Bal Sokhi-Bulley

Originally published in *Discover Society*, JULY 16, 2020

I have always known it as Melton Road. The street sign says Belgrave Road. And the brown and white tourist attraction sign says "Golden Mile". These street names feel metaphoric for how we see, or at least saw, Leicester. For some, like me, it was familiar, home; Melton Road was just where we went to eat out and window shop for jewelry and clothes. Melton Road is called the Golden Mile for the rows of jewelry shops that adorn it; many of these are owned by East African Asians who emigrated to the UK in the 1960s and 70s from Kenya and Uganda.

Set in the East Midlands, Leicester is the exotic heart of Britain, a "city of diversity" that sells the idea of Britain as an integrated, inclusive, multicultural society[124]. But in the last few weeks, the story has changed. Leicester was the first area in the United Kingdom to face a second, or local, lockdown on 29 June 2020 following a significant resurgence of COVID-19 (with a current daily incidence measurement of 16.3 per 100,000 population)[125]. Literal red lines were drawn around areas of the city—including all areas of Oadby and Wigston, parts of Blaby District and Charnwood—penning people in[126].

To say that it is the virus that has colonized the city, by drawing lines on a map as colonizers do, is too easy. It is more than that; this is about a government that has drawn lines around its national shame and produced dirt out of exoticism by neglecting its people. It is a re-colonizing of Leicester—where the combination of the virus and state mismanagement has produced a narrative that this is "the sweatshop of Europe," containing irresponsible BAME (Black, Asian, and minority ethnic) communities and tyrannical factory owners[127].

The double-sided colonial gaze, capable at once of defining attraction and revulsion, has reverted from exoticism to a representation of Leicester as "dirty," lacking reason, initiative, and even kindness. The pandemic has revealed the other side of the colonial gaze, which turns the exoticism of Black and brown British citizens into dirt. The anthropologist Mary Douglas[128] defines *dirt* as "matter out of place," as a sort of *disorder* of things (p. 36). Leicester was always out of place in White supremacist Britain; now, it is out of place as it represents mismanagement of disease.

"How can this have happened in Britain?," asks Anushka Astana on *The Guardian*'s "Today in Focus" podcast, where senior reporter Archie Bland describes this as one of "the most shocking" stories he's worked on[129]. The story goes that manufacturers in Leicester's garment factories have been recklessly flouting lockdown rules to keep up with the heavy demand for fast fashion and satisfy relentless online retailers like the now-infamous Boohoo. The conditions in which workers have had to work are alarming; they have been paid below the £8.72 per hour minimum wage (sometimes as low as £3.00 an hour); they have been forced to come to work even when diagnosed with COVID-19; they have been threatened with lack of pay for not showing up; they have been subjected to furlough fraud.

Who are "they"? These are women from African, Asian and minority ethnic communities. Media reports describe them as amongst the most vulnerable in our society; some not able to speak very good English, many coming from Leicester's Gujarati community (who incidentally received poor guidance on how to respond to the pandemic); some perhaps undocumented. Why is it so shocking? Because these people are effectively working in sweatshops; if this were, say, Bangladesh, you'd be less surprised. But this is Britain. We promote exoticism, not dirt; we respect our workers, we don't dispose of them.

I confess to it being hard to imagine the area of North Evington as the "garment district," as it is now being called. It was just "home." I went grocery shopping with my grandmother on the now infamous St. Saviour's Road, which was adjacent to the road I lived on. In the opposite direction to Kooners (the grocery store) was the Crown Hill's playground, where my granddad often took me. It is hard for me to separate the personal from the political here. But then, why should I? As a product of the labor of grandparents who worked in these very garment factories and in other industries of the city of Leicester, it is personal.

As Bennie Kara, author of *Diversity in Schools*, recently tweeted, it is hard to come to terms with the spreading of the inevitable logic of "brown people spread disease" that the government's penning in has produced[130]. As Claudia Webb MP for Leicester East has stated, there is a blaming of Black and ethnic minority communities here; hence her call to reject this blame and to focus instead on the racial and class inequalities that working class people, migrants, and minority ethnic communities suffer—which means they are already at greater risk of exposure to COVID-19 and suffering its worst effects[131].

How do we respond? First, with recognition that this is about the hostile environment; Leicester's lockdown reveals the disposability of certain lives—Black and brown lives that are having their labor exploited in the name of exoticism, only to be branded as dirt. This is evidence of what El-Enany[132] calls the "colonial theft" of labor and culture. To say that the focus on race is "cultural sensitivity" that has stopped the police from addressing the sweatshops in Britain's fast fashion industry, as Priti Patel did last weekend, is to distract from the hostile environment[133]. These same "cultural sensitivities" did not prevent institutional racism within the UK police, nor the cultural *neglect* that has created the conditions for the factories to thrive in the first place.

Many workers have the immigration status of No Recourse to Public Funds (NRPF); many are not eligible for statutory sick pay; they are employed by firms with no union recognition, and that lack health and safety provisions[134]. Moreover, the same hostile environment that makes Britain unwelcoming towards illegal immigrants extends this hostility to all those it deems do not belong (because, as in this case, they are diseased) and who are not desirable because they represent disease. As Ben Rogaly discusses in his recent blog, questions of space and place arise: "What does this place stand for? To whom does this place belong?"[135] It stood for diversity; it belonged to us. Now it stands for dirt; it belongs to the re-colonizers, who get to define us as dirty. The place is Fanon's[136] "crouching village, a town on its knees, a town wallowing in the *mire*" (p. 30).

The situation in Leicester raises huge human rights issues. Demands to enforce the minimum wage for all garment factory workers in Leicester, to work with trade unions to protect and promote labor rights and to strengthen the *Modern Slavery Act* to require due diligence on the part of large companies and fashion brands must be made. Yet this, and the urge to create and promote *more* rights and protections cannot be all.

Now more than ever we need to pursue the radical potential of "friendship" as a way of life; a mode of life that creates culture, to respond to disposability with recognition and that sees the imperative "take care of yourself," so often cited in our personal responses to COVID-19, as taking care of the other from whom we are estranged[137]. "The bigger question", says Anushka Astana in *The Guardian* podcast, "is about society." It is about the way in which we consume goods. I add to it is also about how we treat the Black and brown estranged other of British society—not with abandonment and caging in, but with generosity, kindness, and right treatment. Something more akin to "love"—a doing, as bell hooks[138] terms it, rather than a feeling. We need to become friends; not in the sense of companions or buddies but in a sense where we respect the ways in which we are estranged and the ways in which the behavior of the other may have betrayed us (by going to work, by not "staying at home and saving lives").

This is the potential of radical friendship; to offer a critique of the hostile environment and indeed of the distraction that rights discourse itself presents as a response to it[139]. Radical friendship requires a coming together. At the intersection of St. Savior's Road is East Park Road, where (turning right) you come to Milan's—the vegetarian sweet shop that almost every visit back home entails a stop at. "Milan" means union, or meeting, in Hindi. How do we respond? We must meet, or come together, or unite against "blaming" our Black, Asian and minority ethnic communities who have been made "dirty" by a hostile environment. As Rogaly[140] has suggested, nothing frightens them more than unity.

1.6

The Myth of Black Immunity: Racialized Disease During the COVID-19 Pandemic

by Chelsey Carter & Ezelle Sanford, III

Originally published in *Black Perspectives*, APRIL 3, 2020

As the novel coronavirus 2019 (COVID-19) pandemic sweeps across the world, troubling associations between race and disease have gone viral. On social media, theories of Black people's immunity to the novel coronavirus spread rapidly and widely, with the initially small number of cases in Africa often cited as evidence[141]. Since then, the virus has spread to the continent and will surely exacerbate already compromised health systems. The virus was also erroneously labelled as the "Kung Fu Flu" and the "China Virus," among other epithets, by members of the United States Presidential administration—including the President himself[142]. While these labels may have the air of jest, White supremacists have sought to use the novel coronavirus for bioterrorism, targeting racial minorities specifically[143]. Claims of immunity falsely suggest that Black people across the entire Diaspora cannot contract the disease. Meanwhile, labels that construct the disease as Chinese obscure the vital pathways the contagion has taken irrespective of racial categories. These claims are more than just racist and xenophobic—they are dangerous to *everyone's* health.

It is times like these, amid existential fear and anxiety, where we must be most attuned to the ways in which race is deployed, to the historical origins from which these ideas emerge, and to how these ideas undergird social fear and political inaction. Race has no biological basis. Rather, it is historically, politically, culturally, and affectively produced not only by systems and structures, but by moments, just like the one we are presently in. The embedded effects of oppression, marginalization, and racism have very real biological consequences. We must consistently ask ourselves: (1) What does the racialization of disease reveal and what does it occlude? (2) What meanings do we attach to a condition and create in these processes of racialization? (3) How do these meanings impact people's day-to-day lives both now and in the future?

COVID-19 is an infectious disease caused by the novel coronavirus, SARS-CoV-2. The disease causes respiratory illness (like influenza) with symptoms such as cough, fever, and in more severe cases, difficulty breathing. This virus disproportionately impacts the elderly and people with "preexisting conditions." We know that 50 to 129 million non-elderly Americans have such conditions[144]. This figure increases substantially when you consider individuals over the age of 55. Black, brown, and Indigenous communities bear a disparate burden of these conditions. We *know* that COVID-19 will disproportionately impact communities of color[145]. The racialized experience of COVID-19 will be further exacerbated at the intersections of class, gender, and age.

These racialized associations, new and old, have historical roots and have been the subjects of scholarly critical analysis for decades. Claims of "Black immunity" and the "Chinese" or "Wuhan" virus, are not wholly distinct. Rather, they are two sides of the same coin. These claims have erased the suffering of marginalized people and continue to do so. As these individuals succumb to disease, they are inevitably blamed, if not entirely feared and demonized as vectors of disease. These pervasive ideas of racialized disease are dangerous for our health.

Assertions of Black immunity to COVID-19 represent the persistent afterlife of slavery and the pervasive power of white supremacist thought[146]. As historian Rana Hogarth argues, these theories emerged in the era of enslavement, as the system itself made such observations of racial difference possible in the Atlantic world. According to Hogarth, "Slavery apologists would, of course, eventually use this claim to suggest that Black people's peculiarities were a sign of their fitness for servitude"[147]. While a pandemic of this size and scope is unprecedented in our generation, the world bore witness to major outbreaks of the past. Black immunity theories emerged, perhaps most prominently, in Philadelphia in the late eighteenth century in the face of successive Yellow Fever outbreaks. Prominent Declaration of Independence signatory and abolitionist, Dr. Benjamin Rush, ardently believed that African Americans were immune to the disease as a result of their purportedly acclimatized bodies. In Philadelphia, Rush worked with African Methodist Episcopal ministers Absalom Jones and Richard Allen to recruit the city's free Black community to care for dying white citizens. When African Americans themselves succumbed to disease, their suffering was ultimately erased, unexplained by immunity.

Even today medical students are taught to quickly associate disease with racial and ethnic identity. Sickle cell anemia is associated with African Americans, cystic fibrosis with European descendants, and Tay-Sachs disease with Ashkenazi Jews[148]. While these shorthand associations facilitate consultation speed and efficiency, they are dangerous and sometimes fatal. A classic case of the consequences of associating race and disease has been shared widely by legal scholar and critical race theorist, Dorothy Roberts[149]. Roberts recounts a *Pediatrics* journal article on the misuses of racialized diagnosis when a young Black girl repeatedly returned to the emergency room for pneumonia or respiratory concerns over a six-year period[150]. At a subsequent ER visit, the eight-year-old's X-rays were examined by a radiologist, who exclaimed, "Who's the kid with cystic fibrosis?" Her medical records illuminate a narrative of racialized assumptions that rendered her invisible to the myriad clinicians who treated her over the years—because of her skin color. Instead of getting a treatment-targeting diagnosis, she went untreated for years.

Diseases without clear etiologies—like ALS, which has been dubbed a "White" disease[151]—often accrue false, racialized narratives as well. Scholars have discovered that Western medicine's beliefs that particular races cannot contract certain diseases does not just impact patient diagnosis or misdiagnosis but impacts the entire care system. While some scientists and physicians rely heavily on associations between race and disease, less attention is devoted to serious analysis of the social determinants of health, i.e., the structural forces that often lead to disparate disease burden in racial minorities. A preliminary paper by a group of epidemiologists in Wuhan, China drew on myths about minority immunity based on blood type, claiming, "#COVID19 deaths likely higher in Europe but less so in Asia/India (more B) or Latin Americans (more O)"[152]. Yet, who was the first person to die of COVID-19 in Brazil? A Black female domestic worker[153]. The first person to die of COVID-19 in St. Louis, Missouri, a hyper-segregated city and home of "Ferguson," was an older Black woman who worked as a nurse[154]. Beyond social media arguments, we have not attended to the real reasons that Black people are showing up around the globe with lower rates of COVID-19.

Those that are the most invisible, most marginalized, and who lead the most precarious lives will be the ones most affected by COVID-19. They certainly are not always the first individuals diagnosed, but they are usually the first to die[155]. COVID-19 spread globally for two chief reasons: (1) a particularly high R0, the "reproduction number" indicating how contagious an infectious disease is, and (2) individuals who had access to resources which allowed them to travel. Thus, in locations like St. Louis, the first case of COVID-19 emerged in a White-majority county suburb—a White student was infected in Italy before returning to St. Louis[156]. Early on, it was easy to "joke" that the virus was a "White disease." And then a Black woman succumbed first. In Brazil, most people cannot get a COVID-19 test, leaving those without money or sick-time undiagnosed and ultimately invisible to public health workers.

When we consider the afterlife of slavery[157], ongoing medical racism[158], global histories of medical mutilation and experimentation, and Black invisibility within White supremacist medical systems—asking why Black people would joke about our own susceptibility is warranted. Theories of Black immunity sound like the perfect reward for generations of racialized violence, amid a dystopian global nightmare. The reality is, regardless of diagnosis, we are particularly susceptible and arguably among the most vulnerable.

As we attempt to identify who COVID-19 most severely impacts, we must resist the rapid, yet uncritical definition of certain risk populations. Currently the disease is propagandized as a "Chinese" virus. Elderly populations are considered the most vulnerable. And yet, there is powerful anecdotal evidence that such conclusions are flawed: take the example of Dez-Ann Romain, a 38-year-old New York City School principal who succumbed to the disease[159], or Judy

Wilson-Griffin, a Black nurse beloved by coworkers and family members who became St. Louis's first COVID-19-related death[160].

In an effort to find control in chaos, racialized claims like Black immunity ultimately represent a scrambling for power and a desire to make sense of uncertainty. We deploy these ideas that ultimately play into our own oppression *and* the oppression of others, however. Although the history of race and the cultural innovations created in response to oppression do give communities of color resilience in the time of great anxiety, racialized rhetoric about diseases can be dangerous for your health[161]. This language is as dangerous when Black people co-opt it. COVID-19 has no demonstrated biological association with any racial or ethnic group—viruses do not discriminate. Popular Black British actor, Idris Elba, himself impacted by COVID-19, responded directly to the "conspiracy theory" of Black immunity[162]. In fact, the virus has the ability to infect us all and will inevitably indirectly touch each and every human life in the world. Its most severe impact will be on those who are most socially vulnerable—the incarcerated, the unemployed, the unhoused, the uninsured—groups in which Black and brown individuals are disproportionally represented. Racializing disease on those grounds alone has no impact other than to promulgate dangerous assumptions. Seemingly banal claims of "Black immunity" may bring some semblance of humorous communal bonding, but they are not funny. These claims are not Black people's invention—instead they are White people's invention, driven by White supremacy, and they ultimately leave us biologically disadvantaged. We must uproot the myth of Black immunity and the related myth labeling the virus as a Chinese pathogen. The stakes are entirely too high!

1.7

On the Minds of Black Lives Matter Protesters: A Racist Health System

by Akilah Johnson

Originally published in *ProPublica*, JUNE 5, 2020

Black lives are being lost to COVID-19 at twice the rate of others. For protesters we talked to, that's one more reason to be on the street. "If it's not police beating us up, it's us dying in a hospital from the pandemic," one said.

On Tuesday, when he decided to protest, William Smith, 27, used a red marker to write a message on the back of a flattened cardboard box: "Kill Racism, Not Me."

As he stood alone, somber, he thought about George Floyd, a fellow Black man whom he'd watched die on video as a Minneapolis cop kneeled on his neck eight days earlier. "Seeing the life leave his body was finally the last straw that broke the camel's back for me," he said.

But he also thought about people he knew, a handful of them, who died after catching the new coronavirus. "They were living in impoverished areas. Couldn't get proper treatment. Lived in crowded conditions, so social distancing was hard to do. And they were still forced to go to work and be put in harm's way."

When speaking out against the loss of Black lives, it is tough to separate those who die at the hands of police from those who die in a pandemic that has laid bare the structural racism baked into the American health system. Floyd himself had tested positive for the coronavirus. Eighteen Black protesters interviewed by *ProPublica* were well aware that Black lives were being lost to the virus at more than twice the rate of others, and that societal barriers have compounded for generations to put them at higher risk[163].

It was fueling their desire to protest and their anxiety about joining the crowd. But they flocked to the White House on Tuesday afternoon, one day after peaceful protesters there were tear-gassed so that President Donald Trump could hold up a bible for a photo op at St. John's Episcopal Church. There were tanks on the streets, along with a battalion of federal agents, military troops and police. Many of the protesters said they were willing to sacrifice their bodies, either to violence or the virus, to be heard.

In front of the White House stood Caleb Jordan, who turns 21 on Saturday. He showed up with an overstuffed backpack to make sure his 62-year-old grandmother, Carolyn Jackson, had enough water to drink and a hoodie to protect her arms in case of violence. "I don't know what I would do if anything happened to her," he said. Some people had on masks. Some did not. Some pulled their masks down to talk or breathe. "I'm not comfortable with that," he said. She's got a chronic lung condition, and he had been so worried about her catching the coronavirus in the past few months that he wouldn't hug her. But then she mentioned that she drove by the protests on Sunday, and immediately he asked, "Why didn't you take me?"

He had been losing sleep over what he was seeing in social media and on TV, having nightmares in which he was fighting a "real-Jim-Crow-looking White guy in a white button-down shirt, black tie, sleeves rolled up." His mom told him he was fighting racism. "It's like obstacle after obstacle," he said. "If it's not police beating us up, it's us dying in a hospital from the pandemic. I'm tired of being tired. I'm so tired, I can't sleep." It was something he continued thinking about until he couldn't help himself, sending a text at 3 a.m. asking his grandmother if they could attend together. "I thought about it and said, 'This is a teachable moment,'" she recalled.

So Jackson took the day off from her job as an accountant at a hospice organization and put on some peace sign earrings and a T-shirt from the 20th anniversary of the Million Man March. On the car ride into the city, her grandson asked about her struggles with race. She explained what it's like being a professional Black woman with over 30 years' experience who still feels overlooked for opportunities because of questions about her qualifications. Her awareness of being treated differently dates back to how her White paternal grandmother favored her lighter-skinned cousins. She found solace in her Black maternal grandmother, who would comb her hair while she sat between her legs. Jackson wants her grandson to feel that kind of comfort from her.

That desire extends to her mission to help the Black community understand palliative care is an option that can offer dignity and support at the end of life. "Because when people hear hospice, their hands go up and they say, 'I don't want to hear it.'" She's also heard that resistance when it comes to getting tested for the coronavirus; she has gotten tested twice and plans to get tested again. She feared being exposed on Tuesday, but being here with her grandson was too important to miss. "We internalized a lot with my generation," she said, "but I think it's important for him to see this."

N.W.A.'s "Fuck Tha Police" blared from a nearby speaker outside St. John's Episcopal Church until an interfaith group of men and women bowed their heads and began to pray. Among them was Timothy Freeman, pastor at Trinity African Methodist Episcopal Zion Church, who wore a brightly colored kente cloth-inspired mask, its vibrant yellows and reds standing in stark contrast to his ministerial black suit and white clerical collar.

Freeman, 42, knows eight people who have been diagnosed with the virus; one died. For two weeks, a sick friend had a fever and could barely move from fatigue but refused to get tested, running through all the scenarios of what might happen if he had it: What if he wound up isolated in an ICU with no one to advocate at his bedside? Another sick friend worried an ambulance would take him to a hospital that he didn't trust. These conversations, the pastor said, are always infused with an awareness of the medical system's record of neglect and abuse of Black people, from dismissing their pain[164] to using their bodies for research without consent[165]. The virus has forced this all top of mind.

A licensed occupational therapist for 19 years who spent a decade managing a skilled rehab facility, Freeman said he has seen racial disparities in health care firsthand and that access to adequate insurance coverage is crucial. "I have seen diagnostic tests not performed…and hospitalizations cut extremely short—or not happen at all—because of insurance." COVID-19 is affecting Black and brown people in disproportionate numbers, "and not just because we're Black and brown, but because of the social and economic conditions people are forced to live in," he said.

"All of it comes together. What happened with George Floyd publicized to the world the experience that we live," he said. "It's a conglomeration of everything."

A block away from the prayer group, Elizabeth Tsehai, 53, drove slowly in her BMW SUV, honking her horn, as federal agents in riot gear began to march past the crowd just behind her. She had a Black Lives Matter T-shirt displayed on the dashboard and a bike rack on the top of her car that she joked made her look like the "caricature of a soccer mom."

She stopped her car on the road and remained there as protesters to her left took a knee. There was some heckling from the crowd but no one was in anybody's face. A Secret Service agent warned her to move. Her response: "Arrest me. I can't breathe!" Agents then pulled her from her car and to the ground and handcuffed her. "I didn't resist because I know they just arrest you for resisting arrest," she said. "But the minute they pulled me up on my feet, I was talking all kinds of trash."

Her car was left unlocked in the middle of the street, where it was protected by protesters. She was questioned and released. She said agents told her they were afraid she was going to hit protesters because people have been using their cars as weapons. They told her to move it and leave. The Secret Service did not respond to questions about this incident.

"Ordinarily, I would not get involved," Tsehai said. But George Floyd's death was enraging, as were "all of the things that came before it."

All of the things.

How a White nurse looked her up and down when she arrived at the hospital to give birth to her son and sneered, "Can we help you?"

How her brothers, who live in Minneapolis, recount being pulled over by police for driving while Black.

How a Black man couldn't watch birds in Central Park last week without having the police called on him.

"The pandemic is hitting Black people hard and exposing these structural inequalities," she said. "Then on top of that, you get Amy Cooper ... weaponizing her White privilege at a time when he might end up in jail, where infection is rife[166].

"But when they manhandled protesters who were peaceful, that was a bridge too far," said Tsehai, who grew up in Ethiopia under an authoritarian regime during a period known as Red Terror. She didn't know life without a curfew until she moved to the United States to attend Georgetown University 35 years ago.

"Moments like this are quite unusual," she said. They can also inspire change, a message she shared with her children, ages 12 and 14, when recounting her ordeal with them. "I want these children to live in a different world. It's not enough to read about it and get outraged and talk about it at the dinner table. Silence makes you complicit."

Notes

1 https://www.penguinrandomhouse.com/books/623541/
   the-cancer-journals-by-audre-lorde-foreword-by-tracy-k-smith/
2 https://lareviewofbooks.org/article/quarantine-files-thinkers-self-isolation/#_ftn15
3 https://twitter.com/carolynryan/status/1243363812889071616
4 https://www.theatlantic.com/ideas/archive/2020/04/stop-looking-away-race-covid-19-victims/609250/
5 https://www.theatlantic.com/ideas/archive/2020/04/race-and-blame/609946/
6 https://www.aaihs.org/a-white-man-took-her-trauma-loss-and-grief-among-the-enslaved/
7 https://uncpress.org/book/9780807848296/black-marxism/
8 https://www.aaihs.org/death-grieving-and-the-necessity-of-history/
9 https://www.tandfonline.com/doi/abs/10.1080/00064246.2014.11413684
10 https://www.theatlantic.com/ideas/archive/2020/03/
   humanitys-long-history-of-making-epidemics-worse/607780/
11 https://doi.org/10.1080/14788810.2011.589695
12 https://www.upenn.edu/pennpress/book/15639.html
13 https://www.upenn.edu/pennpress/book/14030.html
14 https://www.jstor.org/stable/10.5406/historypresent.6.2.0184
15 http://www.beacon.org/The-Price-for-Their-Pound-of-Flesh-P1227.aspx
16 https://science.sciencemag.org/content/366/6464/447
17 https://www.aaihs.org/how-black-activists-sought-healthcare-reform-a-new-documentary/
18 https://www.cdc.gov/coronavirus/2019-ncov/downloads/community-mitigation-strategy.pdf
19 https://archive.org/details/loixetconstituti01fran/page/608/mode/2up
20 https://www.theatlantic.com/ideas/archive/2020/03/role-apathy-epidemics/608527/
21 https://uncpress.org/book/9781469632872/medicalizing-blackness/
22 https://www.ncbi.nlm.nih.gov/pmc/articles/PMC2862340/
23 https://www.tandfonline.com/toc/usou20/21/2-3
24 https://www.theatlantic.com/ideas/archive/2020/04/coronavirus-exposing-our-racial-divides/609526/
25 https://www.muse.jhu.edu/article/241115
26 https://doi.org/10.1215/01642472-7145658
27 https://www.worldcat.org/title/dispossessed-lives-enslaved-women-violence-and-the-archive/
   oclc/1009055150&referer=brief_results
28 https://libcom.org/library/"no-humans-involved"-open-letter-my-colleagues
29 https://earlyamericanists.com/2017/05/15/qa-marisa-fuentes-dispossessed-lives/
30 https://www.pbs.org/newshour/health/where-will-the-bodies-go-morgues-plan-as-virus-grows
31 https://www.cnn.com/2020/04/13/health/detroit-hospital-bodies-coronavirus-trnd/index.html
32 https://theintercept.com/2020/03/31/rikers-island-coronavirus-mass-graves/
33 http://a.msn.com/01/en-nz/BB12DfU5?ocid=scu2
34 https://www.jstor.org/stable/pdf/464747.pdf

35   https://www.penguinrandomhouse.com/books/623541/
     the-cancer-journals-by-audre-lorde-foreword-by-tracy-k-smith/
36   http://smallaxe.net/sxarchipelagos/issue03/johnson.html
37   https://www.nbcnews.com/news/us-news/
     awful-beautiful-saying-goodbye-coronavirus-victims-without-funeral-n1175431
38   https://www.aaihs.org/zoombombing-university-lectures-brings-racism-home/
39   https://www.nytimes.com/2020/04/05/us/coronavirus-dilemmas-mourning.html
40   https://www.aaihs.org/mourning-the-loss-of-my-father-wynton-marsalis-on-the-passing-of-ellis-
     marsalis-jr/
41   https://www.hup.harvard.edu/catalog.php?isbn=9780674057128
42   https://www.dukeupress.edu/in-the-wake
43   https://www.aaihs.org/the-imperial-history-of-us-policing-an-interview-with-stuart-schrader/
44   https://www.inquirer.com/health/coronavirus/protest-philadelphia-jails-social-distancing-coronavirus-
     covid-19-20200330.html
45   https://www.inquirer.com/health/coronavirus/coronavirus-covid-19-hahnemann-joel-freedman-
     philadelphia-graffiti-20200330.html
46   https://www.inquirer.com/opinion/coronavirus-racial-disparities-black-americans-testing-
     philadelphia-20200414.html
47   https://www.miamiherald.com/news/coronavirus/article241554991.html
48   https://www.aaihs.org/mapping-resistance-to-surveillance/
49   https://truthout.org/articles/hiv-prison-activists-are-leading-a-freedom-movement-in-the-face-of-
     covid-19/
50   https://itsgoingdown.org/c19-mutual-aid/
51   https://www.aaihs.org/announcement-aaihs-online-roundtable-on-cedric-robinsons-black-marxism/
52   https://news.harvard.edu/gazette/story/2020/04/health-care-disparities-in-the-age-of-coronavirus/
53   https://www.aaihs.org/racializeddiseaseandpandemic/
54   https://twitter.com/CovidWhileBlack
55   https://twitter.com/black_covid?s=20
56   https://www.tandfonline.com/doi/abs/10.1080/10999949.2016.1162596?journalCode=usou20
57   https://www.jstor.org/stable/10.5323/jafriamerhist.95.3-4.0296
58   https://www.upress.umn.edu/book-division/books/body-and-soul
59   https://www.theatlantic.com/magazine/archive/2019/12/elina-matsoukas-queen-and-slim/600907/
60   https://www.nytimes.com/2020/04/13/opinion/protest-social-distancing-covid.html
61   https://www.ft.com/content/a2901ce8-5eb7-4633-b89c-cbdf5b386938
62   http://www.oecd.org/coronavirus/policy-responses/
     evaluating-the-initial-impact-of-covid-19-containment-measures-on-economic-activity-b1f6b68b/
63   http://hdr.undp.org/sites/default/files/covid-19_and_human_development_0.pdf
64   https://www.nber.org/papers/w26948
65   https://ilo.org/global/about-the-ilo/newsroom/news/WCMS_627189/lang--en/index.htm
66   https://theconversation.com/global-poverty-coronavirus-could-drive-it-up-for-the-first-time-since-the-
     1990s-140662
67   https://www.undp.org/content/undp/en/home/librarypage/transitions-series/temporary-basic-income--
     tbi--for-developing-countries.html
68   https://academic.oup.com/qje/article-abstract/131/4/1973/2468874
69   https://www.ncbi.nlm.nih.gov/pmc/articles/PMC6486161/
70   https://www.sciencedirect.com/science/article/pii/S1570677X18303575
71   https://www.sciencedirect.com/science/article/pii/S0304387818300105
72   https://basicincome.org/news/2020/06/emergency-basic-income-in-tuvalu/
73   https://www.theguardian.com/world/2020/jun/03/
     spain-rekindles-a-radical-idea-a-europe-wide-minimum-income
74   https://www.latinamerica.undp.org/content/rblac/en/home/library/crisis_prevention_and_recovery/
     covid-19-and-social-protection-of-poor-and-vulnerable-groups-in-.html
75   https://www.imf.org/external/pubs/ft/wp/2015/wp15250.pdf
76   https://openknowledge.worldbank.org/handle/10986/33589
77   https://www.odi.org/publications/10505-cash-transfers-what-does-evidence-say-rigorous-review-
     impacts-and-role-design-and-implementation
78   https://scholar.harvard.edu/hendren/publications/unified-welfare-analysis-government-policies
79   https://papers.ssrn.com/sol3/papers.cfm?abstract_id=3613239
80   https://assets.publishing.service.gov.uk/government/uploads/system/uploads/attachment_data/
     file/876466/Letter_from_Minister_Hall_to_Local_Authorities.pdf
81   https://www.gov.uk/government/speeches/pm-address-to-the-nation-on-coronavirus-23-march-2020

82 https://www.bbc.com/news/uk-england-northamptonshire-53213147

83 https://www.gov.uk/government/news/
prime-minister-pledges-new-action-to-eliminate-homelessness-and-rough-sleeping

84 https://www.theatlantic.com/international/archive/2020/03/
coronavirus-panic-buying-britain-us-shopping/608731/

85 https://www.theatlantic.com/politics/archive/2020/03/coronavirus-testing-rich-people/608062/

86 https://www.theatlantic.com/ideas/archive/2020/03/quantifying-coming-recession/608443/

87 https://www.abc.net.au/news/2020-04-25/
homeless-put-up-in-four-star-hotel-during-coronavirus/12176942

88 https://www.ft.com/content/8c4cf336-8eb1-4384-8feb-563010d3c911

89 https://www.gov.ca.gov/2020/04/03/at-newly-converted-motel-governor-newsom-launches-project-
roomkey-a-first-in-the-nation-initiative-to-secure-hotel-motel-rooms-to-protect-homeless-individuals-
from-covid-19/

90 https://www.gov.uk/government/speeches/
dame-louise-caseys-statement-on-coronavirus-covid-19-31-may-2020

91 https://www.gov.uk/government/news/6-000-new-supported-homes-as-part-of-landmark-commitment-
to-end-rough-sleeping

92 https://www.communities-ni.gov.uk/news/hargey-pays-tribute-homelessness-sector

93 https://www.gov.scot/publications/coronavirus-covid-19-homelessness/

94 https://gov.wales/welsh-government-announce-new-20-million-fund-transform-homelessness-services

95 https://www.theguardian.com/society/2020/may/29/san-francisco-homeless-deaths-coronavirus

96 https://www.cdc.gov/mmwr/volumes/69/wr/mm6917e2.htm

97 https://www.nbcwashington.com/news/local/coronavirus-tears-through-homeless-shelter-in-dc/2299411/

98 https://www.ons.gov.uk/peoplepopulationandcommunity/birthsdeathsandmarriages/deaths/articles/
navirusanddeathsofhomelesspeopleenglandandwalesdeathsregisteredupto26june2020/2020 -07-10

99 https://www.crisis.org.uk/about-us/media-centre/ons-release-number-of-deaths-of-people-experiencing-
homelessness-involving-coronavirus-during-outbreak-crisis-response/

100 https://www.ons.gov.uk/peoplepopulationandcommunity/housing/articles/
ukhomelessness/2005to2018#demographics

101 https://www.ons.gov.uk/peoplepopulationandcommunity/birthsdeathsandmarriages/deaths/bulletins/
deathsofhomelesspeopleinenglandandwales/2018

102 https://www.homeless.org.uk/facts/homelessness-in-numbers/rough-sleeping/
rough-sleeping-our-analysis

103 https://metro.co.uk/2019/01/31/165-increase-homelessness-since-tories-took-power-8419274/

104 https://www.theguardian.com/cities/2019/jun/03/
its-a-miracle-helsinkis-radical-solution-to-homelessness

105 https://londonist.com/london/housing/shelter-homelessness-in-london

106 https://www.newham.gov.uk/news/article/336/update-about-coronavirus-covid-19-stratford-centre-to-
close-from-8pm-to-5am-for-28-days-in-response-to-pandemic-from-mayor-rokhsana-fiaz-28

107 https://www.bbc.com/news/uk-england-46891392

108 https://www.crisis.org.uk/media/237022/costsofhomelessness_finalweb.pdf

109 https://www.bbc.co.uk/news/business-53104734

110 https://www.gov.uk/government/news/
ban-on-evictions-extended-by-2-months-to-further-protect-renters

111 https://www.gov.uk/government/news/105-million-to-keep-rough-sleepers-safe-and-off-the-streets-
during-coronavirus-pandemic

112 https://www.ft.com/content/83578ab4-4aa8-4c7b-9867-31238dfb3f9a

113 https://blog.shelter.org.uk/2020/06/government-must-support-people-who-have-no-recourse-to-
public-funds/

114 https://www.politicshome.com/news/article/
half-a-million-households-face-homelessness-if-housing-crisis-not-prioritised-councils-warn

115 Throughout this chapter we use the term Indigenous to refer to American Indian, Alaska Native, Native
Hawaiian, and the peoples of Oceania.

116 This research project was supported by a grant from the National Science Foundation (#1947319) led
by Dr. Kimberly Scott (Arizona State University) and Dr. Brenda Jensen (Hawaii Pacific University).

117 We thank Dr. Kimberly Scott (Arizona State University), Dr. Brenda Jensen (Hawaii Pacific
University), Noelani Kalipi (Kalipi Enterprises), and Katie Schwind for their helpful comments.

118 https://nces.ed.gov/programs/digest/d18/tables/dt18_318.45.asp

119 https://www.researchgate.net/publication/227623577_Cultural_processes_in_science_education_
Supporting_the_navigation_of_multiple_epistemologies

120 https://www.semanticscholar.org/paper/Culturally-Responsive-Schooling-for-Indigenous -A-of-Castagno-Brayboy/1a8933db91e10bcdafcf30805df9544a5061e5fe

121 This concept was introduced by Indigenous scholar Gerald Vizenor (1999), who explains in the preface of his book *Manifest Manners: Narratives of Postindian Survivance*, "Survivance is an active sense of presence, the continuance of native stories, not a mere reaction, or a survivable name. Native survivance stories are renunciations of dominance, tragedy and victimry."

122 https://eric.ed.gov/?id=EJ1203738

123 http://www.dissertations.wsu.edu/Dissertations/Spring2008/j_guillory_042408.pdf

124 https://storyofleicester.info/a-place-to-live/the-golden-mile/

125 https://www.theguardian.com/world/2020/jul/11/revealed-20-areas-at-most-risk-of-local-lockdowns

126 https://www.leicestermercury.co.uk/news/leicester-news/map-shows-exact-areas-leicester-4276783

127 https://twitter.com/ClaudiaWebbe/status/1281616603554217986

128 https://www.routledge.com/Purity-and-Danger-An-Analysis-of-Concepts-of-Pollution-and-Taboo/ Douglas/p/book/9780415289955

129 https://www.theguardian.com/news/audio/2020/jul/09/ the-leicester-garment-factories-exposed-by-covid-19

130 https://twitter.com/benniekara/status/1278342063038189568

131 https://www.theguardian.com/commentisfree/2020/jul/05/government-errors-leicester-covid-19-spike

132 https://manchesteruniversitypress.co.uk/9781526145420/

133 https://www.thetimes.co.uk/edition/news/ boohoo-investigation-racism-fears-let-leicester-sweatshops-go-unchecked-says-priti-patel-h23x88k85

134 https://twitter.com/ClaudiaWebbe/status/1281616603554217986

135 https://discoversociety.org/2020/07/01/working-class-unity/

136 https://groveatlantic.com/book/the-wretched-of-the-earth/

137 https://caringlabor.wordpress.com/2010/11/18/michel-foucault-friendship-as-a-way-of-life/

138 https://www.harpercollins.com/products/all-about-love-bell-hooks?variant=32116522090530

139 https://www.historyworkshop.org.uk/gangs-policing-deportation-and-the-criminalisation-of-friendship/

140 https://discoversociety.org/2020/07/01/working-class-unity/

141 https://newsone.com/3910125/coronavirus-Black-people-debunking-myths/

142 https://www.foxnews.com/politics/trump-coronavirus-china-virus-white-house-kung-flu

143 https://www.colorlines.com/articles/white-supremacists-plot-use-covid-19-agent-bioterrorism

144 https://www.cms.gov/CCIIO/Resources/Forms-Reports-and-Other-Resources/preexisting

145 https://www.colorlines.com/articles/ring-alarm-covid-19-presents-grave-danger-communities-color

146 https://www.citylab.com/equity/2020/03/coronavirus-immunity-racism-history-disease-yellow-fever/ 607891/

147 https://uncpress.org/book/9781469632872/medicalizing-blackness/

148 https://www.worldcat.org/title/the-troubled-dream-of-genetic-medicine-ethnicity-and-innovation- in-tay-sachs-cystic-fibrosis-and-sickle-cell-disease/oclc/956771290&referer=brief_results

149 https://thenewpress.com/books/fatal-invention

150 https://www.ncbi.nlm.nih.gov/pubmed/15121958

151 https://anthrosource.onlinelibrary.wiley.com/doi/abs/10.1111/AN.1091?af=R

152 https://twitter.com/mason_lab/status/1240642213668966400

153 http://www.anthropology-news.org/index.php/2019/02/11/its-a-white-disease/

154 http://www.stlamerican.com/news/local_news/nurse-judy-wilson-griffin-is-first-covid--death-in/ article_1d422bea-6b06-11ea-83e1-17bbd703c8fb.html

155 https://www.worldcat.org/title/boundaries-of-blackness-aids-and-the-breakdown-of-black-politics/ oclc/750941929&referer=brief_results

156 https://www.ksdk.com/article/news/health/coronavirus/ coronavirus-st-louis-county-villa-duchesne-amtrak/63-a93ed63a-ba36-4686-b0fe-5fd6c4d29b5a

157 https://www.aaihs.org/1619-2/

158 https://www.aaihs.org/how-black-activists-sought-healthcare-reform-a-new-documentary/

159 https://newsone.com/3916437/who-coronavirus-kills-36-year-old-principal-dies/

160 http://www.stlamerican.com/news/local_news/nurse-judy-wilson-griffin-is-first-covid--death-in/ article_1d422bea-6b06-11ea-83e1-17bbd703c8fb.html

161 https://blavity.com/blavity-original/how-a-history-of-resilience-has-prepared-black-folks- to-survive- the-coronavirus-pandemic

162 https://blavity.com/idris-elba-is-lambasting-conspiracy-theories-about-and-Black-people

163 https://www.apmresearchlab.org/covid/deaths-by-race

164 https://www.pnas.org/content/early/2016/03/30/1516047113.abstract

165 https://www.nber.org/papers/w22323

166 https://www.nytimes.com/2020/05/26/nyregion/amy-cooper-dog-central-park.html

Part Two

The Pandemic of Racism: Exposing the Racial Contract

2.1

Sweat

by Amber Jamilla Musser

Originally published in *Social Text Online*, APRIL 27, 2020

In the time of COVID, I do a lot of laundry. At first it was because I was finally still; no longer traveling so there was more time and a backlog of dirty clothes. Then, it was for other reasons. Partly, because I change my clothes a lot. This gives me a way to demarcate different segments of the day—something that is a challenge in a studio apartment. There were clothes to sleep in, clothes for work Zoom, clothes for Zoom yoga, clothes for grocery shopping, and evening lounging clothes. Despite not wearing anything for an especially long time, the clothes also need to be washed more frequently. This is because of all of the sweating.

I wake up soaked and come back from walks with undershirts stuck to me. The night sweats—fever or anxiety? The day sweats—generally reduced exercise capacity, COVID-induced hypoxia; more anxiety? Someone called it Schrodinger's disease: you must act like you have it and like you don't. This uncertainty, too, producing spirals of anxiety and sweat. Status unknown though likely; but, still, the sweat on my clothes offers a material remainder of the prevailing affects—anxiety and terror. It is a tangible reminder of what life feels like now; illustrative of the fundamental porosity of bodies. The virus, itself, does this too, but whereas its DNA works to produce more and more copies of itself—transforming cells into virus factories while obliterating their original functions—sweat speaks more fundamentally to enmeshment. Even in a time of physical distancing, we are embedded in multiple ecologies.

Some of the anxiety is personal, related to a conception of individual threat. When someone outside starts to get too close (for example), I can feel it in the back of my neck. Grocery shopping makes my armpits sting. These are signs of a "fight or flight response": stress hormones—adrenaline and cortisol—course through the body, activating the apocrine glands, which release a blend of fats, oils, and water that bacteria on the skin's surface, in turn, eat. The pungent odors are a by-product of these cycles. Here, psychology and metabolism are inextricable and the limits of the self, already perceived to be under threat, are rendered laughable. But, sweat is also my pandemic residue in that it links me to larger communities of Blackness in this moment and in the past. So many different forms of structural racism go a long way toward explaining why the coronavirus disproportionately affects Black people and other people of color who have been marginalized in food deserts, health care deserts, and air pollution hot spots, and are geographically distant from their jobs, which are still essential. These are not my particular circumstances, which means that facing the same virus offers connection, guilt, and estrangement—what, aside from donating money, can I do in the immediate face of yet another moment of racial violence and mass death? This is anxiety as existential dread; it is anxiety that activates specters of Black death, possibilities of Black love and care, and knowledge of Black forms of survival. This enmeshment is part of what it is to "consent not to be a single being."[1]

Sweat is also a byproduct of breath. Breathing is the first part of respiration; it brings oxygen into the body where it ends up producing energy, carbon dioxide, and water (sweat). There is, then, the bitter irony of yet another mode of choking off air supply circulating within Black communities that makes "I can't breathe," resonate in other ways. Breath has become an important frame for thinking about the possibility of Black life, particularly in the aftermath of Eric Garner's 2014 death at the hands of police. His last words, "I can't breathe," famously reference the chokehold being used to restrain him. Since then, especially after a grand jury refused to bring criminal charges against the White officer who killed him, the refrain has become a way to describe anti-Blackness. Christina Sharpe references the incident as but one of an endlessly repeating series of incidents that accumulate as an oppressive atmosphere, what she calls the weather: "In my text, the weather is the totality of our environments; the weather is the total climate; and that climate is anti-black"[2] (p. 75). Later, Sharpe works through the term aspiration, another synonym of sorts, in order to ponder the possibility of survival for Black people under these conditions. Survival means allowing for the intake of air; in part it means caring through the multigenerational trauma of the transatlantic slave trade, but it also means fusing breath with something else: "Aspiration here, doubles [...] To the necessity of breath, to breathing space, to the breathtaking spaces in the wake in which we live; and to the ways we respond, 'with wonder and admiration, you are still alive, like hydrogen, like oxygen'"[3] (p. 109). What Sharpe points toward is the affective excess that accompanies survival. It is the place where one might put begin to see beyond the mere conditions of being toward thriving. Since it is surplus, it requires the surplus of breath—the energy that it provides—in order to make this something else real. In some ways, this is the landscape that I describe in relation to brown *jouissance* in that it *creates* beings in its excess even as it remains moored to an ethos of survival.

Ashon Crawley, too, cites Eric Garner as a way to think about the multiple types of violence that engulf Blackness. It is not *just* the (endlessly repeating) legacy to which he refers, but a logic that continues to attempt to suffocate and eradicate in multiple permutations. Thus, this statement becomes a call for abolition and a way to approach breathing anew: "'I can't breathe' charges us to do something, to perform, to produce otherwise than what we have. We are charged to end, to produce abolition against, the episteme that produced for us current iterations of categorical designations of racial hierarchies, class stratifications, gender binaries, mind- body splits" (1)[4]. In this space that circulates around breath; both Crawley and Sharpe point us toward the excess that circulates around breathing. This is what I call the energetic because it reminds us of the connection between breath, respiration, and sweat.

Sweat inflects breath and breathing in other ways. Not only because it introduces smell but because it points us toward the mechanisms of metabolism. This is to say that respiration is intimately connected with the body's materiality, which is not static but part of ever-changing ecologies. In response to the anti-Black violence that accompanied civil rights struggles of the 1960s, Audre Lorde wrote, "One of the most basic Black survival skills is the ability to change, to metabolize experience, good or ill, into something that is useful, lasting, effective"[5] (p. 137). It is unclear what forms survival will take, but I know that my sweaty clothes are testament to being in the midst of an event even when the outcome is uncertain. They index complex forms of affective connection and the persistence of metabolism and transformation. Because I can breathe, I sweat.

2.2

But Your Whiteness Will Not Protect You: White Supremacy and COVID-19

by Lisa M. Anderson

We have seen how a pandemic brings into sharp relief deep and significant structural problems in U.S. society. When we take an intersectional perspective on the pandemic, we can see how COVID-19 impacts communities differentially based on their engagements with race, class, gender, nationality, ability, and age. The pandemic *and* the various responses to it are also strongly influenced by the deep connections to White supremacy that suffuses the U.S. This chapter offers an examination of how media coverage of the pandemic changed perceptions about its effect on different communities, and how media coverage impacted local and national responses along racial lines.

Media Impacts on Policy—Some Historical Notes

Policy decisions in the U.S. are strongly rooted in the perceptions and understandings of 'deserving' versus 'undeserving' populations, which have historically fallen along racial, class, immigration status, and ability lines. We can see this in policy through two examples: 'welfare' programs and drug policy.

When 'welfare' was originally enacted, its purpose was to aid (White) women and their children during the Great Depression. Dorothea Lange's famous photo "Migrant Mother" (1936) is a primary example of this type of image. Rhetoric surrounding these recipients posited that they were widows and therefore 'deserving,' and such recipients were represented by images of White women and their children. Women of color were largely excluded from eligibility. As Patricia Hill Collins deftly explains in *Black Feminist Thought*[6], the image of the Black woman as a 'welfare mother' emerged once Black women had gained access to social welfare programs more broadly, and Aid to Women and Children specifically.

Welfare policy changed when women of color—particularly Black women—became the visual image of the welfare recipient. Efforts to 'reform' welfare and to reduce its rolls, despite the persistent needs of women with young children, took up notions of poor Black and brown women and their children as 'undeserving' populations. The replacement of the image of 'deserving' White mothers with 'undeserving' Black and brown mothers helped drive popular opinion towards reducing and limiting welfare benefits, and strongly played on racist tropes that viewed poor people of color as infantile, non-contributors to society. As Collins notes, "Creating the controlling image of the welfare mother and stigmatizing her as the cause of her own poverty and that of African-American communities shifts the angle of vision away from the structural sources of poverty and blames the victims themselves"[7].

The project of replacing the images of poor White women and children with images of urban poor people of color became a cultural project whose goal was specifically to dismantle the welfare state through White supremacist ideas like the "bootstrap" theory and code words like "personal responsibility." Beginning in the 1980s, this project strongly influenced both elected officials and voters to pursue 'reform' of welfare. In these reforms, limits on benefits hurt all poor families regardless of race. The insidious nature of White supremacy meant even rural Whites who were dependent upon welfare supported the politicians who fought for, and succeeded in, limiting benefits.

In the "War on Drugs," which has shifted over time and become strongly racialized, we see another example of this cultural project. When established during the Nixon administration, the "War on Drugs" was designed to focus primarily on treatment rather than punishment. Its racialization emerged during the 1980s with the "crack epidemic." We can see the deleterious effects of the ways in which controlling images were deployed. "Crack" was rumored to be more addictive than powdered cocaine and justified mandatory minimum sentences; it was also positioned as a driving factor in "gang violence." The perceived danger of the Black drug user was popular in film and television from the late 1980s, and was seen in films such as *Boyz n the Hood*, *New Jack City*, and *Menace II Society*. We saw a revision of harsh penalties for drug users and a return to a focus on treatment when the 'new' epidemics of methamphetamine and opioids, which strongly hit White rural communities, emerged. We can see these visualized and dramatized in the television series *Breaking Bad* and *Ozark*. This marks the shift back from penalties for drug use to rehabilitation for drug use.

In both areas, policy decisions were initially more open and generous. In both cases, significant changes in the policies surrounding these programs at the federal and state levels coincided with the rebranding of both as racialized 'problems' and with the changes in visual imagery. This shift was shortly followed by changes in the attitudes of voters and elected officials about the policies. We can see from these two examples that 'controlling images' persist in negative depictions of Black and brown peoples, and help generate support for policy changes that criminalize or otherwise denigrate people of color.

The U.S. COVID-19 Response: How White Supremacy Put Lives at Risk

In the U.S., reactions to the pandemic were slow and differed among states. Places with the earliest infections quickly enacted restrictions on large gatherings, and as community spread was acknowledged, states made efforts to ramp up testing. Once the virus began to spread on the East Coast, stay-at-home orders were enacted. People seemed to understand that the virus was dangerous and that it was spreading quickly, and large gatherings and places where people congregated—schools, bars and restaurants, and shopping centers—needed to be closed down in order to slow the spread of the virus. In early days, some celebrity positive cases (like that of Tom Hanks) drove home the seriousness of the situation, and, for a while, people were willing to work to help try to slow the spread of the virus. These images, and the images of the dead, were largely of White middle-aged and older people who were hospitalized, or who were memorialized by their families after their deaths[8].

There was a simultaneous narrative in conservative media and by the President that the virus was quickly being contained and would soon be eliminated, and that it was not serious (just the flu). Those communities were surprised when they began to see outbreaks of serious illness in *their* communities. The spikes of cases in places like Louisiana after Mardi Gras shifted the understanding of the virus and made most people amenable to comply with shelter-in-place orders where they were enacted.

It was also obvious that even in shut-down states, some people would need to continue to work. These sectors and workers were deemed "essential." In almost every case, essential workers included first responders, hospital personnel (doctors, nurses, therapists, and housekeeping staff) and other care workers, grocery and drug store employees, people in food production (meatpacking, farmworkers, etc.), and public transportation employees.

Towards the end of March, a new story of the virus emerged. On March 30, the *Charlotte Observer* published an article about how Blacks were being disproportionately affected by COVID-19[9] (Kuznitz, 2020). In this instance, the Black population of Mecklenburg County is about 33% of the population, but Black residents were about 44% of the confirmed cases of the virus. The story made its way to national news outlets. In early April, other organizations like the Kaiser Family Foundation[10] and the Human Rights Campaign[11] posted blog posts on the disproportionate effects of COVID-19 on minority populations. Within a few weeks, COVID-19 was perceived as a minority disease. It was not, of course; but disproportionate was misunderstood to mean that *the people who were getting seriously ill and dying from COVID-19 were mostly*

Black and Latino. The emphasis of this differential effect would have serious implications.

The images associated with various media and reporting on the virus shifted to be specifically of Black and brown people. The virus had already been responsible for a wave of anti-Asian violence. The popular understanding, especially among people who already held a White supremacist perspective, was that this disease just affected minorities. As the story of the virus changed, so did the national response to it. One of the first responses was an almost immediate push, particularly in Republican-run states, to re-open the economy. This push to reopen was strongly supported by the Trump administration. While the CDC and WHO outlined what was necessary to flatten the curve, none of the states that moved aggressively to re-open at the end of April or beginning of May met those guidelines. In all of those states, confirmed cases were on the rise, and their testing and tracing capabilities were minimal.

In Iowa, the spike in COVID-19 cases emerged specifically in businesses deemed essential—meatpacking plants. The state's governor declared 'regular' people were not being infected, so there was no reason to issue stay-at-home orders or to close the meatpacking plants. Many of the workers at meatpacking plants are people of color and immigrants—not 'regular' Iowans (not *White* Iowans).

As the people identified in the media with the virus became less White, the push to reopen came from White communities and officials. In Michigan, the Democratic governor was subject to intimidation by White men with assault weapons at the Capitol, insisting on reopening[12]. These included men who identify with the 'boogaloo' movement, a White supremacist group[13]. These 'protests' occurred in several states, but the demographic was always the same: White[14], often armed[15], and carrying pro-Trump signs and confederate flags[16].

The push to re-open was discussed as an economic issue, and devastating high unemployment was offered as an important reason to re-open as soon as possible. People who work in non-essential businesses (retail workers, hair and nail salon workers, restaurant employees) are some of the most vulnerable in our country. The direct effect of this reopening was the shutting down of unemployment benefits for millions of people who would now essentially be forced to return to work while cases and hospitalizations were rising.

This disregard of the virus and of the people it primarily affects reflect an engagement with an anti-Black, anti-Indigenous culture that simply cannot and does not value those lives. The idea that the most vulnerable communities should be protected through a kind of community 'sacrifice' (keeping stay-at-home orders until the curve had flattened and begun to go down) was viewed as an affront to the rights of some (Whites) to engage in activities that put not only themselves, but others, at risk. The reframing of the virus's story shows the connection between White supremacy and policy. Like in previous years, changing the narrative of public policy to portray that only people of color will benefit turns public sentiment against those policies and results in policy changes that damage everyone, not only people of color. The result of the push to reopen has been a surge in cases, making the U.S. the worst country for COVID-19 infections in the world.

2.3

The Coronavirus Was an Emergency Until Trump Found Out Who Was Dying

by Adam Serwer

Originally published in *The Atlantic*, MAY 8, 2020

Six weeks ago, Ahmaud Arbery went out and never came home. Gregory and Travis McMichael, who saw Arbery running through their neighborhood just outside of Brunswick, Georgia, and who told authorities they thought he was a burglary suspect, armed themselves, pursued Arbery, and then shot him dead.

The local prosecutor, George E. Barnhill, concluded that no crime had been committed[17]. Arbery had tried to wrest a shotgun from Travis McMichael before being shot, Barnhill wrote in a letter to the police chief[18]. The two men who had seen a stranger running, and decided to pick up their firearms and chase him, had therefore acted in self-defense when they confronted and shot him, Barnhill concluded. On Tuesday, as video of the shooting emerged on social media, a different Georgia prosecutor announced that the case would be put to a grand jury[19]; the two men were arrested and charged with murder yesterday evening after video of the incident sparked national outrage across the political spectrum.

To see the sequence of events that led to Arbery's death as benign requires a cascade of assumptions. One must assume that two men arming themselves and chasing down a stranger running through their neighborhood is a normal occurrence. One must assume that the two armed White men had a right to self-defense, and that the Black man suddenly confronted by armed strangers did not. One must assume that state laws are meant to justify an encounter in which two people can decide of their own volition to chase, confront, and kill a person they've never met[20].

But Barnhill's leniency is selective—as *The Appeal's* Josie Duffy Rice notes[21], Barnhill attempted to prosecute Olivia Pearson, a Black woman, for helping another Black voter use an electronic voting machine[22]. A crime does not occur when White men stalk and kill a Black stranger. A crime does occur when Black people vote.

The underlying assumptions of White innocence and Black guilt are all part of what the philosopher Charles Mills calls the "racial contract"[23]. If the social contract is the implicit agreement among members of a society to follow the rules—for example, acting lawfully, adhering to the results of elections, and contesting the agreed-upon rules by nonviolent means—then the racial contract is a codicil rendered in invisible ink, one stating that the rules as written do not apply to non-White people in the same way. The Declaration of Independence states that all men are created equal; the racial contract limits this to White men with property. The law says murder is illegal; the racial contract says it's fine for White people to chase and murder Black people if they have decided that those Black people scare them. "The terms of the Racial Contract," Mills wrote, "mean that non-White sub-personhood is enshrined simultaneously with White personhood."

The racial contract is not partisan—it guides staunch conservatives and sensitive liberals alike—but it works most effectively when it remains imperceptible to its beneficiaries. As long as it is invisible, members of society can proceed as though the provisions of the social contract apply equally to everyone. But when an injustice pushes the racial contract into the open, it forces people to choose whether to embrace, contest, or deny its existence. Video evidence of unjustified shootings of Black people is so jarring in part because it exposes the terms of the racial contract so vividly. But as the process in the Arbery case shows, the racial contract most often operates unnoticed, relying on Americans to have an implicit understanding of who is bound by the rules, and who is exempt from them.

The implied terms of the racial contract are visible everywhere for those willing to see them. A 12-year-old with a toy gun is a dangerous threat who must be met with lethal force[24]; armed militias drawing beads on federal agents are heroes of liberty[25]. Struggling White farmers in Iowa taking billions in federal assistance are hardworking Americans down on their luck[26]; struggling single parents in cities using food stamps are welfare queens. Black Americans struggling in the cocaine epidemic are a "bio-underclass" created by a pathological culture[27]; White Americans struggling with opioid addiction are a national tragedy[28]. Poor European immigrants who flocked to an America with virtually no immigration restrictions came "the right way"[29]; poor Central American immigrants evading a baroque and unforgiving system are gang members and terrorists.

The coronavirus epidemic has rendered the racial contract visible in multiple ways. Once the disproportionate impact of the epidemic was revealed to the American political and financial elite, many began to regard the rising death toll less as a national emergency than as an inconvenience. Temporary measures meant to prevent the spread of the disease by restricting movement, mandating the wearing of masks, or barring large social gatherings have become the foulest tyranny. The lives of workers at the front lines of the pandemic—such as meatpackers, transportation workers, and grocery clerks—have been deemed so worthless that legislators want to immunize their employers from liability even as they force them to work under unsafe conditions[30]. In East New York, police assault Black residents for violating social-distancing rules; in Lower Manhattan, they dole out masks and smiles to White pedestrians[31].

Donald Trump's 2016 election campaign, with its vows to enforce state violence against Mexican immigrants, Muslims, and Black Americans, was built on a promise to enforce terms of the racial contract that Barack Obama had ostensibly neglected, or violated by his presence[32]. Trump's administration, in carrying out an explicitly discriminatory agenda that valorizes cruelty[33], war crimes[34], and the entrenchment of White political power[35], represents a revitalized commitment to the racial contract.

But the pandemic has introduced a new clause to the racial contract. The lives of disproportionately Black and brown workers are being sacrificed to fuel the engine of a faltering economy, by a president who disdains them. This is the COVID contract.

As the first cases of the coronavirus were diagnosed in the United States in late January and early February, the Trump administration and Fox News were eager to play down the risk it posed[36]. But those early cases, tied to international travel, ensnared many members of the global elite: American celebrities[37], world leaders[38], and those with close ties to Trump himself[39]. By March 16, the president had reversed course, declaring a national emergency and asking Americans to avoid social gatherings.

The purpose of the restrictions was to flatten the curve of infections[40], to keep the spread of the virus from overwhelming the nation's medical infrastructure, and to allow the federal government time[41] to build a system of testing and tracing that could contain the outbreak[42]. Although testing capacity is improving, the president has very publicly resisted investing the necessary resources, because testing would reveal more infections; in his words, "by do-ing all of this testing, we make ourselves look bad"[43].

Over the weeks that followed the declaration of an emergency, the pan-demic worsened and the death toll mounted. Yet by mid-April, conservative broadcasters were decrying the restrictions, small bands of armed protesters were descending on state capitols, and the president was pressing to lift the constraints.

In the interim, data about the demographics of COVID-19 victims began to trickle out. On April 7, major outlets began reporting that preliminary data showed that Black and Latino Americans were being disproportionately felled by the coronavirus[44]. That afternoon, Rush Limbaugh complained, "If you dare criticize the mobilization to deal with this, you're going to be immediately tagged as a racist"[45]. That night, Fox News host Tucker Carlson announced, "It hasn't been the disaster that we feared"[46]. His colleague Brit Hume mused that "the disease turned out not to be quite as dangerous as we thought"[47]. The nationwide death toll that day was just 13,000 people; it now stands above 70,000, a mere month later.

As Matt Gertz writes[48], some of these premature celebrations may have been an overreaction to the changes in the prominent coronavirus model de-signed by the Institute for Health Metrics and Evaluation at the University of Washington, which had recently revised its estimates down to about 60,000 deaths by August[49]. But even as the mounting death toll proved that estimate wildly optimistic, the chorus of right-wing elites demanding that the economy reopen grew louder. By April 16, the day the first anti-lockdown protests be-gan, deaths had more than doubled, to more than 30,000.

That more and more Americans were dying was less important than who was dying.

The disease is now "infecting people who cannot afford to miss work or telecommute—grocery store employees, delivery drivers, and construction workers," *The Washington Post* reported[50]. Air travel has largely shut down, and many of the new clusters are in nursing homes, jails and prisons, and factories tied to essential industries. Containing the outbreak was no longer a question of social responsibility, but of personal responsibility. From the White House podium, Surgeon General Jerome Adams told "communities of color" that "we need you to step up and help stop the spread."

Public-health restrictions designed to contain the outbreak were deemed absurd. They seemed, in Carlson's words, "mindless and authoritarian"[51], a "weird kind of arbitrary fascism"[52]. To restrict the freedom of White Americans, just because non-White Americans are dying, is an egregious violation of the racial contract. The wealthy luminaries of conservative media have sought to couch their opposition to restrictions as advocacy on behalf of workers[53], but polling shows that those most vulnerable to both the disease and economic catastrophe want the outbreak contained before they return to work[54].

Although the full picture remains unclear, researchers have found that disproportionately Black counties "account for more than half of coronavirus cases and nearly 60 percent of deaths"[55]. The disproportionate burden that Black and Latino Americans are bearing is in part a direct result of their overrepresentation in professions where they risk exposure[56], and of a racial gap in wealth and income that has left them more vulnerable to being laid off[57]. Black and Latino workers are overrepresented among the essential, the unemployed[58], and the dead[59].

This is a very old and recognizable story—political and financial elites displaying a callous disregard for the workers of any race who make their lives of comfort possible. But in America, where labor and race are so often intertwined, the racial contract has enabled the wealthy to dismiss workers as both undeserving and expendable. White Americans are also suffering, but the perception that the coronavirus is largely a Black and brown problem licenses elites to dismiss its impact. In America, the racial contract has shaped the terms of class war for centuries; the COVID contract shapes it here.

This tangled dynamic played out on Tuesday, during oral arguments over Wisconsin Governor Tony Evers's statewide stay-at-home order before the state Supreme Court, held remotely. Chief Justice Patience Roggensack was listening to Wisconsin Assistant Attorney General Colin Roth defend the order.

"When you see a virus like this one that does not respect county boundaries, this started out predominantly in Madison and Milwaukee; then we just had this outbreak in Brown County very recently in the meatpacking plants," Roth explained. "The cases in Brown County in a span of two weeks surged over tenfold, from 60 to almost 800—".

"Due to the meatpacking, though, that's where Brown County got the flare," Roggensack interrupted to clarify. "It wasn't just the regular folks in Brown County."

Perhaps Roggensack did not mean that the largely Latino workers in Brown County's meatpacking plants—who have told reporters that they have been forced to work in proximity with one another, often without masks or hand sanitizer, and without being notified that their colleagues are infected—are not "regular folks" like the other residents of the state. Perhaps she merely meant that their line of work puts them at greater risk, and so the outbreaks in the meatpacking plants, seen as essential to the nation's food supply, are not rationally related to the governor's stay-at-home order, from which they would be exempt.

Yet either way, Roggensack was drawing a line between "regular folks" and the workers who keep them fed, mobile, safe, and connected. And America's leaders have treated those workers as largely expendable, praising their valor while disregarding their safety.

"There were no masks. There was no distancing inside the plant, only [in the] break room. We worked really close to each other," Raquel Sanchez Alvarado, a worker with American Foods, a Wisconsin meatpacking company, told local reporters in mid-April[60]. "People are scared that they will be fired and that they will not find a job at another company if they express their concerns."

In Colorado, hundreds of workers in meatpacking plants have contracted the coronavirus[61]. In South Dakota, where a Smithfield plant became the site of an outbreak infecting more than 700 workers, a spokesperson told *BuzzFeed News* that the issue was their "large immigrant population"[62]. On Tuesday, when Iowa reported that thousands of workers at meat-processing plants had become infected[63], Governor Kim Reynolds was bragging in *The Washington Post* about how well her approach to the coronavirus had worked[64].

Although, by the official tally, more than 70,000 Americans have died from the coronavirus, many governors are rushing to reopen their states without sufficient testing to contain their outbreaks. (Statistical analyses of excess deaths[65] in comparison with years past suggest that COVID-19 casualties are approaching and may soon exceed 100,000.) Yet the Trump administration is poised to declare "mission accomplished," engaging in the doublespeak of treating the pandemic as though the major risks have passed, while rhetorically preparing the country for thousands more deaths. The worst-case scenarios may not come to pass. But federal policy reflects the president's belief that he has little to lose by gambling with the lives of those Americans most likely to be affected.

"We can't keep our country closed down for years," Trump said Wednesday[66]. But that was no one's plan. The plan was to buy time to take the necessary steps to open the country safely. But the Trump administration did not do that, because it did not consider the lives of the people dying worth the effort or money required to save them[67].

The economic devastation wrought by the pandemic, and the Trump administration's failure to prepare for it even as it crippled the world's richest nations, cannot be overstated. Tens of millions of Americans are unemployed. Tens of thousands line up outside food banks and food pantries each week to obtain sustenance they cannot pay for. Businesses across the country are struggling and failing. The economy cannot be held in stasis indefinitely—the longer it is, the more people will suffer.

Yet the only tension between stopping the virus and reviving the economy is one the Trump administration and its propaganda apparatus have invented. Economists are in near-unanimous agreement that the safest path requires building the capacity to contain the virus before reopening the economy[68]—precisely because new waves of deaths will drive Americans back into self-imposed isolation, destroying the consumer spending that powers economic growth. The federal government can afford the necessary health infrastructure and financial aid; it already shelled out hundreds of billions of dollars in tax cuts to wealthy Americans[69]. But the people in charge do not consider doing so to be worthwhile—Republicans have already dismissed aid to struggling state governments that laid off a million workers this month alone[70] as a "blue-state bailout"[71], while pushing for more tax cuts for the rich[72].

"The people of our country are warriors," Trump told reporters Tuesday[73]. "I'm not saying anything is perfect, and will some people be affected? Yes. Will some people be affected badly? Yes. But we have to get our country open and we have to get it open soon."

The frame of war allows the president to call for the collective sacrifice of laborers without taking the measures necessary to ensure their safety, while the upper classes remain secure at home. But the workers who signed up to harvest food, deliver packages, stack groceries, drive trains and buses, and care for the sick did not sign up for war, and the unwillingness of America's political leadership to protect them is a policy decision, not an inevitability. Trump is acting in accordance with the terms of the racial contract, which values the lives of those most likely to be affected less than the inconveniences necessary to preserve them. The president's language of wartime unity is a veil draped over a federal response that offers little more than contempt for those whose lives are at risk. To this administration, they are simply fuel to keep the glorious Trump economy burning.

Collective solidarity in response to the coronavirus remains largely intact—most Americans support the restrictions and are not eager to sacrifice their lives or those of their loved ones for a few points of gross domestic product. The consistency across incomes and backgrounds is striking in an era of severe partisan polarization[74]. But solidarity with the rest of the nation among elite Republicans—those whose lives and self-conceptions are intertwined with the success of the Trump presidency—began eroding as soon as the disproportionate impact of the outbreak started to emerge.

The president's cavalier attitude is at least in part a reflection of his fear that the economic downturn caused by the coronavirus will doom his political fortunes in November. But what connects the rise of the anti-lockdown protests, the president's dismissal of the carnage predicted by his own administration, and the eagerness of governors all over the country to reopen the economy before developing the capacity to do so safely is the sense that those they consider "regular folks" will be fine.

Many of them will be. People like Ahmaud Arbery, whose lives are depreciated by the terms of the racial contract, will not.

2.4

The Coronavirus Crisis Is Worsening Racial Inequality

by Connor Maxwell

Originally published in *Center for American Progress*, JUNE 10, 2020

In recent weeks, data have demonstrated that people of color—especially Black and Native American people—are contracting and dying from COVID-19 at far higher rates than their White counterparts[75]. Now, new data from the U.S. Census Bureau reveal that families of color are also disproportionately experiencing the negative social, economic, and mental health effects of the coronavirus crisis[76].

In the Wake of the Coronavirus Crisis, People of Color Face Many Disparities
This column provides fresh, racially disaggregated estimates for the percentages of U.S. households experiencing economic, housing, and food insecurity as well as health and health care problems. These analytical findings underscore the importance of a robust and equitable recovery that centers those who have suffered the most during the coronavirus pandemic and current economic recession.

Increased Economic Hardship
The coronavirus crisis has produced stark racial disparities in negative income shocks. Since March 13, an alarming 43 percent of White households have "experienced a loss of employment income"[77]. However, even higher numbers of Asian American, Black, and Hispanic or Latino households have lost income—49 percent, 54 percent, and 63 percent, respectively. Households of color are also much more likely than their White counterparts to expect "a

loss of employment income in the next 4 weeks because of the coronavirus pandemic." Occupational segregation and employment discrimination have long restricted workers of color to jobs with lower pay, fewer benefits, and less security than those of their White counterparts[78]. Without action, the pandemic could deepen and prolong economic hardship in communities across the United States, especially communities of color[79] (See Figure 2.4-1).

Percentage of households currently experiencing or expecting a loss of employment income due to the pandemic, by race

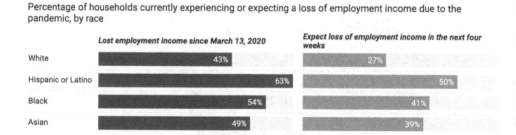

Figure 2.4-1: Households of color are far more likely to experience negative income shocks in the wake of the coronavirus.

Source: Center for American Progress; Author's calculations are based on data from the U.S. Census Bureau, "Household Pulse Survey: May 28-June 2"[80] (accessed June 2020).

Heightened Food Insecurity

Food security in communities of color is not a new problem, but the current crisis has magnified it. People of color have faced substantial barriers to accessing affordable, nutritious food for decades[81]. For example, Black and Hispanic people are much more likely to reside in food deserts than their White counterparts, even after controlling for factors such as poverty[82].

And racial disparities in access to food appear to have only worsened in recent weeks. According to the Census Bureau data, from May 28 to June 2, Black and Hispanic or Latino households were twice as likely as their White counterparts to report that they sometimes or often do not have enough to eat. Among households with children, 21 percent of Hispanic or Latino respondents and 27 percent of Black respondents reported that they are currently experiencing food insecurity, compared with 9 percent of White respondents and 7 percent of Asian respondents. Access to healthy, affordable food is a basic human right. No family should go hungry, especially during a public health crisis (See Figure 2.4-2).

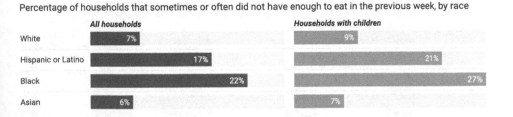

Percentage of households that sometimes or often did not have enough to eat in the previous week, by race

	All households	Households with children
White	7%	9%
Hispanic or Latino	17%	21%
Black	22%	27%
Asian	6%	7%

Figure 2.4-2: The coronavirus crisis has undermined food security in communities of color

Source: Center for American Progress; Author's calculations are based on data from the U.S. Census Bureau, "Household Pulse Survey: May 28-June 2"[83] (accessed June 2020).

High Rates of Housing Instability

Housing instability triggered by the coronavirus pandemic is a growing threat across the United States, especially in communities of color. While 9 percent of White homeowners with a mortgage missed or deferred their mortgage payment last month, a shocking 20 percent of Black homeowners did so. People of color are also twice as likely to have slight or no confidence that they will be able to make next month's payment. Renters are in an even graver situation: 21 percent of White renters, 28 percent of Asian American renters, 45 percent of Hispanic or Latino renters, and 45 percent of Black renters have slight or no confidence that they will be able to pay next month's rent (See Figure 2.4-3). Racial disparities in housing instability are not the product of individual behavior but of decades of housing discrimination and economic degradation[84]. While recent federal, state, and local efforts to establish temporary protections for homeowners and renters are admirable, the nation could experience an avalanche of foreclosures and evictions in the coming weeks and months as these protections expire[85]. These and other second-order consequences of reduced household financial stability could slow the economic recovery and increase racial wealth inequality. Lawmakers must take immediate steps to extend protections, ensure continued assistance, and create more equitable and sustainable housing measures.

Percentage of households that deferred or did not make last month's rent or mortgage payment and percentage of households with no or slight confidence in ability to pay next payment on time, by race

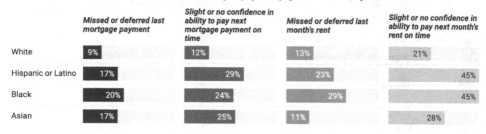

Figure 2.4-3: Homeowners and renters of color are struggling to meet payments

Note: Analysis of homeowners is restricted to households with mortgages. Households with slight/no confidence in ability to pay next month's payment on time include those that plan to defer payments.

Source: Center for American Progress; Author's calculations are based on data from the U.S. Census Bureau, "Household Pulse Survey: May 28-June 2"[86] (accessed June 2020).

Unequal Access to Mental Health Care Services

Millions of Americans, especially people of color, are reporting signs of emotional distress associated with depression and anxiety in the wake of the coronavirus[87]. According to the Census Bureau data, from May 28 to June 2, 51 percent of White Americans, 62 percent of Black Americans, 59 percent of Asian Americans, and 63 percent of Hispanic or Latino Americans were bothered by "not being able to stop or control worrying." Millions also reported "feeling down, depressed, or hopeless"[88] (See Figure 2.4-4). For people of color, increases in reported distress undoubtedly reflect the oppressive social conditions that many of them endure. Further, people of color face substantial barriers to mental health services[89], including language access, stigma, discrimination, lack of affordable high-quality health insurance, and cultural incompetence, as well as refusal to accept insurance among psychiatrists[90]. Lawmakers must ensure that all Americans, regardless of background, have full access to the mental health services they need. Robust and equitable mental health services must be coupled with policies that guarantee access to housing, nutrition, health care, and coronavirus testing and treatment, among other things.

Percentage of Americans reporting signs of emotional distress associated with depression and anxiety at least several days in the previous week, by race

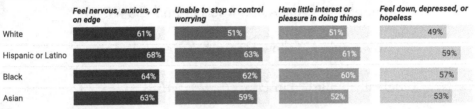

	Feel nervous, anxious, or on edge	Unable to stop or control worrying	Have little interest or pleasure in doing things	Feel down, depressed, or hopeless
White	61%	51%	51%	49%
Hispanic or Latino	68%	63%	61%	59%
Black	64%	62%	60%	57%
Asian	63%	59%	52%	53%

Figure 2.4-4: The pandemic has highlighted the importance of equitable access to mental health services

Note: Estimates include people who reported being bothered by symptoms "at least several days," "at least half the days," or "nearly every day" in the past week.

Source: Center for American Progress; Author's calculations are based on data from the U.S. Census Bureau, "Household Pulse Survey: May 28-June 2"[91] (accessed June 2020).

Conclusion

Data demonstrate that the coronavirus is not the "great equalizer" that some politicians and pundits have purported it to be[92]. On the contrary, inequality has only worsened during the current national hardship. Without bold, prompt policy action, families of color will struggle to recover and be in an even more precarious position when the next crisis arises.

Methodology

To estimate the social and economic effects of the coronavirus crisis on U.S. households, the author utilized data from the U.S. Census Bureau's new weekly Household Pulse Survey, which "ask[s] individuals about their experiences in terms of employment status, spending patterns, food security, housing, physical and mental health, access to health care, and educational disruption"[93]. The nationally representative data presented in this analysis were collected from May 28, 2020, to June 2, 2020. The Census Bureau did not statistically assign missing data, as it would for most survey programs[94]. To most closely match percentages that would result from this statistical imputation, the author based calculations only on the responding cases.

2.5

Xenophobia, Anti-Asian Racism, and COVID-19

by Aggie J. Yellow Horse & Karen J. Leong

Originally published in *Praxis Center*, MARCH 25, 2020

The "coronavirus disease 2019" (COVID-19) is a novel strain of coronavirus that was first detected in Wuhan, China in December 2019. The World Health Organization (WHO) declared the rapidly spreading "COVID-19" as a pandemic (i.e., "a global outbreak of diseases") on March 11, 2020. The first confirmed case of COVID-19 in the United States occurred on January 19, 2020 in Washington State—by a 35-year-old man who traveled to Wuhan and returned to Washington on January 15, 2020[95]. As of March 24, 2020, at least 49,619 people have tested positive for coronavirus in the United States[96].

The response to COVID-19 in the U.S. has unveiled the persistent xenophobia against Asian Americans. Despite the memo sent by WHO to governments and media organizations at the end of February[97] and against CDC recommendation, some U.S. politicians and elements of the media are intentionally using the racialized terms, such as "Chinese Virus" or "Asian Virus"[98]. The term "Wuhan Virus," originated from the media and continued by some politicians, conflates a specific Chinese province with national and continental locations (China and Asia) that historically have been racialized and connected to persons of Asian descent in the U.S. As California representative Ted Lieu tweeted, "[t]he virus was also carried into the U.S. from other countries & U.S. travelers. Calling it Chinese coronavirus is scientifically wrong"[99]. This mislabeling enables xenophobic and racist responses towards Asian/Americans. In fact, the reported cases of racist attacks against Asian Americans have skyrocketed since January and are occurring in all parts of the country, including places with large Asian American populations like New York, and places with smaller Asian American presence, like New Mexico[100].

This hysteria against Asian Americans is not new. The U.S. has a long history of using "others" as scapegoats by associating diseases with "foreigners." In fact, how institutions have shaped meanings of race and citizenship through public health discourses is an important part of Asian American history (and the history of race in the United States)[101]. Late 19th century anti-East Asian racism, deeply rooted in the Yellow Peril xenophobic ideology, viewed East Asians as a threat to the Western world[102]. Nativist policies such as the *Chinese*

Exclusion Act of 1882 and the *Immigration Act* of 1924, singled out Asians and Asian Americans as a racial group targeted for immigration restrictions and quotas, and made ineligible for citizenship. This institutional racism has contributed to the continuing practice of seeing Asian Americans as the *perpetual foreigner stereotype*. Asian Americans thus are perceived as foreign despite the long history of families in the U.S. for generations. This xenophobic "othering" contributes to Asian Americans being targeted for racial stereotyping for interpersonal discrimination through "microaggressions" ("Where are you from?") and racially-motivated hate crimes.

Anti-immigration and anti-Asian sentiments converged on March 10, 2020 when the U.S. President tweeted "We need the Wall more than ever!"[103] in response to Charlie Kirk's March 10 tweet, "With the China Virus spreading across the globe, the U.S. stands a chance if we can control our borders"[104]. This response from the nation's current commander-in-chief contrasts with the actions of former President George W. Bush after the terrorist attack on September 11, 2001. Although his administration did not fully protect the Muslim American community after 9/11, to say the least, Bush visited a mosque six days after the attack and gave a speech in which he explicitly condemned anti-Muslim violence[105]. Brian Levin, a professor of criminal justice who researches hate crimes, has argued that political rhetoric matters, and attributes the sharp drop in hate crimes against Muslim Americans after the speech to Bush's explicit stance[106]. Moreover, by focusing on China as a source of the virus (only as the cause of the problem), we also overlook potential lessons that China and other Asian nations may offer in their efforts to halt its spread[107]. Take for example South Korea's response to the coronavirus. COVID-19 cases dropped sharply in South Korea but are exponentially increasing in the U.S., yet both countries confirmed the first case on the same date—January 19, 2020. What explains these differences? What might we learn from South Korea so that we may better cope with the spread of COVID-19 in the U.S.?[108]

The President's refusal to distance himself from racialized descriptions of the virus only contributes to a climate of fear that disproportionately burdens Asian Americans who are associated with the pandemic[109]. For example, an international student from China enrolled at the University of New Mexico was subject to a "prank" where his dorm room door was sealed off as a biohazard[110]. The student was forced to move off campus out of concerns for his safety. Anecdotal reports of Asian/Americans suggest that verbal harassment and even being forced out of public spaces by threats of violence circulate and spread fear among Asian American communities[111].

The current health strategy to "flatten the curve" of the pandemic has called for "sheltering in place," and "social distancing." To succeed, these critical steps require social cooperation on a large-scale level. It is useful to note, however, that *social distancing already has taken place.* Asian Americans have been shunned, threatened, and harassed—*a different and violent form of distancing that is not informed by science and altruism, but fueled by xenophobic and racist assumptions.* The fears triggered by racial discrimination constitute another threat to our society. Discrimination against Asian Americans and other individuals in the time of a pandemic may have serious consequences for *everyone,* as individuals may try to hide their illness or refuse to seek health care. Our society's gun-centric approach to self-defense also has led some Asian Americans to arm themselves as a form of protection, regardless of its actual effectiveness[112].

The absence of a clear national message condemning xenophobic and racist assumptions allows ignorance and fear to multiply, and feeds violence. While we have seen local leaders and celebrities step up to address these fears and urge caution and care, it is on all of us to think carefully about our response to this crisis. As some agencies and volunteers are reaching out to elderly persons who are practicing isolation to ensure they are not alone, or as some are securing necessities for those who fear exposure to the virus, *how can we also reach out and support those who fear exposure to hatred and violence, including Asian Americans, immigrants, and foreign visitors and residents?*

During World War II, some Japanese American railroad workers in Winslow, Arizona were involuntarily confined to their housing by the Santa Fe Railway company as a "security measure." Some American Indian workers, who lived next to the Japanese American workers, brought food so that the workers and their families would not starve during this frightening time[113]. Other European American neighbors and Mexican American workers supported Japanese American families in Mesa and Glendale, Arizona by selling their farm produce at the market when the Japanese Americans were not allowed to cross into military zones. In these precarious times, these are the examples of how our best protection against this pandemic might be looking out for each other, especially those most vulnerable due to health, age, race and nationality. How we increase social cohesion and collaboration in time of "social distancing" requires acknowledging our social interdependence with each other, even as we practice physical distancing to protect each and every one from harm.

2.6

Coronavirus Is Triggering Historical Trauma—and Real Life Consequences—for Native Americans

by Erika T. Wurth

Originally published in *Bitch Media*, MAY 12, 2020

COVID-19 has been a disaster on every level for every community around the world. But the virus has been particularly deadly for a number of vulnerable communities: the elderly, front-line workers, low-income families, and especially minorities. People whose jobs are classified as essential tend to be folks of color and/or working-class Whites[114]. This version of the coronavirus has also had a terrifying impact on Native American communities, who already live in a state of extreme vulnerability. Indian Health Services, the government-sponsored program that supports Native American citizens, is vastly underfunded. And the lack of personal protective equipment—combined with close living quarters, a lack of running water, and a history of diabetes, asthma, and heart disease—has increased the impact of the coronavirus. For example, if the Navajo Nation was a U.S. state, it would rank behind only New York and New Jersey when it comes to per-capita confirmed cases[115]. In fact, the governor of New Mexico has warned that the virus could potentially wipe out entire tribes in that state, a shattering reality for communities already living with the legacy of genocide[116].

Despite these obvious vulnerabilities, the Trump administration wanted to give tribes literally nothing, and the Republican-controlled Senate designated very few resources to tribes in the recently passed stimulus bill. And adding insult to injury[117], much of the allocated funding is being funneled into state-chartered corporations that don't actually benefit tribally enrolled citizens at all, moving most of the $8 billion allocated primarily to those corporations[118]. As a number of Native writers and scholars, including Rebecca Nagle[119], have noted, this attempt at modern-day genocide has been triggering, to say the least, for communities that historically suffered widespread genocide[120]. More recently these same communities have lived the through the traumatic legacy of boarding and day schools—a continuation of 20th-century genocide[121]. It's undeniable that many Native people on reservations and in urban and rural communities live in a state of poverty. They also often live in close quarters and many times with elders, which is only exacerbating the impact of the virus[122].

Beyond the immediate danger COVID-19 poses to Native lives, it's also disheartening to consider how this pandemic will curtail burgeoning Native art movements and the resurgence of Native languages. Thanks to numerous financial strides[123]—some of which can be attributed to progressive legislation—the Cherokee Nation of Oklahoma, for example, has been able to move its citizens toward a stronger economic position and stronger cultural sovereignty (self-governance), which has made a significant difference in the everyday lives of its citizens. And recently, three Cherokee citizens have released books through large publishers, which is a historic first. Margaret Verble's 2015 novel, *Maud's Line*[124], was a finalist for the Pulitzer Prize in Literature[125]. Brandon Hobson's 2018 novel, *Where the Dead Sit Talking*[126], was shortlisted for a National Book Award. And, a story excerpted from Kelli Jo Ford's forthcoming novel, *Crooked Hallelujah*[127], won the *Paris Review*'s coveted Plimpton Prize.

After such victories, it's worrying to consider how the virus could impact the Cherokee Nation—for example, considering how financially solvent its citizens have become. One only has to look at the numerous educational scholarships available to its citizens[128]—which certainly affect the amount of folks who might become writers—to worry. Now we must wonder if Native American families will survive this pandemic, and what this will mean long-term for artists in these vulnerable communities. COVID-19 also poses an inherent threat to language revitalization since so many elders—the people in many communities who typically speak their Indigenous languages fluently—are at risk[129]. There's a legitimate fear that these cultural movements, not to mention the people leading them, will disappear just as there's been an uptick in the usage of Native American languages, and certainly in their proficiency[130].

These particular issues might seem abstract during a global pandemic, but losing momentum around Native art and languages will have concrete, real-life consequences for everyday American Indians. For example, there have been a number of studies that show that high-school graduation rates increase for American Indians when schools prioritize teaching Indigenous languages[131]. Fueling pride in one's background through language—one of the most fundamental aspects of culture—instills a sense of self-worth that translates to tangible life outcomes. And it goes without saying that art gives people charge to do more than survive, to express themselves, and to think and feel more deeply about who they are and where they come from[132].

The absence of Native people in everyday American mediums only magnifies the strides schools and creators have been making and reinforces the importance of art and language movements from Indian country: reservations, urban, and everywhere in-between. When American Indians are able to create complex art that, when purchased or experienced by non-Natives, offers a fuller portrait of our humanity, there's an increased likelihood that non-Natives will consider supporting our economic and cultural sovereignty. American Indians being able to purchase or receive art from other Natives directly opposes the damage that one-dimensional art about Natives has caused. For instance, though Indian mascots have been deemed harmless by some, many studies show that growing up with mascots, which provide ugly, cartoonish representations of Native people, has a negative impact on our overall self-esteem[133], which is deeply important to develop considering the high suicide rates in Indian country[134].

Throughout history, American Indians have lived in times of termination—where the federal government actively seeks out the destruction of our sovereignty[135]—as well as acts of governance that respect our sovereignty and work to bolster it[136]. American Indians had already been living in a time of termination under the Trump administration, and the virus has considerably worsened this reality. But there are still glimmers of hope: The three aforementioned Cherokee Nation authors are merely the tip of the emerging Native Renaissance: Arapaho/Cheyenne author Tommy Orange's bestselling 2018 novel, *There There*, was nominated for nearly every major literary award, including a National Book Award[137]. Pueblo author Rebecca Roanhorse's 2018 fantasy novel, *Trail of Lightning*, won a Hugo Award, making her the first Native American author to win[138]. Though the coronavirus has dealt a blow to the publishing industry, these authors aren't going away.

There has also been progress in the fashion and art industries, and considering that many of these businesses, such as B.Yellowtail[139] and Eighth Generation[140], already operate online, it's increasingly clear that Native art has the potential to survive this pandemic. Yellowtail will still be a political and fashionista force—and she's currently giving all proceeds from selling goods to the artists whose work she sells alongside her own. Eighth Generation's Louie Gong, a multidimensional artist whose work includes phone cases, earrings, and furniture, is now manufacturing face masks for Seattle's Indian community[141]. And through it all, U.S. citizens should look to Indigenous life to better understand the importance of self-governing, especially for Natives.

We should look to the Lummi Nation, which took independent and immediate action in January 2020 to combat COVID-19. Before the coronavirus hit the United States, the Lummi Nation had already begun using tribal money to build a better healthcare system. And according to *The Seattle Times*, once it realized the potential global impact of the coronavirus, it began "gathering medical supplies, including test kits from a range of sources—including a vendor now sold out—and personal protective equipment in February, and reached out to the [University of Washington] to arrange test processing. The tribe had 300 tests on hand as other clinics around the region were scrambling"[142]. Like the rest of the world, Indian country is scared, and it has even more reason to be. But Native people also know that our languages, our arts, and our right to self-govern will save us.

It's ironic that some U.S. citizens believe that any attempt at a rational, science-based government mandate is oppressive[143]. Many of these same citizens are descendants of those responsible for the genocide of many Native tribes, but now they are staking a claim to their form of self-governance, without realizing the inherent privilege in being able to stay home and watch or read art about people who look just like them, to exercise their right to vote unimpeded, to have officials working for their survival or to have the right to—as usual—endanger the lives of so many of us without a second thought. Perhaps taking a closer look at the people they ignore, look down on, and deride, the people whose identities they often co-opt, could lead them to an enlightened future.

2.7

Stop Blaming Black People for Dying of the Coronavirus

by Ibram X. Kendi

Originally published in *The Atlantic*, APRIL 14, 2020

New data from 29 states confirm the extent of the racial disparities.

I grew up in the Christian Church, the second son of two ministers. I'm not one for making biblical references about my life, but I can't say the same about my father.

Two weeks ago, Dad likened me to John the Baptist, a voice crying out in the wilderness for racial data on the pandemic[144]. I had to remind him that, unlike John, I was not crying out alone. Senator Elizabeth Warren, Representative Ayanna Pressley, and a quintet of Black doctors[145] at the University of Virginia had also raised the alarm[146].

But we were indeed in the wilderness. On April 1, hardly any states, counties, hospitals, or private labs had released the racial demographics of the people who had been tested for, infected with, hospitalized with, or killed by COVID-19. Five days later, citing racial disparities in infection or death rates from five states or counties and the racial demographics of the worst corona-virus hot spots, I speculated that America was facing a racial pandemic within the viral pandemic[147]. But we needed more racial data to know for sure.

Now—after so many Americans joined our chorus, after so many states and counties released their first sets of racial demographic data, after so many data sets showed appalling racial disparities—we know for sure.

At least 29 states have released the racial demographics of confirmed corona-virus cases, death rates, or both, according to the COVID Racial Data Tracker. The tracker, a collaboration between *The Atlantic*'s COVID Tracking Project[148] and my colleagues at the Antiracist Research and Policy Center[149], is being developed to track, analyze, and regularly update racial data on the pandemic within the United States. These initial data provide a still-incomplete picture of the national outbreak's disparities. In 38 percent of the 194,000 cases that these 29 states had reported as of April 12, no racial data were attached. And some states mix racial and ethnic categories in reporting their numbers. But the federal government's failure to assemble these data has left it to us to produce this resource, however incomplete, for researchers, advocates, and the public.

And the picture keeps looking worse by the day. In New York City's ground zero, Latinos make up 34 percent of the known deaths from the coronavirus, higher than their 29.1 percent share of the city's population. Two small Native American pueblos in New Mexico had higher infection rates than any U.S. county as of Friday[150].

But at this point in the pandemic, the disparities between the size of the Black population and the percentage of Black people infected with, hospital-ized with, or dead from COVID-19 appear to be the most severe. A *Washington Post* analysis found that majority-Black counties had infection rates three times the rate of majority-White counties[151]. A Centers for Disease Control and Prevention analysis of nearly 1500 hospitalizations across 14 states found that Black people made up a third of the hospitalizations, despite accounting for 18 percent of the population in the areas studied.[152] An *Associated Press* anal-ysis of available death data found that Black people constituted 42 percent of the victims, doubling their share of the populations of the states the analysis included[153]. In Louisiana, more than 70 percent of the people who have died so far from COVID-19 were Black, more than twice their 32 percent share of the state's population, and well above the 60 percent share of the population of New Orleans, where the outbreak is worst[154]. In New York, African Americans comprise 9 percent of the state population and 17 percent of the deaths[155].

Amid all these data drops last week, a few antiracist voices came out of the wilderness, stood a brief moment at the clearing, then were moved back again into the wilderness. Today, the racial disparities are undeniable. But Americans don't know for sure that there is racism behind those racial disparities. The racism itself remains deniable. So yet again, our voices are crying out in the wilderness for a miracle to save America from its original sin—the sin Americans can't ever seem to confess.

Over the past two weeks, each answer led to new questions. Should states be collecting racial data? Yes. Do those data show racial disparities? They do. And that led to the question Americans have been arguing over since the beginning of the republic: *Why do racial disparities exist?* Why are Black people generally being infected and dying at higher rates than other racial groups? This is the question of the hour. And too many Americans are answering this new question in the old, familiar way. They are blaming poverty, but refusing to recognize how racism distinguishes Black poverty from White poverty, and makes Black poverty more vulnerable to a lethal contagion.

And Americans are blaming Black people. To explain the disparities in the mortality rate, too many politicians and commentators are noting that Black people have more underlying medical conditions but, crucially, they're *not explaining why*. Or they blame the choices made by Black people, or poverty, or obesity—but not racism.

"Now, if you have diabetes, obesity, hypertension, then African Americans are going to have more of those receptors" the coronavirus likes to hit, Senator Bill Cassidy said on NPR's *Morning Edition*. "Now, as a physician, I would say we need to address the obesity epidemic, which disproportionately affects African Americans. That would lower the prevalence of diabetes, of hypertension"[156].

When pressed on whether these "underlying health conditions" are "rooted in years of systemic racism," Cassidy responded: "That's rhetoric, and it may be. But as a physician, I'm looking at science."

Without question, African Americans suffer disproportionately from chronic diseases such as hypertension, cardiovascular disease, diabetes, lung disease, obesity, and asthma, which make it harder for them to survive COVID-19. But if Cassidy were looking at science, then he'd also be asking: *Why are African American suffering more from these chronic diseases? Why are African Americans more likely to be obese than Latinos and Whites?*[157]

Defending Cassidy, Rod Dreher, a senior editor at *The American Conservative*, argued that "in the South, country White people and country Black people eat the same kind of food" and wondered "to what extent Black folks all over the country still eat the traditional soul food diet with lots of grease, salt, pork, sugar, and carbs"[158]. To which one of Dreher's readers responded: "I am especially amused by the implication that a racist conspiracy is keeping Brussels sprouts and kale from Black neighborhoods. If people wanted fresh vegetables and salads and tofu, stores would provide them." If there are food deserts, it seems, then Black people are to blame.

If Black people receive inferior care from hospitals and doctors, are Black people to blame? If Black people are less likely to be insured, are Black people are to blame? If hospitals in majority-Black counties are overloaded with coronavirus patients, are Black people to blame?

According to this logic, racism is not murderous; Black people are killing themselves. To be Black in America is to be suicidal. Black people are to blame for showing up in so many morgues across this godforsaken land.

Others have embraced a different theory of Black culpability. "An information vacuum in some Black communities … allowed false rumors to fester that Black people were immune to the disease," *The New York Times* reported[159]. "While farfetched, the early rumors of Black immunity to the COVID-19 virus gave some African Americans a fantastical hope," the *Los Angeles Sentinel* stated[160].

"Now we're playing catch-up with the messaging and spreading the word that it can affect any one of us," explained Philadelphia city-council member Cindy Bass[161]. "Influential figures in Black communities need to unite and overcorrect for the misinformation running rampant about African Americans being immune to COVID-19," CNN's Van Jones declared[162]. Or as the Los Angeles activist Najee Ali told the *Los Angeles Times*, "That myth spread like wildfire on social media, but there was never a concentrated effort from leaders to dispel that myth"[163].

What actually spread like wildfire was another myth: that the fable of Black immunity affected Black behavior. Where's the evidence that this was widely believed by Black people? Where's the evidence that it caused Black people to not take the virus as seriously as other groups did? Anecdotes offer evidence of individual behavior, not group behavior.

Then again, when it comes to Black people, whenever Americans see a Black *individual* acting in a self-destructive manner, they see Black *people* acting in a self-destructive manner. Whenever Americans see a Black *individual* not social distancing, they see Black *people* not social distancing. Whenever Americans see a group of Black *individuals* congregating at a party or a funeral, they see Black *America* congregating at a party or a funeral. Black individuals are all, always, stand-ins for their race, never individuals. As Barack Obama intoned in *Dreams From My Father*, "Only White culture had individuals"[164].

That many Americans generalized the behavior of Black individuals, claiming Black people are being infected and killed by COVID-19 at higher rates because they are not taking the threat seriously or social distancing appropriately, should not be surprising. "The message of social distancing doesn't seem to be hitting home, with people still playing basketball, having card parties and hosting sleepovers, say Black mayors," *USA Today* reported[165]. "I don't think our community is taking it as seriously as it should," said Lovely Warren, the mayor of Rochester, New York, and the second vice president of the African American Mayors Association[166]. Instead, African Americans have taken a "lackadaisical approach to social distancing," surmised Representative Marc Veasey of Fort Worth, Texas[167]. A Cleveland nurse made it plain: "Ignorance is causing us to have a rapid increase"[168].

Because they believe the cause of higher Black infection rates is Black ignorance and skepticism, a group of Dallas-area pastors and community leaders recently launched the #WeNeed2Survive campaign, aimed at "preventing misinformation," "educating skeptics about social distancing," and "raising awareness without fear"[169]. As the director Tyler Perry pleaded in an Instagram message to Black people: "Please, please, please, I beg you to take this seriously"[170].

There is nothing wrong with begging all Americans to take this vicious virus seriously. There is nothing wrong with begging one's Black grandfather or White daughter or Latina sister or Asian father or Native friend to social distance. There is everything wrong with lecturing a racial group to behave better as a solution to racial disparities, as U.S. Surgeon General Jerome Adams did on Friday during a White House press conference[171].

Too many Americans are infected with the belief that *a* cause or *the* cause of higher Black infection or death rates is that Black people are not taking the viral threat seriously, and that White people have lower infection and death rates because they *are* taking COVID-19 seriously.

But the evidence points in the opposite direction. A national survey conducted by the Pew Research Center between March 10 and 16, long before racial disparities in infection rates were documented, found that Black respondents, at 46 percent, were more than twice as likely as White respondents, at 21 percent, to view the coronavirus as a major threat to their own health[172]. An additional 32 percent of Black respondents considered it a minor threat. Slightly more White respondents (23 percent) than Black respondents (21 percent) considered the coronavirus to not be a threat.

Days later, Pew and Dynata conducted a survey that again found that Black people (59 percent) were significantly more likely than White people (44 percent) to be very concerned about their health during this pandemic[173]. According to the survey, Black people were more likely than White people to be buying nonperishable foods, hand sanitizer, cleaning products, toilet paper, and bottled water. Ironically, the very people calling Black people ignorant are ignorant about Black people.

What if Black people *are* taking the coronavirus as seriously as White people? What if Black people have been taking the coronavirus *more* seriously than White people for weeks, as the survey data suggest? What if despite all that, Black people are *still* being infected and dying at higher rates from COVID-19?

The answer of the hour can be heard. Our voices are still crying out in the wilderness: *Black people are not to blame for racial disparities. Racism is to blame.*

I want to imagine the day when the wilderness finally clears for good, when our antiracist voices are heard for good, when Americans will no longer blame Black people for Black death. I want to imagine the day when every valley shall be lifted up, and every mountain and hill made low; the uneven ground will become smooth, and the rugged land a plain.

But I cannot see that day right now, because I remain in the wilderness.

2.8

Stolen Breaths

by Rachel R. Hardeman, Eduardo M. Medina, & Rhea W. Boyd

Originally published in *The New England Journal of Medicine*, JULY 16, 2020

In Minnesota, where Black Americans account for 6% of the population but 14% of COVID-19 cases and 33% of COVID-19 deaths, George Floyd died at the hands of police.

"Please—I can't *breathe*."

He was a Black man detained on suspicion of forgery, an alleged offense that was never litigated or even charged, but for which he received an extrajudicial death sentence.

"Please—I can't *breathe*."

He was only 46 years old.

"Please—I can't *breathe*."

And he was loved.

But despite onlookers' pleas and his own calls of distress, with his face against the pavement, three officers on his back, and a knee in his neck, he was murdered.

"Please—I can't *breathe*."

While trained officers and paramedics stood by, and a horrified community witnessed, Floyd was denied the basic rights of due process and the basic dignity of life support.

"Please—I can't *breathe*."

In the wake of his public execution, uprisings have ignited in cities throughout the United States and the world, many of them led by young Black people. Despite potential risks of exposure to COVID-19, demonstrators are laying bare the deep pain that persists for Black people fighting to live under the crushing weight of injustice that has long been at our necks. The words "I can't breathe" hang heavy in the air. But they are so much more than a rallying cry. They are indictments.

"Please—I can't *breathe*."

The truth is Black people cannot breathe because police violence is a major cause of premature death, of stolen lives and stolen breaths in America. And it is a particularly deadly exposure for Black Americans.

"Please—I can't *breathe*."

The truth is Black people cannot breathe because as many mourn George Floyd, we also mourn Breonna Taylor and Tony McDade, and the nearly 1000 people who are killed by police each year, an outsized proportion of whom are Black.

"Please—I can't *breathe*."

The truth is Black people cannot breathe because we are preemptively grieving the 1 in 1000 Black men and boys who will be killed by police[174].

"Please—I can't *breathe*."

We are holding our children closer and tighter because we know Black girls will be presumed to be older, less innocent, and less in need of protection than White girls as early as 5 years old[175], and Black boys by 10 years old. We know the risks that may meet them when they leave our sides, and we hide our silent devastation when we prepare them for those risks—risks that no amount of guidance may deter.

"Please—I can't *breathe*."

The truth is Black people cannot breathe because the legacies of segregation and White flight, practices of gentrification and environmental racism, and local zoning ordinances combine to confine us in residential areas where we are disproportionately exposed to toxins and pollutants. As a result, Black populations have higher rates of asthma and cancer. And recent data suggest that chronic exposures to particulate matter in the air may contribute to a risk of death from COVID-19 as much as 15% higher for Black Americans than that faced by White Americans.[176]

"Please—I can't *breathe*."

The truth is Black people cannot breathe because we are currently battling at least two public health emergencies, and that is a conservative estimate. One of every 1850 Black Americans have lost their lives in this global fight against a novel virus that could have harmed anyone[177]. And yet—because of racism and the ways humans use it to hoard resources and power for some, while depriving others—it has killed an enormous number of Black people.

"Please—I can't *breathe*."

And Black people are three times as likely to be killed by police as White people.[178] Both these realities are acutely threatening Black lives right now. But prevailing gaps in maternal and infant mortality have long threatened our survival beginning before we are even born.

"Please—I can't *breathe*."

In the face of literal gasps, as Black communities bear the physical burdens of centuries of injustice, toxic exposures, racism, and White supremacist violence, too many either do not know what our communities endure or are aware but choose not to act. Too many "leaders" wonder how we got here and what we can do to move forward, as if the answers have not been ever-present.

We got here, as the sociologist Ruha Benjamin expertly notes, because "Racism is productive"[179]. We got here because we live in a country established by Indigenous dispossession and genocide. Because slavery and the racial ordering of humans and goods it established constructed a political economy predicated on devaluing Black labor, demeaning Black bodies, and denying Black humanity. We got here because stolen lives and stolen breaths are profitable and we work in systems that continue to reap the gains.

"Please—I can't *breathe*."

Any solution to racial health inequities must be rooted in the material conditions in which those inequities thrive. Therefore, we must insist that for the health of the Black community and, in turn, the health of the nation, we address the social, economic, political, legal, educational, and health care systems that maintain structural racism. Because as the COVID-19 pandemic so expeditiously illustrated, all policy is health policy.

We expect the deployment of these solutions to meet the urgency of this moment and the dire needs it has evidenced. We have confidence that these changes can be made rapidly, given the agility with which health care systems have reorganized in the face of COVID-19—many establishing new practice patterns, payment models, and delivery mechanisms. The response to the pandemic has made at least one thing clear: systemic change can in fact happen overnight.

Although there is much to do, we recommend that health care systems engage, at the very least, in five practices to dismantle structural racism and improve the health and well-being of the Black community and the country:

Divest from racial health inequities. Racial health inequities are not signs of a system malfunction: they are the by-product of health care systems functioning as intended. For example, the U.S. health insurance market enables a tiered and sometimes racially segregated health care delivery structure to provide different quality of care to different patient populations. This business model results in gaps in access to care between racial and ethnic groups and devastating disparities like those seen in maternal mortality. Universal single-payer health care holds the promise of removing insurance as a barrier to equitable care.

Desegregate the health care workforce. The health care workforce is predominantly White at essentially every level, from student and staff to CEO. This lack of diversity must be understood as a form of racial exclusion[180] that affects the economic mobility and thus the health of non-White groups. For example, health care systems are often the economic engines and largest employers in their communities. Extending employment opportunities to those communities can extend the employer-based insurance pool, raise the median wage, support the local tax base, and counter the gentrification and residential segregation that often surrounds major medical centers—each of which improves population health.

Make "mastering the health effects of structural racism" a professional medical competency. In 2016, we asked individual clinicians to "learn, understand and accept America's racist roots"[181]. In 2020, it is clear that clinicians need to master learning the ways in which structural racism affects health. We believe that medical schools and training programs should equip every clinician, in every role, to address racism. And licensing, accreditation, and qualifying procedures should test this knowledge as an essential professional competency.

Mandate and measure equitable outcomes. Just as health care systems are required to meet rigorous safety and quality performance standards for accreditation, they should be required to meet rigorous standards for addressing structural racism and achieving equity in outcomes.

Protect and serve. Health care systems must play a role in protecting and advocating for their patients. Victims of state-sanctioned brutality are also patients, who may present with injuries or disabilities or mental health impairments, and their interests must be defended. Health care systems should also be on the forefront of advocating for an end to police brutality as a cause of preventable death in the United States. They should take a clear position that the disproportionate killing of Black (and Indigenous and Latinx) people at the hands of police runs counter to their commitment to ensuring the health, safety, and well-being of patients.

"Please—I can't *breathe*."

Police violence, racial inequities in COVID-19, and other forms of structural racism are concurrent and compounding public health crises in the United States.

"Please—I can't *breathe*."

Postmortem evidence indicates that George Floyd tested positive for COVID-19, underscoring this reality. The choice before the health care system now is to show, not tell, that Black Lives Matter.

Because, like George Floyd, Black people are loved.

Notes

1   https://www.dukeupress.edu/black-and-blur
2   https://www.dukeupress.edu/in-the-wake
3   https://www.dukeupress.edu/in-the-wake
4   https://www.fordhampress.com/9780823274550/blackpentecostal-breath/
5   https://en.wikipedia.org/wiki/Sister_Outsider
6   https://books.google.com/books/about/Black_Feminist_Thought.html?id=cdtYsU3zR14C
7   https://books.google.com/books/about/Black_Feminist_Thought.html?id=cdtYsU3zR14C (p. 80)
8   *The New York Times'* memorial page set up specifically for coronavirus victims and their obituaries reveals the contours of the virus's effects, and highlights that the deaths were mostly older people, many in care facilities, who had 'underlying conditions.'
9   https://www.charlotteobserver.com/news/coronavirus/article241625916.html
10 https://www.kff.org/coronavirus-covid-19/issue-brief/communities-of-color-at-higher-risk-for-health-and-economic-challenges-due-to-covid-19/
11 https://www.hrc.org/blog/hrc-president-on-the-disproportionate-impact-of-covid-19-on-marginalized-po
12 https://www.vox.com/2020/4/19/21225195/stay-at-home-protests-trump-tea-party-reelection
13 https://theconversation.com/why-are-white-supremacists-protesting-to-reopen-the-us-economy-137044
14 https://www.nytimes.com/2020/05/03/us/coronavirus-extremists.html
15 https://www.foreignaffairs.com/articles/united-states/2020-06-23/growing-white-supremacist-menace
16 https://www.vox.com/first-person/2020/4/25/21234774/coronavirus-covid-19-protest-anti-lockdown
17 https://www.nytimes.com/2020/04/26/us/ahmed-arbery-shooting-georgia.html
18 https://int.nyt.com/data/documenthelper/6916-george-barnhill-letter-to-glyn/b52fa09cdc974b970b79/optimized/full.pdf
19 https://www.nytimes.com/2020/05/05/us/ahmaud-arbery-killing-georgia.html
20 https://www.theatlantic.com/ideas/archive/2020/05/ahmaud-arbery/611539/
21 https://twitter.com/jduffyrice/status/1258414240450457606
22 https://www.ajc.com/blog/investigations/jury-quickly-says-not-guilty-georgia-elections-case/uxbnZO4AUxmBQfTmVGZjXK/
23 https://www.amazon.com/Racial-Contract-Charles-W-Mills/dp/0801484634
24 https://www.nytimes.com/2015/01/23/us/in-tamir-rice-shooting-in-cleveland-many-errors-by-police-then-a-fatal-one.html
25 https://www.mediamatters.org/sean-hannity/fox-news-attacks-black-lives-matter-lawless-after-cheering-cliven-bundys-lawless
26 https://www.politico.com/news/2020/04/17/white-house-farmer-aid-193180
27 https://www.washingtonpost.com/archive/opinions/1989/07/30/children-of-cocaine/41a8b4db-dee2-4906-a686-a8a5720bf52a/
28 https://www.theatlantic.com/politics/archive/2017/07/what-the-crack-baby-panic-reveals-about-the-opioid-epidemic/533763/

29 https://www.americanimmigrationcouncil.org/research/
    did-my-family-really-come-legally-todays-immigration-laws-created-a-new-reality
30 https://www.latimes.com/politics/story/2020-05-06/
    business-groups-lobby-congress-to-ease-their-liability-to-corornavirus
31 https://www.nytimes.com/2020/05/07/nyregion/nypd-social-distancing-race-coronavirus.html
32 https://www.theatlantic.com/politics/archive/2017/11/the-nationalists-delusion/546356/
33 https://www.theatlantic.com/ideas/archive/2018/10/the-cruelty-is-the-point/572104/
34 https://www.theatlantic.com/ideas/archive/2019/11/trump-war-crimes/602731/
35 https://www.theatlantic.com/ideas/archive/2019/06/
    census-case-about-white-mans-government/590977/
36 https://www.theatlantic.com/ideas/archive/2020/03/donald-trump-menace-public-health/608449/
37 https://www.vulture.com/article/famous-people-celebrities-with-coronavirus.html
38 https://www.nbcnews.com/politics/donald-trump/
    brazilian-official-who-met-trump-mar-lago-tests-positive-coronavirus-n1156861
39 https://www.washingtonpost.com/investigations/the-inside-story-of-the-cpac-scare-when-
    the-coronavirus-passed-within-a-handshake-of-the-president-no-public-health-agency-took-
    charge/2020/03/19/8fbebe42-67a3-11ea-b313-df458622c2cc_story.html
40 https://www.theatlantic.com/health/archive/2020/04/
    pandemic-summer-coronavirus-reopening-back-normal/609940/
41 https://www.washingtonpost.com/health/2020/03/10/social-distancing-coronavirus/
42 https://www.nbcnews.com/politics/politics-news/
    fact-check-trump-says-u-s-ready-contain-covid-19-n1195621
43 https://www.whitehouse.gov/briefings-statements/
    remarks-president-trump-vice-president-pence-meeting-governor-reynolds-iowa/
44 https://www.nytimes.com/2020/04/07/us/coronavirus-race.html
45 https://www.mediamatters.org/coronavirus-covid-19/
    rush-limbaugh-slams-news-coverage-coronavirus-racial-disparity-how-they-stop
46 https://www.mediamatters.org/coronavirus-covid-19/
    tucker-carlson-coronavirus-crisis-may-have-passed-well-see-it-looks-it-may
47 https://twitter.com/BadFoxGraphics/status/1247684528698777600
48 https://www.mediamatters.org/fox-news/
    fox-news-dangerous-coronavirus-mission-accomplished-moment
49 https://www.washingtonpost.com/politics/2020/04/08/
    leading-model-now-estimates-tens-thousands-fewer-covid-19-deaths-by-summer/
50 https://www.washingtonpost.com/local/new-coronavirus-cases-despite-shutdown/2020/04/30/
    a8e5685e-8566-11ea-878a-86477a724bdb_story.html
51 https://www.mediamatters.org/tucker-carlson/
    tucker-carlson-praises-michigan-protest-against-coronavirus-mitigation-efforts
52 https://www.mediamatters.org/coronavirus-covid-19/
    defending-protests-against-social-distancing-tucker-carlson-takes-democratic
53 https://www.mediamatters.org/coronavirus-covid-19/
    defending-protests-against-social-distancing-tucker-carlson-takes-democratic
54 https://www.ipsos.com/en-us/news-polls/abc-news-coronavirus-poll
55 https://www.washingtonpost.com/nation/2020/05/06/study-finds-that-disproportionately-black-
    counties-account-more-than-half-covid-19-cases-us-nearly-60-percent-deaths/
56 https://cepr.net/a-basic-demographic-profile-of-workers-in-frontline-industries/
57 https://www.pewsocialtrends.org/2020/04/21/
    about-half-of-lower-income-americans-report-household-job-or-wage-loss-due-to-covid-19/
58 https://trib.al/mB5fUk4
59 https://www.washingtonpost.com/nation/2020/05/06/study-finds-that-disproportionately-black-
    counties-account-more-than-half-covid-19-cases-us-nearly-60-percent-deaths/
60 https://www.wuwm.com/post/workers-are-scared-says-wisconsin-meatpacking-plant-worker-who-
    tested-positive-covid-19#stream/0
61 https://www.cpr.org/2020/05/03/were-not-heroes-were-sacrificial-workers-carry-the-burden-of-
    colorados-food-supply-chain/
62 https://www.buzzfeednews.com/article/albertsamaha/smithfield-foods-coronavirus-outbreak
63 https://www.desmoinesregister.com/story/news/health/2020/05/05/
    coronavirus-infects-thousands-iowa-meatpacking-plant-workers-covid-19-waterloo-perry/5170796002/
64 https://www.washingtonpost.com/opinions/2020/05/05/
    republican-governors-our-states-stayed-open-covid-19-pandemic-heres-why-our-approach-worked/
65 https://www.nytimes.com/interactive/2020/04/28/us/coronavirus-death-toll-total.html

66 https://www.whitehouse.gov/briefings-statements/
remarks-president-trump-signing-proclamation-honor-national-nurses-day/
67 https://www.nytimes.com/2020/04/27/us/politics/trump-coronavirus-testing.html
68 https://www.nytimes.com/2020/04/26/opinion/coronavirus-economy-reopen.html
69 https://www.npr.org/2020/04/30/848321204/
how-the-cares-act-became-a-tax-break-bonanza-for-the-rich-explained
70 https://www.bls.gov/news.release/empsit.nr0.htm
71 https://nypost.com/2020/05/05/trump-blue-state-coronavirus-bailouts-are-unfair-to-republicans/
72 https://www.nytimes.com/2020/05/05/business/economy/trump-tax-cuts-coronavirus-stimulus.html
73 https://www.cnbc.com/2020/05/05/trump-acknowledges-some-coronavirus-deaths-will-result-from-reopening.html
74 http://maristpoll.marist.edu/wp-content/uploads/2020/04/NPR_PBS-NewsHour_Marist-Poll_USA-NOS-and-Tables_202004280852.pdf#page=3
75 https://www.cdc.gov/coronavirus/2019-ncov/need-extra-precautions/racial-ethnic-minorities.html
76 https://www.census.gov/householdpulsedata
77 https://www2.census.gov/data/experimental-data-products/household-pulse-survey/household-pulse-survey-questionnaire.pdf?
78 https://www.americanprogress.org/issues/race/reports/2019/08/07/472910/
systematic-inequality-economic-opportunity/
79 https://www.americanprogress.org/issues/race/news/2020/04/14/483125/
economic-fallout-coronavirus-people-color/
80 https://www.census.gov/data/experimental-data-products/household-pulse-survey.html
81 https://tcf.org/content/commentary/
covid-19-lays-bare-vulnerabilities-u-s-food-security/?session=1&session=1
82 https://hub.jhu.edu/magazine/2014/spring/racial-food-deserts/
83 https://www.census.gov/data/experimental-data-products/household-pulse-survey.html
84 https://www.americanprogress.org/issues/race/reports/2019/08/07/472617/
systemic-inequality-displacement-exclusion-segregation/
85 https://evictionlab.org/covid-policy-scorecard/
86 https://www.census.gov/data/experimental-data-products/household-pulse-survey.html
87 https://www.washingtonpost.com/health/2020/05/26/
americans-with-depression-anxiety-pandemic/?arc404=true
88 https://www2.census.gov/data/experimental-data-products/household-pulse-survey/household-pulse-survey-questionnaire.pdf?
89 https://www.law.georgetown.edu/poverty-inequality-center/wp-content/uploads/sites/14/2019/12/
Mental-Health-and-Communities-of-Color.pdf
90 https://ps.psychiatryonline.org/doi/full/10.1176/appi.ps.201800014
91 https://www.census.gov/data/experimental-data-products/household-pulse-survey.html
92 https://www.npr.org/sections/coronavirus-live-updates/2020/03/31/824555135/
chris-cuomo-says-he-tested-positive-for-coronavirus
93 https://www.census.gov/householdpulsedata
94 https://www2.census.gov/programs-surveys/demo/technical-documentation/hhp/2020-Household-Pulse-Survey-User-Notes.pdf
95 Holshue, M. L., DeBolt, C., Lindquist, S., Lofy, K. H., Wiesman, J., Bruce, H., & Diaz, G. (2020). First case of 2019 novel coronavirus in the United States. *New England Journal of Medicine.*
96 https://www.nytimes.com/interactive/2020/us/coronavirus-us-cases.html
97 https://www.who.int/docs/default-source/coronaviruse/covid19-stigma-guide.pdf
98 https://www.theguardian.com/world/2020/mar/10/
republicans-face-backlash-racist-labeling-coronavirus-china-wuhan
99 https://twitter.com/tedlieu/status/1237218087004295168
100 https://drive.google.com/file/d/1gkrjw4tfOQLoF_T2YztgExtzexGi0jNX/view
101 Shah, N. (2001). *Contagious Divides: Epidemics and race in San Francisco's Chinatown.* University of California Press. Molina, N. (2006). *Fit to be Citizens? Public health and race in Los Angeles, 1879-1939.* University of California Press. The authors also acknowledge that blaming specific ethnic communities for disease and epidemics has a long history worldwide, such as the persecution of Jewish people throughout Europe during the spread of the bubonic plague in the mid-14th century.
102 Lyman, S. M. (2000). The "Yellow Peril" Mystique: Origins and Vicissitudes of a Racist Discourse. *International Journal of Politics, Culture and Society, Vol. 13* (4): 683-747. Lyman credits Kaiser Wilhelm with using the term to specifically refer to China as a military threat in 1895, with Arthur de Gobineau using the term to refer to the economic threat Chinese poised to labor in the early 20th century (p. 688).

103 "Build the Wall" is a frequently use anti-Mexican, anti-Latinx trope that this president employs as a political mobilization tactic: https://twitter.com/realDonaldTrump/status/1237334397172490240

104 https://twitter.com/charliekirk11/status/1237306970429775872

105 https://www.c-span.org/video/?c4552363/user-clip-bushs-911-speech-mosque.

106 https://www.newsweek.com/islamophobia-america-rise-hate-crimes-against-muslims-proves-what-politicians-640184

107 https://www.nytimes.com/2020/03/19/opinion/coronavirus-testing.html

108 https://www.sciencemag.org/news/2020/03/coronavirus-cases-have-dropped-sharply-south-korea-whats-secret-its-success

109 https://www.nytimes.com/2020/03/18/us/politics/china-virus.html

110 https://www.kob.com/albuquerque-news/chinese-student-at-unm-subject-of-racist-prank/5673113/

111 https://www.npr.org/2020/03/02/811363404/when-xenophobia-spreads-like-a-virus

112 https://www.newsweek.com/coronavirus-gun-sales-asian-california-washington-1491891

113 Russell, A. B. (2003). *American Dreams Derailed: Japanese Railroad and Mine Communities of the Interior West*. PhD dissertation, Department of History, Arizona State University.

114 https://www.vox.com/covid-19-coronavirus-explainers/2020/4/23/21228971/essential-workers-stories-coronavirus-hazard-pay-stimulus-covid-19

115 https://www.sltrib.com/news/2020/04/19/navajo-nation-has-higher/

116 https://abcnews.go.com/Politics/mexicos-governor-warns-tribal-nations-wiped-coronavirus/story?id=69884997

117 https://www.huffpost.com/entry/tribes-stimulus-coronavirus-white-house-republicans_n_5e839c10c5b6871702a5dc10

118 https://newrepublic.com/article/157345/coronavirus-emergency-aid-become-disaster-indian-country

119 https://twitter.com/rebeccanagle/status/1241360492507078657?s=20

120 https://www.vice.com/en_us/article/m7qwnv/the-us-has-neglected-indian-country-for-years-now-comes-a-pandemic

121 https://www.history.com/news/how-boarding-schools-tried-to-kill-the-indian-through-assimilation

122 https://www.washingtonpost.com/climate-environment/2020/04/04/native-american-coronavirus/

123 https://www.muskogeephoenix.com/news/notes-from-the-chief-making-great-strides-in-economic-growth/article_b2cb0066-366e-5197-ac65-03eb9782fdca.html

124 http://bookshop.org/books/maud-s-line/9780544705241

125 https://www.pulitzer.org/finalists/margaret-verble

126 http://bookshop.org/books/where-the-dead-sit-talking/9781641290173

127 http://bookshop.org/books/crooked-hallelujah/9780802149121

128 https://www.cherokee.org/all-services/education-services/college-resources/

129 https://newrepublic.com/article/157070/protecting-native-elders-pandemic

130 https://www.acf.hhs.gov/sites/default/files/ana/a_new_chapter_for_native_american_languages_in_the_united.pdf

131 https://www.chronicle.com/article/For-Native-Students/237210

132 https://www.arts.gov/sites/default/files/nea_arts/neaARTS_2013_v1.pdf

133 https://www.changethemascot.org/wp-content/uploads/2013/10/DrFriedmanReport.pdf

134 http://www.usatoday.com/story/news/nation/2019/06/21/suicide-rate-native-american-indian-women-men-since-1999/1524007001/

135 https://www.smithsonianmag.com/history/the-cherokees-vs-andrew-jackson-277394/

136 https://obamawhitehouse.archives.gov/the-press-office/2011/12/02/executive-order-13592-improving-american-indian-and-alaska-native-educat

137 http://bookshop.org/books/there-there-9780525436140/9780525436140

138 https://rameylady.com/2019/04/28/review-trail-of-lightning-rebecca-roanhorse-hugo-award-reads/

139 https://byellowtail.com/

140 https://eighthgeneration.com

141 https://eighthgeneration.com/blogs/blog/eighth-generation-donates-over-10-000-ppe

142 https://www.seattletimes.com/seattle-news/a-lummi-nation-doctor-is-self-quarantined-but-the-tribe-has-been-preparing-for-weeks-for-a-coronavirus-outbreak/

143 https://www.newsweek.com/majority-americans-oppose-protests-against-coronavirus-measures-poll-1499127

144 https://www.theatlantic.com/ideas/archive/2020/04/stop-looking-away-race-covid-19-victims/609250/

145 https://www.buzzfeednews.com/article/nidhiprakash/coronavirus-tests-covid-19-black

146 https://hosted.ap.org/article/c0e58c2e0de70169ef000ce3666c285a/democratic-lawmakers-call-racial-data-virus-testing

147 https://www.theatlantic.com/ideas/archive/2020/04/coronavirus-exposing-our-racial-divides/609526/

148 https://covidtracking.com/data

149 https://antiracismcenter.com/
150 https://indiancountrytoday.com/news/
two-pueblos-have-some-of-the-highest-infection-rates-in-us-5IAXXwxfsU6gLdWcR74tnA
151 https://www.washingtonpost.com/nation/2020/04/07/coronavirus-is-infecting-killing-black-americans-
an-alarmingly-high-rate-post-analysis-shows/?arc404=true
152 https://www.cdc.gov/mmwr/volumes/69/wr/mm6915e3.htm
153 https://abcnews.go.com/US/wireStory/outcry-racial-data-grows-virus-slams-black-americans-70050611
154 https://www.wwno.org/post/black-communities-are-hit-hardest-covid-19-louisiana-and-elsewhere
155 https://covid19tracker.health.ny.gov/views/NYS-COVID19-Tracker/NYSDOHCOVID-19Tracker-Fat
alities?%3Aembed=yes&%3Atoolbar=no&%3Atabs=n
156 https://www.npr.org/2020/04/07/828715984/
sen-bill-cassidy-on-his-states-racial-disparites-in-coronavirus-deaths
157 https://www.cdc.gov/obesity/data/adult.html
158 https://www.theamericanconservative.com/dreher/class-race-coronavirus-cuisine/
159 https://www.nytimes.com/2020/04/07/us/coronavirus-race.html
160 https://lasentinel.net/more-coronavirus-cases-dispel-black-immunity-myth.html
161 https://www.inquirer.com/news/philadelphia-coronavirus-race-african-american-cases-rising-20200403.
html
162 https://www.cnn.com/2020/04/06/opinions/african-americans-covid-19-risk-jones/index.html
163 https://www.latimes.com/california/story/2020-04-07/l-a-releases-first-racial-breakdown-of-
coronavirus-fatalities-african-americans-have-higher-death-rate
164 https://www.penguinrandomhouse.com/books/123909/dreams-from-my-father-by-barack-obama/
165 https://www.dispatch.com/news/20200408/why-are-so-many-black-people-dying-from-coronavirus
166 https://www.dispatch.com/news/20200408/why-are-so-many-black-people-dying-from-coronavirus
167 https://www.star-telegram.com/news/special-reports/article241880466.html
168 https://www.fox19.com/2020/04/09/cleveland-nurse-hoping-educate-african-americans-alarming-
racial-disparities-with-covid-deaths/
169 https://www.wfaa.com/article/news/health/coronavirus/black-covid-19-patients-dallas-county-
nationwide-higher-rates-hospitalized/287-8eacaf04-e7dd-48d5-a204-f053215b3098
170 https://www.instagram.com/p/B-vkUYbn7eP/
171 https://www.vox.com/2020/4/11/21217428/surgeon-general-jerome-adams-big-mama-coronavirus
172 https://www.people-press.org/2020/03/18/u-s-public-sees-multiple-threats-from-the-coronavirus-and-
concerns-are-growing/
173 https://www.wsj.com/articles/the-hand-sanitzer-divide-coronavirus-behaviors-vary-by-race-
party-11584795601
174 https://www.pnas.org/content/116/34/16793
175 https://www.law.georgetown.edu/poverty-inequality-center/wp-content/uploads/sites/14/2017/08/
girlhood-interrupted.pdf.
176 https://www.medrxiv.org/content/10.1101/2020.04.05.20054502v2
177 https://apmresearchlab.org/
178 https://mappingpoliceviolence.org/
179 https://belonging.berkeley.edu/video-ruha-benjamin
180 https://pubmed.ncbi.nlm.nih.gov/31232362/
181 https://www.nejm.org/doi/full/10.1056/NEJMp1609535

Part Three

Investments in Coronavirus Capitalism

3.1

Coronavirus Is the Perfect Disaster for 'Disaster Capitalism'

by Marie Solis

Originally published in *VICE*, MARCH 13, 2020

Naomi Klein explains how governments and the global elite will exploit a pandemic.

The coronavirus is officially a global pandemic[1] that has so far infected 10 times more people[2] than SARS did. Schools, university systems, museums, and theaters across the U.S. are shutting down, and soon, entire cities[3] may be too. Experts warn[4] that some people who suspect they may be sick with the virus, also known as COVID-19, are going about their daily routines, either because their jobs do not provide paid time off or because of systemic failures in our privatized health care system.

Most of us aren't exactly sure what to do[5] or who to listen to. President Donald Trump has contradicted recommendations from the Centers for Disease Control and Prevention, and these mixed messages[6] have narrowed our window of time to mitigate harm from the highly contagious virus.

These are the perfect conditions for governments and the global elite to implement political agendas that would otherwise be met with great opposition if we weren't all so disoriented. This chain of events isn't unique to the crisis sparked by the coronavirus; it's the blueprint politicians and governments have been following for decades known as the "shock doctrine," a term coined by activist and author Naomi Klein in a 2007 book[7] of the same name.

History is a chronicle of "shocks"—the shocks of wars, natural disasters, and economic crises—and their aftermath. This aftermath is characterized by "disaster capitalism"[8], calculated, free-market "solutions" to crises that exploit and exacerbate existing inequalities.

Klein says we're already seeing disaster capitalism play out on the national stage: In response to the coronavirus, Trump has proposed a $700 billion[9] stimulus package that would include cuts to payroll taxes[10] (which would devastate Social Security) and provide assistance to industries that will lose business as a result of the pandemic.

"They're not doing this because they think it's the most effective way to alleviate suffering during a pandemic—they have these ideas lying around[11] that they now see an opportunity to implement," Klein said.

VICE spoke to Klein about how the "shock" of coronavirus is giving way to the chain of events she outlined more than a decade ago in *The Shock Doctrine*.

This interview has been lightly edited for length and clarity.

Let's start with the basics. What is disaster capitalism? What is its relationship to the "shock doctrine"?

Naomi Klein: The way I define disaster capitalism is really straightforward: It describes the way private industries spring up to directly profit from large-scale crises. Disaster profiteering and war profiteering isn't a new concept, but it really deepened under the Bush administration after 9/11, when the administration declared this sort of never-ending security crisis, and simultaneously privatized it and outsourced it—this included the domestic, privatized security state, as well as the [privatized] invasion and occupation[12] of Iraq and Afghanistan.

The "shock doctrine" is the political strategy of using large-scale crises to push through policies that systematically deepen inequality, enrich elites, and undercut everyone else. In moments of crisis, people tend to focus on the daily emergencies of surviving that crisis, whatever it is, and tend to put too much trust in those in power. We take our eyes off the ball a little bit in moments of crisis.

Where does that political strategy come from? How do you trace its history in American politics?

NK: The shock-doctrine strategy was a response to the original New Deal under FDR. [Economist] Milton Friedman believes everything went wrong[13] in America under the New Deal: As a response to the Great Depression and the Dust Bowl, a much more activist government emerged in the country, which made it its mission to directly solve the economic crisis of the day by creating government employment and offering direct relief.

If you're a hard-core free-market economist, you understand that when markets fail it lends itself to progressive change much more organically than it does the kind of deregulatory policies that favor large corporations. So, the shock doctrine was developed as a way to prevent crises from giving way to organic moments where progressive policies emerge. Political and economic elites understand that moments of crisis is their chance to push through their wish list of unpopular policies that further polarize wealth in this country and around the world.

Right now, we have multiple crises happening: a pandemic, a lack of infrastructure to manage it, and the crashing stock market. Can you outline how each of these components fit into the schema you outline in The Shock Doctrine?

NK: The shock really is the virus itself. And it has been managed in a way that is maximizing confusion and minimizing protection. I don't think that's a conspiracy, that's just the way the U.S. government and Trump have utterly mismanaged this crisis. Trump has so far treated this not as a public health crisis but as a crisis of perception[14], and a potential problem for his reelection.

It's the worst-case scenario, especially combined with the fact that the U.S. doesn't have a national health care program and its protections for workers are abysmal. This combination of forces has delivered a maximum shock. It's going to be exploited to bail out industries that are at the heart of most extreme crises that we face, like the climate crisis: the airline industry[15], the gas and oil industry[16], the cruise industry[17]—they want to prop all of this up.

How have we seen this play out before?

NK: In *The Shock Doctrine*, I talk about how this happened after Hurricane Katrina. Washington think tanks like the Heritage Foundation met and came up with a wish list of "pro-free market" solutions to Katrina. We can be sure that exactly the same kinds of meetings will happen now— in fact, the person who chaired the Katrina group was Mike Pence[18]. In 2008, you saw this play out in the original [bank] bailout, where countries wrote these blank checks to banks, which eventually added up to many trillions of dollars. But the real cost of that came in the form of economic austerity [later cuts to social services]. So it's not just about what's going on right now, but how they're going to pay for it down the road when the bill for all of this comes due.

Is there anything people can do to mitigate the harm of disaster capitalism we're already seeing in the response to the coronavirus? Are we in a better or worse position than we were during Hurricane Katrina or the last global recession?

NK: When we're tested by crisis we either regress and fall apart, or we grow up, and find reserves of strengths and compassion we didn't know we were capable of. This will be one of those tests. The reason I have some hope that we might choose to evolve is that—unlike in 2008—we have such an actual political alternative[19] that is proposing a different kind of response to the crisis that gets at the root causes behind our vulnerability, and a larger political movement that supports it.

This is what all of the work around the Green New Deal has been about: preparing for a moment like this. We just can't lose our courage; we have to fight harder than ever before for universal health care, universal child care, paid sick leave—it's all intimately connected.

If our governments and the global elite are going to exploit this crisis for their own ends, what can people do to take care of each other?

NK: "I'll take care of me and my own, we can get the best insurance there is, and if you don't have good insurance it's probably your fault, that's not my problem": This is what this sort of winners-take-all economy does to our brains. What a moment of crisis like this unveils is our porousness to one another. We're seeing in real time that we are so much more interconnected to one another than our quite brutal economic system would have us believe.

We might think we'll be safe if we have good health care, but if the person making our food, or delivering our food, or packing our boxes doesn't have health care and can't afford to get tested—let alone stay home from work because they don't have paid sick leave—we won't be safe. If we don't take care of each other, none of us is cared for. We are enmeshed.

Different ways of organizing society light up different parts of ourselves. If you're in a system you know isn't taking care of people and isn't distributing resources in an equitable way, then the hoarding part of you is going to be lit up. So be aware of that and think about how, instead of hoarding and thinking about how you can take care of yourself and your family, you can pivot to sharing with your neighbors and checking in on the people who are most vulnerable.

3.2

'Disaster Socialism': Will Coronavirus Crisis Finally Change How Americans See the Safety Net?

by Will Bunch

Originally published in *The Philadelphia Inquirer*, MARCH 12, 2020

Diana Hernández has one foot in the Ivy League, where she's an assistant professor of sociomedical sciences at Columbia University's Mailman School of Public Health, and another in the grittier streets of the South Bronx, the mostly working-class area where she lives. Walking down a Bronx boulevard the other day, she witnessed scenes much different from the TV-news version of the coronavirus crisis, where suburbanites stuff payloads of squeezably soft toilet paper and price-gouged Purell in the back of luxury SUVs.

Instead, Hernández wrote[20] that she witnessed Bronx shoppers at her local Dollar Tree stocking up on bleach, a tiny four-pack of toilet paper or a three-pack of Cup Noodles—stockpiles for families that lack cash for day-to-day emergencies, let alone the uncertainties of a global pandemic. She called it emblematic of how hard the coronavirus crisis is for people living on the margins—who can't simply work from home when their job is cleaning hospital floors or frying fast-food burgers, who can only get around on crowded buses or subways, who can't take paid sick days or don't have child care when their kids' schools shut down.

"The Black and brown folks who work for these corporations have to show up on their line or at their cleaning facility, because they're taking care of the things that can't be taken care of remotely," Hernández told me by phone. I'd called her after reading her op-ed[21] on how a public health crisis has laid bare what so many have tried to ignore for so long—the many ways that the cruel inequalities of modern U.S. capitalism weigh on working people.

The public-health emergency even has some lawmakers who've worked for decades to cut the social safety net now supporting a universal paid sick leave—at least for this one virus[22], if not for the 900 or whatever other things that could make workers ill—and/or even funding what might be called Medicaid-for-all ... people with coronavirus symptoms[23], so that the uninsured or under-insured will get free testing[24], at least.

In 2020, a liberal is a conservative who's been exposed to the coronavirus. It was almost surreal to watch a suddenly kinder, gentler-sounding Mike Pence declare[25] that "[w]hen we tell people, 'If you're sick, stay home,' the president has tasked the team with developing economic policies that will make it very, very clear that we're going to stand by those hardworking Americans." Aren't these the same people fighting in court to deny health insurance to hardworking Americans with other types of pre-existing medical conditions? (Spoiler alert: Yes, they are[26].)

It's fascinating to watch how a pandemic-inspired fear of the unknown—flavored by the fact that COVID-19 initially tended to spread through the things that more affluent Americans do, like travel overseas, book cruise-ship vacations or attend business conferences—has finally caused at least a slight bump in awareness of the kind of problems that everyday folks, working two or three jobs in a gig economy, have been screaming about for years.

Many experts noted that America's mad scramble to suddenly guarantee paid sick days or coverage for necessary medical procedures must look strange to Europeans, or other developed societies with a generous safety social net, where leaders don't think the only solution to every problem is to throw more tax breaks at corporations and pray that a few dollars trickle down. *The New York Times* recently noted[27] that Germany, France, Denmark, and the Netherlands are among the nations where workers have a right to paid sick leave—and that sense of security, along with the knowledge that folks won't get surprise medical bills, have dampened both the economic fallout and some of the fear from the pandemic.

On this side of the Atlantic, in the land of unfettered free-market capitalism and "rugged individualism," things are a little different. With no federal law in place, about a dozen, mostly blue states[28], D.C., and about 30 municipalities (including Philadelphia[29], for most employers, in 2015) have mandated paid sick leave, often over the objection of business lobbyists[30] offering dire predictions of profit shrinkage.

In arguably the most well-timed paper in the history of American academia, research co-led by a Temple University professor[31]—and dropped by the National Bureau of Economic Research on Monday, in the heat of the coronavirus debate—found that the economic costs of paid sick leave are surprisingly low while other gains are high.

Temple economist Johanna Catherine Maclean and her two colleagues, using a treasure trove of wage and benefit data reported to the U.S. Labor Department from 2009 to 2017, when a number of state and local mandatory paid-leave laws were enacted, found workers in those jurisdictions took just two more sick days a year. There was no significant effect on business, and the researchers calculated the per worker cost at 20 cents per hour. But the workers were healthier and better off, and probably had better morale. And they weren't making their co-workers sick when they could afford to stay home—even before the coronavirus reached America.

Maclean told me on Wednesday that "sometimes it takes a crisis" for leaders to see the benefits of something like paid sick leave, even though polls before the coronavirus showed roughly 75 percent of Americans support such laws. "We see this pattern," she said, "where it takes a troubling development to rise the value of a policy change to policy makers."

Well, yes and no. As is so often the case in today's American oligarchy, corporations are responding faster and better to the public outcry than government. In the last week, we've seen big businesses like Amazon[32] to Darden Restaurants[33] to gig economy icon Uber[34] agree to some form of coronavirus sick leave—the same kind of thing they've been fighting against for workers came down with, say, Influenza Classic, which may kill 30,000 Americans this year[35].

But up on Capitol Hill, GOP Sen. Lamar Alexander—even while making the concession, seemingly remarkable for a top Republican, that a bill mandating 14 days of paid sick leave in a national health emergency is "a good idea"[36]— then blocked that good idea (which also allowed workers to accrue seven days of conventional paid sick days a year) because he believes that government and its bottomless pasta bowl of debt should pay the tab, not the industrialists who coincidentally finance the Republican Party.

The legislative state-of-play on Thursday—with the nation reeling[37] from a bear market, the suspension of NBA basketball, and news that Tom Hanks and his wife Rita Wilson are the first celebrity cases—is the same-old gridlock, for now. The new plan from House Democrats[38] is people-oriented—sick leave, widespread free testing, food aid, and unemployment insurance—while Trump is talking typical GOP corporate welfare and tax cuts[39]. But the pressure of a worsening crisis could be the thing—maybe the only thing, in 2020's divided America—that leads to common ground.

There's a notion that's gained credence over the last decade or two—"the shock doctrine"[40], as named by the writer Naomi Klein, also known as "disaster capitalism"—that our modern kleptocracy uses tragedies, from natural (like hurricanes) to manmade (like, um, stock market crashes) to impose policies[41] such as privatization of government services that the public would never go for in normal times. But can it work in reverse? Can the shock of a pandemic— and the realization that our cruel capitalist constructs have made it harder to deal with—cause a reversal of fortune?

Will the coronavirus crisis spark a kind of "disaster socialism," to finally embrace the social safety net that's the norm in so many other countries?

The political irony is that 2020 started out with two high-profile presidential candidates calling for the kind of radical change that would have made a public-health crisis like the current moment easier for everyday Americans: Sens. Elizabeth Warren[42] and Bernie Sanders[43]. Now Warren is gone and Sanders is on the ropes, as voters in the earlier stage of the coronavirus crisis focus less on policy and more on the kind of familiar leadership offered by Joe Biden.

But despite their flaws, the thing about Biden and, arguably, President Trump is that both men are not rigid ideologues. They have been known to bend to the moment. Trump, after all, used to be a pro-choice Democrat while Biden was a Catholic moderate of the 1970s who evolved into championing gay marriage. Today, rising to meet this crisis means embracing the security that working Americans need to pay their medical bills or call out sick or put their kid in child care. If there was ever a time for a Nixon-in-China[44] transformation, it's now.

And if calling this "disaster socialism" makes you politically uncomfortable, then just call it simply a more humane America. But the coronavirus has exposed an underlying sickness in modern U.S. society that too many of us have tried to avoid for too long. It's time to embrace the cure.

3.3

I Don't Feel Like Buying Stuff Anymore

by Anne Helen Petersen

Originally published in *BuzzFeed News*, MAY 18, 2020

Our economy is built on Americans of all class levels buying things. What happens when the ability—and desire—to do so goes away?

I didn't even realize I'd lost my desire to shop until one day, about six weeks into isolation, I absentmindedly clicked on a Madewell email offering an additional sale on a sale. I don't even have anywhere to wear the jumpsuits I already own, let alone one that would require *heels*. Every work trip, every speaking gig, every quick vacation had already been canceled, even as my calendar still had reminders of the life I had planned in advance, on a different timeline, for myself. But in a matter of weeks, those, too, would be gone. I feel very lucky to spend my days walking my dog on the same loop I always take. But that walk, for the foreseeable future, requires no new purchases.

I don't need new makeup, because I've stopped wearing it. I have Zoom calls with my friends after they've put their kids to bed, and everyone's hair is just as wild, their faces just as makeup-less, as mine. I'm still lucky enough to be working. Others have been furloughed or laid off. Those changes may shape the tenor of our shared but separate isolation, but not its fundamental character. The aperture of my world feels very small, its rhythms incredibly repetitive. Sometimes, it's almost calming. Other times, it's incredibly claustrophobic. Either way, there are only so many pairs of leggings I need to navigate this new life.

Not wanting to buy things feels as bizarre as not wanting to sleep or not wanting to eat. It's been ingrained in us, as Americans, as an unspoken component of residency. Before the coronavirus[45] pandemic, I'd find myself clicking on the emails that overflowed the Promotions tab in Gmail, seemingly from every store I'd ever patronized. I'd online shop while I was traveling for work, while stressed, while avoiding a seemingly insurmountable number of *other* emails in my inbox. Buying things, especially things on sale, provided a momentary sense of comfort: I was fixing some problem, completing some task, simply by clicking "Buy Now."

We're trained to buy often, buy cheap, and buy *a lot*. And I'm not just talking about food, which everyone has to acquire in some capacity, or clothes. I mean all the other small purchases of daily life: a new face lotion, a houseplant holder, a wine glass name trinket, an office supply organizer, a vegetable spiralizer, a cute set of hand towels, a pair of nicer sunglasses, a pair of sports sunglasses, a pair of throwaway sunglasses. The stuff, in other words, that you don't even know that you want until it somehow finds its way to your cart at Target or T.J. Maxx.

In post–World War II America, the vast majority of things we buy are often not what we actually need. But they're indisputably *things we want*: manifestations of personal and collective abundance. We buy because we're bored, or because planned obsolescence[46] forces us to replace items we can't fix. We buy to accumulate objects meant to communicate our class and what sort of person we are[47]. We buy because we want to feel something or change something, and purchasing something is the quickest way to do so. When that doesn't work, we buy "an experience," whether it's a night at Color Me Mine or a weekend bachelorette trip to Nashville[48]. We buy because, from the Great Depression onward, how we consume has become deeply intertwined[49] with how we think of ourselves as citizens.

The U.S. didn't become a nation of consumers because everyone has ample amounts of discretionary cash. Before the pandemic, income inequality had reached its highest levels[50] since the Depression. Most Americans' wages, when adjusted for inflation and purchasing power, have barely risen[51] in four decades. In 2018, with the economy at its most robust in years, 61% of Americans said they could not cover a surprise expense of $400. In 2019, a study by the AARP[52] found that 53% of American households did not have an emergency savings account—including a quarter of those who earn more than $150,000 a year.

So how do Americans buy so much when we have so little discretionary money? Massive amounts of credit. Payday loans, credit cards, quick and easy car loans, and the newly common "Afterpay" function in online checkouts incentivize spending beyond our means. The average American has a startling $6,194 in credit card debt[53], with an average interest rate of 16.88%. Over the last decade, auto debt has gone up[54] 40%, and the average auto loan for a new car[55] is a whopping $32,199. In April 2019, Americans reported borrowing[56] $88 billion over the previous year just to cover medical costs. The middle class is going deeper and deeper into debt[57] to maintain the expenditures of middle-class identity. The working class has done the same—borrowing for cars, for tuition[58], for everyday expenditures—only often at much higher interest rates[59].

And yet we keep spending: As of 2018, the average household expenditure was $61,224[60]. That's rent and groceries, but also nonessential items: entertainment, vacation, clothes, plus all that other random stuff that ends up in your shopping cart.

That kind of spending is what our current economic model is based on: Americans of all class levels buying things and always wanting to buy more, regardless of their actual means. But when a society-throttling, economy-decimating pandemic comes along, what happens when that ability—and, just importantly, that *desire*—goes away? In April, retail sales fell an astonishing 16.4%[61], far more than the 12.3% economists had predicted. Clothing store purchases went down by 78.8%; furniture and home furnishings plummeted 58.7%. If you feel like you're buying far less than at any point in recent history, you're very much not alone. But will American identities and habits actually change, or will we just figure out a new and COVID-19-compatible way to consume at the same rate as before?

In many ways, the pandemic has functioned as a great clarifier[62], making it impossible to ignore the dilapidated state of so many American systems. It's highlighted whose work is actually essential[63], which leaders actually care about people who aren't like them[64], and whose lives[65] are considered expendable[66].

The supply chain is broken; the social safety net is in shambles. And a whole lot of things we thought of as *needs* have revealed themselves to be pretty deeply unnecessary.

Any attempt to suggest otherwise—as various clothing shops have attempted to do ("Perfect Tops for Zoom Calls!")—feels desperate or obtuse. "I've cut back on some of the beauty products I was using," Jordan, who's 40, works in tech, and still has her job, told me. "I realized just how many promises those products were making: *I'll look refreshed!* Or *My skin won't look like the Cryptkeeper's!* But I don't need all that shit if I hydrate and look after myself. I find myself wanting to be sold to *less*." In the early weeks of the pandemic, Els, who's 29 and lives in Houston, found herself sucked into the sales offers in her inbox. "But when I put the clothes in my cart, I kept thinking: *When am I really going to wear these? Jeans? In* this *economy?*"

As unemployment numbers continue to rise and most of the country is still in some sort of lockdown, any marketing that frames a new shirt as a "quarantine necessity" feels like a con. Especially when you factor in a newfound awareness (and attention to) the human cost of each purchase: For everything you buy online, there are people in factories packaging it, others in warehouses distributing it, and still more in trucks delivering it. Some companies have taken steps to provide adequate personal protective equipment and paid sick leave. But many, including Amazon[67], have been slow to act—and assurances from workplaces concerning worker and warehouse safety have been[68] refuted[69] by employees[70]. (A spokesperson for Amazon said they expect to invest approximately $4 billion from April to June on COVID-related initiatives to get products to customers and keep employees safe.)

Tania, who's 34 and works for a nonprofit, is telecommuting and collecting her usual salary, as is her husband. With significant guilt and consternation, they've made the decision to leave their small apartment and move in, after 14 days of isolation, with her parents in another state. They've been living out of the three suitcases they brought for themselves and their two young children for several months and plan to keep doing so for the foreseeable future.

"Everything I've bought has been for my kids, who are growing out of their clothes," Tania told me. "And I have agonized over every purchase. The calculus for every decision is: Do I need to put an essential worker in harm's way to get this? Can I do without it? Can I afford it? Do we have anything that could work in its place? Can I wait 10 days for it, since that's the average shipping time? And if I can't have something immediately, do I really want it?"

Ann, 56, lives outside of Torrey, Utah, 50 miles from the closest Walmart. For her, bulk shopping has been a way of life: Apart from a monthly trip to the city, she and her family get everything from friends or online. "Let's put it this way: Our UPS driver has a personal relationship with not just us, but our dogs and farm critters," she told me.

Now they're just trying to make do with less, generally—but they still have to go to the feed store for their animals. ("There's no such thing as UberFeed," Ann said.) They drive 17 miles into town for contactless grocery orders. "I just did a meal plan for four weeks instead of one," Ann explained. They got a CSA share for a quarter of a cow and a year's worth of poultry. Cutting out trips to the big city (Salt Lake) means cutting out a significant number of expenses. "I am so grateful that where we live, at least in our circle, dressing up means clean denim and fleece," she said.

Ann misses musicians coming through the area; she's worried about how dips in tourism will affect everyone she knows. But she also refuses to participate in a plan to revive the economy that places the burden on the consumer. "After 9/11, and again after the 2008 recession, there was the idea that consumers should somehow patriotically spend to revive the economy," she said. "And who benefited disproportionately? Billionaires. This time, the billionaires can do the heavy lifting, not me."

What Ann's referring to is the larger idea of *citizenship*—Americanness, patriotism, loyalty—through consumerism. In *A Consumers' Republic: The Politics of Mass Consumption in Postwar America*[71], historian Lizabeth Cohen traces the origins of this ideology to the 1930s, as the needs, protection, and veneration of the consumer began to supersede those of the worker. The consumer could do their American duty (and preserve the food chain) by *not* buying during World War II—and funneling any excess money into war bonds. But once the war was over, Americanism was expressed by engagement in mass consumption. The more Americans bought, the more American factories produced—and the more America could assert its status as a new global superpower.

This idea was ingrained in the American psyche, sometimes quite explicitly. Cohen points to a *Life* magazine photo spread from 1947, published under the headline "Family Status Must Improve: It Should Buy More for Itself to Better the Living of Others." The piece argued that "a health and decency standard for everyone" meant every American family buying, well, a whole lot of stuff: a washing machine, a suit for Dad, a high chair, new cabinets, a new telephone.

In this figuration, mass consumption wasn't indulgent or selfish but a way of creating "full employment and improved living standards for the rest of the nation."

At the time, many American families were going from deprivation to abundance, transitioning from living with their parents or military service to marriage and new homes—at least for White families—purchased with the help of the GI Bill. War bonds were cashed out; new construction in the suburbs was plentiful; American manufacturing recentered its ambition from wartime production to domestic goods and automobiles. And buying all this stuff did make life better for a much larger swath of the population: The growth in manufacturing, combined with robust unions, allowed blue-collar workers to enter the rapidly expanding middle class.

During this so-called golden age of American capitalism, real per capita income rose 2.25% *a year*[72]. That period only lasted 20 years—from around 1950 to 1970—but it has cast a long shadow over Americans' understanding of themselves: what's possible, what's necessary, what each of us deserves, and what conditions make America "great." The enduring myths of the white picket fence, "working your way through college," the sustainability of a single-income household, the superiority of the single-family home, the car as essential, the primacy of the nuclear family, the family vacation, even the widespread commercialization of holidays—these all grew in the fertile economic soil of the time.

But even as that economy began to sour—for various, tangled reasons, first in the '70s, and again with rolling mini recessions through the '80s and '90s—those myths continued to endure. As did the idea that buying things was a form of civic responsibility, even as the rolling deregulatory actions of the Reagan, Bush, and Clinton administrations, coupled with nationwide union busting and the gradual "tempification" of the workplace, meant fewer and fewer Americans were actually benefiting much at all from those purchases. Before, the idea went: You bought a washing machine so that everyone else could buy a washing machine. Now, you bought one so the men in charge of the washing machine company could buy a new jet.

Two weeks after 9/11, President George W. Bush famously called upon Americans to soothe their grief by shopping. "Get down to Disney World in Florida," he said. "Take your families and enjoy life the way we want it to be enjoyed." The country had already been in a mini recession since the previous March, and the sharp decrease in travel and entertainment that followed 9/11 threatened to deepen it. However laughable that messaging seems today, it was effective at the time: After declining sharply in September 2001, personal consumer spending rose sharply[73] just a month later. The recession ended shortly thereafter[74].

"The president's political message was also clear," Charles F. McGovern writes about Bush in *Sold American: Consumption and Citizenship, 1890–1945*[75]. "The citizen's duty was not mandatory military service to combat terrorism (although the rate of volunteers rose), or civic engagement to strengthen social bonds in the wake of national disaster and shock. The citizen's duty certainly did not include sincere questioning or reexamination of national security and diplomacy, although millions of Americans did just that. Instead, the president urged everyone to resume business as usual: individual, atomized consumption was best for the nation as a whole. Americans faced trauma, doubt, and fear; the White House directed them to the nearest mall."

Because the recession was so brief—and because the "forever wars" that followed in Afghanistan and Iraq only directly affected a portion of Americans—few would look back at the period following 9/11 and think of any substantial changes in their consumption. Some lost money on the stock market over the course of the dot-com boom; others boycotted french fries. Ideas about Muslims and torture, about "the axis of evil" and America's place in the world, all changed. But not our shopping—at least not until 2008.

The popular understanding of the financial crisis — largely gleaned, at this point, from *The Big Short*, *Margin Call*, and the "Giant Pool of Money"[76] podcast—is that Wall Street, through a series of complicated machinations, screwed itself over by pretending that bad debt was good debt. But that "bad" debt, in the form of subprime mortgages, was the result of hundreds of thousands of Americans being convinced, and then convincing *themselves*, that they could afford to take on massive debt for massive homes they couldn't actually afford. The most shocking stories of the crisis focused on the people who didn't have jobs, didn't have any form of savings, and still managed to buy a home that would require a $2000-a-month mortgage. But many of those stories were also about people who were convinced they could afford a second home, either as an investment or vacation property: Between 2000 and 2007, the percentage of Americans with second homes rose from 20% to 35%.

But what does "afford" really mean, anyway? Few people can "afford" the full price tag of a college education, but we go anyway. Someone might be able to cover the cost of a mortgage or rent, but they might need to use credit cards to cover the cost of incidentals. The availability of credit makes nearly anything *seem* affordable. Between 1990 and 2007, consumer (e.g., everything from credit card balances to car loans) and mortgage debt went from 77% to 127% of disposable income. That sort of increase means we weren't just spending more than we had. We were normalizing it.

But the particularities of the 2008 recession meant that people all over the United States started losing their homes—an estimated 10 million in all[77]. And that, to many Americans, burst a foundational understanding of self. People and businesses—including the current president's—go bankrupt all the time in

America. But going from being a homeowner back to being a renter suggested something fundamentally broken at the core of the American project. Experts, lenders, banks—they all said that you *qualified* for this loan. You *qualified* for homeownership. What you dreamed of could be yours. People said it was the housing "bubble" that burst, but it was actually one of those original postwar myths of what it meant to be an American that overinflated to the point of collapse. And when that happened, there was so little left of the rest of the American dream to assuage them: so few good jobs, no robust social safety net, nothing to buoy you financially when you can no longer work. Just more debt on top of existing debt, a mirage of success hiding at the bottom of a well.

The grief and disillusionment following that collapse translated, briefly, into consumer frugality. Consumer spending in 2008 dropped sharply[78]; in *The Economist*, an analyst for Morgan Stanley predicted[79] that "the golden age of spending for the American consumer has ended and a new age of thrift likely has begun." *The New York Times* ran a piece in 2009 about consumers reveling in the new, miserly normal, describing[80] how "the gleefully frugal happily seek new ways to economize and take pride in outsaving the Joneses." In 2011, the paper profiled[81] the movement to repair and recycle older items, pointing to early data that consumers were holding on to items—like cars—longer than before. Personal savings rates, which had plummeted to as low as 2.2%[82] amid the massive influx of consumer credit in the '80s, '90s, and '00s, climbed to 12% in December 2012.

But within a year, those personal savings rates were nearly cut in half. Then-president Barack Obama was elected to a second term, and the Occupy Wall Street movement—sparked by anger over the growing income inequality—fizzled. Sure, the jobs added back to the economy were low-paying and, in the vast number of cases, part of the precarious new gig economy; sure, healthcare costs continued to rise and millennials gradually began to internalize the fact that milestones of adulthood might remain permanently outside their reach. But the economy was in "recovery"—which meant a return to spending (and saving) norms.

As Sheldon Garon, author of *Beyond Our Means: Why America Spends While the World Saves*, explained[83] back in 2012, most Americans weren't actually able to substantively change their saving habits: "Those in the middle- and lower-income strata have made efforts to reduce debt, but they are so indebted and have so little savings that it's been difficult for them to significantly increase savings." You might not be able to save, but with readily available home equity loans and credit cards, at least you could still *buy*—and that felt like you were doing *something*.

But that feeling, for many, has soured. Stephanie is 36, unemployed, and "swimming in debt"—but her husband's job is secure, so they're "okay on monthly expenses," at least for the time being. Like many others I've heard from, she's cautious about predicting any sort of long-term shift in spending behaviors—in part because *buying things* has become so central to our understanding of recovery from economic trauma.

"The consumption-as-civic-duty, billionaires-as-job-creators ethos is toxic for so many things," she said. "I feel like a lot of rich folks I know genuinely think they're 'doing good' when they get a manicure or go shopping because they're stimulating the economy. And it's hard to disagree when the American economy really is built on consumer spending and confidence."

The "economy" is technically all of the resources of a given area: all of its production, all of its consumption. But many people—including a whole lot of politicians—use the word "economy" in situations when they really mean "the stock market." The *economy* is built on consumer spending; the *stock market* is built on projections. Or, as I like to think about it, a bunch of guys (and they're almost entirely guys) sitting around, making periodically educated yet often irrational and emotional bets about the future. The economy and the stock market are not disarticulated from each other, but they are also far from the same thing; it's no coincidence, after all, that the highest levels of income inequality have coincided with record-breaking numbers on the stock market.

But the stock market *signals* economic health. It's what gets broadcast, it's what Trump talks about at his rallies, it determines politicians' polling numbers. It doesn't matter if you, yourself, don't feel that financial security and everyone else you know is barely keeping above water.

If the "economy" is thriving, everyone else must be, too, right? Hence the growing indebtedness necessary to maintain middle-class status: It takes a lot of debt to keep up with the illusion that the entire country is doing great.

And this is where the pandemic, and the economic collapse that's accompanied it, comes in. Its wreckage is so vast, so all-encompassing, that no amount of presidential rhetoric, no calls for patriotic mass consumption, can conceal it. The illusion has been shattered. We're buying less because we're scared for the economic future and concerned for the workers who make buying things possible, but we're also buying less because the actual act of purchasing—at least in person—is a risk.

The amount of new "revolving" credit extended to individuals (in most cases: credit cards) went down 31%[84] between February and March, the most extreme drop since 1989. According to Visa, credit card spending collapsed in all categories except food and drugstores, while savings rates grew[85] from

8% in February to 13.1% in March—the highest since 1981. No one knows when or how long COVID-19 measures will be in place (or if they will be reimplemented). Very few people feel secure in their economic futures[86]. "People have seriously reined in their spending," one analyst told[87] CNN. "You have to wonder when they will feel comfortable splurging." It won't be for some time—regardless of when states begin to open. "The current pandemic mood of consumers cannot be easily or quickly reversed," Richard Curtin, director of the University of Michigan's Surveys of Consumers, wrote[88] earlier this month. "Moods are remarkably independent of conscious control."

But what if…we don't ever go back? People are still buying things right now, but the things many people are seeking out, apart from necessities, offer an experience: a way to create something or otherwise distract themselves. Cooking and bartending implements, craft supplies, mini trampolines, gardening tools, Pelotons. An employee at my local bike store said they've had their busiest three-month period on record. Home improvement stores are as packed as a store can be at this point. Shopping still creates a momentary feeling of control—something all of us are lacking right now. But so, too, does making something, growing something, mastering something, or weeding something.

Natalie, 29, lives in St. Paul with her husband and is currently on unemployment. "I have been going nuts, needing projects to keep me busy, so I'm spending more than I did before on home improvement–type things, like gardening and pantry organization," she said. "I spend a lot of time trying to find things I can afford from 'cool independent retailers' that I would like to support, but most of that is too expensive for me. But I just say no to Amazon and only shop at places where they have made a concrete statement about what they are actively doing for their workers."

Some of these home improvements can be done with items on hand. Some require purchases. And some can be facilitated by newly vibrant bartering communities. Tania (the one living out of three suitcases) is still getting emails from the parents group she was a part of back in the city. Usually, it's filled with parents selling and giving away baby items; now, she said, "it's in overdrive."

"You don't need to buy *anything*," she said. "You just post to the listserv what you need, and someone will give it to you. I've also seen an amazing trade economy emerge: trading yeast for flour, toys for sourdough bread, passing clothes from one family to the next."

I've seen a similar activity in my local "Buy Nothing Sell Nothing" Facebook Groups here in Montana: people making and giving away masks, using 3D printers to manufacture dupe N95 masks, giving away children's toys and electronics in a "contactless exchange." Just because you're not buying anything (or buying less) doesn't mean you're not experiencing new things, doing new things, figuring out new things.

I know a lot of people—especially those who live in small apartments—have become fatigued with their spaces. Being with your stuff all the time can make you resent it. There's a reason, after all, that those "Buy Nothing" Facebook Groups and parenting listservs are flooded with people trying to give things away right now. But I also know people who have found a deep appreciation for all that they *do* have—the marvelous comfort of a bed or a fuzzy blanket, a small and sunny corner with houseplants you check on every day, a pile of books arranged just so—that just feel *right* and *yours*. But the things you chose, instead of just accumulated, become all the more cherished.

Some of these practices can feel like the same sort of performative change in behavior that was featured in *The New York Times* trend piece on frugality[89] after the 2008 recession: a real estate investor, married to a plastic surgeon, who's gotten really into borrowing books from the library instead of buying them. Regrowing scallions on your windowsill—and posting photos of them to Instagram—is simply the latest version. But the extent of the crisis, and the nebulous but lingering physical and psychological barriers to buying, makes these behaviors feel *different*.

This might, of course, be a misguided proclamation coming from the inside of a pandemic. But in addition to the actual risk (to oneself, to others) of buying things, the pandemic has afforded many Americans, whether in isolation or out of work, with something they haven't had in years: time and mental space to actually think about the way we spend and its effects on others.

Farrah, 33, lives in San Jose, where she works two part-time jobs and has $80,000 in student loan debt. She describes her current economic situation as "fairly precarious." "I knew that Amazon was terrible before this, and I continued to buy from them," she said. "But the plague has really laid all of this out in a way that I can't ignore: people being fired for organizing for basic protection, the risk involved in getting people things (essential and very inessential alike) and Bezos/Amazon raking in money all the while. COVID-19 has made me realize how fragile and fucked our whole supply chain is." (Amazon has disputed this in a previous story[90].)

Evan, 32, works in private education and described himself as "comfortable and stable upper-middle-class for New York." Since going into quarantine, he's bought a pair of painters overalls and a puzzle, both from Amazon, which he justified because he was using a gift card and didn't buy on a Strike Day. He's getting groceries once a week, but only at local stores; he's been buying higher-quality foods via mail-order meat subscriptions or the neighborhood butcher shop. "Between the distancing rules and the cognizance of my privilege, I feel like there's more impediments to me spending, both physically and mentally," he said. "I'm spending less than half what I used to on a monthly basis, maybe even less."

"The thing that's staying with me is how many of these bad shit purchases are attempts to create control and satisfaction from circumstances where I (seem to) have little," he continued. "I'm incredibly lucky that my isolation has brought me less stress and more time for myself. And it's amazing how, in that state, I am better able to act on good ethics and self-care and just spend less. If our jobs and commutes weren't wringing us emotionally dry on a daily basis, we'd be much more ethical consumers, maybe?"

And that's the thing: If you do have time to think about your consumption choices right now, you have time free from stress, period. Beatrice, 26, is a "middle-class renter" in South Dakota with no kids and no debt. She lives an hour outside the nearest town; before COVID-19, she relied heavily on Amazon. She's still ordering a few necessities online—just direct from retailers—but otherwise donating what she's saved to organizations helping those in need. But she's wary of making any pronouncements about how others should be internalizing the lessons of the pandemic.

"I'm a middle-class White lady," she said. "You can say, 'We should focus on buying only high-quality goods that last'—but for so many folks, fast fashion and particleboard furniture is all they can afford. Ideally we would stay the fuck out of other people's business and ignore what others are buying, but I don't think humans are wired that way. So maybe instead we tax the hell out of people who can afford to buy tons and tons of stuff and redistribute that so that everyone can have high-quality items if they want them."

This is where pandemic-induced reductions in spending, decadelong resentment over income inequality[91], the resurgent progressive and labor movements[92], sustained millennial/Gen X burnout[93] and precarity, and burgeoning Gen Z idealism collide. What if we decided that things didn't have to be the way they were before all of this happened? Part of that shift would involve taxing the rich and disarticulating healthcare from employment; it would involve forming and protecting unions and focusing on reimplementing regulatory systems, decentralizing production, and restoring the supply chain. And it could also mean disabusing ourselves of the idea that buying things is a solution to our problems.

In this moment, the primary tension in America is how, and when, life is going to "return to normal." But that "normal" was an economy that, even before COVID-19, was built on a form of consumption that felt compulsory, with household debt as normalized as the exploitative work conditions that make those daily consumption habits possible. A "normal" in which the vast majority of people still felt economically precarious, burned out[94], and swallowed by their student debt[95], and most still struggled to cobble together enough savings to protect them from medical or financial catastrophe. A "normal" in which the various manifestations of the gig economy—and the lack of healthcare, labor protections, or the general safety net that accompanies them—have been, well, *normalized*.

So, what if we don't actually want to go back to that? John is 37, single, and has no kids because, in his words, he can't afford them. He told me he's making minimum wage with a part-time job at Starbucks, where he works for the health insurance. Pre–COVID-19, he also worked the door at a local comedy club for some spending money. He has a very small amount of savings; like a lot of people his age, he feels like he's stuck treading water. "Being part of the service class is really tough," he said. "During this time, some eyes have been opened to how hard it can be. But I really hope more than a few of those eyes stay open once this is all part of the new normal."

A *New* Normal. One that doesn't just have to be socially distanced tables in restaurants or masks on airplanes. It could also be, as John puts it, "embracing slowness and focusing more on humaneness. We could put less emphasis on 'now, I need it now!' and more attention on 'how are you feeling? Are you OK?'"

Part of the reticence to reopen the economy is rooted in the very real fear of widespread infection. And part, I'd argue, is a manifestation of a desire to reject that old way of living entirely. There are different ways of being with each other as a society, different ways of caring and knowing and growing. As cheesy as all of that sounds, it's certainly better than being told to do your part to save the country by going to Disney World or trying to distract ourselves from our exhaustion and fear by buying skincare products[96].

As Richard Curtin, the director of the University of Michigan's Surveys of Consumers, pointed out[97], "The pandemic highlighted the basic mismatch between the current economic policy dependence on growth and market efficiency, and the new emphasis on equity, not only of income and wealth, but also in the availability of health care, and educational opportunities."

The old way wasn't just unsustainable for millions of Americans. It was also deeply unsatisfying. Consumer sentiment—and behavior—suggests we're hungry, even desperate, for something different.

"I don't want to return to a choice of unemployment versus burnout," Natalie, who's 36 and has been searching for a job since January, told me. "I want just enough of an income and just enough health insurance that I don't have to check my bank account on a daily basis. I just want to be comfortable and content.

"I don't know that there are any answers to this," she said. "I just don't want to return to the world as it was."

3.4

Compassionate Consumption: What Is It and Why It Won't Solve Society's Problems

by Christine Schwobel-Patel

Originally published in Teen Vogue, JUNE 25, 2020

This op-ed argues that the brands won't save us.

Eating chocolate in your home, and at the same time saving lives: sounds like a sweet deal. Wearing a cute T-shirt, and at the same time sharing messages of hope: another win-win situation. But these offers to spend your way towards addressing the novel coronavirus pandemic read as just another form of regressive "compassionate consumption."

Many corporations are now advertising special products that allow customers to show appreciation for essential workers and compassion for those physically, mentally, and financially harmed by the pandemic. One of the corporations that has invited us to shop pandemic products is Hershey's. Under the banner of "Togetherness during the COVID-19 health crisis"[98], the U.S. chocolate giant rolled out a "superhero" chocolate collaboration with DC Comics this summer. The first batch, depicting cartoon heroes like Wonder Woman and Batman, will be sent to frontline workers, the "everyday heroes"[99]. Meanwhile, on Instagram, you can show your followers your appreciation by wearing rainbow-adorned "thank you" T-shirts[100], with all proceeds ostensibly going to healthcare services in the United Kingdom. Shopping to show appreciation seems like one simple solution to a complicated problem.

As many people's lives are made smaller by restrictions on who to meet and where to go, there is an understandable need to be part of a community of compassion. We want to show that we care. Giving priority to our consumer identities seems to make sense at this moment. After all, the story of COVID-19 has also been a story of consumer habits. Remember the toilet paper memes[101]? People in many countries are also unhappy about how their governments are dealing with the crisis. In the absence of trust in governments, some hoped the private sector could step up to help address societal issues[102]. This question has become even more pressing in light of the global response to the recent police killings of George Floyd and Breonna Taylor, which saw mass protests break out across the world. But all crises have winners and losers; and there is a distinct possibility that compassionate consumption puts us on the side of the powerful and exploitative, not the vulnerable and disenfranchised.

Brands Solving Societal Problems

During the pandemic, brands have been providing equipment where chronically underfunded public services could not. Car companies like General Motors and Ford[103] offered to source and manufacture ventilators. Clothing giants like H&M[104], Madewell[105], and Barbour[106] have turned to manufacturing much-needed personal protective equipment (PPE) like gowns and face masks. Billionaire and millionaire philanthropists[107] have also been donating, and many big brands have professed solidarity[108] with the Black Lives Matter movement. One might think that this is the kind of trickle-down economics that capitalist societies have been hoping for, with lightly taxed and regulated corporations and entrepreneurs free to allow the wealth they've accumulated to trickle down to the rest of us. After all, the societal problems of years of cuts to health-care services could not have been more evident during this pandemic. In the United Kingdom, for example, the National Health Service has been suffering from debilitating funding cuts: by 2021, the budget for public health services will have been cut[109] by 25% from its 2015 level in real terms. It was only in February of this year that President Trump proposed a 10% cut to federal health-care agencies and programs[110] for the next fiscal year.

The problem is that many big brands have not only enjoyed a corporate-friendly tax environment and a stabilizing network of international laws; they have also benefited from the mystifications of global value chains through clever marketing. Global value chains are the networks of resources and production, often across multiple countries, behind products and services. Tracking them allows us to see where value is added to a product, and where exploitation occurs in the interest of profits. Analyzing global value chains provides insight into workers' interests—like decent pay, safe working conditions, healthcare support, and a healthy balance between work and rest—and whether they are being neglected for profits. Paying workers too little or extracting resources without considering environmental impact, then marketing the product to a higher price, creates profits, or surplus value[111].

Workers who are part of the production process for multinational corporations are often part of an exploited (and racialized) domestic work force, or, more commonly, live in the Global South. Due to the imbalance of power towards the Global North's interests[112] in the global trade order, appeals to social justice tend to be silenced. Political power lies with capital, not with labor. So, when a brand invokes "togetherness" during the pandemic, this often excludes the cocoa growers, sweatshop or warehouse workers, or mineral miners at the "wrong" end of the global value chain.

Past Compassionate Consumption and Backlashes Against It

This is not the first pandemic in which we have been invited to shop to "save lives" as a form of compassionate capitalism. During the HIV/AIDS pandemic, U2 singer Bono co-founded RED[113]. From iPhones to condoms, the brands that partner with RED sell select products in the color red and redirect some of the profits to HIV/AIDS programs in sub-Saharan Africa. Perhaps tellingly, RED was launched at the World Economic Forum in Davos, the annual meeting of the world's capitalist elite.

There have also been backlashes[114] against this form of consumerism. Remember PepsiCo having to pull its "Live for Now"[115] ad featuring Kendall Jenner? Viewers were outraged[116] by the spot, which saw the reality star joining a march and uniting police officers with protesters over a can of soda. It is not that capitalism doesn't *see* contemporary problems, it's that they are, as cultural theorist Stuart Hall observed[117], "falsely attended to." "Togetherness," Hall commented, is "part of a process of cultural degeneration": It creates a false identification with a group and distracts from structural inequalities.

How to Engage Our Political Selves

So how do the good intentions behind compassion consumerism get turned into something politically productive? We might start with acts of kindness that are not calculated against our own social capital like, say, non-Instagrammable acts of generosity. This could be the first step of de-commodifying our relationship with kindness. In other words, we need to question why we want to buy stuff when we want to come together socially and when we want to help.

Karl Marx famously explained this displacement in terms of "commodity fetishism"[118]. Building on the Marxist theory, we should first think about how we displace human relationships through our relationship with the stuff we buy. Brands create the idea that we are connecting with others through buying—but really, buying products is a highly individualized act. Second, we need to question who makes the coronavirus-related products, how they are distributed, and how they are sold. When it comes to Hershey's, we need to question whether "togetherness" includes a commitment to follow through with the company's promised steps towards ending the use of child labor[119] within its cocoa supply chain. For T-shirt activism, this includes questioning the conditions for workers and the environmental impact of the cotton grown for fast fashion. More than anything, we should engage in structural thinking of who gains from a crisis[120], and organize around anti-marketization of social justice[121]. Let's make "togetherness" politically meaningful through seeking opportunities of kindness and solidarity over opportunities of compassion consumption.

3.5

Disaster Capitalism in the Wake of Coronavirus

by Samantha Klein

Originally published in *Currents: A Student Blog*, JUNE 1, 2020

One day in late March, while walking along the Burke Gilman trail, I encountered a man advertising chicken coop building services in order to "keep your family fed". At the start of the stay-at-home order, I also began to notice advertisements on Craigslist exploiting the fear surrounding food shortages and enthusiasm for greater self-sufficiency. These advertisements were for raised-bed boxes for "summer survival gardens" and small greenhouses to "get ready for the apocalypse". Despite the tongue and cheek wording of these advertisements, I worry that the urge to take advantage of the anxieties of others to make money reveals a sickening dimension of capitalism. As people in urban areas spend more time gardening and growing their own food[122], what exactly does this reveal about broader economic and social trends?

From panic-buying baby chicks[123] to hoarding toilet paper and dried beans, the coronavirus pandemic has changed how Americans interact with the economy and how economic institutions interact with us. As COVID-19 takes a particularly heavy toll on low-income[124] folks, Black communities[125], and Native nations[126] across the U.S., it makes me question, is the surge in backyard coops and gardens indicative of the impulse to resist corporate food systems? Or is this just an example of high-income families using their wealth and new free time to invest in individualistic leisure activities, producing heirloom vegetables in their yards, walled off from less privileged folks?

In response to the pandemic, fear mongering about food shortages and sickness has led to hoarding[127] and price gouging[128] of essential sanitation supplies like hand sanitizer[129] and antibacterial wipes. Instead of distributing these supplies to those in need, some have bought enormous quantities to sell at exorbitant prices when stocks run out from conventional retailers.

While the scale and motivations may be less insidious, these local and decentralized efforts are mirrored by the actions of the large corporations that use their resources to exploit those most desperate in times of crisis. On Instagram, I see targeted ads from MiracleGro urging you to "plant your #victorygarden today". MiracleGro is the brand name for products sold by Scotts Miracle-Gro, a company that sells fertilizer, seeds, and plants for at-home gardening. In 2012 Scotts Miracle-Gro[130] was fined $12.5 million for selling 70 million units of birdseed that were coated with the pesticides Actellic 5E and Storcide II, which are prohibited by the EPA and known to be deadly[131] to birds and fish. I can't help but think that their slogan—encouraging people to plant victory gardens—doesn't come from concern for the physical and mental wellbeing of their targeted audience.

Another example of large corporations profiting off of this pandemic is Amazon. Due to virus related surges in online shopping and streaming, Amazon shares have increased in value by 28%[132] compared to last year. Meanwhile they have fired[133] warehouse employees that organized to demand greater protections against the health impacts caused by increased workload during the pandemic. On May 14th, the company announced that the $2 per hour hazard[134] pay will stop at the end of May. As of May 27th, the eighth[135] Amazon employee has died from COVID-19.

While many small businesses are still struggling to survive, hedge funds and private equity firms see this as a good time to offer high interest loans[136] to these businesses. Since these businesses do not have other options, many of them may take these risky loans and make these firms rich in the process.

With now 20.5 million lost jobs[137] due to COVID-19 restrictions and layoffs, this health crisis will be exacerbated by financial struggles for months or years to come. On a large scale, the uncertainty and fear caused by this pandemic may enable the roll out of unfavorable economic policies and political agendas that under normal circumstances would not be tolerated by the general public. Naomi Klein refers to this concept as disaster capitalism[138] in her book, *The Shock Doctrine*. Klein defines disaster capitalism as "the way private industries spring up to directly profit from large-scale crises" and shock doctrine as "a political strategy of using large-scale crises to push through policies that systematically deepen inequality, enrich elites, and undercut everyone else." In a recent interview[139], Klein uses the Trump-proposed, $700 billion dollar[140] stimulus plan as an example of disaster capitalism. Trump's stimulus plan would eliminate payroll taxes through the end of the year leading to a reduction in social security funding[141]. This could further cut funding to programs such as Federal Old-Age (Retirement), Survivors and Disability Insurance (OASDI), Temporary Assistance for Needy Families (TANF), and Health Insurance for Aged and Disabled and Medicare. These programs are crucial right now.

The situation seems bleak, but for as many instances of disaster capitalism I have seen in the last couple months, I have also seen remarkable examples of communities coming together to provide services for those most vulnerable to the COVID-19 and virus-related hardships. In Seattle, mutual aid networks[142] have sprung up to deliver groceries and sanitary supplies to the homes of folks who are financially struggling or sick, primarily the hardest hit being low income communities of color[143]. These networks have also organized flower sales to support Hmong and Mien[144] flower farmers who can no longer sell their flowers at their regular markets and florists. Additionally, they have collaborated with incarcerated folks and their families and striking farm workers[145] to demand better COVID-19 policies and protections. These networks are the direct antithesis to capitalism's response to the virus; instead of exploiting the situation for financial gain, these grassroots organizations freely provide resources to communities that were left vulnerable by pre-COVID inequalities.

There are also international examples of effective mutual aid networks. As the virus began to spread in January in my hometown of Hong Kong, the Hong Kong government refused[146] to close borders and advised against widespread mask-wearing[147]. However, the city has kept the number of infections surprisingly low, partly because of its digital and in-person mutual aid networks[148] set up by citizens during the city's ongoing anti-extradition movement. Volunteers distributed hand sanitizer in low income apartment buildings and posted informative art about proper mask wearing and how to keep yourself safe during the pandemic.

These remarkable acts of community aid can help us cope with the effects of COVID-19. This support can also help our communities address and fight against underlying societal inequalities that have been amplified by this pandemic. Go ahead, plant your garden, get some chickens! But that cannot be the only thing you do during this pandemic. Instead of taking advantage of one another in this hard time for personal gain and falling prey to disaster capitalism, we can harness our collective power and resources to help those most in need.

3.6

Vampiric Affect: The Afterlife of a Metaphor in a Global Pandemic

by Ian Liujia Tian

Originally published in *Social Text Online*, JUNE 17, 2020

What does the politics of gratitude do in our shared public health crisis? In almost all nation-states, essential workers are heroized and appreciated on numerous social media platforms. These campaigns produce particular affect in our traumatic times, and when we send our heartfelt "thank-yous," the politics of gratitude circulates elated feelings of supposed solidarity while obscuring the politics of doing good. Thus, such politics often fail to materialize into concrete political and social transformation. In this textual analysis, I deploy "blood-soaked steamed buns" (人血饅頭), a metaphor used by the famous Chinese novelist and critic Lu Xun in Republic-era China to think about the vampiric nature of the affective politics of gratitude.

In a well-known novel, *Medicine*[149], Lu Xun wrote about the superstition of curing tuberculosis by eating steamed buns soaked in blood. Set in the early Republic-era China (1911-1949), the story narrates the efforts to cure the main character, Hua Xiaoshuang, who suffered from tuberculosis. After unsuccessful attempts, his rich parents eventually bought a steamed bun soaked in the blood of an executed revolutionary, Xia Yu. For them, Xia is a talking point, and the sacrificial blood of Xia is the best cure for their son's disease. In my interpretation, the metaphor "eating blood-soaked steamed buns," although sometimes described as being "moralistic," offers a critique of the senselessness of public belief and the difficulty of critical consciousness at the time of the writing. "Blood-soaked steamed buns" remains in use in Mandurian, serving as the indictment of the vampiric nature of capitalism. However, this metaphor is more than a moralistic critique of profit-making, regardless of human costs. In our social media and affective economic era, steamed buns are important affective placebos mined and valorized in the process of value generation, in which the affective fulfillment of the general population hides the blood-sucking "vampires" known as capital, as Marx[150] once articulated. As the global pandemic renders affective needs ever more present, the cost of feeling good is soaked in the corporeal sacrifices of the front-liners, those who cannot not work.

In post-socialist China, the best examples are the gendered state propaganda of one nurse who returned to work just days after her abortion and another who stayed to treat COVID-19 patients while being pregnant. In these instances, similar to buns soaked in persecuted revolutionaries' blood as "medicine" for tuberculosis, gendered bodies are sacrifices offered up as a "cure" to elevate the population from the national trauma of COVID-19, and as the "channel" for the affective circulation of popular gratitude towards medical workers. The affective gratitude towards feminized bodies continues the state socialist practices of romanticizing "sacrifices" and obscures the lack of nationalized free healthcare, the decades-long changes and shifts in the public health sector since it was integrated into global capitalism, the increasing pressure of privatization, and the violence and repressions produced by state capitalism.

These vampiric and cannibalistic tropes are not unique to post-socialist China. In the Canadian context, for example, "clap for essential workers" or "honk for essential workers," although initiated not directly by the state, are recognitional politics that do not engage with migrant struggles and labor rights. Instead, the affective politics of gratitude costs the lives of frontline workers in cannibalistic ways. Temporary migrant workers in farms and meat factories have been praised and heroized as the COVID-19 cases and mortality rates climb. In Calgary, migrant workers in meat factories have been working in conditions where they are unable to social distance, and life has vanished because of COVID-19[151].

The gratitude for frontliners' corporeal sacrifice renders the vampiric extraction of bodily capacities within capitalist production invisible via appreciation. The affective politics of gratitude operates as the process of "eating blood-soaked steamed buns"; the difference lies in the fact that these "steamed buns," the essential workers, are honored—but simultaneously offered up for the affective fulfillment of the workers who are able to stay home.

At the end of *Medicine*, Mother Hua and Mother Xia are at the cemetery to see their sons. It is later revealed to the readers that Xia Yu and Hua Xiaoshuang are buried beside each other, separated by a narrow path. It is not clear if both women recognize each other, yet the fact that their sons' lives are entangled even after death requires contemplating. I tend to believe that Lu Xun offers us a way to think about social relations in tragedy: we eventually return to the land, what we think might separates us are just spatial lines on the surface, while deep down, lives merge. In the time of COVID-19, frontline workers are indeed risking their lives, and many are doing so because of the nature of their work (e.g., nurses) or because of the shortage of labor (e.g., farm workers or sanitation workers). An affective politics that does more than recognition would center the deeply embedded relations we share and would fight for what front-liners need. After all, our bodily sovereignty and capacities are the effect of laboring by, for, or with others. What are we if we are not the relations we inhabit? Are we, sitting at home, ready to labor for our collective life?

Notes

1 https://www.npr.org/sections/goatsandsoda/2020/03/11/814474930/coronavirus-covid-19-is-now-officially-a-pandemic-who-says
2 https://www.nbcnews.com/health/health-news/coronavirus-diseases-comparing-covid-19-sars-mers-numbers-n1150321
3 https://www.nytimes.com/2020/03/12/nyregion/coronavirus-new-york-update.html
4 https://www.nytimes.com/2020/03/01/upshot/coronavirus-sick-days-service-workers.html
5 https://www.vice.com/en_us/article/y3meg7/what-do-i-do-coronavirus-travel-public-transit-guidelines
6 https://www.nbcnews.com/politics/white-house/mixed-white-house-messaging-coronavirus-sparks-internal-frustration-n1152606
7 https://tsd.naomiklein.org/shock-doctrine.html
8 https://theintercept.com/2017/01/24/get-ready-for-the-first-shocks-of-trumps-disaster-capitalism/
9 https://www.nytimes.com/2020/03/10/us/politics/trump-coronavirus-relief-package.html
10 https://www.nytimes.com/2020/03/12/business/trump-tax-cut-coronavirus.html
11 https://www.vox.com/2020/3/6/21168038/trump-on-entitlements-fox-news-town-hall
12 https://www.washingtonpost.com/news/monkey-cage/wp/2018/09/11/privatizing-the-u-s-effort-in-afghanistan-seemed-a-bad-idea-now-its-even-worse/
13 https://www.forbes.com/2009/02/12/stimulus-depression-deficits-opinions-columnists_0213_bruce_bartlett.html#58cf8f6e6680
14 https://www.politico.com/news/2020/03/11/trump-emergency-declaration-coronavirus-message-125902
15 https://www.npr.org/2020/03/10/813979266/trump-vows-to-help-cruise-airline-industries-amid-coronavirus-concerns
16 https://www.washingtonpost.com/
17 https://www.npr.org/2020/03/10/813979266/trump-vows-to-help-cruise-airline-industries-amid-coronavirus-concerns
18 https://theintercept.com/2017/01/24/get-ready-for-the-first-shocks-of-trumps-disaster-capitalism/
19 https://www.vice.com/en_us/article/qjdeq5/there-are-no-private-solutions-to-a-public-health-crisis
20 https://www.nydailynews.com/opinion/ny-oped-how-the-have-nots-are-coping-with-coronavirus-20200310-jdj7t2rlobasjjhkwqhj2y5dr4-story.html
21 https://www.nydailynews.com/opinion/ny-oped-how-the-have-nots-are-coping-with-coronavirus-20200310-jdj7t2rlobasjjhkwqhj2y5dr4-story.html
22 https://thehill.com/policy/finance/486876-trump-throws-support-behind-paid-sick-leave
23 https://www.chicagotribune.com/opinion/ct-nyt-farhad-manjoo-pandemic-column-20200311-jzsvjv22jfg2fmlcjfiu6dekmq-story.html
24 https://www.elderlawanswers.com/medicare-and-medicaid-will-cover-coronavirus-testing-17631
25 https://www.whitehouse.gov/briefings-statements/remarks-president-trump-vice-president-pence-members-white-house-coronavirus-task-force-press-briefing/
26 https://www.nytimes.com/2020/01/13/upshot/trump-tweets-health-care.html
27 https://www.nytimes.com/2020/03/06/business/europe-coronavirus-labor-help.html
28 https://www.zenefits.com/workest/the-definitive-list-of-states-and-cities-with-paid-sick-leave-laws/
29 https://www.inquirer.com/philly/news/politics/20150513_Philly_s_paid_sick_leave_goes_into_effect_Wednesday.html
30 https://philly.metro.us/advocates-comcast-is-trying-to-block-phillys-paid-sick-leave-law/
31 https://www.sltrib.com/news/politics/2020/03/10/coronavirus-brings-new/
32 https://www.cnbc.com/2020/03/09/amazon-adjusts-attendance-policy-for-warehouse-workers-amid-coronavirus-outbreak.html
33 https://popular.info/p/free-breadsticks-during-a-coronavirus
34 https://www.cnn.com/2020/03/07/tech/uber-coronavirus-sick-leave/index.html
35 https://www.health.com/condition/cold-flu-sinus/how-many-people-die-of-the-flu-every-year
36 https://www.commondreams.org/news/2020/03/11/unconscionable-senate-republicans-block-emergency-paid-sick-leave-bill-experts
37 https://www.inquirer.com/health/coronavirus/live/coronavirus-covid19-philadelphia-pennsylvania-new-jersey-confirmed-case-updates-news-20200312.html

38   https://www.politico.com/news/2020/03/11/nancy-pelosi-coronavirus-stimulus-package-125564
39   https://abcnews.go.com/Health/wireStory/
     trump-plans-payroll-tax-relief-response-coronavirus-69497755
40   https://en.wikipedia.org/wiki/The_Shock_Doctrine
41   https://www.theguardian.com/us-news/2017/jul/06/naomi-klein-how-power-profits-from-disaster
42   https://www.inquirer.com/opinion/commentary/elizabeth-warren-best-candidate-2020-democratic-
     primary-20200112.html
43   https://www.inquirer.com/opinion/bernie-sanders-leads-california-primary-biden-bloomberg-super-
     tuesday-20200302.html
44   https://en.wikipedia.org/wiki/Nixon_goes_to_China
45   https://www.buzzfeednews.com/collection/coronavirus
46   https://www.theguardian.com/technology/2020/apr/15/
     the-right-to-repair-planned-obsolescence-electronic-waste-mountain
47   https://press.princeton.edu/books/paperback/9780691183176/the-sum-of-small-things
48   https://www.buzzfeednews.com/article/annehelenpetersen/
     how-nashville-became-one-big-bachelorette-party
49   https://books.google.com/books/about/A_Consumer_s_Republic.html?id=tHj3cNJLBo4C
50   https://www.huffpost.com/entry/400-richest-own-more-than-150-million-
     poorest_n_5c60f627e4b0eec79b250c34
51   https://www.pewresearch.org/fact-tank/2018/08/07/
     for-most-us-workers-real-wages-have-barely-budged-for-decades/
52   https://www.aarp.org/content/dam/aarp/ppi/2019/10/unlocking-potential-emergency-savings-
     accounts.doi.10.26419ppi.00084.001.pdf
53   https://www.usatoday.com/story/money/2020/02/23/
     average-americans-credit-card-debt-how-much-it-costs-them/111330144/
54   https://www.wsj.com/articles/auto-lenders-ramp-up-risk-to-win-more-customers-
     1528639200?mod=article_inline
55   https://www.wsj.com/articles/the-seven-year-auto-loan-americas-middle-class-cant-afford-their-
     cars-11569941215
56   https://news.gallup.com/poll/248081/westhealth-gallup-us-healthcare-cost-crisis.aspx
57   https://www.wsj.com/articles/families-go-deep-in-debt-to-stay-in-the-middle-class-
     11564673734?mod=article_inline
58   https://thenewpress.com/books/lower-ed
59   https://www.forbes.com/sites/advisor/2019/10/27/the-true-cost-of-payday-loans/#7945b2e76947
60   https://www.statista.com/statistics/237203/average-expenditures-of-united-states-households/
61   https://www.cnbc.com/2020/05/15/us-retail-sales-april-2020.html
62   https://annehelen.substack.com/p/foreword
63   https://www.nytimes.com/2020/04/18/us/coronavirus-women-essential-workers.html
64   https://www.buzzfeednews.com/article/kadiagoba/
     coronavirus-new-york-brooklyn-essential-workers-black-poc
65   https://www.buzzfeednews.com/article/emmanuelfelton/
     coronavirus-hospital-healthcare-staff-no-health-insurance
66   https://www.nytimes.com/2020/05/05/opinion/coronavirus-nyc-subway.html
67   https://www.buzzfeednews.com/article/carolineodonovan/
     amazon-employee-positive-coronavirus-one-month-no-pay
68   https://www.buzzfeednews.com/article/briannasacks/
     costco-workers-coronavirus-social-distancing-measures
69   https://www.buzzfeednews.com/article/briannasacks/costco-thriving-coronavirus-pandemic-workers-pay
70   https://www.buzzfeednews.com/article/nishitajha/coronavirus-zara-spain-inditex-myanmar
71   https://books.google.com/books/about/A_Consumers_Republic.html?id=YuZPy6JqutIC
72   https://www.theatlantic.com/magazine/archive/1996/07/
     the-forces-making-for-an-economic-collapse/376621/
73   https://fred.stlouisfed.org/series/PCE
74   https://files.stlouisfed.org/files/htdocs/publications/review/03/09/Kliesen.pdf
75   https://uncpress.org/book/9780807856765/sold-american/
76   https://www.thisamericanlife.org/355/the-giant-pool-of-money
77   https://www.marketplace.org/2018/12/17/what-we-learned-housing/
78   https://money.cnn.com/2008/11/26/news/economy/personal_income_spending/index.htm
79   https://www.economist.com/united-states/2008/11/20/the-end-of-the-affair
80   https://www.nytimes.com/2009/04/11/business/economy/11cheap.html
81   https://www.nytimes.com/2011/02/26/business/26upgrade.html

82   https://fred.stlouisfed.org/series/PSAVERT
83   https://globalpublicsquare.blogs.cnn.com/2012/02/16/why-america-spends-while-the-world-saves/
84   https://www.federalreserve.gov/releases/g19/current/
85   https://www.cnn.com/2020/05/12/investing/jobs-coronavirus-consumer-spending-debt/index.html
86   https://www.buzzfeednews.com/article/venessawong/coronavirus-americans-scared-future-economy
87   https://www.cnn.com/2020/05/12/investing/jobs-coronavirus-consumer-spending-debt/index.html
88   https://data.sca.isr.umich.edu/fetchdoc.php?docid=65214
89   https://www.nytimes.com/2009/04/11/business/economy/11cheap.html
90   https://www.buzzfeednews.com/article/carolineodonovan/
      amazon-fired-employee-involved-in-workplace-organizing-in
91   https://www.washingtonpost.com/
92   https://www.vice.com/en_us/article/ney387/
      the-resurgence-of-the-labor-movement-the-year-in-workers-power
93   https://www.buzzfeednews.com/article/annehelenpetersen/millennials-burnout-generation-debt-work
94   https://www.buzzfeednews.com/article/annehelenpetersen/millennials-burnout-generation-debt-work
95   https://www.buzzfeednews.com/article/annehelenpetersen/
      student-debt-college-public-service-loan-forgiveness
96   https://www.newyorker.com/culture/cultural-comment/
      the-year-that-skin-care-became-a-coping-mechanism
97   https://data.sca.isr.umich.edu/fetchdoc.php?docid=65214
98   https://www.thehersheycompany.com/en_us/sustainability/shared-communities/our-response-to-
      covid-19.html
99   https://www.thehersheycompany.com/en_us/blog/giving-back-to-the-real-super-heroes.html
100   https://www.standard.co.uk/fashion/rainbow-tshirt-nhs-clapforourcarers-a4410476.html
101   https://www.insider.com/toilet-paper-memes-coronavirus-quarantine-shortage-tiktoks-2020-3
102   https://www.marketingweek.com/brand-purpose-coronavirus-crisis/
103   https://www.theverge.com/2020/4/15/21222219/
      general-motors-ventec-ventilators-ford-tesla-coronavirus-covid-19
104   https://hmgroup.com/media/news/general-news-2020/h-m-group-to-supply-protective-equipment-for-
      hospitals.html
105   https://www.madewell.com/womens/accessories/masks
106   https://www.barbour.com/us/barbour-service-update
107   https://www.forbes.com/sites/hayleycuccinello/2020/04/15/
      jack-dorsey-bill-gates-and-at-least-75-other-billionaires-donating-to-pandemic-relief/#2053a82c21bd
108   https://www.jacobinmag.com/2020/06/brands-corporate-publicity-racial-justice
109   https://nhsfunding.info/symptoms/10-effects-of-underfunding/cuts-to-frontline-services/
110   https://www.whitehouse.gov/wp-content/uploads/2020/02/budget_fy21.pdf
111   https://www.britannica.com/topic/surplus-value
112   https://www.cambridge.org/core/books/sugar-and-the-making-of-international-trade-law/948C7B3F03
      EEF69BCAFF85CF8DBCFFE8#fndtn-information
113   https://www.red.org/how-red-works
114   https://brandaidworld.wordpress.com/
115   https://www.theguardian.com/fashion/2017/apr/04/kendall-jenner-pepsi-ad-protest-black-lives-matter
116   https://www.theguardian.com/fashion/2017/apr/04/kendall-jenner-pepsi-ad-protest-black-lives-matter
117   http://banmarchive.org.uk/collections/ulr/05_26.pdf
118   https://www.marxists.org/archive/marx/works/1867-c1/ch01.htm
119   https://www.washingtonpost.com/
120   https://naomiklein.org/the-shock-doctrine/
121   https://www.cambridge.org/core/books/marketing-global-justice/D33A067EA3D92F1015FC00133EB
      2EC74
122   https://www.latimes.com/lifestyle/story/2020-04-16/
      shop-safely-for-plants-with-patience-and-the-internet
123   https://www.nytimes.com/2020/03/28/style/chicken-eggs-coronavirus.html
124   https://time.com/5800930/how-coronavirus-will-hurt-the-poor/
125   https://depts.washington.edu/urbanuw/news/
      data-suggests-coronavirus-is-disproportionately-affecting-black-communities-in-the-us/
126   https://www.aljazeera.com/news/2020/05/navajo-nation-hit-hard-coronavirus-200526171504037.html
127   https://abcnews.go.com/US/york-man-accused-hoarding-covid-19-materials-price/story?id=70333494
128   https://abcnews.go.com/US/york-man-accused-hoarding-covid-19-materials-price/story?id=70333494
129   https://www.nytimes.com/2020/03/14/technology/coronavirus-purell-wipes-amazon-sellers.html
130   https://www.audubon.org/news/pesticides-bird-seed-scotts-miracle-gro-fined-125-million

131 https://abcbirds.org/article/4-5-million-fine-for-scotts-highlights-need-for-monitoring-bird-seed-safety/
132 https://www.forbes.com/sites/isabeltogoh/2020/05/14/
     jeff-bezos-trillionaire-is-trending-on-twitter-heres-why/#77455ae22e3d
133 https://www.cbsnews.com/news/amazon-worker-fired-coronavirus-maren-costa-emily-cunningham/
134 https://www.businessinsider.com/amazon-dropping-covid-19-hazard-pay-warehouse-workers-
     may-2020-5
135 https://www.latimes.com/business/technology/story/2020-05-27/
     la-fi-tn-amazon-worker-dead-hiring-wave
136 https://www.nytimes.com/2020/04/03/business/private-equity-hedge-funds-coronavirus.html
137 https://www.nytimes.com/interactive/2020/05/08/business/economy/april-jobs-report.html
138 https://www.vice.com/en_us/article/5dmqyk/
     naomi-klein-interview-on-coronavirus-and-disaster-capitalism-shock-doctrine
139 https://www.vice.com/en_us/article/5dmqyk/
     naomi-klein-interview-on-coronavirus-and-disaster-capitalism-shock-doctrine
140 https://www.nytimes.com/2020/03/10/us/politics/trump-coronavirus-relief-package.html
141 https://www.forbes.com/sites/ebauer/2020/05/04/
     whats-so-wrong-about-trumps-payroll-tax-cut-call/#3b0ba2894d4c
142 https://www.newyorker.com/magazine/2020/05/18/what-mutual-aid-can-do-during-a-pandemic
143 https://www.seattletimes.com/seattle-news/health/
     king-county-has-big-racial-disparities-in-coronavirus-cases-and-deaths-according-to-public-health-data/
144 https://docs.google.com/forms/d/e/1FAIpQLSePq1Ik5UfYwJQ6itjPxzWioYkwUEIF
     jx84-7nFxDEQeaYDSQ/viewform
145 https://www.gofundme.com/f/didyoueattoday?utm_source=customer&utm_medium=copy_link-
     tip&utm_campaign=p_cp+share-sheet
146 https://www.scmp.com/news/hong-kong/politics/article/3049111/
     coronavirus-why-wont-carrie-lam-shut-hong-kongs-border
147 https://www.scmp.com/news/hong-kong/health-environment/article/3048883/
     coronavirus-carrie-lam-warns-hong-kong-officials
148 https://www.theatlantic.com/technology/archive/2020/05/
     how-hong-kong-beating-coronavirus/611524/
149 https://www.marxists.org/archive/lu-xun/1919/04/x01.htm
150 https://www.marxists.org/archive/marx/works/download/pdf/Capital-Volume-I.pdf
151 https://www.cbc.ca/news/canada/calgary/food-inspector-union-meat-plant-1.5554848

Part Four

The Politics of Exposure and Protection

4.1

How Asia's Clothing Factories Switched to Making PPE—But Sweatshop Problems Live On

by Alessandra Mezzadri & Kanchana N. Ruwanpura

Originally published in *The Conversation,* JUNE 29, 2020

Personal protective equipment (PPE) has arguably become the most sought-after commodity in the world. The COVID-19 pandemic has led to a global shortage[1] of this equipment. This has created an opportunity for garment factories across Asia, which have lots of spare capacity because their clothing is in much less demand than usual.

High street chains in the UK and elsewhere could have immediately paid their garment suppliers to make PPE rather than clothes, but did not. Many simply cancelled[2] millions of orders, which ended up putting thousands of Asian workers[3] out on the streets. Many garment workers didn't even receive monthly wages[4] due to these cancelled orders. This was despite global campaigning by trade unions, such as those in Bangladesh.[5]

Only a few western brands such as Barbour[6] eventually started converting their supply chains to make PPE. In most cases, Asian manufacturers just took their own initiative.

Asia's Big Shift

China was already the largest PPE exporter before the pandemic, providing almost half[7] of the world supply of face masks, protective gowns, gloves and goggles in 2018. In the first two months of 2020, China's PPE exports dipped by about 15%[8] as its own demand for these products rose sharply, with the government preventing some consignments from leaving the country.

However, from March, Chinese PPE exports rebounded as the virus spread west. China was able to meet these orders with help from many garment manufacturers, in a bid to answer mounting calls from other countries for tighter quality control[9] of PPE.

Elsewhere, Sri Lanka has secured a significant niche in the PPE supply chain, having won at least[10] U.S.$500 million (£402 million) in orders during the crisis. Notably, lingerie manufacturer MAS Holdings advertised a move into PPE production using its trademark slogan, "Change is Courage"[11].

Malaysia has enjoyed a massive rise in rubber gloves exports.[12] With as much as 65% of all medical gloves made in the country, the U.S. embassy tweeted in March that "the world relies on Malaysia"[13]. The country has also seen[14] numerous garment businesses moving into PPE.

Meanwhile, India is now the second largest PPE producer[15] after China, having only started making this equipment earlier in the year. India was manufacturing 450,000 PPE suits a day[16] in May, and aiming to hit 2 million[17] by the end of June. While Indian production has so far only targeted the domestic market, the government has just announced it will soon allow the export of[18] 5 million PPE suits a month.

Bangalore is producing 50% of India's[19] PPE kits, thanks to a garment center dominated by the Gokaldas empire, which employs thousands of women. Production has also risen massively[20] in Tiruppur in Tamil Nadu state, normally a T-shirt center. Over 600 Indian companies are now lab-certified[21] for PPE, including top garment and textile exporters Alok Industries, JCT Phagwara, Gokaldas Exports, and Aditya Birla.

With a population of well over a billion, with around 37,000 public health facilities[22], India needs a staggering quantity of PPE as the pandemic worsens[23]. As it emerges from a tough lockdown that still threatens an economic crisis, the country should arguably make PPE[24] for all workers[25] in sectors that need to reopen, such as agriculture. This would get the economy moving, while employing even more people in PPE production.

Yet producing billions of PPE kits may be unviable—even the fast-fashion supply chain can only churn things out so fast. There are also serious issues about environmental waste and disposable equipment[26], both in India and around the world.

Beyond Asia, the PPE supply chain has also extended to garment factories in countries such as Kenya and Madagascar. This is being supported by[27] the World Bank, again with a view to sustaining employment.

Job Opportunities and Abuses

On the positive side, this shift into PPE has protected and created jobs. In India, where global buyers like H&M continue cancelling orders and labor protests roll on, PPE production may mean re-employing at least some of the hundreds of thousands of garment workers who joined the exodus of migrant labor leaving[28] cities early in the pandemic. In Sri Lanka, PPE is potentially providing[29] a livelihood for 300,000 workers.

On the other hand, there's so much pressure[30] to keep up with orders that it is possible that many factories are running[31] sweatshop conditions and other abusive practices carried over from their usual operations. The PPE supply chain was already known[32] for labor abuses. For instance, recent evidence[33] indicated the use of child labor in surgical instruments production in Pakistan. In Malaysia, there are media reports[34] of Nepali migrant workers in rubber glove factories being subjected to severe abuse.

In China, recent findings[35] suggest the widespread use of Uighur forced labor in numerous sectors, potentially including PPE. During lockdown in India, some states have suspended existing legislation, making it possible for factories to use forced labor. Others have passed legislation extending the working day[36] from eight to 12 hours. At the same time, it is worth pointing out that some countries such as Sri Lanka are known to impose more rigorous standards on their factories.

More generally, garment workers worldwide may not[37] actually have access to the PPE equipment they make. They deserve to be included in the list of key workers in responding to the pandemic. We tend to think of the key workers helping us as only being in our own country, but this is clearly mistaken.

As such, we should be particularly concerned about labor abuses, and do whatever we can to oppose them. Those who are saving our lives should not themselves live their lives under threat. These workers who were the backbone of the global economy are now stitching its safety net.

4.2

What Lies Beneath? COVID-19 and the Racial Politics of Face Masks

by Shakira Hussein & Scheherazade Bloul

Originally published in *ABC Religion and Ethics*, JULY 14, 2020

As the number of COVID-19 cases began to spike in Melbourne in June 2020, Dr. Norman Swan, whose daily ABC podcast, *Coronacast*[38], has become the nation's most trusted source for information on the pandemic, tweeted: "Why isn't Victoria insisting on masks? @victorianCHO[39], Given you can't really go back to full lockdown, a month of masks might give you the extra help you need. A real shame it's got to this. Victoria seems to have done everything right."

In the early stages of the pandemic, the advice from the World Health Organization was that facial masks were not necessary[40] except for people who were sick and showing symptoms and those caring for them. Health practitioners and policymakers in Australia, Europe, and North America discouraged the use of face masks as a means of infection control on the grounds that the general public lacked the knowledge to wear them correctly. Given the shortage of personal protective equipment at the time, there were also concerns that the widespread use of disposable facemasks would come at the expense of frontline medical workers.

However, fabric facial coverings have been a routine public health measure in East Asian societies such as China, Hong Kong, Taiwan, and Japan since the 2003 SARS epidemic. In Australian cities too, it has become commonplace to see people of East Asian background wearing face masks during the winter flu season.

As evidence mounted for the effectiveness of fabric face masks in reducing disease transmission, the failure to learn from the expertise gained by East Asian health professionals during the SARS epidemic seemed increasingly misguided and bodies such as the World Health Organization and the U.S. Center for Disease Control have shifted their guidelines accordingly. The Victorian government now "strongly urges" adults to cover their faces in circumstances when social distancing is difficult, but has refrained from following the examples of countries including France, Austria, and Spain by making them mandatory in such circumstances.

Medical face masks have become a signifier of East Asian identity and as Sinophobia rose[41] along with the COVID-19 death toll, those wearing them were singled out for racist abuse and harassment.

We suggest that the institutional skepticism and community hostility towards facial covering mirror the moral panic generated by the "burqa ban" debates which located face-coverings as emblems in a civilizational conflict during the decade preceding the pandemic. The "clash of civilizations" forecast by Samuel Huntington[42] back in the 1990s has now transitioned from the battle between Islam and the West, to one that Huntington termed "the West versus the rest"—with the so-called "Confucian civilization" prominent among "the rest." Just as visibly Muslim women were vilified as carriers of terrorism, people of East Asian appearance are now scapegoated as carriers of the so-called "Chinese virus."

Face masks have become flashpoints for disputes over national identity, liberty, and the limits of state power in a range of locations—perhaps nowhere more so than the United States. The uncovered face has become an important political signifier, with President Donald Trump until very recently[43] refusing to wear a face mask and mocking those who choose to do so. With Trump reportedly believing that wearing a mask would make him appear "weak," his uncovered face illustrates his persona as the simultaneously invincible and victimized leader.

As the death toll mounted in the Republican heartland, senior party leaders began to soften their opposition to face masks, with Vice President Mike Pence among those photographed wearing masks and some Republican governors mandating their use[44] in confined spaces in order to mitigate the risks of reopening the economy.

The Worthy and the Unworthy

Thanks to the nation's high-profile burqa ban, the uncovered face has been promoted as a symbol, not only of French national identity, but of "the Enlightenment Legacy" for which France is the self-appointed guardian. Government-issued posters[45] circulated when the ban was introduced showed the image of Marianne, the symbol of the French Republic, alongside the proclamation "The Republic lives with its face uncovered" (*La République se vit à visage découvert*). Like the ban on visible religious symbols in state schools which had preceded it, the legislation outlawing facial coverings was carefully worded so as not to single out a particular religious community, while being clearly understood as targeting Muslim religious practices in particular.

Masks worn for medical purposes are exempt from France's ban on facial covering (which, as the Chinese embassy noted in a warning to its nationals in February, did not prevent fraudsters posing as police from imposing "fines"[46] on Chinese visitors to the country), and laws have been introduced requiring French citizens to wear facemasks on public transport and in other enclosed public spaces to protect against the spread of COVID-19—while no changes were made to the 2010 religious veiling law. This double-standard points, we believe, to an inherently imperial, blatantly Islamophobic (and racist) exercise of state power over its "unworthy" citizens.

A similar distinction between worthy and unworthy citizens can be seen in the Victorian state government's reluctance to impose mandatory face masks upon "mainstream Australians" while showing no such reluctance to impose the full force of the state upon the residents of nine public housing towers in Melbourne[47] that had been found to have dangerously high rates of COVID-19. These "unworthy people" who are poor, (mostly) Black, brown, and/or Muslim, have been held in a prison-style lockdown, while their neighbors in "the world's most livable city" are trusted to leave their homes while adhering to COVID-safe regulations.

The difference between the two cohorts is not only household income but also skin color, physical features, and religious identity. This type of eugenic categorization is embedded in the colonial hierarchies that have permeated the structures of the modern state since its founding as a penal colony and the genocide of Aboriginal people[48].

In contrast to their right-wing critics, protestors at Black Lives Matter rallies in locations ranging from Melbourne to Sydney to Los Angeles, Seattle, and Minnesota have embraced the use of face masks as a way of staying safe while continuing to engage in acts of dissent and civil disobedience. Politicians and media commentators have blamed the "selfish" protestors[49] for a spike in COVID-19 cases, despite no such spike having materialized within the relevant time frame. Similarly, the volunteers who stepped in to provide basic necessities to the residents living under hard lockdown in the nine public housing towers in Melbourne wore face masks to mitigate the risk of falling sick themselves.

The Politics of Fashion

Unsurprisingly, the fashion industry has capitalized on the crisis by turning their factories into mask and PPE-making facilities. As previously seen during the bushfire crisis, designer brands are turning a profit[50] from face-masks, with those from higher-end brands selling for just under US$200 and on Ebay for upwards of US$250. These masks are manufactured[51] under the same exploitative conditions as other products of the garment industry, with women and girls in developing societies often working under slave-like conditions. Only a few weeks ago, workers in factories making clothes for Zara and Primark in Myanmar were fired after forming unions[52]—the reason management gave was related to COVID-19 austerity measures.

At the other end of the market, many small businesses and newly unemployed workers have begun to sew facial masks in an attempt to survive the economic recession, while some community organizations are making masks to give away to those on low-incomes.

Although designer face masks are becoming a fashion must-have for those mainstream consumers who can afford them, wearing a face cover of any description remains a hazardous undertaking for members of racialized minorities. For those of East Asian background, the protection that masks may offer against infection must be balanced against the increased likelihood of being targeted by racial abuse. One of the authors of this paper (who is visibly brown-skinned, although not East Asian) was harassed on the streets of Melbourne while wearing a fabric mask by an older White male who breached social distance guidelines to shout, "The masks don't work!" at close range.

For others, the risks associated with covering the face are potentially lethal. African American men are understandably reluctant to cover their faces for fear that it will see them racially profiled as criminals by the police. The misclassification already exists in the form of the hooded, dangerous Black man, posing a threat to the White (especially) women. This is why 17-year-old Trayvon Martin was murdered—and countless others with him. It does not matter what items of clothing you put on your person: if you're Black or brown, you'll be profiled, harassed, and potentially killed.

Whose Values?

Evidence to date suggests that while face masks may provide some protection to the person wearing them, their primary value lies in the preventing them from infecting others around them, should they already be infected. Hence[53]: "My mask protects you; your mask protects me." They are, then, an inherently communitarian instrument. Those opposed to the use of face masks justify their stance in terms of libertarian individualism, while those promoting them speak in terms of community and mutual support. Their use by Black Lives Matter protestors are consistent with the values of empathy, loving engagement, and collective community, which are listed among the movement's thirteen guiding principles[54].

In East Asia, face masks are regarded as hallmarks of courtesy and good manners—long stereotyped as "Asian values" in contrast to the supposed "Western values" of individual choice and liberty. Masks are fast acquiring similar connotations of empathy and care in other communities as well, as societies adjust to the no-longer-new normal of the pandemic. The true "clash" has always been *within* rather than *between* civilizations—but never more so than now.

It remains clear, however, that much of the discourse around face covering is much more concerned with the color of the face beneath the mask than with the mask itself.

4.3

New York City's Coronavirus Essential Workers are Overwhelmingly People of Color

by Kadia Goba

Originally published in *BuzzFeed News*, APRIL 21, 2020

"We're telling you that no one should be out here because it's dangerous, but we're sending you out there and we're not giving out any masks."

For one essential worker, there's a specific time when coronavirus[55]-related anxiety is at its highest: the moment she pulls into a crowded bus stop.

Forcing people to enter the rear doors helps a little to ease the tension for the Brooklyn bus operator who is still working during the pandemic. But now that the Metropolitan Transit Authority has restricted passengers from sitting in seats closest to the driver, the bus seems even more packed.

"I'm more concerned about my son than myself, of course, because he has an underlying health issue as well," she told *BuzzFeed News* to explain why they decided to buy their own masks and cleaning products a month before the MTA began distributing them to workers. *The New York Times* reported[56] some MTA employees were reprimanded for using precautionary measures themselves.

"It was every man for himself," she said and added that once the MTA began to distribute masks, it only provided one per employee. "I'm very nervous. I think I got more serious about the situation with the passing of coworkers."

As of Monday, April 20, 71 MTA employees have died of COVID-19, the disease caused by the novel coronavirus. The first MTA death occurred on March 26, a day before transit union officials negotiated a deal with the MTA to provide masks to workers, according to Jim Gannon, a spokesperson for transit union workers. Bus operators—whom the city considers essential workers—account for at least 20 of those deaths.

An MTA spokesperson said the agency had given out one million masks and three million pairs of gloves, "including masks to all employees days before the CDC changed course and recommended it. We are doing everything possible to protect our customers and employees, frontline heroes moving the doctors, nurses, first responders, pharmacy and grocery workers, transit colleagues and other essential workers who are saving lives every day."

The bus driver, who declined to be named for fear of losing her job, is one of hundreds of thousands of Brooklynites still working essential jobs, even as the borough is hit hard by the coronavirus. Twenty-eight percent of New York City's essential workers live in Brooklyn—the most in any borough—and the vast majority of them are people of color. In Brooklyn, the number of deaths outpaced those in Queens[57] on Sunday. Brooklyn has more than 2606 confirmed COVID-19 deaths and 865 "probable" COVID-19 deaths, according to NYC data released April 19.

"It's not a secret and it's very clear… We divided the city at the beginning of the coronavirus into essential employees and nonessential employees and that term was used all over the city," Brooklyn Borough President Eric Adams told *BuzzFeed News* during a phone interview last week. "I heard it. I said, 'This is coded language.'"

Black, Hispanic, and Asian people make up more than 70% of the city's essential workers, including transit, childcare, health care, cleaning service, and postal employees. More than 40% of transit workers are Black and 60% of frontline cleaning workers are Hispanic, according to a report[58] released in March by New York City Comptroller Scott Stringer's office. In addition to racial data on frontline workers, Stringer, who is running for New York City mayor, offered solutions to protect those people, including free protective gear, hazard pay, and guaranteed health care.

"Black and brown people went to service this city and then went home and spread the virus among their citizens," Adams told *BuzzFeed News*. "Just look at the numbers."

Adams said he personally has lost five close friends in the span of a week. "The impact is very real, and you become almost even afraid to pick up your phone," Adams told *BuzzFeed News*, saying he was haunted by the words "Did you hear…"

The same racial divide is consistent[59] in Milwaukee, Chicago, New Orleans, and other major cities and experts say the disparity adds to the outsize number of COVID-19 cases throughout Black and Latino communities.

"Essential workers are absolutely more vulnerable," Mary Osirim, provost and professor of sociology at Bryn Mawr College, told *BuzzFeed News*. "While there are certain professionals that are of every ethnicity and race in the country, it is also the case that many on the front lines are low-wage … low-status workers and they're often very disproportionately African American and Latinx."

And many lack access to basic protective gear as they continue to go to work. Adams, who is also running for New York City mayor, began addressing that problem on March 25, when he held a press conference in front of a Brooklyn MTA bus depot and demanded[60], "Give us the goddamn masks."

"Yes, we're telling you that people should be six feet apart from each other. Yes, we're telling you that everyone should shelter in place," he told *BuzzFeed News* during a phone interview. "Yes, we're telling you that no one should be out here because it's dangerous, but we're sending you out there and we're not giving out any masks, coverings, gloves, or anything else while you service the city and service the country."

Employees at the U.S. Postal Service have similar concerns, especially mail carriers who interact with close to 1000 New Yorkers every day at work. African Americans make up 21% of postal employees and 13% of the U.S. population.

One USPS worker in Brooklyn told *BuzzFeed News* they now have a ritual when they get home from work: "I immediately remove my shoes, my postal pants…I take off my jacket, my sweater and coat and I leave everything in my room in a corner. When I *had* Lysol I would spray everything down."

The USPS worker is practicing social distancing inside their home as well, so as not to infect vulnerable loved ones—hugs and kisses are replaced with a distant "hi."

The same USPS employee told *BuzzFeed News* that protective supplies, including gloves, began to dwindle as early as March 1. More pressing is the lack of communication from management amid a public health crisis, they said.

"We started hearing [from coworkers] 'at this particular post office, this person is infected,' but [management] wasn't saying anything. I noticed a clerk went out sick," they said, adding that two more followed within the same week.

There's signage posted about proper hygiene, but no one from management had personally spoken to staff at this particular Brooklyn branch as of late

March. "We're finding out things on our own, like 'Why is this person not here? Why do we have this skeleton crew?'" At a separate Brooklyn USPS location, employees said management gathers employees for updates on COVID-19 but not on a daily basis.

"They'll call everyone around the desk and basically read off what they have."

Approximately 1000 of the 630,000 employees have tested positive for COVID-19 "with some deaths," USPS spokesperson David Partenheimer told *BuzzFeed News* in a statement.

One USPS employee contrasted the coronavirus response with the 2001 anthrax scare, when letters carrying spores that caused the infectious disease were mailed to news outlets and elected officials, resulting in five deaths and 17 injuries.

"[In 2001], they were on top of it. We got all of this information. We got flu shots," one employee said. "But this time, no one is saying anything to us."

Adams also pointed out that while the CDC specified susceptible communities[61], there is no government plan to protect the most vulnerable. Black people are at greater risk of illnesses that can lead to more severe cases of COVID-19, including diabetes and heart disease. Adams himself reversed his diabetes diagnosis by exercising and changing his eating habits in 2018.

"There was not one plan that was rolled out that said 'let's go after the people who we know if they get it, they may die from it,'" Adams said. "Our plan was an intervention, not prevention. If you look at over 60, preexisting conditions, diabetes, respiratory issues, that's [the New York City Housing Authority]. That's why I was at NYCHA handing out masks and information to NYCHA residents."

Experts have said there's an information gap for some Black and non-English-speaking New Yorkers on the front lines because of inconsistent work hours and differences in the way people consume news. Mayor Bill de Blasio announced a $10 million campaign aimed to inform communities hardest hit by the disease that will include robocalls and flyers directly to homes. The campaign will run in 15 languages and follows an $8 million effort launched early March which ran ads in English, Spanish, Mandarin, and Cantonese. Experts also suggested targeting social media as a part of city-sponsored ad campaigns to counter the misinformation circulating[62] among younger audiences and New Yorkers who speak languages other than English.

"Everybody don't wake up in the morning and run and get *The New York Times* and listen to Trump, Cuomo, and the mayor's briefings," Adams told

BuzzFeed News. "We're talking in echo chambers. You know who we're talking to? We're talking to the 30% who can telecommute."

4.4

'We Are Not Essential. We Are Sacrificial.'

by Sujatha Gidla

Originally published in *The New York Times*, MAY 5, 2020

I'm a New York City subway conductor who had COVID-19. Now I'm going back to work.

When I heard that a co-worker had died from COVID-19—the first in the Metropolitan Transportation Authority[63]—on March 27, I thought, "It's starting." More deaths followed in quick succession, frequently more than once a day. Some of those people I used to see every day and fist bump.

On Facebook, when bad news comes, my co-workers and I express grief and offer condolences to the families. But our spontaneous response is the numb curiosity of an onlooker. We knew this was coming. We knew many among us wouldn't make it through the pandemic.

Every day I see posts on the MTA[64] workers' group pages striking a jaunty tone: "Oh Lord, here we go. I got the symptoms, see you all in 14 days. Or not."

We work at the epicenter of the epicenter, with a mortality rate substantially higher[65] than that of first responders. Common sense tells you that subway trains and platforms are giant vectors of this virus. We breathe it in along with steel dust. As a conductor, when I stick my head out of the car to perform the required platform observation, passengers in many stations are standing 10 inches from my face. At other times, they lean into the cab to ask questions. Bus drivers, whose passengers enter right in front of them, are even worse off.

My co-workers want doors locked on the two cars where the crew rides. Bus drivers want to let passengers enter through the back doors. We want hazard pay and family leave for child care.

In mid-March, a bulletin came out mandating that conductors make an announcement every 15 minutes. Wash hands, soap and water, sanitizer, elbow-sneeze. "Together we can help keep New York safe."

The irony was that we didn't have soap and water. At my terminal at that time, the restrooms were closed for three days after a water main break. Most employee restrooms are in similarly bad shape. Crew rooms are packed.

The MTA takes stern action against workers seen without goggles or cotton knit safety gloves. Yet we had to work without protection against the coronavirus.

At first, we were warned not to wear masks. The MTA said it would panic the public. It said[66] masks were dangerous for us. Later it said we could wear masks we bought ourselves. But by then there were few masks for sale.

One week after the pandemic was declared, a vice president of TWU Local 100 came to my terminal to give a talk. I rose to my feet in outrage and asked why we weren't receiving masks. I was told healthy people didn't need masks and that doctors needed them more. Aren't doctors healthy? No answer. How about rubber gloves and hand sanitizer? No answer.

Finally, the MTA agreed to supply us[67] with personal protective equipment. When signing in, we get an N95 mask and three small packets of wipes the size of those used before a shot at the doctor's office. This is meant to last three days. We also get a small container to fill with hand sanitizer from a bottle in the dispatcher's office.

The masks are cheaply made. My co-workers complain that the masks pinch their noses. The straps break easily. Many masks must be secured with duct tape.

Or so I have heard. Two days after the vice president's visit, I developed severe body aches, chills, and a dry cough. On March 27, I woke up at 6 a.m. to go to the bathroom and collapsed. I made a quick call to a close friend and then dialed 911. An ambulance took me to NYU Langone Medical Center, where I was treated and discharged. I stayed isolated for 14 days, after which I felt better. My co-workers told me about a place where I could get tested. On April 15, I tested positive. Further quarantine. My direct-deposit statement shows $692: less than half my wages for the first pay period and nothing thereafter. (I had used up all of my sick days).

The third death I heard about was a Black co-worker I used to see every day who once saw me reading Michelle Alexander's *The New Jim Crow*. He wanted to know why a woman from India was interested in the condition of Black people. From then on, whenever we ran into each other we hugged and cheek-kissed.

I used to talk to another co-worker across the platform when his N train and my R train reached Atlantic Avenue. He was one of only two Orthodox Jews in the rapid transit operation. A train buff, he once noticed that a cable that connects one car to another had come loose and was hanging dangerously near the third rail. He may have saved lives that day. Now he's dead, too.

We are stumbling upon dead bodies. I know of two cases. A train operator nearly tripped over one while walking between cars. The other person was sitting upright on a bench right outside the conductor's window and discovered to be dead only at the end of an eight-hour shift after my co-workers kept noticing the person on each trip.

The conditions created by the pandemic drive home the fact that we essential workers—workers in general—are the ones who keep the social order from sinking into chaos. Yet we are treated with the utmost disrespect, as though we're expendable. Since March 27, at least 98 New York transit workers have died of COVID-19. My co-workers say bitterly: "We are not essential. We are sacrificial."

That may be true individually, but not in our numbers. Hopefully this experience will make us see clearly the crucial role we play in keeping society running so that we can stand up for our interests, for our lives. Like the Pittsburgh sanitation workers walking out to demand protective equipment. Like the G.E. workers calling on the company to repurpose plants to make ventilators instead of jet engines.

I took my second test on April 30. It was negative. Tomorrow, I will go back to work.

4.5

How Millions of Women Became the Most Essential Workers in America

by Campbell Robertson & Robert Gebeloff

Originally published in *The New York Times*, APRIL 18, 2020

One in three jobs held by women has been designated as essential.

Every day, Constance Warren stands behind the cold cuts counter at a grocery store in New Orleans, watching the regular customers come and go.

They thank Ms. Warren and tell her they do not like being stuck indoors, waiting out the epidemic. She wraps their honey-smoked turkey and smiles.

It is good to have a job right now, the mixed fortune of being deemed an essential worker[68]. But she wonders whether, once everyday life is safe again, people will remember the role she played when it was not.

"Don't forget that we were open to serve you in your time of need," she said on a break one recent workday afternoon. "You never know when you might need us again."

From the cashier to the emergency room nurse to the drugstore pharmacist to the home health aide taking the bus to check on her older client, the soldier on the front lines of the current national emergency is most likely a woman.

One in three jobs held by women has been designated as essential, according to a *New York Times* analysis of census data crossed with the federal government's essential worker guidelines. Non-White women are more likely to be doing essential jobs than anyone else.

The work they do has often been underpaid and undervalued an unseen labor force that keeps the country running and takes care of those most in need, whether or not there is a pandemic.

Women make up nearly nine out of 10 nurses and nursing assistants, most respiratory therapists, a majority of pharmacists, and an overwhelming majority of pharmacy aides and technicians. More than two-thirds of the workers at grocery store checkouts and fast food counters are women.

In normal times, men are a majority of the overall workforce. But this crisis has flipped that. In March, the Department of Homeland Security released a memo identifying "Essential Critical Infrastructure Workers," an advisory guide for state and federal officials. It listed scores of jobs, suggesting they were too vital to be halted even as cities and whole states were on lockdown. A majority of those jobs are held by women.

Among all male workers, 28 percent have jobs deemed part of this essential workforce. Some of the biggest employers of men in the United States are building trades, like construction and carpentry—lines of work that are now, for the most part, on hold.

Men do make up a majority of workers in a number of essential sectors, including law enforcement, transit and public utilities, and millions face serious and unquestionable risk as they head to work every day. But there are simply not as many of these jobs as there are in the industry at the forefront: health care. There are 19 million health care workers nationwide, nearly three times as many as in agriculture, law enforcement, and the package delivery industry combined. Long before the outbreak, in an aging and ailing country, the demand for health care was almost limitless. The size of this workforce has ballooned over the decades as medical advances extended the lives of the sick and well alike.

There are now four registered nurses for every police officer, and still hospitals raise alarms about nursing shortages. Within this massive, ever-growing and now indispensable part of the economy, nearly four out of five workers are women. This is reflected in another grim statistic: While male doctors and nurses[69] have died on the front lines, a recent report[70] from the Centers for Disease Control and Prevention found that women account for 73 percent of the U.S. health care workers who have been infected since the outbreak began.

The nation's health care industry spreads far beyond hospitals, encompassing a vast army of people who tend to the young, old, sick, and infirm. This "care workforce," said Mignon Duffy, a professor at the University of Massachusetts Lowell who studies women and labor, "is part of the infrastructure of our whole society. It holds everything together." Yet it has long been undervalued, she said, a neglect that is as obvious as ever right now, with acute shortages nationwide of basic safety gear.

"But now we're being forced to identify who the essential workers are," Dr. Duffy said. "And guess who they are?"

Aurora Ozanick, the five-year-old daughter of a nurse and a construction worker in Pittsburgh, makes sense of her parents' jobs this way: "Mommy fixes people," she says. "Daddy fixes things."

These days, Bobbi Ozanick—"Mommy"—continues to report to work at the hospital. Her husband, who was laid off when his job site was shut down, stays home with Aurora. Fixing things can wait. This has been hard to digest for both parents.

"The concept of it was one of the weirdest conversations we've ever had," Ms. Ozanick, 33, said. She told her husband that if things got bad, keeping her at work for long hours and putting the health of those around her in jeopardy, he should go with their daughter to a relative's house. He wanted none of that. "His plan is to go apply for what's deemed essential. He used to work in a hospital cafeteria years ago."

But being essential does not at all mean being well compensated or even noticed.

While women have steadily increased their share of high-end health care jobs like surgeons and other physicians, they have also been filling the unseen jobs proliferating on the lowest end of the wage scale, the workers who spend long and little-rewarded days bathing, feeding and medicating some of the most vulnerable people in the country. Of the 5.8 million people working health care jobs that pay less than $30,000 a year, half are non-White and 83 percent are women.

Home health and personal care aides, jobs that earn little more than minimum wage and until recently were even exempt from basic labor protections[71], are two of the fastest growing occupations[72] in the entire U.S. job market. More than eight in 10 of these aides are women.

"We're still a part of health care and we're not recognized at all," said Pam Ramsey, 56, who has gone years without health insurance working as a home health aide in rural Pennsylvania.

Ms. Ramsey did not set out to do this. In her 20s, she earned a degree from a trade school in auto body and mechanics, one of just three women in her graduating class of 115. But her father was badly hurt working in a coal mine, and the duty of taking care of him fell to her rather than her brothers. She has been taking care of people, paid and unpaid, ever since.

If protective equipment is in dangerously short supply at big city hospitals, it is virtually nonexistent in Ms. Ramsey's job. She goes to work with no gear beyond what she can find at the dollar store. She does not have a formal letter, like many others have, identifying her as an essential worker. A policeman recently stopped and questioned her when she was out buying medicine.

"People don't look at us because we have no license, no certificate, no proof that we're as good as they are," Ms. Ramsey said. But still she goes to work, bringing whatever rubbing alcohol and peroxide she can get her hands on.

Ms. Ramsey is not alone in having to improvise. While some child care centers are still open for the children of essential workers, this is not true everywhere.

And though educators nationwide are spending long and demanding days teaching online, a young student at home needs an adult there, too. (The federal classification of educator jobs is unclear, so they were not included in the analysis of the essential workforce; if they had been, the women's share of the workforce would have been substantially higher.)

As a result, many single mothers who have essential jobs are also facing the added emergency of 24-hour child care.

"This one is helping watch this one's child while she works the night shift, then she watches hers for the 7-3 shift," said Keshia Williams, 44, a certified nursing assistant at a nursing home in Scranton, Pa., where the staff members—"99.9 percent of them" women—are trying to cover an ever-growing list of rotations left unfilled by infected or quarantined co-workers.

"Now we are apparently essential," Ms. Williams said dryly, before describing the critical lack of protective gear where she works. Some N95 masks recently arrived, but she is limited to one a week, an uneasy regimen given that she spends each morning screening residents for the virus. Still, dealing with people face to face is what drew her to her job in the first place. The pandemic has not changed that.

That millions of care workers are "driven by incentives other than purely economic incentives" is in part why this work has traditionally been so undervalued, said Gabriel Winant, a labor historian at the University of Chicago.

It is a type of work that does not produce an object that can be traded or sold, he said; it is simply work that has to be done. "There is a whole system in place to make us not think of this as critical infrastructure," he said.

Until that system gets a shock.

"I didn't sign up for a pandemic," said Andrea Lindley, 34, an ICU nurse at a Philadelphia hospital where scores of coronavirus patients have been admitted. "But I am not going to walk away when people need me."

Growing up, she wanted to become a doctor, watching her mother come back exhausted and back-sore from long hours as a licensed practical nurse. Health care is harder physical work than people realize—workers in health care and social assistance suffer nonfatal injuries[73] on the job at a rate higher than workers in construction or manufacturing. Ms. Lindley's mother described the job to her this way: "You work too hard and you don't get paid enough."

But Ms. Lindley was attracted to the personal, hands-on practice of nursing. "We are in the rooms way more than the doctors," she said. It is what she still loves about the job. These days, with her husband unable to find carpentry work and her daughter recovering from leukemia, it is also what makes the job so dangerous.

"I have horrible nightmares knowing I'm going into the hospital the next day," she said. She felt a sense of deep relief when, on a recent shift, she was transferred to the burn unit.

Across the state, in southwestern Pennsylvania, Crystal Patterson heads to work. Her stepfather was laid off from his airport job, and her parents are unsure what they will do.

For Ms. Patterson, 30, a home health aide, there is less uncertainty. Yes, she has to manage caring for her son, but there is a client in her 90s who is depending on her. So for around $10 an hour, she stays on the job. There is a fundamental question before her, one faced by countless other women keeping the country alive: If she does not do this, who will?

"As a woman, this is nothing new to me," Ms. Patterson said. "That's how it's always been in this country: 'When we're sick, get us through this.'"

4.6

COVID-19 Exacerbates Gender Inequality. Let's Ensure PPE Doesn't Neglect Women's Bodies

by Jennifer Weiss-Wolf

Originally published in *Ms. Magazine*, MAY 11, 2020

Across the country, women occupy the vast majority[74] of roles deemed essential to the coronavirus crisis response.

According to *The New York Times*[75]:

> From the cashier to the emergency room nurse to the drugstore pharmacist to the home health aide taking the bus to check on her older client, the soldier on the front lines of the current national emergency is most likely a woman.

One key commonality is the need for adequate safety gear. By now, we're all too fluent in the vernacular of PPE—personal protective equipment—and its importance in shielding those who risk exposure to COVID-19.

But what happens when PPE is treated as a "one-size-fits-all" proposition? And when the default is the body and experience of a cisgender male? Two recent news stories highlight the dangers.

Menstrual Products as Part of PPE

First, is the often-overlooked consideration of menstrual products as part of the PPE package.

Back when hospitalizations peaked in China's Hubei province, medical providers there spoke out[76] about the challenge of working long shifts in full-body protective jumpsuits while managing their periods. Many made complaints to officials about the dearth of readily available menstrual products and infrequent bathroom breaks—only to be met with derision. Some were chided that they "lacked the spirit of devotion"[77].

A nightmarish response ensued when a hospital in Shanghai announced[78] it would donate hormonal birth control pills to suppress menstruation—as its leaders put it, to "postpone female team members' 'unspeakable' special periods."

Finally, a viral social media post shared on a local site spurred a much-needed supply of donated pads, tampons, period underwear, and even adult diapers.

Weeks later, another cohort posed a similar need—actual frontline soldiers. Of the nearly 5000 members of the U.S. Navy on board the USS Theodore

Roosevelt, the aircraft carrier hit with coronavirus[79], approximately one thousand were women. The Washington, D.C.-based nonprofit I Support the Girls[80] was summoned to provide an emergency donation of tampons and pads for these sailors, after being flagged that many were left high and dry during quarantine with limited access to these and other essential hygiene products.

Periods should never be cause for shame or deprivation of bodily autonomy and integrity. At a minimum, governments must ensure that those they employ to do crucial work on the front lines are able to readily manage normal bodily functions—including menstruation. Donation drives filled an emergency gap in both of these scenarios but are no substitute for public and policy interventions.

PPE Treats Men's Bodies as the Default

And second is rising awareness that standardized PPE itself is not constructed for all bodies, either. Unisex gear often is made for the male physique.

A recent *Refinery 29* [81] report shed light on this problem among British health providers. Although the Department of Health announced that its PPE kits of gloves, masks, gowns and visors were designed to protect "both genders," much of it has proved ineffective—and too big for many of the women who make up 77 percent of the NHS workforce. One surgeon observed[82] that the (ill-fitting) mask she received came in a box that featured a man's face; a headline from *The Guardian*[83] blared, "PPE is designed for a 6-foot-3 bloke built like a rugby player."

It is not hard to see how this poses significant, even life-threatening harm—not only to the legions of women forced to don gear that wasn't made to fit, but also those whom they serve and encounter, from vulnerable patients to the public at large.

And the solution should be stunningly simple: Right-size the PPE, acknowledge the reality and array of women's bodies and lose the assumption that men are the default.

This is the argument at the heart of Caroline Criado-Perez's extraordinary book, *Invisible Women: Exposing Data Bias in a World Designed for Men.* In it, she addresses PPE in particular: *"Respiratory protective equipment is designed for a male face, and if it doesn't fit, it won't protect."*

It is 2020 and women simply no longer can be treated as 'the other'—not ever, and surely not when occupying crucial positions to save us in crisis, while simultaneously bearing the brunt of its toll.

There are myriad ways that the global pandemic exacerbates gender inequality. Let's be sure that the size, shape and function of our bodies is not one of them.

4.7

The Anti-Mask League: Lockdown Protests Draw Parallels to 1918 Pandemic

by Peter Lawrence Kane

Originally published in *The Guardian*, APRIL 29, 2020

California has succeeded in flattening the curve of infections, but will it learn a lesson from a similar pandemic a century ago?

San Francisco seems to have done a good job of flattening the coronavirus curve. Initially perceived as an overreaction, the shelter-in-place order issued on March 16 now seems prudent in light of the sustained public health crisis that New York has endured.

San Francisco has seen roughly 1450 confirmed coronavirus cases and 23 deaths but the city wasn't always so good at heeding the advice of experts.

A century ago, the influenza pandemic hit San Francisco harder than any other major U.S. city, with 45,000 infections and 3000 deaths. As NPR's Tim Mak pointed out in a Twitter thread[84] on April 19, protests in late 1918 and early 1919 helped turn a manageable public-health situation into a disaster—courtesy of a now-forgotten movement known as the Anti-Mask League.

It began after the initial wave of infections in the fall of 1918 died down, the approximate juncture where California is now vis-à-vis COVID-19. But instead of flattening the curve, hostility to common sense measures on grounds of personal liberty turned that curve into a double hump. Cases spiked in October, and mask use became mandatory, but only for four weeks. As of November 21, they were no longer required.

Seemingly clear of danger, the city reopened, and a populace weary from the first world war and the widespread destruction of the 1906 earthquake and fire jumped back into the conviviality of life. Predictably, this led to a second wave of illness and death, and the city became convulsed by debates over the efficacy of masks and whether their use should be compulsory or not.

Then as now, a loose alliance of constitutional conservatives and economic boosters coalesced in opposition to the idea of masks, even as the caseload exploded to more than 600 a week by January 1919. A port city of 500,000 couldn't seal itself off from the world[85] the way a remote mountain town like Gunnison, Colorado, could, and ultimately around 3000 residents would succumb to the flu. All the while, civic-minded physicians coaxed people into adopting masks as a kind of fashionable accessory, with one claiming[86] that "chiffon veils for women and children have been as satisfactory as the common gauze masks." But the Anti-Mask League complained bitterly that an obligation to cover one's nose and mouth was an unconstitutional affront to the principles of a free society.

The San Francisco Board of Supervisors nonetheless reinstated the mask requirement on January 17, 1919. People caught without one were typically fined $5 or $10, money that was donated to the Red Cross, although a minority of scofflaws were sentenced to brief jail terms. In one case, a zealous public health official shot three people[87] on a downtown street.

The League "seems to have been an ad hoc thing that was set up to respond to the board of supervisors reinstituting the mandate that citizens wear masks," says Brian Dolan, a professor at the University of California San Francisco school of medicine. Local denim manufacturer Levi Strauss was a major producer of masks, Dolan adds, lending credence to the suspicion that profit was the real motive.

The medical literature was scant, with a Canadian health official casting doubt on mask effectiveness as well. "He said it was quite clear from the epidemiological evidence: when people across the world were asked to wear masks, the numbers still went up," Dolan says. "So people began to lose confidence against this measure, and his recommendation as a result was to focus on quarantine and isolation: what we're calling social distancing."

Only a week after the supervisors took action, some 4500 League members—far more than any gathering this month in Sacramento or Lansing—assembled at the long-gone Dreamland skating rink. After that show of force, the chair of the Anti-Mask League, one Mrs. E. C. Harrington, implored[88] the board of supervisors to grant "speedy relief" from the "burdensome" requirement. At least one supervisor rose to question the science behind masks as a preventive public health measure, claiming that unemployment among recently demobilized soldiers was a more urgent problem. Yet the city remained resolute, under the leadership of the health commissioner, Dr. William C Hassler, the Dr. Anthony Fauci of his day.

"Hassler and the mayor, whose wife was ill, called for remasking," says historian John M. Barry, a professor at Tulane University's school of public health and the author of *The Great Influenza*. "But this time around, the outbreak was much less severe than in October and November and pushback was intense. Even the state board of health said masks were unnecessary. A bomb was even sent to Hassler—though it went to the wrong address, and no one was hurt. The business community and unions had both supported all control measures the first time around, and both opposed remasking."

Parochialism and a wariness toward outsiders armed with expertise played roles very similar to today, says Bill Issel, professor emeritus of history at San Francisco State University. Social workers—often single, college-educated women—were met with "contemptuous criticism" in working-class neighborhoods. But what compounded that phenomenon in San Francisco was a widespread perception of municipal incompetence.

"The protests back in 1918 and 1919 were organized. That sort of distrust of experts, distrust of the government's point of view was very strong," Issel says. "The San Francisco of 1870 to 1920 was only gradually moving away from a city that had a huge problem raising enough money through bond issues and taxation to put sidewalks in the street."

In other words, it was a question of the legitimacy of state power, underscored by the discomfort of citizens who could not see one another's faces. Publicly concealing oneself has always been associated with lawlessness and behaviors deemed antisocial or deviant, from the bandannas worn by train robbers to the Guy Fawkes masks found on Antifa street protesters to the beaked plague doctor costume found at masquerades and Edwardian balls.

While ordinary PPE isn't nearly as grotesque, it's still fraught. Even though New York's Governor Andrew Cuomo has made public mask use mandatory, the state's penal code still considers the wearing of a disguise on the street to be a form of loitering[89]. In San Francisco today, enforcement of the mask requirement falls to restaurateurs and small-business owners who are already under serious financial strain. Chastising would-be patrons for violating a public health ordinance doesn't create an atmosphere of hospitality, it's true. Hopefully San Francisco learned its lesson from the last pandemic.

4.8

The Dudes Who Won't Wear Masks

by Julia Marcus

Originally published in *The Atlantic*, JUNE 23, 2020

Face coverings are a powerful tool, but health authorities can't simply ignore the reasons some people refuse to use them.

Last week, the former Major League Baseball player Aubrey Huff announced on Twitter[90] that he was no longer going to wear a mask inside any business. "It's unconstitutional to enforce," he wrote. "Let's make this bullshit stop now! Who's with me?" In a video[91] that went viral the following day, he said his critics had tried to shame him for "threatening the lives of millions of innocent people" and insisted that he considered dying from the coronavirus preferable to "wearing a damn mask."

Thousands of people responded to Huff. Many called him a social disgrace for disrespecting his community, abdicating his civic duty, and putting Grandma at risk. The anger toward mask naysayers is understandable, and shaming can feel relieving in the moment. Yet those responses did nothing to persuade Huff to wear a mask. Instead, they played right into his notions about the finger-wagging, "elitist" public-health experts who want to take away the freedoms of ordinary Americans.

During a health crisis, some people quickly accommodate a major shift in behavioral norms. But long-standing habits—such as not wearing a mask to the grocery store—are difficult to break, and until recently few American adults have been called upon to do so. Some have, though, and the parallels are instructive.

Americans are figuring out how to live with a deadly new virus now, just as gay men did in the early years of AIDS. Abstinence from sex wasn't sustainable, and condoms became a ticket to greater sexual freedom. Likewise, Americans can't abstain from human interaction forever[92], and widespread masking may be a ticket to more social and economic freedom. But trying to shame people into wearing condoms didn't work—and it won't work for masks either.

The public-health messaging around masks during the coronavirus pandemic has been muddled and confusing. The federal government recommended against face coverings for the public in March, with some public-health officials positing[93] that they may even cause more harm than good. But a growing body of science, including evidence[94] that people can transmit the virus when they don't have symptoms, indicates that masks are an important tool[95] for mitigating coronavirus transmission, especially in combination with physical distancing, hand hygiene, and other preventive strategies. Indeed, public-health concerns may justify mask mandates in some settings, including indoor spaces where many people gather for extended periods of time. But mandates have major downsides: Any enforcement is likely to disproportionately affect[96] communities that are already marginalized, and some Americans—including some elected leaders[97] in states facing serious coronavirus outbreaks—believe that requiring people to wear masks is an infringement on civil liberties. In practice, if Americans are going to mask up, public-health officials will have to cajole, not compel.

This will not be easy. When the president mocks mask-wearers for appearing weak[98] and sees face coverings as a political statement against him[99], it's no surprise that some Americans are loudly declining[100] to wear them. Mask-refusers are more likely to be politically conservative[101], an ominous trend when new coronavirus cases and hospitalizations are increasing steeply in some red states—the very states where mask mandates are least likely to be adopted. As one research team[102] noted, men are especially likely to opt out of wearing masks, believing them to be "shameful," "a sign of weakness," and "not cool"—even though men are at higher risk[103] than women of dying from coronavirus infection. A similar pattern has emerged during prior pandemics[104] and across other areas of health[105]: Men—especially those who endorse[106] traditional masculine gender norms—have been less likely than women to engage in protective health behaviors.

But even macho men like Huff, whose Twitter bio declares[107], "I support Toxic Masculinity," aren't immune to public-health advice: In his video, he appears to be wearing a seatbelt[108]. Yet unlike a seatbelt, which directly benefits the user, masks primarily protect everyone else, particularly people who are older or have underlying health conditions that make them vulnerable to the coronavirus. Huff seems to understand this; he just thinks those people should "stay the fuck home"[109]. As Representative Tom Rice, a South Carolina Republican, told *The Wall Street Journal*[110] after refusing to wear a mask on the House floor and contracting the coronavirus, "A mask doesn't really protect you as much as it protects other people. I don't think it would have made much of a difference." The message seems to have gotten across that masks are mainly about protecting others; these men are simply choosing not to do so.

Still, trying to shame people into healthier behavior generally doesn't work—and actually can make things worse[111].

Public-health professionals have learned this lesson before. In 1987, Congress banned the use of federal funds for HIV-prevention campaigns that might "promote or encourage, directly or indirectly, homosexual activities." As a result, public-health campaigns avoided sex-positive imagery and messaging, and instead associated condom use with virtue and condomless sex with irresponsibility, disease, and death. According to one particularly foreboding poster[112], which featured an image of a gravestone: "A bad reputation isn't all you can get from sleeping around." But those moralistic, fear-mongering health messages often fell flat. Other HIV-prevention campaigns began to adopt a harm-reduction approach[113], which empathizes with people's basic human needs and offers them strategies to limit potential dangers. For some men, condoms got in the way[114] of what they valued most about sex: pleasure and intimacy. Not surprisingly, HIV-prevention campaigns that put pleasure and intimacy at the center of their safer-sex messaging tended to work[115].

Summoning compassion for people who have a hard time wearing masks, or even the people who flat-out object to them, isn't such a tall order. Many Americans genuinely want to keep their community safe, and recognize that masks reduce the risk of coronavirus transmission. But just like the well-intended condom on the nightstand that never makes it out of its wrapper, some masks don't make it onto someone's face—often for relatable reasons. And while ideologues who entirely eschew masks will be less persuadable, people who support the use of masks may find shared ground with them. Lamenting the way that face coverings impede social interactions with the cashiers ringing up his groceries, Huff says[116], "The two ladies that were checking me out were wearing these masks. And I love to make people like that smile and laugh and have a great conversation. You couldn't even see the wrinkles in their eyes with their smiles. They looked so beat-down and run-down."

Let's be real: Americans *are* beat-down and run-down after months of loss and social isolation. Masks do keep people from seeing facial expressions and hearing voices clearly, both vital elements of social connection. Masks don't deprive people of oxygen[117], but they do make it harder to breathe freely. They fog up people's glasses. They make noses itch and faces sweat. Many masks feel decidedly uncool. They are yet another thing to remember when walking out the front door. And, most of all, masks are a constant reminder of what Americans so desperately want to forget: that despite all of our sacrifices, the pandemic hasn't gone anywhere.

Empathy has its own kind of power. Acknowledging what people dislike about a public-health strategy enables a connection with them rather than alienating them further. And when the barriers are understood, they become addressable. When it became clear that people needed better condoms, companies began making them in all different shapes, sizes, and styles—ribbed, studded, impossibly thin, even glow-in-the-dark—to improve comfort, sensation, and people's sense of individuality. Likewise, the government needs to support businesses in developing masks that are not only effective, but also fit well and feel good[118]. People need a range of options, including face shields[119], that can help meet their personal needs and preferences. And people need face coverings that make them feel stylish, cool, and—yes—even manly.

When the public-health community talks about harm reduction, we often talk of "meeting people where they are." A fundamental part of that is, well, literally meeting people where they are. Just like the buckets of free condoms stationed in gay bars, masks need to be dispensed where they're needed most: at the front of every bus and the entrance to every airport, grocery store, and workplace. Masks should become ubiquitous, but distribution should begin in areas where the coronavirus has hit hardest, including Black and Latino neighborhoods[120]. (That Black men who wear masks may be at heightened risk of violence is one more grim illustration of why[121] combatting racism is inextricable from public health.) What matters most is that people choose to wear a mask when they are indoors or in close proximity to others—and that choice needs to be rendered as effortless as possible.

The decision of whether to wear a mask is a far more visible one than the decision of whether to wear a condom, making an individual's choice to go without an easy target for scorn. But trying to shame people into wearing masks will only cement their resistance—and perhaps even drive them to socialize behind closed doors, where being unmasked is higher risk. Public health works best when it recognizes and supports people's needs and desires without judgment. If Americans do this right, Huff might even find that his wearing a mask is the very thing that makes those checkout ladies smile.

Notes

1   https://www.who.int/news-room/detail/03-03-2020-shortage-of-personal-protective-equipment-endangering-health-workers-worldwide

2   https://www.theguardian.com/global-development/2020/apr/15/arcadia-group-cancels-over-100m-of-orders-as-garment-industry-faces-ruin

3   https://cleanclothes.org/news/2020/live-blog-on-how-the-coronavirus-influences-workers-in-supply-chains

4   https://apnews.com/181650f23661c91c8757d85c5491c883

5   https://www.business-humanrights.org/en/latest-news/bangladesh-trade-unions-to-launch-global-campaign-against-retailers-that-cancel-or-suspend-orders/

6   https://www.retailgazette.co.uk/blog/2020/04/barbour-supplies-ppe-nhs-frontline-healthcare-workers/
7   https://www.piie.com/blogs/trade-and-investment-policy-watch/
      covid-19-chinas-exports-medical-supplies-provide-ray-hope
8   https://www.piie.com/blogs/trade-and-investment-policy-watch/
      covid-19-chinas-exports-medical-supplies-provide-ray-hope
9   https://www.reuters.com/article/us-heath-coronavirus-usa-china/u-s-asks-china-to-revise-export-rules-
      for-coronavirus-medical-gear-idUSKBN21Z07G
10   http://www.xinhuanet.com/english/2020-05/22/c_139079934.htm
11   https://www.youtube.com/watch?v=zrHYOujdrCQ&feature=youtu.be
12   https://www.business-humanrights.org/en/latest-news/malaysia-medical-glove-manufacturers-see-surge-
      in-orders-due-to-covid-19-amid-forced-labour-concerns/
13   https://www.telegraph.co.uk/global-health/science-and-disease/
      dont-forget-people-behind-ppe-migrant-workersmeeting-surge/
14   https://www.thestar.com.my/news/nation/2020/04/17/group-seeks-industrial-help-to-make-ppe
15   https://swarajyamag.com/insta/india-becomes-worlds-2nd-largest-ppe-kit-producer-in-just-two-
      months-develops-world-first-reusable-ppe-suit
16   https://www.livemint.com/news/india/india-now-manufactures-4-5-lakh-ppe-suits-a-day-in-the-fight-
      against-covid-19-11589951566951.html
17   https://timesofindia.indiatimes.com/india/covid-19-india-likely-to-produce-2-crore-ppe-by-june-end/
      articleshow/75769392.cms
18   https://www.hindustantimes.com/india-news/covid-19-outbreak-export-of-5-million-ppe-suits-a-
      month-on-cards/story-xWPand59JAdkKe3CdWAJRK.html
19   https://thelogicalindian.com/news/bengaluru-is-manufacturing-50-of-ppe-kits-in-india-20829
20   https://theprint.in/india/tirupur-moves-from-hm-tommy-hilfiger-marks-spencer-to-making-masks-
      and-ppe-kits/400898/
21   https://duexpress.in/ppe-production-in-india/
22   https://pib.gov.in/PressReleasePage.aspx?PRID=1539877
23   https://theconversation.com/coronavirus-in-india-and-brazil-new-forecasts-for-when-economic-giants-
      will-hit-peak-140672
24   https://www.thehindu.com/opinion/op-ed/a-way-out-of-the-covid-19-crisis/article31504195.ece
25   https://thewire.in/political-economy/the-modi-sarkars-project-for-indias-informal-economy
26   https://www.economist.com/international/2020/04/19/
      why-countries-cant-meet-the-demand-for-gear-against-covid-19
27   https://blogs.worldbank.org/nasikiliza/
      working-africas-apparel-makers-produce-personal-protective-equipment
28   https://indianexpress.com/article/explained/
      coronavirus-how-many-migrant-workers-displaced-a-range-of-estimates-6447840/
29   http://www.xinhuanet.com/english/2020-05/22/c_139079934.htm
30   https://laborrights.org/releases/covid-19-related-worker-protections-needed-garmentppe-production-us
31   https://www.instyle.com/fashion/fashion-industry-garment-workers-making-ppe
32   http://sro.sussex.ac.uk/id/eprint/91196/
33   https://www.chinalawblog.com/2020/03/chinas-other-supply-chain-infection-forced-labor.html
34   https://www.aljazeera.com/news/2020/04/malaysia-concerns-labour-abuse-meet-rubber-gloves-
      demand-200420101808177.html
35   https://www.chinalawblog.com/2020/03/chinas-other-supply-chain-infection-forced-labor.html
36   https://economictimes.indiatimes.com/news/economy/policy/states-extend-working-hours-from-8-to-
      12-hours-in-factories/articleshow/75342462.cms?from=mdr
37   https://www.instyle.com/fashion/fashion-industry-garment-workers-making-ppe
38   https://www.abc.net.au/radio/programs/coronacast/
39   https://twitter.com/VictorianCHO?s=20
40   https://apnews.com/d951324af9a6e5a4bcb3dd3c3c6b4c28
41   https://www.abc.net.au/religion/andrew-jakubowicz-sinophobia-goes-viral/11983714
42   https://www.simonandschuster.com/books/
      The-Clash-of-Civilizations-and-the-Remaking-of-World-Order/Samuel-P-Huntington/9781451628975
43   https://www.nytimes.com/2020/07/12/style/president-trump-face-mask.html
44   https://www.nytimes.com/2020/07/01/us/coronavirus-masks.html
45   https://archives.var.fr/article.php?laref=11188&titre=affiche-la-republique-se-vit-a-visage-decouvert-
46   https://www.rfi.fr/en/france/20200309-coronavirus-french-fake-policemen-fine-chinese-students-
      wearing-face-masks-crime
47   https://www.theguardian.com/world/2020/jul/04/melbournes-hard-lockdown-orders-residents-of-nine-
      public-housing-towers-to-stay-home-as-coronavirus-cases-surge

48   https://www.3cr.org.au/thursday-breakfast/episode-201808090700/
     special-program-enough-enough-beyond-africangangs
49   https://www.rmit.edu.au/news/all-news/2020/jun/coronacheck-blm-protests
50   https://truthout.org/articles/as-fashion-lines-are-praised-for-making-face-masks-dont-ignore-garment-
     workers/
51   https://www.hrw.org/news/2020/04/22/protecting-garment-workers-during-covid-19-crisis
52   https://www.theguardian.com/fashion/2020/jun/24/
     zara-primark-factory-workers-myanmar-fired-union
53   https://www.amt.org.au/downloads/COVID-19/Mask-poster-A3.pdf
54   https://blacklivesmatter.com/what-we-believe/
55   https://www.buzzfeednews.com/collection/coronavirus
56   https://www.nytimes.com/2020/04/08/nyregion/coronavirus-nyc-mta-subway.html
57   https://www1.nyc.gov/assets/doh/downloads/pdf/imm/covid-19-deaths-confirmed-probable-
     daily-04192020.pdf
58   https://comptroller.nyc.gov/reports/new-york-citys-frontline-workers/
59   https://www.buzzfeednews.com/article/danvergano/coronavirus-black-americans-covid19
60   https://www.instagram.com/p/B-KfwrCpMiN/?utm_source=ig_web_copy_link
61   https://www.cdc.gov/coronavirus/2019-ncov/need-extra-precautions/index.html
62   https://www.buzzfeednews.com/article/janelytvynenko/
     coronavirus-fake-news-disinformation-rumors-hoaxes
63   https://www.nytimes.com/2020/06/10/nyregion/mta-subway-coronavirus.html
64   https://www.nytimes.com/2020/06/10/nyregion/mta-subway-coronavirus.html
65   https://www.nydailynews.com/coronavirus/ny-coronavirus-mta-nyc-transit-workers-deaths-20200408-
     f37damz5tjdmnc4pahurf3cjay-story.html
66   https://ti.org/pdfs/March6MTAMemo.pdf
67   https://www.nytimes.com/2020/04/08/nyregion/coronavirus-nyc-mta-subway.html
68   https://www.nytimes.com/2020/07/14/business/coronavirus-essential-workers-pay-raises.html
69   https://www.nytimes.com/2020/03/26/nyregion/nurse-dies-coronavirus-mount-sinai.html
70   https://www.cdc.gov/mmwr/volumes/69/wr/mm6915e6.htm?s_cid=mm6915e6_x
71   https://www.shrm.org/resourcesandtools/legal-and-compliance/employment-law/pages/home-care-rule-
     left-in-place.aspx
72   https://www.bls.gov/ooh/healthcare/home-health-aides-and-personal-care-aides.htm#tab-6
73   https://www.bls.gov/iif/osch0062.pdf
74   https://msmagazine.com/2020/03/13/
     coronavirus-covid19-gender-gap-women-workers-nurses-teachers-flight-airline-attendants/
75   https://www.nytimes.com/2020/04/18/us/coronavirus-women-essential-workers.html
76   https://www.inkstonenews.com/health/
     coronavirus-womens-advocates-ship-period-products-center-outbreak/article/3050653
77   https://www.nytimes.com/2020/02/26/business/coronavirus-china-nurse-menstruation.html
78   https://www.straitstimes.com/asia/east-asia/
     china-coronavirus-fight-sparks-outcry-over-female-frontline-staff
79   https://www.cnn.com/2020/04/28/politics/sailors-return-uss-theodore-roosevelt-aircraft-carrier-
     coronavirus/index.html
80   https://twitter.com/I_Support_Girls/status/1255871636391198721
81   https://www.refinery29.com/en-gb/women-ppe-risk-coronavirus
82   https://www.refinery29.com/en-gb/women-ppe-risk-coronavirus
83   https://www.theguardian.com/world/2020/apr/24/
     sexism-on-the-covid-19-frontline-ppe-is-made-for-a-6ft-3in-rugby-player
84   https://twitter.com/timkmak/status/1251936242834563073
85   https://www.theguardian.com/world/2020/mar/01/
     gunnison-colorado-the-town-that-dodged-the-1918-spanish-flu-pandemic
86   https://www.influenzaarchive.org/cities/city-sanfrancisco.html#
87   https://www.theatlantic.com/ideas/archive/2020/03/how-fragmented-country-fights-pandemic/608284/
88   https://books.google.com/books?id=zMMbAAAAIAAJ&newbks=0&printsec=frontcover&pg=PA50&d
     q=anti-mask+league+of+1919&hl=en#v=onepage&q=anti-mask%20league%20of%201919&f=false
89   https://twitter.com/srfeld/status/1251228271645208577
90   https://twitter.com/aubrey_huff/status/1272545366773096453?s=20
91   https://twitter.com/aubrey_huff/status/1273018665391099904?s=21
92   https://www.theatlantic.com/ideas/archive/2020/05/
     quarantine-fatigue-real-and-shaming-people-wont-help/611482/
93   https://www.businessinsider.com/americans-dont-need-masks-pence-says-as-demand-increases-2020-2

94   https://www.cdc.gov/coronavirus/2019-ncov/prevent-getting-sick/cloth-face-cover-guidance.html
95   https://www.healthaffairs.org/doi/full/10.1377/hlthaff.2020.00818
96   https://www.nytimes.com/2020/05/07/nyregion/nypd-social-distancing-race-coronavirus.html
97   https://miami.cbslocal.com/2020/06/19/florida-governor-ron-desantis-says-masks-should-be-voluntary/
98   https://www.washingtonpost.com/politics/trumps-mockery-of-wearing-masks-divides-
     republicans/2020/05/26/2c2bdc02-9f61-11ea-81bb-c2f70f01034b_story.html
99   https://www.businessinsider.com/trump-americans-wearing-masks-show-disapproval-not-as-preventive-
     measure-2020-6
100 https://abcnews.go.com/US/conservative-activist-kicked-off-plane-refusing-wear-mask/
     story?id=71313066&cid=social_twitter_abcnp
101 https://www.nytimes.com/2020/06/02/health/coronavirus-face-masks-surveys.html
102 https://psyarxiv.com/tg7vz/
103 https://www.vox.com/2020/4/9/21215063/coronavirus-covid-19-deaths-men-women-sex-dying-why
104 https://onlinelibrary.wiley.com/doi/full/10.1348/135910710X485826
105 https://journals.sagepub.com/doi/abs/10.1177/1466424007073205
106 https://psycnet.apa.org/record/2005-07547-005
107 https://twitter.com/aubrey_huff
108 https://twitter.com/aubrey_huff/status/1273018665391099904?s=21
109 https://twitter.com/aubrey_huff/status/1273018665391099904?s=21
110 https://www.wsj.com/articles/gop-rep-tom-rice-fell-ill-from-coronavirus-11592263448
111 https://www.theatlantic.com/ideas/archive/2020/05/
     quarantine-fatigue-real-and-shaming-people-wont-help/611482/
112 https://www.nlm.nih.gov/exhibition/survivingandthriving/digitalgallery/detail-A028179.html
113 https://www.theatlantic.com/ideas/archive/2020/05/
     no-one-telling-americans-how-reopen-their-lives/612172/
114 https://www.theatlantic.com/health/archive/2013/04/why-still-so-few-use-condoms/275301/
115 https://www.tandfonline.com/doi/full/10.1016/S0968-8080(06)28254-5
116 https://twitter.com/aubrey_huff/status/1273018665391099904?s=21
117 https://www.usatoday.com/story/news/factcheck/2020/05/30/
     fact-check-wearing-face-mask-not-cause-hypoxia-hypercapnia/5260106002/
118 https://hbr.org/2020/06/we-need-better-masks
119 https://www.cbc.ca/news/business/buckner-face-shields-demand-1.5613976
120 https://www.npr.org/sections/health-shots/2020/05/30/865413079/
     what-do-coronavirus-racial-disparities-look-like-state-by-state
121 https://www.nytimes.com/2020/04/14/us/coronavirus-masks-racism-african-americans.html

Part Five

The Politics of Space

5.1

Pandemic, Race, and Moral Panic

by Zuleyka Zevallos

Originally published in *The Other Sociologist*, JULY 5, 2020

Since the Coronavirus COVID-19 pandemic reached Australia in January 2020, I've been working on a couple of COVID-19 research posts for you. I was ready to post one of these on Monday, but I have decided to first address a race and public health response that is presently unfolding.

In the afternoon of 4 July 2020, Victorian Premier Daniel Andrews, gave a press conference announcing that two more postcodes are being added to COVID-19 lockdown (making 12 in total)[1]. The new postcodes under Stage-3 lockdown are 3031 Flemington and 3051 North Melbourne.

Additionally, the Victorian Government is effectively criminalizing the poor: nine public housing towers are being put into complete lockdown. The Premier said: "There's no reason to leave for five days, effective immediately." This affects 1345 public housing units, and approximately 3000 residents.

Public housing lockdown is made under Public Order laws. Residents will be under police-enforced lockdown for a minimum of five days, and up to 14 days, to enable "everyone to be tested."

How do we know this public housing order is about criminalizing the poor, and driven by race? The discourse that the Premier used to legitimize this decision echoes historical moral panics and paternalistic policies that are harmful.

Let's take a look at the moral panics over the pandemic in Australia, and how race and class are affecting the policing of "voluntary" testing.

I support continued social distancing, self-isolation for myself and others who can afford to work from home, quarantine for people who are infected so they can get the care they need without infecting others, and widespread testing for affected regions. These outcomes are best achieved through targeted public communication campaigns that address the misconceptions of the pandemic and forward the benefits of testing for different groups, making clear the support available for people who test positive, and addressing the structural barriers that limit people's ability to comply with public health measures.

Moral Panics

There have been multiple race moral panics following public health responses to the pandemic. A moral panic is a situation or group that is positioned as a threat to social values, usually in response to rising fear during periods of widespread social stress or change[2]. Sociologist Stanley Cohen demonstrates that moral panics follow a predicable formula of contradictory states:

- Moral panics identify a *new* threat, but rely on *old* notions of "well-known evils;"

- They are both *damaging in themselves* and representative of *warning signs* of a much deeper problem in society; and

- They simultaneously point to a *transparent issue* that everyone can see, but one which poses an *opaque threat* that requires experts to explain the hidden perils.

Public leaders, elites, the media or other influential people will act as "moral entrepreneurs," using negative stereotypes, rumors and accusations to assign blame to a "folk devil" accused of being responsible for perceived moral or social damage[3]. These influential people will call for punishment of "deviants," and a return to imagined "proper" social norms. Such action, of course, serves to consolidate their social status and power.

COVID-19 has dusted up a predictable moral panic. Poor people, migrants, refugees and Aboriginal people are, on the one hand, positioned as vulnerable and in need of additional state intervention because they are at higher risk of infection. On the other hand, these disadvantaged groups are simultaneously characterized as "folk devils" who are responsible for spreading the infection. Either way, the moral panic is used to justify increased policing of disadvantaged groups.

As of 4 July 2020, the World Health Organization (2020) reports 10.9 million confirmed cases of COVID-19; 523,011 confirmed deaths; and 216 countries, areas, and territories with cases.

The first confirmed case in Australia was on 25 January 2020[4]. Victoria was the first state to declare a state of emergency, on 16 March. Other states soon followed. International and domestic travel was heavily restricted from 19 March and soon halted altogether. The Federal Government officially announced that the pandemic was "deadly serious" on 22 March, and lockdown restrictions came into effect around the country.

To date, there have been 8362 confirmed cases in Australia, 104 deaths, and 2.7 million tests conducted[5]. There have been 113 new confirmed cases in the past 24 hours; 108 of these in the state of Victoria. The Australian Government has identified five groups to be at greater risk of serious illness due to COVID-19[6]. They are: Aboriginal and Torres Strait Islander people and people living in remote communities; older people; people in aged care facilities; people with chronic conditions or compromised immune systems; and people with disability.

A Short History of Moral Panics During the Pandemic

March–April 2020: Anti-Asian Racism
As the outbreak spread, one-third of racism complaints to the Human Rights Commission were COVID-19-related[7] and the Asian Australian Alliance COVID-19 Racism survey received 178 reports in its first two weeks[8] in April 2020. Chinese Australians were being blamed for the virus, because the first recorded cases were in Wuhan, China. And yet the Government allowed multiple cruise ships to dock in Australia throughout March, without quarantining these 7000 passengers[9,10]. One of these ships—the Ruby Princess—alone accounted for 10% of Australia's national cases by the end of March[11]. It is these and other relatively wealthier overseas travelers who unwittingly spread the infection, not Asian-Australians specifically.

April 2020: Fines in Working-Class Multicultural Suburbs
In New South Wales, in early April, social distancing fines were being unevenly policed[12]. One-third of infringements were being issued in highly multicultural suburbs, such as South-West Sydney, even though this region had a relatively low transmission rate. Yet the top four local government areas (Waverley, Northern Beaches, Inner West, and Randwick) had one quarter (23%) of locally acquired COVID-19 cases, but only one infringement. These are majority Anglo, White and affluent suburbs.

May–June 2020: Over-Policing Remote Aboriginal Communities and Black Lives Matter Protests

Aboriginal communities reported that they are being policed more severely than other groups. Aboriginal communities successfully[13] implemented social distancing pre-emptively to protect their people, due to being at higher risk of COVID-19. As time evolved, racial inequalities of restrictions emerged. For example, in late May 2020, Yarrabah Aboriginal Shire Council[14], in Far North Queensland, sought an exemption from lockdown as they were unable to get essential items. In mid-June, Aboriginal communities in Tennant Creek, Northern Territory[15], were facing strong police sanctions and sought to have this lifted. At the same time, Cape York in Far North Queensland wanted lockdown to remain[16], to protect vulnerable community members, but were not being adequately supported to do so.

On 5 June 2020, the New South Wales Police went to the Supreme Court and temporarily blocked the Black Lives Matter protests in metro Sydney, under the grounds of public health, citing the COVID-19 restrictions. The decision was overturned[17] the following day, minutes before the protest was set to begin. Regardless, 10,000 protesters[18] had already showed up. The protests around the country were organized by Aboriginal women, to shed light on Black deaths in custody. This too is a public health issue; 434 Aboriginal people have died at the hands of police[19], or due to their negligence, as well as being denied medical care whilst in custody. Yet public discussions have ignored this national emergency, blaming protests for the resurgence of COVID-19. This has been proven false by Australia's Chief Medical Officer[20].

End June–Early July 2020: Lockdown of Multicultural Suburbs and Policing Social Housing

At the end of June, the Victorian Government, which is dealing with a worrying rate of COVID-19 infection, re-introduced Stage-3 Restrictions for only 10 suburbs. Stage 3 means people in the 12 suburbs must always stay home, until at least 29 July.

Much like in New South Wales, these Victorian suburbs targeted for lockdown have a high number of migrant residents; however, these suburbs account for only half (52%) of the new confirmed cases[21]. Targeting only multicultural suburbs for lockdown, but not others, is highly troubling.

Racist media commentators were quick to blame Muslims and Ramadan, as well as South Sudanese migrants for secret mass gatherings and hiding infections amongst families. None of this is remotely true[22,23]. For starters, the majority of South Sudanese in Australia are Christian, not Muslim. Yet religion and race are fueling moral panic. The Premier himself specified that no one religion or ethnic group was responsible for the resurgence of cases in Victoria, giving an example of a wealthy (presumably White) family who returned from a holiday in Aspen, Colorado and led to a new cluster[24].

With the Andrews Government facing a dip in popularity due to the re-introduced restrictions, and questions about the mismanagement of hotel quarantine[25], it seems a populist show of power has reared its head.

Criminization of the Poor

As Victorian Premier Daniel Andrews discussed that residents would be "fed and given what they need," he also listed "drug and alcohol support." Many people have alcohol and other drug issues, across all classes; but it's only the poor who are overpoliced[26].

Andrews explained that public housing's "common lifts, entrances and walkways" made lockdown the only logical measure the Government could consider. The Premier said:

> On expert advice by the Chief Health Officer, this presents an acute challenge going forward . . . This is not dissimilar to aged care if there's an outbreak. Such is the *vulnerability* and *susceptibility* of residents in those towers. . . To do anything else would . . . pose an unacceptable risk to residents of those towers and the rest of Victoria. [my emphasis]

Here, poor people are being used as a scaremongering tool. A better approach would have been to address the public health requirements for testing early, tailoring information to different communities.

Poor people are (rightfully) distrustful of the Government. People who receive social welfare are in a precarious position. As researchers Linda Brennan, Zuleyka Zevallos, and Wayne Binney point out, they are afraid of reporting to Government, and even reaching out for help when they experience financial hardship, for fear that they will lose their entitlements[27]. They have legitimate concerns because they live from pay to pay, and many are stuck in a cycle of poverty. They worry that their kids will be removed if they're seen to be doing something wrong. It's no wonder that, during a pandemic, they might be afraid of testing, especially when they don't understand the nature of the pandemic, their data privacy, and their rights. They might also fear that they might lose their jobs or be kicked out of social housing if they're identified as being COVID-19 positive.

Additionally, migrants and refugees have many other reasonable fears of COVID-19 testing[28]. For example, they may harbor trauma about government officials due to political persecution in their countries-of-origin. Plus, they have not received sufficient public health information from the Australian Government in their native languages.

Testing and Misinformation

Many people misunderstand testing. Highly educated people (from university professors to executive directors of companies) have publicly complained about testing, the COVID app, and other public health decisions on grounds of "surveillance," and other misunderstandings of public health measures. Health officials say conspiracy theories about COVID-19 are fueling people's refusal to be tested[29]. In this light, over the past week, 10,000 people in the priority suburbs have refused to be tested. Is it any wonder? These suburbs are the only places in Australia that are being urged to be tested via door-to-door visits. Disparate treatment only heightens public distrust.

Around one-third of international travelers in quarantine in Melbourne hotels have refused testing: that's 5400 people[30]. By law, they must stay in quarantine for at least 14 days. At the end of June, it was revealed that most known cases could be traced back to the quarantine hotels, and so quarantine period for travelers is now 24 days. But they can still refuse to be tested at that time and they get to go home, free to move through the community if they are not in the priority suburbs under lockdown. Refusal to be tested is therefore commonplace, and not dictated by postcode or class.

Middle-class people are equally likely to be misinformed about COVID-19, as are poor and working-class people; and yet affluent people happily air views, and take many health risks at huge department stores[31] and packed beaches[32] with little consequence. Poor people don't simply get to ignore social distancing—and nor should they, nor anyone else! Yet it is only working class and disadvantaged people who have officials knocking at their door, and police barricading them in.

The public, across all sociodemographic groups, distrusts government. In fact, a study by the Australian National University found that, by December 2019, only 25% of Australians were confident in political leaders and institutions. This is a 40-year low in public trust in government[33]. But the pandemic has shown that only poor and working-class people—especially Aboriginal people, migrants and refugees—are being demonized and criminalized as a result of this erosion of trust.

Public health campaigns at the beginning of the COVID-19 pandemic could have more usefully dealt with public suspicion of health governance, instead of assuming everyone will just comply with testing and social distancing.

During the social housing announcement, the Premier said emphatically: "There is no mandatory testing." However, he also said: "Door to door, every resident will be tested. If they don't agree, the lockdown will be extended." All of this adds up to de facto mandatory testing through coercion:

- Police oversee the operation.

- No resident can leave their apartment, not even on compassionate grounds (but they will have medical care available).

- The Premier warns these public housing tenants will be fined if they try to leave.

- If people refuse to be tested, they will be required to stay locked in their houses for longer, and possibly this may extend to their entire building.

Differential Treatment of "Clusters"

Victorian rates of transmission are alarmingly high and require redress. But public housing tenants do not deserve to be singled out by brute force.

Overnight, Victoria recorded 108 new confirmed cases of COVID-19. That's unacceptably high. The Government is right to take swift action. Yet less than one quarter are linked to the public housing estates. How is police barricade warranted?

The Deputy Chief Health Officer confirms 23 cases *across* the nine housing towers were linked to one COVID-19 cluster at start of the day on 4 July. She expects up to 30 cases by end day. However, more broadly, she also reports 389 active cases as a result of community transmission without a known source; this is an increase of 26 cases since yesterday. While troubling, these other clusters are *not* being forced into what's effectively house arrest. That's how we know this is an ill-conceived and discriminatory measure.

One of the journalists' questions during the press conference alluded to the ways in which inequality can fuel transmission and, subsequently, lead to this heavy-handed policy response: public housing units are typically overcrowded because poor people have no other choice. They cannot self-isolate. They do not have sick leave. As of 20 June, the Victorian Government is offering $1500 support payment to people who self-isolate if they have no sick leave[34]. This is excellent, but it has been a recent initiative as yet not widely promoted.

Widespread testing is important! But everyone should have the same rights. Public health legislation allows for individual autonomy to be overridden, which is why social distancing has been put into place. Our individual freedom to move through public spaces is not more important than the health of people most at risk of dying from this pandemic. Social distancing is our collective duty. But when we have only some residents being put into a precarious position led by police, we need to question the rationale.

On my social media, I have been regularly advocating for maintaining stricter social distancing, especially for all those who are able to work from home. I also promote testing for people with the mildest symptoms, and anyone living in priority suburbs with confirmed cases. I would happily support mandatory testing if that's what's required. At this point in time, however, Australia is not enforcing mandatory testing. The Victorian Government only set out to voluntarily test 50% of residents in the priority suburbs, regardless of symptoms. The rest of us are being urged to get tested if we show minor symptoms, if we're in high-risk categories, or if we come into contact with known cases. We need to ask why only the most disadvantaged are being effectively forced to comply with testing while the rest of us are not.

It is understandable that some people are afraid of doorknocks asking for a genetic sample when they don't know better. Testing is safe. People's data and genetic material are protected by the *Privacy Act*. But even highly educated people don't necessarily understand this. So why would other groups be expected to submit to testing? Poor people cannot help it that they are forced to live in sub-optimal infrastructure. Many migrants and refugees live in these housing estates as they work to achieve some social mobility. With increased housing prices, it's even harder for them to move out of these places than it was for those of us who arrived in the 1970s and 1980s. It's not luck, or hard work, that makes refugees or migrants upwardly mobile: it is the social policies and community infrastructures that are in place at the time we migrate. Social housing should not be a public health trap.

Why is the Public Housing Measure a Racist Policy Response?

The housing estates that are being locked down are in migrant majority suburbs. Almost half of Flemington residents are overseas born (47.3% compared to 33.3% of rest of Australia). Most of them are from Vietnam 5.2%, Ethiopia 3.3%, Somalia 2.2%, New Zealand 1.9%, and China (excluding SARs and Taiwan) 1.8%[35]. Many people from these top three groups have arrived in Australia as refugees. In North Melbourne, 58.3% of residents were born overseas. Mostly from China 13.5%, Malaysia 2.9%, Vietnam 2.4%, England 2.3%, and New Zealand 2.2%[36]. Coinciding with a rising racist moral panic about migrants being responsible for the mass infection (even though this is not true), this latest measure by the Andrews Government is paternalistic racism at its worst.

Anglo-majority suburbs are part of the active clusters and they have had far higher number of infected people at other points in the pandemic. But they do not have police at their doors. By the Victorian Government's own analysis, a

Sociological features of a moral panic*	Construction of disadvantaged groups as folk devils of the pandemic
The moral threat is new: "hard to recognise; deceptively ordinary and routine, but invisibly creeping up the moral horizon"	COVID-19 is a virus that does not discriminate, and yet its impact is disparately experienced by different social groups. As with all new infections, data on the spread and treatment of COVID-19 are evolving. But because it originates from Wuhan, China, Chinese people were blamed for its spread. In reality, global interconnectedness of travel, under-resourcing of pandemic research and preparedness, have helped its spread.
The moral threat is old: "camouflaged versions of traditional and well-known evils"	Racial minorities are positioned as the threat. Aboriginal protest is framed as uncivil, as it has been since invasion; the "yellow peril" discourses of the 1940s play out in blame of Chinese migrants; post 9-11 Islamophobia and mythical "African gangs" of the 2000s are blamed for unwillingness to test. In fact, overseas travellers returning to affluent, White, Anglo-majority suburbs contributed to spread of infection and they continue to refuse testing at high rates.
The threat is damaging and a warning sign: it's "a much deeper and more prevalent condition"	The moral panic goes like this: Aboriginal people, migrants and refugees refuse to assimilate to Anglo norms and their actions put everyone else at risk. Poor people deserve can't be trusted to self-isolate and need be punished. This allows for state mismanagement of quarantine to fly under the radar, and for middle class and affluent people to evade Stage-3 lockdowns, which have made the Government unpopular.
The moral threat is transparent, but its true nature is also opaque: there's an evident problem but only "accredited experts must explain the perils hidden behind the superficially harmless"	Everyone can see that there is a virus impacting everyone across the world, but many people also misjudge the extend of personal risk. People also mistrust the Government's decisions about restrictions. It is more palatable to use folk devils (multicultural suburbs, residents in social housing) to lockdown some suburbs to get ahead of testing, rather than doing the inevitable, which is to put the entire state of Victoria back into lockdown, and making testing more widely accepted.

Adapted from Cohen (1972)

Table 5.1-1: Construction of a Moral Panic of COVID-19

Source: This table appears in the blog post, Pandemic, Race, and Moral Panic, by Dr. Zuleyka Zevallos, https://othersociologist.com/2020/07/05/pandemic-race-and-moral-panic/

big source of transmission is traced back to security guards and staff working at quarantine hotels[37]. In recent days, it has been revealed that the private security companies running quarantine hotels did not go through a transparent tender process[38]. Guards have been engaging in unethical and poor public health practices and received poor training.

The Victorian Government has done much good during the pandemic, but it has also made questionable decisions, specifically on policing. Targeting public housing tenants is a bad public health response.

Table 5.1 summarizes how this racist moral panic has played out to date. Further down, I conclude with a brief discussion of paternalism.

Benevolent Paternalism

During the press conference, Andrews used the term "vulnerable" multiple times, along with similar familiar phrases such as "It's in their best interests" and "We're protecting them."

Benevolent paternalism has been a key narrative used to facilitate racist policies since invasion. This phrase refers to the state creating policies on the premise that the Government is better able to make decisions on behalf of citizens, by largely restricting or removing the autonomy of individuals[39].

People do not make optimal choices for good reasons (e.g. due to poverty). Let's address structural inequality, but without penalizing the poor. By Premier Daniel Andrews' own words, the problem is structural inequality quite literally: it is the social housing buildings that create a public health emergency ("Common lifts, entrances and walkways").

The federal Government has housed returning overseas travelers into 5-star hotels as part of its quarantine strategy. It's telling that this does not seem to be an option for public housing residents, even though their homes, built and maintained under Government contract, are inadequate. Instead, the poor will stay shut up in sub-optimal housing.

The problem with social housing infrastructure is well documented. Governments saw fit not to fix this. Knowing the risks, officials did not act to protect public housing tenants at the beginning of the pandemic. And now disadvantaged people bear the consequences.

This is inequality by design.

5.2

Confinement and Disease from Slavery to the COVID-19 Pandemic

by Gabriella Onikoro-Arkell

Originally published in *Black Perspectives*, MAY 14, 2020

As many college students as well as others have moved back home during the current pandemic[40], people's houses are feeling more cramped than ever. The conditions of small living spaces feel even more confining as communities are tasked with staying inside as much as possible with orders to shelter in place still intact in some locations. These conditions have left many feeling restless, bored, agitated and sad as they try to carve out private space and a sense of normalcy in such an uncertain time. The feelings of confinement ordinary people are facing contrasts starkly with the views of celebrity housing available through live streams, photos, and videos on social media. Gal Gadot and several other celebrities, for example, released a video of them singing John Lennon's "Imagine." The video was posted to Gadot's Instagram[41] with the caption "We are in this together, we will get through it together. Let's imagine together. Sing with us. All love to you, from me and my dear friends." Immediately, people on Instagram and Twitter noted the emptiness of these gestures coming from wealthy celebrities without the addition of material action.

The pandemic has drawn to a head the inequalities in housing and wealth defining the contemporary US. The nation's majority have been left scrambling to make rent for their tiny apartments while watching the wealthy squirrel away in large open concept mansions with lush lawns and huge pools.

For Black communities, these contradictions are nothing new, as forced immobility and confinement have defined their historical and contemporary experiences with regard to the matters of space. As West Africans were rendered slaves, one of their primary spatial experiences was confinement, first in slave castles like El Mina in modern Ghana and then aboard the thousands of slave ships[42] that traversed the Atlantic across five centuries. Africans crossed the ocean packed in and chained together with little room to move.

The carceral space aboard the slave ship[43] put captives in a position of increased vulnerability to diseases and illness. Despite slave traders' efforts to bring only "healthy" Africans[44] across the sea, many ships suffered numerous casualties due to yellow fever, smallpox, scurvy, malaria, flux, and several other diseases. Sowande' Mustakeem[45] has noted that the isolation caused by the sea voyage along with the cramped and unsanitary conditions captives were held in created unique and devastating encounters with disease. The spread of disease was further aggravated by the violent treatment of captives aboard these ships as well as poor nutrition. As people's bodies attempted to heal from physical and psychological injuries as well as illness, they faced an environment that only further deteriorated their capacities to fight infection.

In the North American context, despite variation in housing circumstances across different regions and time, the enslaved were forced to live in confining spaces. Whether awaiting sale[46] in a dingy and overcrowded slave pen[47] in Richmond, living in overcrowded gender-segregated barracks in Charleston, or making lives in a drafty and inadequately sized cabin on a rural sugar plantation in New Orleans' hinterland[48], slaves experienced the quotidian violence of tight living irrespective of other differences in their social conditions and labor. This contrasts sharply with White slave owners who demonstrated their power with sprawling homes on sprawling estates. Consider for example, Thomas Jefferson's Albemarle County, Virginia mansion, Monticello[49] in contrast to the small and poorly insulated log cabin structures in which the people he enslaved lived. The contrasts between Black and White space also had another dimension related to mobility. Especially in the wake of the Jacksonian era, White people moved freely, while enslaved people's movements were legally regulated and violently circumscribed. Even free Black people, especially after Nat Turner's[50] bloody 1831 rebellion, were strictly delimited in their abilities to move freely. Confinement and immobility were twinned conditions for slaves. As Katherine McKittrick analyzes[51], Harriet Ann Jacobs[52] spent seven years in her grandmother's garret or attic space, unable to fully stand upright in nine-foot-long, seven-foot-wide, three-foot-tall space. She hid in this space, carving it as a "loophole of retreat" in order to evade the violence of her master and eventually to escape. For Jacobs, freedom required a subtle reworking of the confinement enforced on Black life and Black geographies[53].

This lack of mobility and confinement continued after slavery as part of its afterlives along with the related condition of predisposition to contagious disease and premature death. In Chicago between the World Wars, Black migrant communities were forced into the West and Southside by legally sanctioned segregation, policing, and vigilante violence. Black families rented small apartments called kitchenettes at exorbitant rates, and as St. Clair Drake and Horace Cayton characterized[54] in their influential study, lived in cramped poorly heated and congested conditions. As Rashad Shabazz[55] argues, in the spaces of kitchenettes, Black Chicagoans experienced an expression of carceral power in their ordinary lives, manifest in the arrangement of their housing. He writes, "by creating close associations between people, the kitchenette made privacy of any kind impossible, shaming its residents by putting all actions under the forced gaze of others in the room."[56] This kind of housing arrangement is psychologically wearing, as Richard Wright's *Native Son*[57] disturbingly and dramatically fictionalizes. Many Black Chicagoans, across generations, experienced lifelong emotional states like the frustration, restlessness, and captivity some people stuck in their homes due to the pandemic currently are experiencing for the first time.

This confining geography extending out from kitchenette also had deadly effects. In 1918 and 1919, the Spanish Flu pandemic caused mass death and tremendous social upheaval that anticipated and rehearsed what Black communities are currently experiencing with COVID-19. Prisoners today are among the most vulnerable to COVID-19—the highest number of cases tied to a location is a prison in Ohio[58], where 80% of the prisoners have tested positive. This resonates with the history of the Spanish Flu in Chicago. As one *Chicago Defender* writer noted, "Chicago police stations are doing more to breed disease than any other agency supposed to be working for the good of Chicago"[59]. The journalist went on to note the way Chicago jails "huddle prisoners together" without medical examinations and how this led to the spread of the deadly flu.[60] The carcerality of the kitchenette also made its residents vulnerable. Shabazz notes that Black Chicagoans had higher rates of mental illness, disease, and death all of which were influenced by their crowded and rundown living conditions. These kinds of vulnerabilities tied to spatial confinement are ongoing in Chicago[61] where 50% of the deaths from COVID are Black, and where segregation and carcerality continue to define the landscape[62].

Blackness's tie to tight spatial control and confinement, extending between living spaces and formal carceral institutions, and from slavery to the present, puts Black people at greater risk for disease and infection exacerbated by the mental health effects of confinement. This greater vulnerability tied to spatial confinement, overcrowding, and other effects of our nation's anti-Black geography buttresses the spatial advantages White communities enjoyed historically and which they continue to enjoy. White slave owners profited from the confinement and forced vulnerability of their slaves. White landowners in Chicago profited from overcharging their Black tenants for poor quality housing. The risk of death, disease, and mental illbeing that Black people live with exists to produce White safety and comfort, guaranteed in exclusive geographies away from lead paint, rusty water, over-policing, and gratuitous violence. In order to mitigate the unequal deadly effects of COVID-19 and to prevent the future of devastating conditions disproportionately affecting Black people, we must reimagine the American landscape outside this history defined by the twinned and reinforcing structures of Black immobility and confinement.

5.3

Many Deaf Women Aren't Safer at Home

by Sarah Katz

Originally published in *Bitch Media*, JUNE 22, 2020

Ana Martinez was speaking to her 16-year-old adopted son in his room at her home in Portland, Oregon, last month when he flew into a rage over his phone calls being monitored by his parents. He punched a hole in a wall just inches from her face, picked up a metal chair, and then hurled it at her. Fortunately, she didn't sustain any injuries, and her two younger children weren't present. Though Martinez called the police, they only issued her son a warning and left without arresting him. Martinez—who's hard of hearing and uses American Sign Language and English to communicate—was surprised by her hearing son's violent behavior. He had been living with her, her hearing husband, Pedro, and their other children for nine months. While she knew that he was capable of being emotionally abusive and destroying property in fits of anger, this was the first time "he came at us," Martinez wrote in an email.

Cases of domestic violence[63] have spiked worldwide under the mandatory lockdowns meant to curb the spread of COVID-19. These mandates have trapped survivors in their homes with their abusers, isolating them from people who can help and worsening already dire situations. Domestic violence is committed against family members, whether it be a spouse, partner, parent, child, or the elderly, and it can take a number of forms, including physical, sexual, verbal, emotional, and financial abuse. Domestic disputes often escalate into homicides; according to a 2015 FBI report[64], 42 percent of homicide victims had some sort of relationship with their perpetrator.

Before the spread of coronavirus, one in four American women[65] experienced domestic violence, and on average, more than three women were murdered[66] by their intimate partners daily. State agencies and advocacy groups are concerned that these numbers will continue to climb in the coming months, since resources available for domestic violence survivors are being depleted and there's growing financial insecurity. In April 2020, the United Nations warned[67] that six months of quarantine could lead to 31 million additional cases of domestic violence globally—but the outlook for deaf women is especially dire. According to a representative from the National Deaf Domestic Violence Hotline—which serves deaf and hard of hearing victims of domestic violence and is reachable by email, live chat, or video—reports of abuse have increased by more than 200 percent since April.

Shelters across the United States have been inundated with new domestic violence cases, but many of them aren't equipped with the resources to meet the needs of deaf, deafblind, or other survivors with disabilities. While deaf and hard of hearing people experience the same forms of violence that hearing people do, they are 1.5 times more likely than hearing people[68] to experience domestic violence in their lifetime. Estimates[69] also show that deaf and disabled women are frequently victims of sexual violence: 83 percent of women with disabilities are sexually assaulted at some point in their lives. Sexual violence is typically perpetrated by a person the victim knows—eight out of 10[70] rapes are committed by a known person, and 33 percent of rapes[71] are committed by a spouse or partner.

Martinez is among the approximately 48 million deaf or hard of hearing people[72] in the United States at risk of domestic violence during the lockdown, yet several systemic barriers are preventing survivors like her from accessing necessary resources during the pandemic. Because abusers are now always at home and able to monitor conversations, it's become more challenging for survivors to reach out to domestic violence agencies and hotlines for support. But even if survivors could safely reach out, many of these agencies and hotlines can't support them, since these organizations often lack qualified sign language interpreters and other accessible means of communication. (ASL, which is derived from early 19th-century French Sign Language[73], is grammatically different from English, so for those whose primary language is ASL, using English to communicate isn't an option.)

What's worse, some domestic violence organizations make communication demands that ignore the realities of many deaf people's lives, said Najma Johnson, the executive director of DAWN, a domestic violence agency based in Washington, D.C. that serves deaf and hard of hearing survivors, including those with other disabilities. Some require deaf survivors to reach out to them using teletypewriters (TTY), an antiquated telephone device invented in the 1960s, though many prefer to use IP Relay, a service that allows users to make and receive calls through text over the Internet, or Video Relay Services (VRS), which allow for communication through a remote sign language interpreter over smartphones and computers. "DAWN usually has to step in and explain why [VRS are] the better choice…and break down confidentiality laws to ease discomfort about using third-party communication," Johnson said.

While there are some state-level organizations like DAWN that specifically serve deaf and hard of hearing people, there are "not enough deaf [domestic violence] organizations nationwide, so the survivors are not getting [the] local support they need," Megan Erasmus, supervisor of the National Deaf Domestic Violence Hotline, told *Bitch*. The lack of accessible information about the coronavirus in ASL is compounding the domestic violence crisis for deaf survivors. "Information deprivation increases risks [of] isolation and abuse," Erasmus said. Isolation was an ongoing issue before the coronavirus, and now, "[deaf] survivors are more isolated than ever, increasing their risk for abuse."

Many deaf women are also in precarious financial situations, which affect their ability to escape. "Leaving an abusive partner often involves secretly saving money," Lore Ameloot, the director of development at the Abused Deaf Women's Advocacy Services in Seattle, an agency that serves deaf survivors of domestic violence, and where the National Deaf Domestic Violence Hotline is housed, told *Bitch*. Deaf women are less likely to have the financial resources they need to leave because they face higher rates of unemployment than both deaf and hearing men. As we enter one of the worst economic downturns[74] since the Great Depression, Ameloot noted that "This will be more difficult if survivors have lost their jobs." According to a 2019 report by the National Deaf Center[75], only 53.3 percent of working-age deaf people are employed, compared to 75.8 percent of hearing people—an employment gap of 22.5 percent. Among those, 61.1 percent of deaf men are in the workforce, while only 50.5 percent of deaf women are employed. Unemployment rates increase with each additional intersection of marginalized identities, including race or additional disabilities.

Al Mascarenas, a resource advocate at DOVE, another domestic violence agency that serves deaf and hard of hearing survivors in Colorado, said that some abusers have been withholding COVID-19 stimulus checks, "forcing survivors to return home or to meet their partners in person to receive the check that belongs to them." Domestic violence is costly. According to the Justice Department's Office on Violence Against Women[76], domestic violence costs the United States more than $5.8 billion in healthcare costs annually, the majority of which goes toward medical care and mental health services. Collectively, survivors lose 8 million days of paid work and 5.6 million days of household productivity to domestic violence each year. Given that deaf people tend to experience greater healthcare inequities[77] than hearing people, it is safe to assume that the financial cost of being a deaf survivor would likely be much higher than it would be for a hearing survivor.

Law enforcement and the criminal legal system also frequently fail deaf women who are survivors of abuse. On the most basic level, it's harder for deaf women to report abuse to the police because there are fewer communication options for them. Howard Rosenblum, the chief executive officer at the National Association of the Deaf (NAD), said in an email interview that his organization hopes to change this. He's encouraging all municipalities to implement text-to-911 systems, which are only available in 19 percent of the country, "even though the data shows that more and more people (not just deaf and hard of hearing people) are using text-to-911 during the pandemic."

Some courts are also holding remote hearings during the pandemic, which may not be accessible for deaf survivors. Even before the pandemic, though, the NAD reported cases where courts didn't make hearings accessible[78] to this population. One in eight[79] people over the age of 12 are deaf or hard of hearing. In order to safeguard deaf survivors from harm during the pandemic, government agencies, domestic violence hotlines, agencies, and courts must familiarize themselves with the needs and realities of this demographic and establish inclusive programs and services that ensure compliance with the *Americans with Disabilities Act*[80]. If they don't, they risk further endangering millions of deaf and hard of hearing women like Martinez, who need help at a time when interlocking crises are destabilizing families and compromising public safety.

Editor's Note: The name of a domestic violence survivor has been changed in this article to protect their identity.

5.4

Rural America Is Starting to Feel the Impact of the Coronavirus

By Olugbenga Ajilore

Originally published in *The Center for American Progress*, APRIL 28, 2020

Policymakers are already discussing plans to reopen the U.S. economy—even though the COVID-19 pandemic is still ravaging the United States and has killed more than 40,000 people[81]. While some of the hardest-hit cities may be flattening the curve, these discussions ignore the many parts of the country that have not even come close to reaching the peak of the outbreak. For example, a large pork plant in Sioux Falls, South Dakota, was forced to shut down because of a severe coronavirus outbreak[82]. Tribal communities in the Southwest are also beginning to get hit hard[83]. While Congress has passed several packages to deal with both the public health crisis and the economic crisis, it is premature to think about an exit strategy before the extent of the pandemic has been realized.

The Coronavirus Aid, Relief, and Economic Security (CARES) *Act* was the third of these packages, providing resources and relief to the U.S. economy as the country combats the COVID-19 pandemic. The package included direct payment assistance to individuals, expanded unemployment insurance, a $500 billion fund to industries, and $350 billion for small businesses. In addition, the package allocated $150 billion to the states for relief as state and local governments face severe budget constraints.

While $150 billion will help states and localities, their needs call for much more resources. One of the major problems resulting from this pandemic is the decimation of state budgets[84]. Due to social distancing and shelter-in-place ordinances, sales taxes are going to fall precipitously. States have followed the federal government and pushed their income tax deadlines to the summer, which means the income tax revenue that is normally expected in the spring will not come until the summer or fall[85]. In addition, efforts to combat the outbreak and fight the spread of the virus will strain public services. These issues—coupled with the fact that many states face a balanced budget amendment—mean that an economic disaster is brewing across the country. States will have to cut services, furlough workers, or raise taxes when the economy can least afford these cuts. In fact, falling revenues have already forced states to engage in budget cuts[86].

The struggles states face will have dire consequences for rural areas. Beyond some funding for rural health care and telemedicine, rural communities were practically left out of the policy debate surrounding all three federal relief packages[87]. Supporting rural areas is not something that should be left only to the states; the federal government needs to directly invest in these communities. The spread of the coronavirus is a national challenge, not one that should be left to states by themselves, as the virus does not care where people live.

The coronavirus is already hitting rural America, and existing structural barriers are making the pandemic worse. Rural areas are in need of targeted relief, which has been missing in the previous COVID-19 relief packages. Policymakers must address these omissions by expanding Medicaid in the states that have not yet done so, and the federal government must increase funding to states to support Medicaid. In addition, the lack of a national stay-at-home order is slowing the response, since the virus is spreading in places that have failed to implement these orders[88]. Physical distancing is effective at fighting the spread of the coronavirus[89]. A national stay-at-home order would take the decision out of the hands of governors who have refused to adhere to the science.[90,91] Policymakers cannot wait to help rural communities because delays in combating this pandemic will lead to an increase in the number of preventable deaths.

The Spread of the Coronavirus in Rural Communities

While major metropolitan cities are being hit hard and have the largest outbreaks, COVID-19 has already started to spread in rural communities. Due to the lack of health care infrastructure resulting from hospital closures and a population with a high level of chronic health issues, these communities will be less able to successfully combat the virus[92,93]. Kaiser Health News produced a sobering map showing that the vast majority of rural counties either have no intensive care units in their hospitals or no hospitals at all[94]. Yet, the problem is more than just a lack of access to health care facilities. Rural residents generally have to travel long distances to access goods and services such as local food markets and educational institutions. Transportation has always been an issue for rural communities, but it takes on a greater weight during this crisis for seniors and people with disabilities[95,96].

There are concerns that the number of deaths caused by COVID-19 are underreported. The extent of the spread is unknown, since there are likely people who were not tested but who contracted COVID-19 or people who died due to complications from the disease[97].

Graying America communities are rural areas that have a high prevalence of aging retirees. They are located in recreation-dependent counties predominantly in the western part of the country. These areas have seen a lot of tourism, which has helped boost their economies but has now led to a rise in COVID-19 cases[98,99]. The African American South is a collection of counties synonymous with the so-called Black Belt region of the United States, a series of counties running from the Mississippi Delta, past the Carolinas, and up to Virginia. This area has persistent poverty, low educational attainment, and high uninsured rates[100]. These factors make individuals in the region more susceptible to public health crises, and the data now bear this out[101].

There were very few reported COVID-19 cases in rural areas during the first two weeks of March. Then, the number of cases started to rise, especially in three rural community categories: Graying America, Rural Middle America, and Evangelical Hubs. However, in the African American South, cases did not begin to rise until mid-March. Cases in this region then proceeded to surpass those in Evangelical Hubs and then caught up to those in Graying America and Rural Middle America by the end of the month. Graying America had its first case on March 6 and, as of April 1, had 1690 cases. The African American South had its first outbreak on March 10 and, as of April 1, had 1452 cases. Rural Middle America had its first case on March 2 and, as of April 1, had 1545 cases. Evangelical Hubs also had their first case on March 6 and, as of April 1, had 802 cases.

Defining Urban and Rural Communities

Using a detailed breakdown of rurality, a recent Center for American Progress issue brief outlined what has happened in rural communities since the Great Recession[102]. One takeaway was that while rural communities have continued to struggle since the Great Recession, some have seen modest growth. This breakdown of rurality provides a more precise analysis of the labor market dynamics occurring in rural communities. Now, it is possible to provide even further precision on what is happening in urban and rural communities using a new classification system: the American Communities Project (ACP)[103]. A project from George Washington University, the ACP created a typology of counties that incorporates demographic and socioeconomic data (see Figure 5.4-1 and Figure 5.4-2)

African Americans in rural southern communities are more likely to contract the virus and to have a higher death rate. In fact, while Graying America has more confirmed cases than the African American South, as of April 2, there were more than twice as many deaths—53 compared with 24—in the African American South. A number of these counties are in states that refuse to expand Medicaid, especially those communities in the South such as the African American South and Evangelical Hubs[104]. The communities are in states that also have lower public expenditures on programs that support low- to middle-income residents[105]. Due to the lack of government resources, these numbers are only going to grow and translate into more preventable deaths. Now that the virus has reached them, these communities will need funds and resources to fight the epidemic.

Even When States Get Money, Some Towns Are Left Behind

Funding for rural communities comes from a variety of sources, both federal and state. The CARES Act allocates $150 billion to the states and about $30 billion to localities, but this leaves many localities without the help they need. The $30 billion designated to localities will go only to cities with populations of at least 500,000 people. Given the fact that the $150 billion is already not

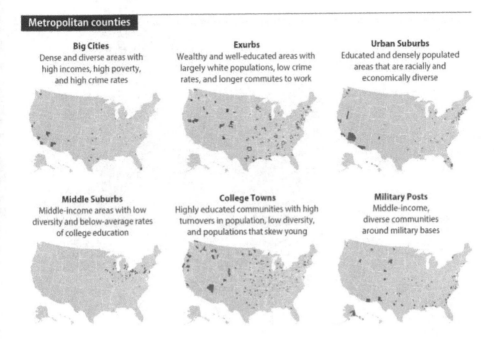

Figure 5.4-1: American Communities Project Urban and Rural Universe, Description and Geography of ACP Community Classification: Metropolitan Counties

Source: American Communities Project, "The American Communities: Map," available at https://www.americancommunities.org/#map; Figure 5.4-1 appears in the online article, "Rural America is Starting to Feel the Impact of the Coronavirus," by Olugbenga Ajilore, https://www.americanprogress.org/issues/economy/reports/2020/04/28/484016/rural-america-starting-feel-impact-coronavirus/

enough for state budgets[106], rural communities are going to be at a disadvantage in accessing these resources. These communities have already been bypassed for needed resources even when they have applied for emergency funding[107]. Small towns are already at a disadvantage when competing for grants since large cities have teams dedicated to securing funding. Meanwhile, in small towns, mayors are often responsible for securing grants while also having a day job. This pandemic is only going to exacerbate this inequality. Rural towns have been left behind in past economic recoveries—none more so than after the Great Recession.

Policymakers need to find a way to provide resources to rural communities if they want to avoid a repeat of the lackluster recovery from the Great Recession. Rural communities are going to be especially hard hit from this pandemic because of the lack of infrastructure, dwindling health care resources,

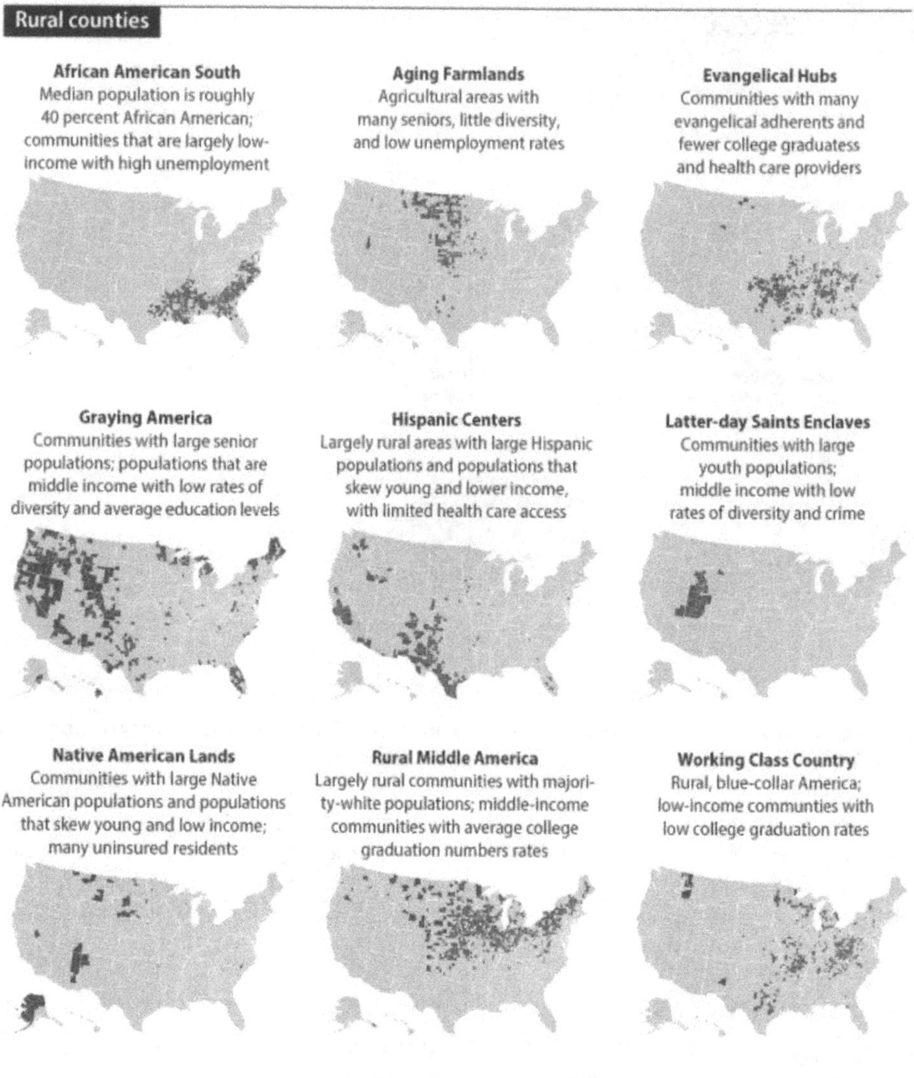

Rural counties

African American South
Median population is roughly
40 percent African American;
communities that are largely low-
income with high unemployment

Aging Farmlands
Agricultural areas with
many seniors, little diversity,
and low unemployment rates

Evangelical Hubs
Communities with many
evangelical adherents and
fewer college graduatess
and health care providers

Graying America
Communities with large senior
populations; populations that are
middle income with low rates of
diversity and average education levels

Hispanic Centers
Largely rural areas with large Hispanic
populations and populations that
skew young and lower income,
with limited health care access

Latter-day Saints Enclaves
Communities with large
youth populations;
middle income with low
rates of diversity and crime

Native American Lands
Communities with large Native
American populations and populations
that skew young and low income;
many uninsured residents

Rural Middle America
Largely rural communities with majority-white populations; middle-income
communities with average college
graduation numbers rates

Working Class Country
Rural, blue-collar America;
low-income communties with
low college graduation rates

Figure 5.4-2: American Communities Project Urban and Rural Universe, Description and Geography of ACP Community Classification: Rural Counties

Source: American Communities Project, "The American Communities: Map," available at https://www.americancommunities.org/#map; Figure 5.4-2 appears in the online article, "Rural America is Starting to Feel the Impact of the Coronavirus, by Olugbenga Ajilore," https://www.americanprogress.org/issues/economy/reports/2020/04/28/484016/rural-america-starting-feel-impact-coronavirus/

and an aging population and higher prevalence of people with disabilities—all factors that highlight how these communities are in need of immediate support[108]. In addition, some rural localities do not have a large enough tax base to match the level of services needed.

In addition to budget difficulties, many in rural communities will struggle with the public health aspect of this pandemic. People in rural areas are already more likely to skip health care and to have medical debt due to an unexpected health emergency. Rural residents are more likely to not seek medical care until it is too late, partially due to a lack of nearby health facilities[109]. They tend to only seek care when health issues become a serious emergency, leading to large medical expenses. These trends are true across race and educational attainment. It is particularly a concern for both African Americans and noncollege-educated individuals in rural communities.

This troubling reality will make it difficult for these communities to fight the spread of the coronavirus if people do not immediately seek medical help when they experience symptoms. Seeking medical care is difficult because of the many closures of rural hospitals and emergency centers[110]. And the lack of Medicaid expansion has been detrimental to many rural communities, particularly in southern states[111]. Moreover, the availability of testing for COVID-19 in rural areas has fallen far behind that of urban areas, although steps have been taken to close this gap[112].

Preventing the collapse of small-town America is crucial now that policymakers and scholars are recognizing the importance of place-based policies for revitalizing communities and reversing decades of regional divergence[113]. Telling rural residents to move to opportunity in urban areas is no longer a viable strategy because urban wage premiums over rural areas no longer exist[114].

Policy Recommendations

Even though Congress and the Trump administration have put together several packages amounting to more than $3 trillion to help stabilize the economy and combat the coronavirus, there is still more to be done, and policymakers are discussing further measures[115]. Additional spending for states and localities—spending that is sizable, flexible, and able to cover programmatic shortfalls—must be a part of a future bill so that these areas can continue to provide necessary services and ensure effective functioning of government[116]. Spending for rural areas also needs to be a part of the bill. The following are four recommendations to help rural areas fight this epidemic:

- First, rural areas need help strengthening and expanding their health care infrastructure. The first thing that states can do, if they haven't already, is expand Medicaid. Medicaid expansion has been responsible for saving thousands of lives and has helped with lowering medical debt—something that has plagued many rural residents, especially African Americans[117]. Medicaid expansion would also help with rural hospitals' financial solvency through lower levels of uncompensated care. In addition, the state attorneys general leading the *California v. Texas* case must withdraw their participation so that those with health insurance can get and keep the medical help they will need if they get infected[118].

- Second, to counteract states' falling revenues, the federal government must build on earlier COVID-19 response legislation. The second package increased the federal government's share of Medicaid payments—the Federal Medicaid Assistance Percentages—by 6.2 percentage points for the duration of public health emergencies. Congress must raise the share increase to at least 10 percentage points for both traditional and expansion Medicaid. This aid must be extended for the duration of any future recession—not simply for the current public health emergency. Moreover, this type of relief should also be automatically pegged to increases in state unemployment rates, which will ensure continued aid during future economic downturns.

- Third, policymakers need to implement a national stay-at-home policy to curb the outbreak. Physical distancing can limit the outbreak and, along with massive testing, allow for the suppression of transmission[119]. The reluctance of certain states to impose these orders and moves to prematurely lift them provide justification for a national policy.

- Finally, policymakers can create dedicated funding streams for micropolitan areas and small towns with populations below 50,000. These are the areas that have been struggling with rural hospital closures and other infrastructure issues such as the lack of broadband access[120]. This will help with the problem of small communities having to compete with larger municipalities for scarce federal and state resources.

Conclusion

Policymakers have pushed three packages through Congress to tackle the coronavirus pandemic. Unfortunately, these packages have failed to provide sufficient resources to support African Americans[121], people with disabilities[122], and state and local governments[123]. Rural communities have also been left behind and must be a part of the policy debate. Providing resources to rural areas is one pathway to help the many communities of color and people with disabilities fight back against the coronavirus[124].

5.5

Another Dull Quarantine Weekend at Home, Target, Chipotle, Home Depot, and Our Niece's Graduation Party

by Katherine Shonk

Originally published in *McSweeney's Internet Tendency*, JULY 20, 2020

I can't believe how careless people are being about this virus. At our house, we have been taking the strictest precautions since March. We stay inside all the time and never go anywhere. When we do go somewhere, we always bring masks, except when we won't need them. We stayed at home all weekend. On Friday night, neither Ethan or I felt like cooking again—we'd been cooking every night since March, except for Takeout Tuesdays and Pickup Thursdays and Delivery Mondays—so we decided to go to a restaurant. It was the first time we'd gone out to dinner since March, except for last Sunday and the Friday before that, so we were excited. We piled the kids into the car with our masks and drove to a restaurant with outdoor seating. We were shocked to see that the tables were close together and that many people clearly were from different households. Most were not wearing masks, and you could practically see the spit flying between them as they talked. It really turned us off.

There was a fifteen-minute wait for an outside table, so we had to sit inside. There weren't that many people—maybe 20, 25% not occupied—and a window was open, so it felt safe. My parents met us—we hadn't seen them since March, except for dinner last Tuesday and the Friday before that, and at Ethan's backyard birthday, and Janey's drive-by birthday, and their weekly lunches in our backyard. We gave each other jokey air hugs, and Mom choked up to finally see her grandkids. We all wore our masks, except when we were eating, drinking, and talking, and we didn't share any food, except for a few appetizers and desserts. Mom kept feeding Janey her French fries, but she always does that. It's sort of a tradition.

When we got outside, we put our masks on and strolled down to the beach. Dozens of people in masks were enjoying the break in the heat in little clumps—it was disgusting. We turned around and left. We came back with a blanket from the car and found a spot by a family we knew from Janey and Petey's school. We hadn't seen them in months, except at Janey's drive-by birthday, when they briefly got out of the car and the kids played in the family room while us parents sat six feet apart in the yard, and that time we all met up at the playground because the police tape had blown away. It was so good to finally see them!

We stayed inside the rest of the weekend, except Saturday morning, when we needed to do curbside pickup at Target. We felt giddy, piling into the car—jailbreak! We brought our masks, of course, and a Target employee loaded the trunk. We would have gone straight home, but Janey had to pee, so we put on our masks and went inside. Ethan took Petey to look at the Legos, while I stood outside the stall and whispered to Janey not to flush. She flushed anyway and said, "Oops, Mommy, I forgot!" but that can't be helped. We got the kids hot-dogs and went straight home after stopping at Old Navy and dropping Janey off at a drive-by birthday party for a couple of hours with her mask.

On Saturday night, there was a big vigil against racism in our town. While we are being very safe, it is also important to us to raise our kids to be antiracist. So we drove over to the square with our masks, but there was no street parking anywhere. The parking structures didn't seem safe—to avoid the elevator, we'd have to walk down multiple flights of stairs, and we had Janey's stroller. So we went home, after stopping at Chipotle and Cold Stone Creamery, because after all that nonsense with the parking and the vigil, we were starving.

It actually turned out to be a nice night. A bunch of us neighbors positioned our chairs six feet apart and blocked off the street with cars so the kids could ride bikes and play tag—an impromptu socially distanced block party. We talked about how scary the virus is and how we can't wait for school to start so we can work from home in peace. After the kids were in bed, it started to rain, so we all got hammered in the Petersons' basement, six feet apart. I wish more people understood how much fun you can have while socially distancing.

We stayed home all day on Sunday. In the morning, though, a local church held a drive-in service in the parking lot, so we drove over because it's important to us to give the kids some kind of spiritual foundation. But the parking lot was almost full, and we wouldn't have been able to see the minister. At that point, we were starving. We hadn't had brunch in an actual restaurant since two Sundays ago. Lots of other people had the same idea, but after about an hour, we had a table inside. We hadn't brought our masks because we hadn't been planning to leave our car, so we kept our breathing shallow.

We literally did nothing the rest of the day. I did some gardening, and Ethan fixed the porch lights—the home improvement never ends! He had to go to Home Depot twice because he got the wrong bulbs. Luckily, everyone stays six feet apart and wears masks, so it feels very safe. On Sunday night, we stayed home, except for our niece's drive-by graduation party. We all drove by with our cars decorated and parked and went to the backyard. My parents were there, and some of my niece's friends and their families. There was a little jazz combo from the high school, and a taco truck in the alley. The little kids played in the basement, but everyone else stood outside, holding masks, just in case. It was a beautiful night. I said to Ethan, "Isn't it nice to be out with people, finally?" It was the first party we'd been to during quarantine, except for the drive-by birthday parties and the other graduation parties, and his mom's 70th birthday weekend in Milwaukee, and his Uncle Jim's funeral.

Life is tough right now, but there are still ways to connect with other people safely. I wish more people would recognize that because then life might finally get back to normal.

Notes

1   https://www.theage.com.au/national/victoria/more-suburbs-in-lockdown-as-victoria-records-108-new-coronavirus-cases-20200704-p558zp.html
2   Goode, E., & Ben-Yehuda, N. (1994). Moral panics: Culture, politics, and social construction. *Annual Review of Sociology, 20*(1), 149-171.
3   Cohen, S. (1972). *Folk Devils and Moral Panics: The Creation of the Mods and Rockers.* Routledge.
4   https://www.health.gov.au/ministers/the-hon-greg-hunt-mp/media/first-confirmed-case-of-novel-coronavirus-in-australia
5   https://www.health.gov.au/news/health-alerts/novel-coronavirus-2019-ncov-health-alert/coronavirus-covid-19-current-situation-and-case-numbers
6   https://www.health.gov.au/news/health-alerts/novel-coronavirus-2019-ncov-health-alert/advice-for-people-at-risk-of-coronavirus-covid-19
7   https://humanrights.gov.au/about/news/opinions/wheres-all-data-covid-19-racism
8   https://www.theguardian.com/world/2020/apr/17/survey-of-covid-19-racism-against-asian-australians-records-178-incidents-in-two-weeks
9   3,500 from *The Ovation of the Season* 18 March; 2,700 from the *Ruby Princess* on 19 March; others from *Voyager of the Seas* on 18 March; and 850 from the *Artania* on 27 March. While all of these carried infected passengers who disembarked across Australia, the *Ruby Princess* led to 662 positive cases, five of whom died by 30 March.
10 https://www.theguardian.com/world/2020/may/02/australias-coronavirus-lockdown-the-first-50-days
11 https://www.theguardian.com/australia-news/2020/mar/31/more-than-400-coronavirus-cases-australia-total-ruby-princess-cruise-ship
12 https://www.sbs.com.au/news/concerns-police-using-coronavirus-powers-to-target-marginalised-communities-in-australia
13 https://www.thesaturdaypaper.com.au/news/health/2020/04/25/aboriginal-community-healths-success-with-covid-19/15877368009740
14 https://www.dailymail.co.uk/news/article-8363999/One-Australias-biggest-Indigenous-communities-demands-exempted-coronavirus-laws.html
15 https://www.abc.net.au/news/2020-05-14/tennant-creek-coronavirus-nt-police-defence-force-adf-afp/12241766
16 https://www.abc.net.au/news/2020-06-11/travel-restrictions-to-lift-from-remote-queensland-communities/12343822
17 https://www.theguardian.com/australia-news/2020/jun/06/black-lives-matter-protests-nsw-police-minister-says-officers-prepared-for-anyone-who-flouts-the-law
18 https://edition.cnn.com/2020/06/06/australia/australia-black-lives-matter-protests-intl-hnk/index.html
19 https://othersociologist.com/2020/05/31/police-violence-in-australia/
20 https://www.sbs.com.au/news/did-australia-s-black-lives-matter-protests-cause-a-spike-in-covid-19-cases

21 https://www.theaustralian.com.au/nation/coronavirus-australia-live-news-victoria-exporting-cases-across-the-nation/news-story/0655717b6cbe30e6d7a80c1e4dbdd549?keyevent=4.55 pm

22 https://www.theguardian.com/world/2020/jun/25/reports-melbourne-coronavirus-cluster-originated-at-eid-party-could-stoke-islamophobia-say-muslim-leaders

23 https://www.theage.com.au/national/victoria/young-south-sudanese-leaders-share-pain-of-unfounded-covid-blame-20200704-p558yh.html

24 https://www.facebook.com/watch/live/?v=273081550584895

25 https://www.theage.com.au/politics/victoria/has-victoria-s-outbreak-caused-daniel-andrews-crown-to-slip-20200703-p558v5.html

26 https://othersociologist.com/2012/11/24/middle-class-substance-abuse/

27 https://www.sciencedirect.com/science/article/abs/pii/S1441358211000449

28 https://theconversation.com/why-some-people-dont-want-to-take-a-covid-19-test-141794

29 https://www.theage.com.au/national/victoria/health-minister-raises-conspiracy-concern-as-10-000-refuse-virus-test-20200703-p558va.html

30 https://www.smh.com.au/politics/federal/states-divided-on-compulsory-testing-of-international-travellers-20200626-p556pa.html

31 https://www.abc.net.au/news/2020-05-09/shoppers-raise-alarm-over-coronavirus-social-distancing/12231780

32 https://www.theguardian.com/australia-news/2020/mar/21/bondi-beach-closed-down-after-crowds-defy-ban-on-gatherings-of-more-than-500-people

33 https://www.sbs.com.au/news/australians-trust-in-government-reaches-new-all-time-low-study-shows

34 https://www.dhhs.vic.gov.au/covid-19-worker-support-payment

35 https://quickstats.censusdata.abs.gov.au/census_services/getproduct/census/2016/quickstat/SSC20923?opendocument

36 https://quickstats.censusdata.abs.gov.au/census_services/getproduct/census/2016/quickstat/SSC21954

37 https://www.theage.com.au/politics/victoria/quarantine-hotels-to-get-more-health-workers-as-new-virus-cases-emerge-20200622-p55520.html

38 https://www.theage.com.au/national/victoria/how-hotel-quarantine-let-covid-19-out-of-the-bag-in-victoria-20200703-p558og.html?fbclid=IwAR1np0-5yn-KAnLpugb2RMc9b1LFwbmsB2mpnOy5Eaenzi_SDzKRhFKoXjE

39 https://www.aph.gov.au/About_Parliament/Parliamentary_Departments/Parliamentary_Library/pubs/rp/rp1011/11rp08#_Toc280187799

40 https://www.aaihs.org/racializeddiseaseandpandemic/

41 https://www.instagram.com/tv/B95M4kNhbzz/

42 https://www.aaihs.org/1619-2/

43 https://www.slavevoyages.org/voyage/database

44 https://www.worldcat.org/title/saltwater-slavery-a-middle-passage-from-africa-to-american-diaspora/oclc/436298967

45 https://www.worldcat.org/title/i-never-have-such-a-sickly-ship-before-diet-disease-and-mortality-in-18th-century-atlantic-slaving-voyages/oclc/5545880038&referer=brief_results

46 https://www.worldcat.org/title/price-for-their-pound-of-flesh-the-value-of-the-enslaved-from-womb-to-grave-in-the-building-of-a-nation/oclc/987398204&referer=brief_results

47 https://www.worldcat.org/title/soul-by-soul-life-inside-the-antebellum-slave-market/oclc/1004015073&referer=brief_results

48 https://www.worldcat.org/title/black-womens-geographies-and-the-afterlives-of-the-sugar-plantation/oclc/8253186435&referer=brief_results

49 https://www.aaihs.org/politics-public-history-and-memory-an-interview-with-niya-bates/

50 https://www.aaihs.org/politics-public-history-and-memory-an-interview-with-niya-bates/

51 https://www.worldcat.org/title/demonic-grounds-black-women-and-the-cartographies-of-struggle/oclc/266083335&referer=brief_results

52 https://www.worldcat.org/title/incidents-in-the-life-of-a-slave-girl/oclc/945612098&referer=brief_results

53 https://www.worldcat.org/title/demonic-grounds-black-women-and-the-cartographies-of-struggle/oclc/266083335&referer=brief_results

54 https://www.worldcat.org/title/black-metropolis-a-study-of-negro-life-in-a-northern-city/oclc/893609551&referer=brief_results

55 https://www.worldcat.org/title/spatializing-blackness-architectures-of-confinement-and-black-masculinity -in-chicago/oclc/1004368675&referer=brief_results

56 Rashad Shabazz, *Spacializing Blackness: Architectures of Confinement and Black Masculinity in Chicago.* (Chicago: University of Illinois Press, 2015), 50.
57 https://www.aaihs.org/politics-public-history-and-memory-an-interview-with-niya-bates/
58 https://www.npr.org/2020/04/23/843310088/covid-19-is-sweeping-through-ohio-prisons
59 "Spanish Plague Raging in Chicago: All Places of Public Assemblage Ordered Closed by Health Officials," Chicago Defender (Chicago, IL), Oct. 19, 1918.
60 Ibid.
61 https://www.chicago.gov/city/en/sites/covid-19/home/latest-data.html
62 "The Color of Caronavirus: COVID-19 Deaths by Race and Ethnicity in the US." APM Research LAB, May 5th, 2020. https://www.apmresearchlab.org/covid/deaths-by-race.
63 https://abcnews.go.com/US/domestic-violence-centers-navigate-coronavirus-crisis-calls-spike/story?id=70902362
64 https://ovc.ojp.gov/sites/g/files/xyckuh226/files/ncvrw2018/info_flyers/fact_sheets/2018NCVRW_Homicide_508_QC.pdf
65 https://www.justice.gov/lair/file/826531/download
66 https://www.justice.gov/lair/file/826531/download
67 https://www.cbsnews.com/news/domestic-violence-additional-31-million-cases-worldwide/
68 https://www.rit.edu/news/college-survey-indicates-relationship-violence-higher-deaf-community
69 https://www.ncbi.nlm.nih.gov/pmc/articles/PMC4161008/
70 https://www.rainn.org/statistics/perpetrators-sexual-violence
71 https://www.rainn.org/statistics/perpetrators-sexual-violence
72 https://www.ncbi.nlm.nih.gov/pmc/articles/PMC3564588/
73 https://www.nidcd.nih.gov/health/american-sign-language
74 https://time.com/5837442/first-global-depression-our-lifetimes/
75 https://www.nationaldeafcenter.org/sites/default/files/Deaf%20Employment%20Report_final.pdf
76 https://www.justice.gov/lair/file/826531/download
77 https://www.apa.org/pi/disability/resources/publications/newsletter/2013/11/deaf-community
78 https://www.nad.org/resources/justice/courts/communication-access-in-state-and-local-courts/
79 https://www.nidcd.nih.gov/health/statistics/quick-statistics-hearing
80 https://www.ada.gov/2010_regs.htm
81 https://thehill.com/homenews/administration/493041-trump-says-white-house-to-release-guidelines-on-relaxing-social
82 https://www.npr.org/2020/04/14/834470141/how-one-city-mayor-forced-a-pork-giant-to-close-its-virus-stricken-plant
83 https://www.nytimes.com/2020/04/09/us/coronavirus-navajo-nation.html?login=smartlock&auth=login-smartlock
84 https://www.taxadmin.org/covid19-federal-impact
85 https://www.wsj.com/articles/u-s-income-tax-delay-to-strain-states-11585143724
86 https://www.bloomberg.com/news/articles/2020-04-01/billion-dollar-blows-to-u-s-states-crater-spending-plans?sref=vuYGislZ
87 https://www.dailyyonder.com/rural-america-and-the-senates-economic-stimulus-package/2020/03/26/
88 https://www.cnn.com/2020/04/17/politics/republican-governors-stay-at-home-coronavirus/index.html
89 https://www.americanprogress.org/issues/healthcare/news/2020/04/03/482613/national-state-plan-end-coronavirus-crisis/
90 https://www.ajc.com/news/one-month-after-warnings-kemp-puts-georgia-lockdown/db6Aodv3LzftEV89WA1EOI/
91 https://www.al.com/news/2020/04/gov-kay-ivey-to-give-update-on-coronavirus-response.html
92 https://www.dailyyonder.com/research-update-why-coronavirus-could-hit-rural-areas-harder/2020/03/24/
93 https://www.vox.com/2020/3/28/21197421/usa-coronavirus-covid-19-rural-america
94 https://khn.org/news/as-coronavirus-spreads-widely-millions-of-older-americans-live-in-counties-with-no-icu-beds/
95 https://prospect.org/economy/revving-rural-public-transit/
96 https://www.americanprogress.org/issues/economy/reports/2019/07/17/471877/redefining-rural-america/
97 https://www.reuters.com/article/us-health-coronavirus-fdny/at-home-covid-19-deaths-may-be-significantly-undercounted-in-new-york-city-idUSKBN21P3KF
98 https://www.americanprogress.org/issues/economy/reports/2020/02/20/480129/economic-recovery-business-dynamism-rural-america/
99 https://www.dailyyonder.com/rural-counties-with-recreation-economies-show-higher-infection-rates/2020/03/25/

100　https://www.americanprogress.org/issues/economy/
　　　reports/2019/08/06/470913/3-ways-improve-outcomes-african-americans-rural-south/
101　https://www.americanprogress.org/issues/race/news/2020/03/27/482337/
　　　coronavirus-compounds-inequality-endangers-communities-color/
102　https://www.americanprogress.org/issues/economy/reports/2019/10/21/476097/
　　　adversity-assets-identifying-rural-opportunities/
103　https://www.americancommunities.org/
104　https://www.kff.org/medicaid/issue-brief/status-of-state-medicaid-expansion-decisions-interactive-map/
105　https://www.theatlantic.com/business/archive/2017/06/race-safety-net-welfare/529203/
106　https://thehill.com/opinion/finance/491259-fiscal-freefall-for-state-and-local-governments-the-crisis-
　　　we-are-not-yet
107　https://www.americancommunities.org/kansas-aging-farmland-fighting-through-covid-19-crisis/
108　https://www.americanprogress.org/issues/economy/news/2020/03/05/481340/
　　　rural-communities-vulnerable-coronavirus/
109　https://inthesetimes.com/features/rural-hospital-closing-crisis-appalachia-ballad-merger.html
110　https://www.americanprogress.org/issues/healthcare/reports/2019/09/09/474001/
　　　rural-hospital-closures-reduce-access-emergency-care/
111　https://www.americanprogress.org/issues/healthcare/reports/2018/10/24/459676/
　　　expanding-medicaid-states-save-14000-lives-per-year/
112　https://www.politico.com/news/2020/04/02/indian-health-service-rural-coronavirus-test-162493
113　https://www.nber.org/papers/w24548
114　https://www.nber.org/papers/w25588
115　https://www.politico.com/news/2020/04/03/pelosi-phase-4-coronavirus-relief-package-163072
116　https://www.americanprogress.org/issues/economy/news/2020/04/17/483461/
　　　coronavirus-recovery-demands-substantial-durable-aid-state-local-governments/
117　https://www.americanprogress.org/issues/healthcare/reports/2019/09/09/474001/
　　　rural-hospital-closures-reduce-access-emergency-care/
118　https://www.americanprogress.org/issues/healthcare/news/2019/12/19/478930/
　　　court-ruling-aca-hurts-patients-destabilizes-health-insurance-markets/
119　https://www.americanprogress.org/issues/healthcare/news/2020/04/03/482613/
　　　national-state-plan-end-coronavirus-crisis/
120　https://www.citylab.com/equity/2020/02/
　　　internet-access-rural-broadband-digital-divide-map-fcc-data/606424/
121　https://jointcenter.org/joint-center-hosts-online-policy-forum-with-cbc-chair-karen-bass-d-ca-on-the-
　　　implications-of-congressional-responses-to-covid-19-on-black-communities/
122　https://www.americanprogress.org/issues/disability/news/2020/03/27/482378/
　　　coronavirus-proposals-leave-disability-community-behind/
123　https://www.epi.org/blog/the-cares-acts-aid-to-state-and-local-governments-isnt-enough-to-shield-vital-
　　　public-services-from-the-coronavirus-shock-lessons-from-the-great-recession-tell-us-why/
124　https://www.americanprogress.org/issues/economy/reports/2019/07/17/471877/
　　　redefining-rural-america/

Part Six

Ecologies of Justice

6.1

COVID-19 Flares Up in America's Polluted 'Sacrifice Zones'

by Sidney Fussell

Originally published in *WIRED*, MAY 26, 2020

Researchers find that areas with high levels of airborne dust or toxic chemicals also have more deaths from the coronavirus.

Air is political. Research indicates race is the biggest predictor[1] of whether a person lives near a heavily polluted area. COVID-19[2] is especially lethal for patients with respiratory problems.

Now researchers are studying whether air pollution makes COVID-19 illnesses more severe. They are especially concerned with so-called sacrifice zones[3], areas with pervasive exposure to toxic emissions. For activists, the COVID-19 crisis has been a call to arms to rethink the balance of power between polluters and low-income communities.

In April, scientists at the Harvard T.H. Chan School of Public Health compared death rates from COVID-19 with air pollution levels for each of the nation's 3000 counties. They found that elevated levels[4] of fine particulate matter (an air pollutant abbreviated as PM 2.5) are associated with an increase in the COVID-19 death rate, even after controlling for other factors like income or preexisting conditions.

The authors noted that counties with a higher percentage of Black residents had consistently higher rates of COVID-19 deaths[5], though this was not part of the study. African Americans were more likely than other racial groups to live in counties with elevated levels of PM 2.5. The data is "consistent with previously reported findings that Black Americans are at higher risk of COVID-19 mortality[6] than other groups," the report says.

In a separate study[7], researchers at the Tulane Environmental Law Clinic examined the impact of COVID-19 on a 130-mile strip of southeast Louisiana known as "Cancer Alley"[8]. The region is home to many petrochemical plants, some of which encircle historic Black communities. Eight of the 10 Louisiana parishes with the highest COVID-19 death rates are in Cancer Alley.

"Parishes with more pollution and higher percentages of African Americans have higher COVID-19 death rates," says Kimberly Terrell, director of community outreach at the Tulane clinic. "And that is not explained by poverty, by unemployment, by diabetes, or by obesity."

Terrell looked at two types of air pollution: the PM 2.5 dust particles examined in the Harvard study and toxic chemicals listed in the EPA's National Air Toxics Assessment[9]. For both measures, Terrell says that even when controlling for other potential factors, parishes with higher rates of air pollution had more Black citizens and higher COVID-19 death rates.

Levels of PM 2.5 have dropped in Louisiana in recent decades. But they dropped less in heavily Black areas, where industrial pollution stayed constant or increased, as new plants opened to process natural gas.

"When it's a facility that's coming into the White residential neighborhood or near one the proposal gets shut down quickly," Terrell says. "But when it's an African American community, it's rubber stamped and ushered through, again and again and again."

"These communities are being sacrificed to the benefits of other communities," says Sacoby Wilson, an associate professor at the University of Maryland–College Park's School of Public Health. "They do not have to live with the petrochemical operations, the oil factories, the incinerators or paper mills."

Sacrifice zones are not exclusive to non-White communities. The defining factor of a sacrifice zone is an exploitive dynamic where industrial pollution is driven into a neighborhood, but the energy or economic benefits generated go elsewhere. "Your community is dehumanized," Wilson explains, "but at the same time it becomes a commodity."

In Massachusetts, the predominantly Latinx city of Chelsea has the state's highest infection and death rates, prompting a May report[10] from the attorney general's office. The report cites research[11] from the Boston University School of Public Health mapping COVID-19 hotspots alongside areas with heavy housing, environmental, and income burdens. "Areas with the lowest environmental quality are largely communities of color and current COVID-19 hot spots," the attorney general's report notes.

The report calls for more environmental enforcement, more robust air quality monitoring, and tougher standards when considering permits for facilities that risk increased air pollution or other environmental hazards. Any enforcement likely will have to happen at the state level. In March, the Trump administration suspended enforcement of some environmental regulations[12] during the pandemic.

That compounds the frustration of activists trying to address environmental hazards. "Normally you would be able to knock on someone's door," says Justin Onwenu, an environmental justice organizer for the Detroit chapter of the Sierra Club. "And say, 'Hey, there is this company that is two blocks away from you that wants to increase levels of lead in your neighborhood. Can you come out on Tuesday?'" With lockdowns in place, that's not possible.

Roughly 15 percent of Michigan residents are Black, but Blacks account for 40 percent[13] of COVID-19 deaths. Near Detroit, where emissions from an oil refinery prompted a shelter-in-place[14] advisory last year before the coronavirus, Onwenu says energy companies are seeking approval for facilities that would increase pollution. He says activists have organized letter-writing campaigns to oppose the proposals, but "we're seeing the impact of not having systems in place that we need to."

"I don't think that we should be moving permits to increase emissions in environmental justice communities," Onwenu says, "especially given what we know about the relationship between heavy air pollution and COVID."

Wilson, the Maryland professor, says the nation hasn't learned lessons from past disasters that hurt vulnerable communities. "Whether it be Katrina, this is the 15th anniversary this year, the 25th anniversary of the Chicago heat wave," he says. "Why aren't we investing in protecting the most vulnerable? I think that's where we fail in this response to the pandemic."

6.2

Environmental Impacts of Coronavirus Crisis, Challenges Ahead

by Robert Hamwey

Originally published in *United Nations Conference on Trade and Development*,
APRIL 20, 2020

As the number of coronavirus infections grew exponentially in Europe and North America in March, restrictive public health measures to stave off a worsening pandemic were put in place.

They included stay-at-home orders, which were first issued in Italy and then in rapid succession in most other countries around the world.

With entire populations ordered to stay home, schools, offices and factories limited their activities, road traffic dwindled to a minimum and airlines reduced scheduled flights[15] by 60% to 95%.

Slashed Greenhouse Emissions

While these developments have inflicted substantial economic and social shocks as global production, consumption, and employment levels dropped precipitously, they have also been associated with significant reductions in air pollution and greenhouse gas emissions.

As a result, air quality levels in the world's major cities improved dramatically in March and April. Air quality improved[16] largely because of a reduction in factory and road traffic emissions of carbon dioxide (CO_2), nitrogen oxides (NO_x) and related ozone (O_3) formation, and particulate matter (PM).

During the same period, global air traffic dropped[17] by 60%. Taken together, these emissions reductions have led to a temporary dip in CO_2 emissions from their pre-crisis levels, encouraging some to hope that our global society may indeed be able to reduce greenhouse gas emissions substantially over the long term to mitigate impending climate change.

So long as the coronavirus crisis keeps economic activities reduced, emissions will remain relatively low. However, it would be short-sighted to conclude this is a durable environmental improvement as emissions will most likely rise to previous levels when economic activity picks up as the crisis resolves.

Many environmental campaigners are thus demanding[18] that bailout packages for transportation companies and industrial manufacturers include provisions for large emissions reductions in their future operations. Such provisions could help prevent pollutant emission levels from rising to pre-crisis levels going forward.

Not All Positive

But not all the environmental consequences of the crisis have been positive. Volumes of unrecyclable waste have risen; severe cuts in agricultural and fishery export levels have led to the generation of large quantities of organic waste; maintenance and monitoring of natural ecosystems have been temporarily halted; and tourism activity to natural areas has ceased.

Local waste problems have emerged[19] as many municipalities have suspended their recycling activities over fears of virus propagation in recycling centers. Food retailers have resumed using plastic bags at checkout points citing health concerns over consumers' reuse of paper bags. In addition, due to stay-at-home policies, many consumers have increased their consumption of take-away food delivered with single-use packaging. All these developments have created acute challenges for the waste management industry at a time when they are operating with limited capacity due to the coronavirus crisis.

With the emergence of import restrictions in export markets and sharp declines in the availability of cargo transportation services, the coronavirus crisis has led to increased volumes of un-shippable agricultural and fishery commodities[20]. Many export-oriented producers produce volumes far too large for output to be absorbed in local markets, and thus organic waste levels have mounted substantially. Because this waste is left to decay, levels of methane (CH_4) emissions, a greenhouse gas, from decaying produce are expected to rise sharply in the crisis and immediate post-crisis months.

As exports of agricultural and fisheries products have declined, production levels have plummeted, causing unemployment levels in both sectors to grow substantially. Many post-harvest processing workers in these sectors are women supporting households, causing extreme hardships, particularly for low-income women[21] in developing countries where social safety nets are not in place.

Ecosystems at Risk

Natural ecosystems and protected species are at risk[22] during the coronavirus crisis. In many countries, environmental protection workers at national parks and land and marine conservation zones are required to stay at home in lockdown, leaving these areas unmonitored. Their absence has resulted in a rise of illegal deforestation, fishing, and wildlife hunting[23].

The stoppage of ecotourism activity has also left natural ecosystems at risk of illegal harvesting and encroachment. In addition, as ecotourism is often a major economic mainstay in many destinations, rising unemployment caused by the crisis may lead many households to harvest resources from fragile ecosystems[24] unsustainably as they seek alternative means to provide their households with food and income.

Many of the environmental challenges caused by the coronavirus crisis will gradually resolve on their own once the crisis comes to an end and previous levels of economic activity resume.

But it is also true that the benefits of air pollution reductions will also be erased. Overall, the crisis may thus have no permanent environmental effects.

However, what we have learned about the environmental benefits and risks of sharp drops in global economic activity will certainly help us to better understand the mechanics of environmental sustainability, societal consumption patterns, and how we can reduce environmental degradation in a future crisis-free world.

Need for Action

Attention must be given to threats on the environment and natural resource bases as a result of the coronavirus pandemic and consequential social and economic impacts.

Many rural and coastal populations rely on the sustainable use of the local environment and its natural resources whether they be small-holder farmers, small and medium-sized enterprises (SMEs), and micro, small, and medium-sized enterprises (MSMEs) involved in the production of BioTrade, forestry and fishery products, and ecotourism services.

As the crisis causes disruptions in their linkages to both national and international demand-side markets, rural producers, of whom many are women supporting entire households, are now no longer able to fully maintain their business models and livelihoods.

If the crisis is prolonged, many will be forced to abandon existing sustainable production in order to generate income quickly in domestic markets, potentially resulting in further poverty and over-exploitation of natural resources and ecosystems.

What UNCTAD Will Do

Helping rural and coastal producers to adapt to crisis market conditions and take actions for recovery and improved performance in post-crisis markets is a top priority.

UNCTAD's Sustainable Trade and Environment Programme[25] stands ready to assist stakeholders from governments, producer associations, SMEs, MSMEs, independent producers (including women entrepreneurs), and civil society to elaborate coronavirus adaptation and resilience strategies.

Actions taken by producers pursuant to such strategies can help maintain subsistence income levels, while ensuring the sustainable management of agricultural, forestry, marine, and biodiversity-rich ecosystems.

Such strategies are expected to be based on enhanced collaboration by affected producers and public support entities in order to adjust to new market realities. To be effective, such assistance needs to be implemented as soon as travel restrictions are eased.

Follow-up activities will later be provided to assist countries to restore their businesses when the crisis comes to an end.

UNCTAD's support includes methodologies for market assessment and trade-related responses as well as means to reforge direct linkages with sourcing businesses interested in restoring a sustainable flow of natural inputs.

6.3

Unequal Impact: The Deep Links Between Racism and Climate Change

by Beth Gardiner

Originally published in *Yale Environmental 360,* JUNE 9, 2020

Activist Elizabeth Yeampierre has long focused on the connections between racial injustice and the environment and climate change. In the wake of George Floyd's killing and the outsized impact of COVID-19 on communities of color, she hopes people may finally be ready to listen.

The killing of George Floyd by Minneapolis police and the disproportionate impact of COVID-19 on African Americans, Latinos, and Native Americans have cast stark new light on the racism that remains deeply embedded in U.S. society. It is as present in matters of the environment as in other aspects of life: Both historical and present-day injustices have left people of color exposed to far greater environmental health hazards than Whites.

Elizabeth Yeampierre has been an important voice on these issues for more than two decades. As co-chair of the Climate Justice Alliance[26], she leads a coalition of more than 70 organizations focused on addressing racial and economic inequities together with climate change. In an interview with *Yale Environment 360*, Yeampierre draws a direct line from slavery and the rapacious exploitation of natural resources to current issues of environmental justice. "I think about people who got the worst food, the worst health care, the worst treatment, and then when freed, were given lands that were eventually surrounded by things like petrochemical industries," says Yeampierre.

Yeampierre sees the fights against climate change and racial injustice as deeply intertwined, noting that the transition to a low-carbon future is connected to "workers' rights, land use, [and] how people are treated," and she criticizes the mainstream environmental movement, which she says was "built by people who cared about conservation, who cared about wildlife, who cared about trees and open space…but didn't care about Black people."

Yale Environment 360: You've spoken about the big-picture idea that climate change and racial injustice share the same roots and have to be addressed together, and that there is no climate action that is not also about racial justice. Can you describe the links you see connecting these two issues?

Elizabeth Yeampierre: Climate change is the result of a legacy of extraction, of colonialism, of slavery. A lot of times when people talk about environmental justice they go back to the 1970s or '60s. But I think about the slave quarters. I think about people who got the worst food, the worst health care, the worst treatment, and then when freed, were given lands that were eventually surrounded by things like petrochemical industries. The idea of killing Black people or Indigenous people, all of that has a long, long history that is centered on capitalism and the extraction of our land and our labor in this country.

For us, as part of the climate justice movement, to separate those things is impossible. The truth is that the climate justice movement, people of color, Indigenous people, have always worked multi-dimensionally because we have to be able to fight on so many different planes.

When I first came into this work, I was fighting police brutality at the Puerto Rican Legal Defense Fund. We were fighting for racial justice. We were in our 20s and this is how we started. It was only a few years after that I realized that if we couldn't breathe, we couldn't fight for justice and that's how I got into the environmental justice movement. For us, there is no distinction between one and the other.

In our communities, people are suffering from asthma and upper respiratory disease, and we've been fighting for the right to breathe for generations. It's ironic that those are the signs you're seeing in these protests—"I can't breathe." When the police are using chokeholds, literally people who suffer from a history of asthma and respiratory disease, their breath is taken away. When Eric Garner died [in 2014 from a New York City police officer's chokehold], and we heard he had asthma, the first thing we said in my house was, "This is an environmental justice issue."

The communities that are most impacted by COVID, or by pollution, it's not surprising that they're the ones that are going to be most impacted by extreme weather events. And it's not surprising that they're the ones that are targeted for racial violence. It's all the same communities, all over the United States. And you can't treat one part of the problem without the other, because it's so systemic.

e360: Can you more explicitly draw the connection between climate change and the history of slavery and colonialism?

Yeampierre: With the arrival of slavery comes a repurposing of the land, chopping down of trees, disrupting water systems and other ecological systems that comes with supporting the effort to build a capitalist society and to provide resources for the privileged, using the bodies of Black people to facilitate that.

The same thing in terms of the disruption and the stealing of Indigenous land. There was a taking of land, not just for expansion, but to search for gold, to take down mountains and extract fossil fuels out of mountains. All of that is connected, and I don't know how people don't see the connection between the extraction and how Black and Indigenous people suffered as a result of that and continue to suffer, because all of those decisions were made along that historical continuum, all those decisions also came with Jim Crow. They came with literally doing everything necessary to control and squash Black people from having any kind of power.

You need to understand the economics. If you understand that, then you know that climate change is the child of all that destruction, of all of that extraction, of all of those decisions that were made and how those ended up, not just in terms of our freedom and taking away freedom from Black people, but hurting us along the way.

It's all related. You can't say that with Hurricane Maria in Puerto Rico and Hurricane Katrina in New Orleans the loss of lives was simply because there was an extreme weather event. The loss of life comes out of a legacy of neglect and racism. And that's evident even in the rebuilding. It's really interesting to see what happens to the land after people have been displaced, how land speculation and land grabs and investments are made in communities that, when there were Black people living there, had endured not having the things people need to have livable good lives.

These things, to me, are connected. It's comfortable for people to separate them, because remember that the environmental movement, the conservation movement, a lot of those institutions were built by people who cared about conservation, who cared about wildlife, who cared about trees and open space and wanted those privileges while also living in the city, but didn't care about Black people. There is a long history of racism in those movements.

e360: So how do you have a fight for climate action that is intertwined with a fight for racial justice? What are the steps, the policies, that we should be thinking about looking forward?

Yeampierre: With the Green New Deal, for example, we said that it wasn't a Green New Deal unless it was centered on frontline solutions and on ensuring that frontline leadership would be able to move resources to their communities to deal with things like infrastructure and food security. When that happens, we'll be able to move the dial much more efficiently. In New York, for example, we passed the *Climate Leadership and Community Protection Act*, which is aggressive legislation that looks at how you move resources to frontline communities and how you invest in those communities.

Nationally, we need to be looking at stopping pipelines—reducing carbon but also reducing other pollutants. We need to start focusing on regenerative economies, creating community cooperatives and different kinds of economic systems that make it possible for people to thrive economically while at the same time taking us off the grid.

In every community, there are different things people are doing, everything from putting solar in public housing to community-owned solar cooperatives. This is not the '60s or the '70s or the '80s where we follow one iconic leader. This is a time where we need to have numerous people really taking on the charge of directing something that's big and complex.

e360: Can you talk a little bit about the idea of a just transition to a low-carbon future and how that dovetails with anti-racism efforts?

Yeampierre: A just transition is a process that moves us away from a fossil fuel economy to local livable economies, to regenerative economies. Those are different economies of scale that include not just renewable energy, but healthy food and all of the things that people need in order to thrive. The word justice here is important because for a long time, people would talk about sustainability, that you could have sustainability without justice, and the climate movement focused on reducing carbon but didn't really care about other pollutants.

A just transition looks at the process of how we get there, and so it looks at not just the outcomes, which is something that the environmentalists look at, but it looks at the process—workers' rights, land use, how people are treated, whether the process of creating materials that take us to a carbon-neutral environment is toxic and whether it affects the host community where it's being built. It looks at all those different kinds of things.

I can give you one example in New York City. We have been advocates of bringing in offshore wind. One of the things that we learned is that in order for that to happen, the pieces have to come from Europe and be assembled in New York and they would be coming in these huge container ships. Now these ships operate by diesel, and so what happens is they park themselves on the waterfront of an environmental justice community and the climate solution becomes an environmental justice problem. The climate solution is we reduce carbon, but the environmental justice problem is we dump tons of nitrogen oxides and sulfur oxides and PM2.5 [particles] into the lungs of the host community.

We need the climate solution, but then we need to talk about how we electrify the industrial waterfront and how these ships can plug in so they're not burning diesel. While we're doing that, we also need to look at how we create the market instead of following the market—wind turbines that are built in the United States so we don't have to bring the parts in from Europe.

These are the kinds of things that we think about when we're thinking about a just transition. A climate activist will be like, "Okay, we need offshore wind"—right, that's it. But a climate justice activist will be like, "Okay, let's look at it a little closer and let's figure out what the process looks like and how we can engage in remediation to make sure we are not only reducing carbon but we're also reducing co-pollutants, and let's make sure that the people that are hired are hired locally." So, there are all of these other pieces that are involved in a just transition. Climate activists talk about moving at a big, grand scale, and we talk about moving at a local scale, and then replicating those efforts.

e360: Racial justice would presumably have to be at the heart of that.

Yeampierre: It has to be at the center. For example, in Sunset Park [Brooklyn, where Yeampierre runs the Latino community group UPROSE[27]], we just launched the first community-owned solar cooperative in the state. Okay, we want renewable energy. We need to be able to prioritize the people that are going to be most impacted. Low-income communities. People of color. It has to matter to White folks because when our communities succeed and get what they need, everyone benefits from that.

With the cooperative, the community actually owns the utility, owns the energy source. People will be able to access renewable energy, at a reduced cost, be hired locally to build it—and have ownership. So it's really exciting. We're hoping this model will birth more projects like this.

Now, we're reaching out to small businesses. They're struggling because of how COVID-19 has affected the economy. When we started this project, we were thinking it would provide resilience to disruptions of the grid and other systems from extreme weather events. We hadn't anticipated the disruption would be something like COVID. But these models become a real benefit in moments like this where you don't know where your next paycheck is coming from. You have access to energy that is both renewable—which means it has a health benefit—and also benefits your pocketbook.

e360: With the pandemic and its racially disparate impact, and then the killing of George Floyd and the protests that have followed, we're at this moment where these longstanding racial disparities and racism are on vivid display. What would you hope the climate movement and the environmental justice movement take away from this moment and apply going forward?

Yeampierre: I think that this is a moment for them to start thinking internally and thinking about some of the challenges that they're having. I think it's a moment for introspection and a moment to start thinking about how they contribute to a system that makes a police officer think it's okay to put his knee on somebody's neck and kill them, or a woman to call the police on an African-American man who was birdwatching in the park.

These institutions [environmental groups] have to get out of their silos and out of their dated thinking, and really need to look to organizations like the Climate Justice Alliance and Movement Generation and all of the organizations that we work with. There are so many people who have been working with each other now for years and have literally put out tons of information that there's no need to reinvent the wheel. It's all there.

There has to be a fundamental change in the culture of these institutions. If they were thinking strategically, they would be saying, "Hey, let me see. I'm in New York. Who's doing this and how can we support them?" We've had groups of White young people who have contacted us and have said to us, "How can we support you? How can we best use our resources and our skills to support the work that you're doing?" And, we've been like, "You know what? That is the right question. Let's do this together."

This interview has been edited for length and clarity.

6.4

How COVID-19 Could Impact the Climate Crisis

by Daniel Wilkinson & Luciana Téllez-Chávez

Originally published in *Foreign Policy in Focus*, APRIL 16, 2020

Far-right governments are rolling back environmental regulations, while international climate talks stall amid the crisis. But climate activists see opportunity.

Satellite images showing dramatic drops in air pollution in coronavirus hotspots around the globe have circulated widely on social media, offering a silver lining to an otherwise very dark story. But they are also a graphic reminder of the climate crisis that will continue when the pandemic passes.

When the lockdowns are lifted and life returns to what it once was, so too will the pollution that clouds the skies and with it the greenhouse gases that fuel global warming.

In fact, the rebound could be even worse.

In the initial aftermath of the global financial crisis of 2008, global CO2 emissions from fossil fuel combustion and cement production decreased by 1.4 percent, only to rise by 5.9 percent in 2010. And the crisis this time could have a longer-term impact on the environment—at far greater cost to human health, security, and life—if it derails global efforts to address climate change.

This was supposed to be "a pivotal year" for those efforts to address climate change, as UN Secretary General António Guterres put it at a recent briefing[28] on the UN's annual climate summit, which was scheduled to take place in Glasgow in November.

Ahead of the summit, 196 countries were expected to introduce revamped plans[29] to meet the emission reduction goals established under the 2015 Paris Agreement. Yet on April 1, in the face of the spreading coronavirus pandemic, the UN announced that it was postponing[30] the summit until sometime next year.

It was only the latest sign that the casualties of COVID-19 may include global efforts to address climate change. Other international meetings related to climate—on biodiversity and oceans—have also been disrupted[31]. While the need to mobilize governments to act on climate has never been more urgent, the inability to gather world leaders to address the issue could make it all the more difficult to do so.

The coronavirus crisis also threatens local efforts to meet the climate commitments that have already been made.

The European Union has come under pressure to shelve crucial climate initiatives, with Poland calling[32] for a carbon-trading program to be put on hold and the Czech Republic urging[33] that the EU's landmark climate bill be abandoned, while airline companies have pressed[34] regulators to delay emissions-cutting policies. China has already announced[35] such delays, extending deadlines for companies to meet environmental standards and postponing[36] an auction for the right to build several huge solar farms.

In the United States, after a powerful oil lobby petitioned[37] the Trump administration to relax enforcement, the Environmental Protection Agency said[38] it would not penalize companies that fail to comply with federal monitoring or reporting requirements if they could attribute their noncompliance to the pandemic. In recent days, it announced[39] a rollback on car emissions rules that were a central piece of U.S. efforts to reduce greenhouse gas emissions.

In Brazil, the federal environmental agency announced[40] it is cutting back on its enforcement duties, which include protecting the Amazon from accelerating deforestation that could lead[41] to the release of massive amounts of greenhouse gases that are stored in one of the world's most important carbon sinks.

Governments have a human rights obligation to protect people from environmental harm—and this includes a duty to address climate change.

They might conceivably have valid reasons to temporarily relax the enforcement of some environmental rules as they scramble to contain the pandemic and salvage their economies. But these measures could do permanent damage if used to advance the broader anti-environmental agendas of leaders like President Donald Trump and Brazilian President Jair Bolsonaro, who oppose[42] global efforts to address climate change.

The real impact of the coronavirus crisis on climate could depend ultimately on choices made regarding how governments want their economies to look when they recover—and, in particular, how much they will continue to rely on fossil fuels. Meeting the Paris Agreement's central goal of limiting global warming will require reducing this reliance.

And here the crisis might offer some grounds for hope.

Many see the efforts to contain the economic fallout of the pandemic as an opportunity to accelerate the shift to cleaner energy alternatives, such as solar and wind. Options could include ensuring that economic stimulus programs prioritize investments in cleaner energy, or conditioning assistance to businesses, especially in carbon-intensive sectors, on drastic cuts in emissions. Similarly, financial industry bailouts could require banks to invest less in fossil fuel and more in climate change mitigation and resilience efforts.

In the U.S., Congressional Democrats pushed[43] for such measures when negotiating the recent stimulus package. In response, President Trump threatened a veto, tweeting "This is not about the ridiculous Green New Deal." The proposed measures did not survive, though Democrats did manage to block $3 billion that Republicans sought to buy up oil for the strategic reserve.

In Europe, the prospects for green stimulus are more promising. In response to one European leader's call to abandon climate measures, an EU spokesperson was categorical: "While our immediate focus is on combating COVID-19, our work on delivering the European Green Deal continues. The climate crisis is still a reality and necessitates our continued attention and efforts."

The struggle to ensure that human rights protections and climate commitments are not COVID-19 collateral will continue in the U.S., the EU and elsewhere as governments face the task of restarting their economies in the weeks and months to come. The outcome will define our capacity and will to mitigate what threatens to be a global catastrophe far greater even than the viral pandemic.

6.5

Environmental Racism Has Left Black Communities Especially Vulnerable to COVID-19

by Casey Berkovitz

Originally published in *The Century Foundation*, MAY 19, 2020

Racism suffuses nearly every system and institution in the United States, and the COVID-19 crisis has highlighted and magnified that racial inequality, as it has so many other injustices that existed before the pandemic. As a patchwork of demographic data[44] on COVID-19 is released, it is becoming clear[45] that Black communities across the country have been the hardest hit by the pandemic, both contracting and dying from the disease at rates far out of proportion.

The reasons for these disparities are myriad and interconnected. Black Americans are overrepresented in frontline "essential" workforces,[46] and therefore face increased risk of exposure; longstanding disparities in wealth and income mean that Black Americans are more likely to need to continue working rather than distance at home[47]; those same disparities, in combination with a lower rate of health insurance coverage,[48] mean Black Americans are less likely to seek care for a sickness that could be COVID-19 due to fear of the cost;[49] and even those who do seek coverage are more likely to face racism from the health care system, resulting in lack of treatment or misdiagnosis. All of these factors exist in addition to preexisting, widespread racial disparities in health outcomes.[50]

Recent findings about the effects of COVID-19 on the human body, and how it spreads, are highlighting another reason that Black Americans are disproportionately at risk: environmental racism. The interlocking harms of environmental racism and residential segregation, the health effects of those systems, and the particular way that COVID-19 spreads and affects individuals are likely combining to contribute to racial disparities in COVID-19 cases and deaths.

Environmental Racism, Segregation, and Racial Injustice

Environmental racism refers to the many ways that communities of color—in the United States, Black communities in particular—face greater harms from environmental factors. The term, which was first articulated[51] in studies of waste disposal, toxic dumping, and industrial uses, is now understood to encompass everything from the siting of industrial uses; to proximity to power plants and factories; to higher exposure to emissions from mobile sources of pollution, like cars, trucks, and ships; to the disproportionate harm that disasters like Hurricane Katrina do to Black communities.

Environmental racism is inseparable from racial segregation. Residential segregation—which is itself a result of individual and systemic racism, including public policy choices at every level of government and exclusionary choices by financial actors[52]—means that people of color are often concentrated in neighborhoods that have frequently been disempowered, both politically and financially.

For these reasons and more, neighborhoods with large non-White populations have historically seen lower property values[53], meaning that land in those areas is cheaper for industrial actors to acquire—leading to greater pollution. At the same time, policy choices have acted alongside financial factors to drive these dangerous uses toward communities of color and away from wealthier, Whiter neighborhoods, thanks to imbalances in political power. Similarly, the harms of mobile sources of emissions such as cars and trucks have been concentrated in communities of color[54] with less political power to resist them, through the siting of freeways[55] and shipping centers, for example. (In particular, the results of the last half-century's confluence of White flight[56], concentration of Black communities in inner cities, and the construction of freeways[57] explicitly designed to serve suburban communities and break up inner city "slums"[58], even where these trends have mutated or shifted direction recently, continues to cause environmental harm.) In cases where pollution has a geology-specific link—such as mining, oil and gas extraction, or rivers used for dumping—historic patterns of segregation and wealth disparities have allowed White Americans to buy or inherit homes further away, while the forces of segregation and discrimination have prevented Black Americans from doing the same.

This cycle is perpetuated as existing pollution and industrial land use keeps property values low, preventing people of color from building wealth (and power) through property ownership. These environmental factors are used as justification, alongside well-documented reasons like school quality and "quality of life," for White-dominated political systems and individuals to avoid integrating traditionally non-White neighborhoods. Political and financial systems like redlining and zoning amplify and perpetuate this cycle.

Communities of color therefore end up concentrated in areas that face greater environmental harms and are more vulnerable to natural disasters, while the forces of residential segregation create systemic barriers that make it more difficult for individuals to move to less environmentally harmful areas.

Even if these harms are not intentional, conscious decisions keep these injustices in place at each step along the way. Segregation is not the result of natural instincts to separate—it is the result of deliberate choices, conditioned but not inevitable, that include everything racial covenants to redlining[59], municipal secession[60], and exclusionary zoning[61]; and of political leaders who uphold those systems rather than confronting them. Though the placement of polluting facilities is more traditionally thought of as the market at work, this too is the result of policy choices, which allow or ban certain uses of land in certain places. Many of the most high-profile environmental fights in recent years have been over the granting of permits for fossil fuel infrastructure—a choice made by policymakers. By the same token, then, fuel emission standards and wastewater treatment requirements are also policy decisions that officials could choose to strengthen.

Just as policymakers have allowed segregation and environmental racism to persist, they could take steps to turn back the tide. Each decision to issue a mine permit, build a freeway overpass, leave a bus stop exposed to fumes, or deny an affordable housing development is a cog in the machine of racial injustice that could be dismantled rather than reinforced.

The Health Effects of Environmental Racism

These interlocking systems have had hugely detrimental effects on the health of people of color, even before the COVID-19 pandemic broke out. The disparate effects of air pollution alone—hardly the only harm of racism and segregation—have been shown to have adverse health effects. Racial segregation has been shown to be "significantly and positively associated" with exposure to fine particulate matter ($PM_{2.5}$)[62] emitted during combustion from sources like car engines and power plants. $PM_{2.5}$ is a known carcinogen, one which the Environmental Protection Agency (EPA) links[63] to "premature death in people with heart or lung disease, nonfatal heart attacks, irregular heartbeat, aggravated asthma, decreased lung function, [and] increased respiratory symptoms, such as irritation of the airways, coughing or difficulty breathing." Racial disparities in $PM_{2.5}$ exposure hold not only at a national level, but also within most states and counties.[64]

$PM_{2.5}$ is far from the only disparately experienced air pollutant. Communities of color also experience significantly higher rates of exposure to endocrine-disrupting chemicals (EDCs), which can exist in both toxic waste and air pollution and have been linked to higher rates of diabetes[65] for Black Americans. Furthermore, a study of exposure to concentrations of nitrogen dioxide (NO_2),[66] an air pollutant and greenhouse gas, found that people of color had 37 percent higher exposure levels in 2010, concluding that "if people of color had breathed the lower NO_2 levels experienced by Whites in 2010, it would have prevented an estimated 5,000 premature deaths from heart disease among the non-White group." One study focused on Northern California found[67] a significant correlation between historically redlined neighborhoods and asthma-related emergency room visits.

Segregation is an important driver of racial disparities in the social determinants of health far beyond air pollution. As Olivia Chan wrote for The Century Foundation[68],

> Scholars have connected social vulnerability to disaster to the discriminatory housing market; filtering and redlining practices in the real estate and mortgage industries

led lower-income households to inhabit homes and neighborhoods that were physically deteriorated, with poor property values and poor resiliency to storms... Present-day racial and socioeconomic health disparities are influenced by a variety of environmental determinants of health, as well: concentrated poverty; income inequality and segregation; exposure to environmental toxins; exposure to violence; inadequate access to healthy foods; and fewer and lower quality institutional resources, such as child care, schools, and recreational facilities.

How COVID-19 and Environmental Racism Intersect

Though the specific ways that COVID-19 attacks the human body are still being discovered, early consensus is that respiratory and heart ailments are significant risk factors[69] with the virus—conditions that are often also the health effects of environmental racism, and which are likely a factor in the racial disparities in COVID-19 cases and deaths that we are already seeing. The CDC specifically names asthma, lung disease, and diabetes as conditions that put people at higher risk to the virus.

An early study from the Harvard T.H. Chan School of Public Health[70], for example, found that people with COVID-19 who live in counties with higher levels of $PM_{2.5}$ exposure are more likely to die from the virus. A separate study[71] conducted by German researcher Yaron Ogen found a similar link: Ogen says[72] "long-term exposure to [$PM_{2.5}$] may be one of the most important contributors to fatality caused by the COVID-19 virus."

Other studies[73] have[74] linked[75] the regions in Italy and China that were hardest hit by the pandemic with higher levels of air pollution, and presented early hypotheses that air pollution conditions themselves facilitate the broader spread of the disease—one study[76] begins by stating that "an epidemic model based only on respiratory droplets and close contact could not fully explain the regional differences in the spread of" COVID-19. Though early and unconfirmed, these studies suggest that environmental racism could be one cause of wider spread of the virus in communities of color, and not just higher death rate of those infected due to underlying health factors.

The shelter-in-place orders issued in response to the pandemic present both temporary reprieve and new challenges for environmental justice advocates. Emissions from personal vehicles[77] and some industrial uses are dropping as fewer people are driving and some factories temporarily shut down—one study from Europe estimates[78] that 11,000 deaths and 6000 new cases of asthma were avoided in the continent due to the reduction in NO_2 and $PM_{2.5}$ pollution—but the gains made now are unlikely to make up for years of exposure to pollutants. In fact, the pandemic may end with us seeing *higher* levels of pollution than before: air pollution in China, which both shut down and "reopened" before the timeline in the United States, are already above levels at this time last year[79]. Amid the crisis domestically, the Environmental Protection Agency has reduced enforcement[80] of a wide array of environmental regulations during the pandemic, essentially shifting to an honor system of self-enforcement for polluters, and state regulatory agencies responsible for inspection and enforcement have similarly scaled back[81], both because of their own decreased capacity and because the facilities they oversee have requested accommodations. If these rollbacks are maintained even as the economy starts to return to full capacity, it will further exacerbate the health impacts of environmental racism.

What Has Policy Done, and What Should It Do?

The United States remains tragically delinquent in its response to the COVID-19 pandemic. As in other policy areas—paid leave, workplace safety, health care, and financial support for jobseekers, to name just a few—there are longstanding policy proposals that would have helped the health and well-being of Americans before the pandemic, and will help us weather the crisis if implemented today. The EPA's mission of reducing environmental harms, including air pollution and waste management, has meaningfully helped Americans before this crisis, but more comprehensive protection and better enforcement would have left us better prepared for a respiratory pandemic. (The Trump administration has worked to roll back[82] or reduce enforcement of many of the policies implemented to address these harms and disparities— recently, among many other examples[83], by declining to tighten control of $PM_{2.5}$ emissions[84] even after the link to COVID-19 had been established.)

Across the interconnected policy realms of environmental justice, health, and infrastructure, there are a wide variety of proposals that would both help mitigate the effects of the COVID-19 crisis and provide enduring long-term benefits for society.

Existing Environmental Justice Policy Ideas

As discussed above, environmental racism and the current pandemic heavily compound each other's harms; one consequence is that many of the environmental justice proposals that were developed before COVID-19, or without responding to the pandemic as a primary goal, would still substantially alleviate the pandemic's toll. For example, the *Environmental Justice for All Act*[85], similar programs at the regional and local levels, and demands from the community groups at the heart of the environmental justice movement, if enacted, would reduce overall emissions and help to close racial disparities. The benefits of reducing air pollution have been shown to be larger and take effect faster than expected[86], and these policies would boost public health overall in addition to alleviating several key risk factors for COVID-19.

Policies and proposals to integrate neighborhoods[87] have similarly existed long before the COVID-19 pandemic, and could mitigate some of the racial disparities in environmental harms if implemented. In particular, fully funding the Housing Choice Voucher Program[88] (particularly if paired with a ban on source-of-income discrimination) at the federal level and increasing funding for other rental assistance programs at all levels of government would create meaningful residential mobility immediately[89], in addition to providing a significant financial backstop for the millions of American families facing financial uncertainty. Increased funding for repairs and retrofitting of public[90] and affordable housing would improve underlying health conditions for residents. Over a longer period of time, proposals to allow more housing to be built in areas with better access to public transportation would cut down on emissions from personal vehicles, as would making transit more reliable and accessible for existing homes.

The temporary reduction in traffic from personal vehicles also presents an opportunity for local policymakers to try to shift some of those car commuters to less polluting modes of transport[91] by improving bicycle and pedestrian infrastructure, creating more and better bus lanes, and rolling back subsidies for parking.[92] The federal government could encourage these policies by changing how federal transportation funds are structured[93], sharing street design best practices with localities, and ensuring public transportation agencies are adequately funded.[94]

Health-Specific Policies

Other policies should be crafted specifically in response to this health crisis. First and foremost, federal officials must collect and report comprehensive demographic data on COVID-19 cases and deaths. Without that data, and without broadly available testing to ensure cases are accurately being tracked, policymakers and researchers will not have a full understanding of how and why Black Americans are disproportionately affected by the pandemic.

In addition, as policymakers allocate funding to address the health and financial needs of the American people, these resources should be put to use addressing both the immediate and long-term harms of environmental racism. Health care funding should be directed to areas with higher levels of pollution, even if they have not yet been hit hard by the pandemic, as the links between pollution and the disease show that those are the areas likely to be hard hit in the future. Furthermore, expansions to health care coverage must be implemented. In the immediate term, free testing and treatment of COVID-19[95] is essential, as well as incentivizing Medicaid expansion in states that have yet to do so under the *Affordable Care Act*. In the longer term, a universal health care system that supports quality, affordable health care for all is the best solution to prepare the country for pandemic threats in the future.

Green Jobs and Infrastructure

Additionally, future stages of the economic stimulus should include investments in environmental retrofitting and new green infrastructure[96] to reduce emissions and pollutants in the long term, even after this crisis. A letter sent to congressional leadership in late March, whose authorship was led by Representatives A. Donald McEachin (D-VA) and Raúl Grijalva[97] (D-AZ), calls for policies including energy assistance and weatherization programs, development and deployment of zero emission transportation modes, and existing local programs for workforce training and pollution reduction or cleanup. Many of these investments are targeted at "environmental justice communities"—the neighborhoods and communities hit hardest by the harms of pollution and industry—and would also serve as jobs programs for communities that have often suffered from higher-than-average unemployment (for many of the same structural reasons). The *HEROES Act*, recently introduced in the House of Representatives[98], includes $50 million in funding for environmental justice grants targeted to these communities, though this falls far short of environmental justice advocates' targets and more investment is necessary to make a national impact.

This pandemic and ensuing crisis is traveling well-worn paths of inequality in the United States. With the right response, we can not only get through this crisis, but address environmental harms that have disproportionately fallen on Black Americans for decades.

6.6

Why Racial Justice is Climate Justice

by Claire Elise Thompson

Originally published in *Grist*, JUNE 4, 2020

The worst disasters are never colorblind.

We now know that coronavirus—much like police brutality, mass incarceration, and climate change—is not colorblind[99]. It's not that the virus itself differentiates by race[100], but, as with other crises, the factors that make communities of color more susceptible to it are shaped by the United States' long history of discriminatory policies and practices.

Many of the places that have been dealt the harshest blow by COVID-19 are simultaneously dealing with other serious threats to residents' well-being. Even under the cover of the pandemic, environmental rollbacks and pipeline plans[101] continue to threaten the health of people of color. Add to that the outrage and civil unrest that has erupted in many cities in reaction to the death of George Floyd—a Black man on whose neck a White police officer knelt for more than 8 minutes—and you have a veritable witch's brew of community risk.

So what does it mean to have all these calamities come to a head at the same moment? Will policymakers see the compounded threats as a wake-up call to the many ways our society is structured unjustly and unsustainably? What are people doing now to try to build a more resilient, equitable world? How much, and in what way, will things change as cities and states begin to emerge from quarantine?

Even as some folks mumble about getting "back to normal," others are talking about ways[102] to make sure "normal" is never the same again[103]. To that end, we reached out to five environmental justice leaders and Grist Fixers[104] from the West Coast to the East to get their takes on addressing the compounded threats of racial injustice, climate change, and COVID-19. Here's what they had to say.

The following responses have been edited for length and clarity.

Impacted Communities Need to Be Front and Center in a Recovery

Adrien Salazar[105]: Senior campaign strategist for climate equity at Dēmos, New York

Climate justice means racial justice. Today we are in the midst of a political and social upheaval that has exposed the deep structural inequalities of our society in ways that are unignorable. Communities of color are the most threatened by pollution and by COVID-19. And current events have brought into stark relief the lived reality of Black people in particular, whose lives are endangered by police and White-supremacist violence. We must undo the institutions that perpetuate anti-Black racism and White supremacy. This is a precondition to achieving true environmental justice.

Black communities are simultaneously confronted by the acute violence of police brutality and the chronic, slow violence of unequal environmental health impacts. Some people have called COVID-19 a "great equalizer" because the disease is affecting so many. But we now know it is not a great equalizer. Black and brown people are most at risk. Any pandemic or other catastrophe that takes place in an unequal society will have unequal impacts.

Working on climate policy advocacy, I have been navigating the COVID-19 crisis by supporting the immediate needs of the most vulnerable communities. The recent stimulus packages—the CARES Act[106] and the HEROES Act[107]—are imperfect pieces of legislation, largely because they have given a lifeline to corporations (on the order of trillions of dollars) while the basic needs of families and workers struggling to survive continue to be negotiated. People have been fighting for the inclusion of key measures, like rent cancellation and a national utilities shut-off moratorium, in these packages. These are things that people need, a reprieve from their bills when they have lost work in order to feed their families.

Right now, the crises we face are intensifying. People are fed up and compelled to put their lives on the line and take to the streets to demand justice. We have to transform our political and economic systems to end the inequalities aggravated by these overlapping crises. That means policies that end violence in Black and brown communities and a long-term economic recovery that invests in those communities. We have to end making some communities sacrifice zones, and we can do that by building a clean economy, strengthening the resilience of local communities, and ensuring the right to a good life for all.

Health Needs to Be Recognized as a Multi-Pronged Issue

Kerene Tayloe[108]: Director of federal legislative affairs at WE ACT for Environmental Justice, Washington, D.C.

Healthcare isn't just access to doctors and medicine. It's about: Is your home healthy? Is your community healthy? How is that impacting you? It's pretty clear that the legacy pollutants that have existed in Black and brown and Indigenous communities for decades have made people who look like me especially vulnerable to COVID-19. And some of the proposed solutions aren't taking into account the full scope of those inequities. You're asking people to stay home more, for example, but if their apartments aren't kept up—many folks who are in rentals or public housing have homes that aren't up to code, whether it's indoor allergens like mold or a whole host of other things—you're putting those people in harm's way.

Another concern is medical waste. With so many hospitalizations, there's been a rise in the need for PPE and swabs and medical equipment. Well, a lot of waste gets incinerated in communities of color. So then there's potential for increased air pollution that'll come out of that issue. And medical waste isn't something that is typically managed at the federal level; it's managed state by state. There aren't very strong, clear guidelines on how each state is going to handle the situation. In all likelihood, the resulting pollution will get put back into the very same communities that are dying at high rates from COVID-19. It's this very cyclical process of harm.

And it's not just about the lack of access to healthcare or the cumulative exposure to pollution. We are living in a society where people of color are disproportionately incarcerated and killed by the police. In this moment, we have to consider the totality of the inequities that communities of color experience. We need to address all forms of injustice to safeguard our health and well-being.

Because COVID-19 is something that everyone in the country is paying attention to, we can use it to draw attention to all of these longstanding problems and drive toward the solutions we've identified. This is an opportunity to share solutions in areas like climate change that, under other circumstances, leaders probably wouldn't have given the time of day.

It's Imperative We Fill the Gaps in the Social Safety Net
Julian Brave NoiseCat[109]: Writer and VP of policy and strategy at Data for Progress, Washington, D.C.

Just to start, I want to say that Black people, as well as their friends and family across the country, are hurting because the police have become an existential threat to their community. This is not just a social- and racial-justice issue, it is also a public health issue. Black lives matter, and if we truly believe that, we must stand with the people in the street demanding justice and the families mourning the loss of their loved ones. We live in a country built on stolen land and stolen labor. You cannot understand the United States without confronting that ongoing reality.

In Indian Country, what we have seen with the coronavirus is that there is an immense gap in the social safety net in places like the Navajo Nation. I've been reporting this story about the impact of the coronavirus there. The Navajo Nation holds a treaty with the federal government, which is supposed to guarantee them healthcare. But the Indian Health Service (IHS) facilities there are significantly underfunded—IHS spends about $4,000 per person, whereas Medicare spends more than $13,000 per patient.

On top of that, there are very few supermarkets or other places where you might be able to buy hand sanitizer and toilet paper within a reasonable driving distance. And many homes—some of the most overcrowded in the country, by the way—do not have electricity or running water. Imagine being in a pandemic, and the healthcare system where you would go to seek treatment is woefully underfunded and understaffed, and you might live in a home where you can't do something so simple as washing your hands. These are circumstances where the coronavirus has been able to just spread like wildfire.

The whole picture represents the failures of the U.S. government to live up to its legal responsibility to tribes, to provide adequate, modern levels of social rights, healthcare, and welfare for all people. Communities like the Navajo Nation have been filling that gap by taking care of each other. There is a big mutual-aid effort underway right now at the Navajo Nation in which people are delivering food and supplies and medicine and basically doing all of the things that the federal government has failed to do.

Still, in the surveys we've been running at Data for Progress, we've seen a significant jump in support for a more robust social-welfare system. For example, support for the Green New Deal and for green jobs jumped 10 points during the pandemic. Historically, it has not been unusual for moments of positive change and prosperity to follow crises like this.

Tribal Nations Should Assert Their Sovereignty to Survive

Mariah Gladstone[110]: Founder of IndigiKitchen, on the Blackfeet Indian Reservation in Montana

Native communities, in many ways, have stressors that have been exacerbated by the pandemic. But I also think that there are Native communities, especially here in Montana, that I've seen react more proactively than many non-Indigenous communities.

Blackfeet Nation, where I live, has had stay-at-home orders, curfews, and requirements that people wear masks and gloves when entering any store since March. And we're still doing that, even though the state of Montana has started to "reopen." The community is also working on testing all of the residents, which is something that's not happening within a lot of places—but that's the type of action that we need. To date, as far as I know, we've only had one confirmed case on the entire reservation.

That said, we're also a community that relies very heavily on tourist income. We're getting to that point of the year where tourists usually start rushing to Glacier National Park. There's a concern that when the park opens, we will start getting thousands of out-of-state visitors rushing through the reservation, potentially bringing more cases of COVID-19. But there's a simultaneous concern that if the park does not open, all of the businesses that get their annual income from these three months of tourist season won't have that income.

Long term, for this as well as other potential disruptions we may face, it comes down to adaptability. For tribal nations, I think it is essential that we recognize our own sovereignty and our own ability to assert that sovereignty. For example, the Cheyenne River Sioux Reservation[111] has set up roadblocks that are being challenged by the state of South Dakota, but tribal members have been asserting their sovereignty and citing treaty law to say they have the right to control entrance. I think having that local recognition of what's needed and the willingness to take actions that are not popular but are necessary will ultimately help communities thrive and survive.

To Build a Better Tomorrow, We Need to Deal with Root Causes

Alvaro S. Sanchez[112]: Environmental equity director at The Greenlining Institute, Oakland

Racism is the sickness this country has never bothered to cure. The injustice, civil unrest, and oppressive use of force we witnessed last weekend clearly show us that we have a deep need for racial justice. Whether it is a global pandemic, climate change, or police brutality, people of color—particularly Black communities—are always the first and worst hit, and it must end.

COVID-19 really pulled the curtain back to reveal just how quickly people went from kind of getting by, living paycheck to paycheck, to their lives just free falling.

It's no coincidence that the people who are most impacted by this crisis don't look like the protesters who are saying we should open up businesses. Some people are saying, "We can get on with our lives, and it's OK, it's not a big deal," whereas other people are literally dying because of the crisis.

I think it's a tough road ahead. But there are things we can do. Number one, we have to center Black and brown voices in our struggle for a better world. Our response to this crisis must meet the urgent needs of those who are hit hardest by the pandemic and looming recession: frontline workers, immigrants, the unhoused, and Black and brown people. It must be guided by an inclusive vision that deals with the root causes that got us into this crisis and centers climate, economic, and racial justice.

Number two, it's clear that preparation really works—and I equate that to climate change as well. The comparison between New York and San Francisco, I think, is getting a lot of attention, with their respective responses to COVID-19. One of the key differences there was local elected officials listening to their health officials, and making concrete decisions around that information, backed by data. Hopefully, that's a message that comes out of this: We have to listen to the experts, and the government has to reinforce and amplify that message. That's the difference between life and death.

Notes

1   https://www.thenation.com/article/archive/race-best-predicts-whether-you-live-near-pollution/
2   https://www.wired.com/tag/covid-19/
3   https://mitpress.mit.edu/books/sacrifice-zones
4   https://projects.iq.harvard.edu/files/covid-pm/files/pm_and_covid_mortality_med.pdf
5   https://www.wired.com/story/h1n1-crisis-predicted-covid-19-toll-black-americans/
6   https://www.wired.com/story/covid-19-coronavirus-racial-disparities/
7   https://law.tulane.edu/sites/law.tulane.edu/files/Files/Terrell%20-%20COVID-19%20-%20PM%20
     2.5%20Louisiana%202020-5-14%20WEB%20VERSION.pdf
8   https://www.propublica.org/article/welcome-to-cancer-alley-where-toxic-air-is-about-to-get-worse
9   https://www.epa.gov/national-air-toxics-assessment/nata-overview
10   https://www.mass.gov/doc/covid-19s-unequal-effects-in-massachusetts/download
11   https://bucas.maps.arcgis.com/apps/MapSeries/index.
     html?appid=e820a92d6bbc4c9099c59494a4e9367a
12   https://thehill.com/policy/energy-environment/489753-epa-suspends-enforcement-of-environmental-
     laws-amid-coronavirus
13   https://www.michigan.gov/coronavirus/0,9753,7-406-98163_98173---,00.html
14   https://www.detroitnews.com/story/news/local/detroit-city/2019/02/08/
     officials-possible-gas-emissions-during-marathon-repairs/2815858002/
15   https://www.forbes.com/sites/marisagarcia/2020/03/19/
     lufthansa-issues-stark-warning-on-coronavirus-despite-favorable-footing/#1eec33be6046
16   https://www.eea.europa.eu/highlights/air-pollution-goes-down-as
17   https://www.icao.int/sustainability/Documents/COVID-19/ICAO_Coronavirus_Econ_Impact.pdf
18   https://www.theguardian.com/environment/2020/mar/24/
     covid-19-economic-rescue-plans-must-be-green-say-environmentalists
19   https://www.bloomberg.com/news/articles/2020-03-30/
     the-unexpected-environmental-consequences-of-covid-19
20   http://www.fao.org/3/ca8308en/ca8308en.pdf
21   http://www.fao.org/3/x0198e/x0198e02.htm
22   https://www.nationalobserver.com/2020/04/03/news/
     coronavirus-lockdown-threat-many-animals-not-blessing
23   https://www.thejakartapost.com/news/2020/04/09/illegal-fishing-still-rife-in-north-natuna-sea-
     ministry.html
24   https://www.swissinfo.ch/eng/reuters/
     with-tourists-gone--africa-s-conservationists-brace-for-the-worst/45679736
25   https://unctad.org/en/Pages/DITC/Trade-and-Environment.aspx
26   https://climatejusticealliance.org/
27   https://www.uprose.org/
28   https://unfccc.int/news/2020-is-a-pivotal-year-for-climate-un-chief-and-cop26-president
29   https://unfccc.int/process-and-meetings/the-paris-agreement/
     nationally-determined-contributions-ndcs#eq-3
30   https://www.theguardian.com/environment/2020/mar/18/
     cop26-boris-johnson-urged-resist-calls-postpone-climate-talks-coronavirus
31   https://www.sixdegreesnews.com/archives/28076/
     coronavirus-hits-a-critical-year-for-nature-and-the-climate
32   https://www.reuters.com/article/us-health-coronavirus-poland-ets/
     eu-should-scrap-emissions-trading-scheme-polish-official-says-idUSKBN2141RC
33   https://www.euractiv.com/section/energy-environment/news/
     czech-pm-urges-eu-to-ditch-green-deal-amid-virus/
34   https://www.reuters.com/article/health-coronavirus-airlines-climatechang/
     analysis-coronavirus-redraws-battle-lines-on-airline-emissions-idUSL8N2BC5CL
35   https://www.reuters.com/article/us-health-coronavirus-china-environment/china-to-modify-
     environmental-supervision-of-firms-to-boost-post-coronavirus-recovery-idUSKBN20X0AG
36   https://www.economist.com/science-and-technology/2020/03/26/
     the-epidemic-provides-a-chance-to-do-good-by-the-climate
37   https://www.api.org/news-policy-and-issues/letters-or-comments/2020/03/20/
     api-to-president-trump-re-covid-19-response
38   https://www.epa.gov/enforcement/enforcement-policy-guidance-publications
39   https://www.nytimes.com/2020/03/30/climate/trump-fuel-economy.html

40   https://www.reuters.com/article/us-health-coronavirus-brazil-environment/
     exclusive-brazil-scales-back-environmental-enforcement-amid-coronavirus-idUSKBN21E15H
41   https://advances.sciencemag.org/content/5/12/eaba2949
42   https://www.vox.com/energy-and-environment/2019/12/18/21024283/
     climate-change-cop25-us-brazil-australia-japan
43   https://www.nytimes.com/2020/03/25/climate/nyt-climate-newsetter-coronavirus-drought.html
44   https://www.cdc.gov/coronavirus/2019-ncov/cases-updates/cases-in-us.html
45   https://www.motherjones.com/coronavirus-updates/2020/04/
     covid-19-has-infected-and-killed-black-people-at-alarming-rates-this-data-proves-it/
46   https://www.theguardian.com/commentisfree/2020/apr/16/black-workers-coronavirus-covid-19
47   https://www.economist.com/graphic-detail/2020/04/24/
     many-poor-americans-cant-afford-to-isolate-themselves
48   https://www.theguardian.com/commentisfree/2020/apr/16/black-workers-coronavirus-covid-19
49   https://news.gallup.com/poll/309224/avoid-care-likely-covid-due-cost.aspx
50   https://tcf.org/content/report/racism-inequality-health-care-african-americans/
51   https://www.routledge.com/Dumping-In-Dixie-Race-Class-And-Environmental-Quality-Third-Edition/
     Bullard/p/book/9780813367927
52   https://tcf.org/content/report/attacking-black-white-opportunity-gap-comes-residential-segregation/
53   https://www.brookings.edu/research/devaluation-of-assets-in-black-neighborhoods/
54   https://www.theguardian.com/cities/2018/feb/21/roads-nowhere-infrastructure-american-inequality
55   https://www.nytimes.com/interactive/2019/08/14/magazine/traffic-atlanta-segregation.html
56   https://www.nber.org/papers/w22077
57   https://www.vox.com/2015/5/14/8605917/highways-interstate-cities-history
58   https://www.vox.com/2015/5/14/8605917/highways-interstate-cities-history
59   https://www.epi.org/publication/the-color-of-law-a-forgotten-history-of-how-our-government-
     segregated-america/
60   https://www.citylab.com/equity/2018/11/eagles-landing-cityhood-vote-atlanta-stockbridge/571990/
61   https://www.propublica.org/article/how-some-of-americas-richest-towns-fight-affordable-housing
62   https://www.sciencedirect.com/science/article/pii/S0160412016301386
63   https://www.epa.gov/pm-pollution/health-and-environmental-effects-particulate-matter-pm
64   https://ajph.aphapublications.org/doi/10.2105/AJPH.2017.304297
65   https://care.diabetesjournals.org/content/diacare/early/2017/10/20/dc16-2765.full.pdf
66   https://www.washington.edu/news/2017/09/14/
     people-of-color-exposed-to-more-pollution-from-cars-trucks-power-plants-during-10-year-period/
67   https://www.abstractsonline.com/pp8/#!/5789/presentation/22785
68   https://tcf.org/content/commentary/covid-19-wake-call-public-health-preparedness-climate-
     crisis/?session=1
69   https://www.cdc.gov/coronavirus/2019-ncov/need-extra-precautions/groups-at-higher-risk.html
70   https://www.hsph.harvard.edu/news/hsph-in-the-news/
     air-pollution-linked-with-higher-covid-19-death-rates/
71   https://www.sciencedirect.com/science/article/pii/S0048969720321215
72   https://www.theguardian.com/environment/2020/apr/20/
     air-pollution-may-be-key-contributor-to-covid-19-deaths-study
73   https://www.ncbi.nlm.nih.gov/pmc/articles/PMC7151372/
74   https://www.ncbi.nlm.nih.gov/pmc/articles/PMC7151372/4.15.20065995v2
75   https://www.ncbi.nlm.nih.gov/pmc/articles/PMC7156797/#CR6
76   https://www.medrxiv.org/content/10.1101/2020.04.11.20061713v1
77   https://www.nytimes.com/interactive/2020/03/22/climate/coronavirus-usa-traffic.html
78   https://energyandcleanair.org/air-pollution-deaths-avoided-in-europe-as-coal-oil-plummet/
79   https://energyandcleanair.org/china-air-pollution-rebound-briefing/
80   https://www.epa.gov/sites/production/files/2020-03/documents/oecamemooncovid19implications.pdf
81   https://grist.org/energy/coronavirus-has-states-hitting-pause-except-when-it-comes-to-oil-and-gas-
     drilling/
82   https://www.nytimes.com/interactive/2019/climate/trump-environment-rollbacks.html
83   https://www.drillednews.com/post/the-climate-covid-19-policy-tracker
84   https://www.nytimes.com/2020/04/14/climate/coronavirus-soot-clean-air-regulations.html
85   https://www.congress.gov/bill/116th-congress/house-bill/5986/text
86   https://www.atsjournals.org/doi/abs/10.1513/AnnalsATS.201907-538CME
87   https://tcf.org/content/report/attacking-black-white-opportunity-gap-comes-residential-segregation/
88   https://www.cbpp.org/research/introduction-to-the-housing-voucher-program

89   https://www.vox.com/future-perfect/2019/8/4/20726427/
     raj-chetty-segregation-moving-opportunity-seattle-experiment
90   https://thenext100.org/why-we-need-a-green-new-deal-for-public-housing/
91   https://www.citylab.com/transportation/2020/04/
     paris-cars-air-pollution-health-public-transit-bike-lanes/610861/
92   https://www.routledge.com/The-High-Cost-of-Free-Parking-Updated-Edition/Shoupah2/p/
     book/9781932364965
93   https://www.dataforprogress.org/memos/3/17/gnd-city-suburban-transportation
94   http://t4america.org/2020/05/13/house-bill-proposes-15-billion-for-transit-its-not-enough/
95   https://tcf.org/content/commentary/need-covid-19-phase-4-relief-package-heres/
96   http://filesforprogress.org/memos/clean-jumpstart-policy.pdf
97   https://naturalresources.house.gov/imo/media/doc/Grijalva McEachin Letter to House and Senate
     Leaders on Environmental Justice in Virus Response Marh 26 2020.pdf
98   https://docs.house.gov/billsthisweek/20200511/BILLS-116hr6800ih.pdf
99   https://www.nytimes.com/2020/04/29/magazine/racial-disparities-covid-19.html
100 https://www.bostonglobe.com/2020/04/10/opinion/
     being-person-color-isnt-risk-factor-coronavirus-living-racist-country-is/
101 https://grist.org/fix/how-to-protest-pipelines-safely-during-the-coronavirus-era/
102 https://www.today.com/video/getting-back-to-normal-that-to-me-is-the-problem-sheinelle-
     says-84291141614
103 https://www.culturalpower.org/stories/o-going-back-covid-19-cultural-strategy-activation/
104 https://grist.org/about/grist-50/
105 https://grist.org/grist-50/2019/#adrien-salazar
106 https://www.sbc.senate.gov/public/index.cfm/guide-to-the-cares-act
107 https://www.congress.gov/bill/116th-congress/house-bill/6800
108 https://grist.org/grist-50/2019/#kerene-tayloe
109 https://grist.org/grist-50/2020/#julian-brave-noisecat
110 https://grist.org/grist-50/2018/#mariah-gladstone
111 https://www.insideedition.com/how-a-south-dakota-native-american-reservation-successfully-snuffed-
     out-coronavirus-on-its-own
112 https://grist.org/grist-50/2019/#alvaro-s-sanchez

Part Seven

Crises in Leadership: (Confronting) Nationalism and Populism

7.1

The Next Victim of the Coronavirus? American Exceptionalism

by Johann N. Neem

Originally published in *The Washington Post*, MAY 3, 2020

Discarding this myth can be a good thing—if we restore what actually made America great in the past.

The rise of Donald Trump, and the embarrassing failure of the American state to respond effectively to the coronavirus, has proved to the world that the United States is no longer exceptional[1] nor, in President Barack Obama's word, indispensable[2]. The inability[3] of the American government to protect its citizens from a pandemic and provide global leadership vividly illustrates that American exceptionalism is dead.

This might be a good thing. American exceptionalism has allowed Americans on the left and right alike to pretend that we could evade the problems facing other societies. Now is the time to accept the reality that we are part of the world and its history, not exceptions to it.

This requires dismantling aspects of American mythology that have made it harder for us to address deep problems in our society. All nations rely on myths, and perhaps none can survive without them. But today, some of the ideas we hold dear about ourselves—that America is a country of rugged individuals, destined to be the world's first multicultural democracy and too strong and important to falter—are impeding our ability to overcome our most pressing challenges.

These ideas have a history. American exceptionalism is as old as the nation. From the founding, American citizens believed plentiful land and opportunity combined with God's Providence had blessed them as a people. In the 19th century, these ideas became known as Manifest Destiny—the belief that God's goodwill toward us manifested in America's expansion westward, its prosperity, and ultimately its freedom. At the center of this myth stood the rugged individual who pulled himself up by his own bootstraps and tamed the West.

But the self-made man was never made all by himself. The federal government cleared the land for settlement, often using armed force and violence to displace Native Americans. State and federal transportation investments ensured that farmers could bring their crops to domestic and foreign markets. The *Homestead Act*, passed during the Civil War, promised cheap land to Americans willing to improve it. And social mobility was promoted through an expanding system of public schools[4]. In short, American individualism has always relied on government.

Our celebration of individualism has persisted into the 21st century, but our commitment to the public infrastructure that sustains it has withered over the past four decades. Our failure to make the investments[5] necessary to maintain our government's quality and capability has had an impact on all of us—Americans struggle to make ends meet, and social mobility[6] is declining.

Our challenges are not just political but also cultural.

A second myth that inhibits us is the idea that we can become a multicultural society. In the 1970s, multiculturalism emerged as a way to challenge ethnic, religious, and racial prejudice. Today, we rightly celebrate America's diversity. But over time, some advocates of multiculturalism moved beyond demands for political and social equality to proclaim[7] every ethnic group should maintain its own distinct culture without being as attentive to what binds us together.

Unfortunately, the United States is not exempt from the forces that produce conflict and even violence in other places. Democracies depend on social trust, and that trust depends on citizens seeing themselves as part of the nation. As many commentators[8] have noted, today we are at risk of devolving into a society divided[9] by ethnicity, race, and religion. Democratic norms are harder to sustain if we see our opponents as enemies[10] instead of as fellow citizens. At a time when White nationalists are threatening to reclaim America for themselves, it is essential that we balance our differences with what we share as Americans.

A third myth is that somehow American democracy can be taken for granted. This myth emerged after the end of the Cold War when suddenly the

United States found its military and economic primacy unchallenged. Some even believed that we had reached the end of history[11]. With the fall of the Iron Curtain, many hoped that liberal democracy would spread across the globe. Instead, democracy is in retreat[12] around the world. In the United States, voting rights are threatened, money plays an outsized role in politics, false information spreads widely on the Internet and increasing numbers of Americans question[13] the importance of living in a democratic country.

Despite our military and economic might, our democracy is as fragile as any other. For too long, too many American leaders have presumed we are too big to fail. Over the past three decades, no matter how unequal we became, no matter how many jobs were lost, no matter how many people suffered for lack of health care, no matter how many people felt forgotten, while the rich became richer, many political leaders assumed the United States would not have the kind of angry populist response that we have seen (and continue to see) in countries around the globe.

That myth is busted.

In the Trump era, any observer of the United States can see that we are no different from other nation-states. We are divided into hostile camps—rural and urban, White and non-White, evangelical and nonevangelical, rich and poor. These divisions have produced social distrust, and, as students of democracy know, in such times, populist demagogues can feed on the resentment and anger of some while blaming others, tapping into our divisions to gain power. This is happening in the United States just as it is happening in Brazil[14], India[15], and elsewhere.

The framers of our Constitution aspired to establish a government that accounted for the basic facts of human nature, including selfishness and ambition. The Constitution depends on the separate branches of government checking the excesses of the others. As James Madison wrote, "ambition must be made to counteract ambition." That system is being tested. Our democracy is in a state of crisis.

If we believe in democracy, we need to rebuild our institutions[16] and weave back together a national fabric torn apart by decades of culture wars. We must invest in jobs that ensure prosperity and dignity are widely shared. We must nurture democracy, not take it for granted. If American exceptionalism is dead, perhaps we can begin the hard work of remaking our country.

7.2

The Pandemic and Political Order: It Takes A State

by Francis Fukuyama

Originally published in *Foreign Affairs*, JULY/AUGUST, 2020

Major crises have major consequences, usually unforeseen. The Great Depression spurred isolationism, nationalism, fascism, and World War II—but also led to the New Deal, the rise of the United States as a global superpower, and eventually decolonization. The 9/11 attacks produced two failed American interventions, the rise of Iran, and new forms of Islamic radicalism. The 2008 financial crisis generated a surge in antiestablishment populism that replaced leaders across the globe. Future historians will trace comparably large effects to the current coronavirus pandemic; the challenge is figuring them out ahead of time.

It is already clear why some countries have done better than others in dealing with the crisis so far, and there is every reason to think those trends will continue. It is not a matter of regime type. Some democracies have performed well, but others have not, and the same is true for autocracies. The factors responsible for successful pandemic responses have been state capacity, social trust, and leadership. Countries with all three—a competent state apparatus, a government that citizens trust and listen to, and effective leaders—have performed impressively, limiting the damage they have suffered. Countries with dysfunctional states, polarized societies, or poor leadership have done badly, leaving their citizens and economies exposed and vulnerable.

The more that is learned about COVID-19, the disease caused by the novel coronavirus, the more it seems the crisis will be protracted, measured in years rather than quarters. The virus appears less deadly than feared but very contagious[17] and often transmitted asymptomatically. Ebola is highly lethal but hard to catch[18]; victims die quickly before they can pass it on. COVID-19 is the opposite, which means that people tend not to take it as seriously as they should, and so it has, and will continue to, spread widely across the globe, causing vast numbers of deaths. There will be no moment when countries will be able to declare victory over the disease; rather, economies will open up slowly and tentatively[19], with progress slowed by subsequent waves of infections. Hopes for a V-shaped recovery appear wildly optimistic. More likely is an L with a long tail curving upward or a series of Ws. The world economy will not go back to anything like its pre-COVID state anytime soon.

Economically, a protracted crisis will mean more business failures and devastation for industries such as shopping malls, retail chains, and travel. Levels of market concentration in the U.S. economy had been rising steadily for decades, and the pandemic will push the trend still further. Only large companies with deep pockets will be able to ride out the storm, with the technology giants gaining most of all, as digital interactions become ever more important.

The political consequences could be even more significant. Populations can be summoned to heroic acts of collective self-sacrifice for a while, but not forever. A lingering epidemic combined with deep job losses, a prolonged recession, and an unprecedented debt burden will inevitably create tensions that turn into a political backlash—but against whom is as yet unclear.

The global distribution of power will continue to shift eastward since East Asia has done better at managing the situation than Europe or the United States. Even though the pandemic originated in China, and Beijing initially covered it up[20] and allowed it to spread, China will benefit from the crisis, at least in relative terms. As it happened, other governments at first performed poorly and tried to cover it up, too, more visibly and with even deadlier consequences for their citizens. And at least Beijing has been able to regain control of the situation and is moving on to the next challenge, getting its economy back up to speed quickly and sustainably.

The United States, in contrast, has bungled its response badly and seen its prestige slip enormously. The country has vast potential state capacity and had built an impressive track record over previous epidemiological crises, but its current highly polarized society and incompetent leader blocked the state from functioning effectively. The president stoked division rather than promoting unity, politicized the distribution of aid, pushed responsibility onto governors for making key decisions while encouraging protests against them for protecting public health, and attacked international institutions rather than galvanizing them. The world can watch TV, too, and has stood by in amazement, with China quick to make the comparison clear.

Over the years to come, the pandemic could lead to the United States' relative decline, the continued erosion of the liberal international order, and a resurgence of fascism around the globe. It could also lead to a rebirth of liberal democracy, a system that has confounded skeptics many times, showing remarkable powers of resilience and renewal. Elements of both visions will emerge in different places. Unfortunately, unless current trends change dramatically, the general forecast is gloomy.

Rising Fascism?

Pessimistic outcomes are easy to imagine. Nationalism, isolationism, xenophobia, and attacks on the liberal world order have been increasing for years, and that trend will only be accelerated by the pandemic. Governments in Hungary[21] and the Philippines[22] have used the crisis to give themselves emergency powers, moving them still further away from democracy. Many other countries, including China, El Salvador, and Uganda, have taken similar measures. Barriers to the movement of people have appeared everywhere, including within the heart of Europe[23]; rather than cooperate constructively for their common benefit, countries have turned inward, bickered with one another, and made their rivals political scapegoats for their own failures.

The rise of nationalism will increase the possibility of international conflict. Leaders may see fights with foreigners as useful domestic political distractions, or they may be tempted by the weakness or preoccupation of their opponents and take advantage of the pandemic to destabilize favorite targets or create new facts on the ground. Still, given the continued stabilizing force of nuclear weapons and the common challenges facing all major players, international turbulence is less likely than domestic turbulence.

Poor countries with crowded cities and weak public health systems will be hit hard. Not just social distancing but even simple hygiene such as hand washing is extremely difficult[24] in countries where many citizens have no regular access to clean water. And governments have often made matters worse rather than better—whether by design, by inciting communal tensions and undermining social cohesion, or by simple incompetence. India, for example, increased its vulnerability by declaring a sudden nationwide shutdown without thinking through the consequences for the tens of millions[25] of migrant laborers who crowd into every large city. Many went to their rural homes, spreading the disease throughout the country; once the government reversed its position and began to restrict movement, a large number found themselves trapped in cities without work, shelter, or care.

Displacement caused by climate change was already a slow-moving crisis brewing in the global South. The pandemic will compound its effects, bringing large populations in developing countries ever closer to the edge of subsistence. And the crisis has crushed the hopes of hundreds of millions of people in poor countries who have been the beneficiaries of two decades of sustained economic growth. Popular outrage will grow, and dashing citizens' rising expectations is ultimately a classic recipe for revolution. The desperate will seek to migrate, demagogic leaders will exploit the situation to seize power, corrupt politicians will take the opportunity to steal what they can, and many governments will clamp down or collapse. A new wave of attempted migration from the global South to the North, meanwhile, would be met with even less sympathy and more resistance this time around, since migrants could be accused more credibly now of bringing disease and chaos.

Finally, the appearances of so-called black swans are by definition unpredictable but increasingly likely the further out one looks. Past pandemics have fostered apocalyptic visions, cults, and new religions growing up around the extreme anxieties caused by prolonged hardship. Fascism, in fact, could be seen as one such cult, emerging from the violence and dislocation engendered by World War I and its aftermath. Conspiracy theories used to flourish in places such as the Middle East, where ordinary people were disempowered and felt they lacked agency. Today, they have spread widely throughout rich countries, as well, thanks in part to a fractured media environment caused by the Internet and social media, and sustained suffering is likely to provide rich material for populist demagogues to exploit.

Or Resilient Democracy?

Nevertheless, just as the Great Depression not only produced fascism but also reinvigorated liberal democracy, so the pandemic may produce some positive political outcomes, too. It has often taken just such a huge external shock to break sclerotic political systems out of their stasis and create the conditions for long-overdue structural reform, and that pattern is likely to play out again, at least in some places.

The practical realities of handling the pandemic favor professionalism and expertise; demagoguery and incompetence are readily exposed. This should ultimately create a beneficial selection effect, rewarding politicians and governments that do well and penalizing those that do poorly. Brazil's Jair Bolsonaro, who has steadily hollowed out his country's democratic institutions in recent years, tried to bluff his way through the crisis and is now floundering[26] and presiding over a health disaster. Russia's Vladimir Putin tried to play down the importance of the pandemic at first, then claimed that Russia had it under control and will have to change his tune yet again as COVID-19 spreads throughout the country. Putin's legitimacy was already weakening[27] before the crisis, and that process may have accelerated.

The pandemic has shone a bright light on existing institutions everywhere, revealing their inadequacies and weaknesses. The gap between the rich and the poor, both people and countries, has been deepened by the crisis and will increase further during a prolonged economic stagnation. But along with the problems, the crisis has also revealed government's ability to provide solutions, drawing on collective resources in the process. A lingering sense of "alone to-gether" could boost social solidarity and drive the development of more gener-ous social protections down the road, just as the common national sufferings of World War I and the Depression stimulated the growth of welfare states in the 1920s and 1930s.

This might put to rest the extreme forms of neoliberalism, the free-market ideology pioneered by University of Chicago economists such as Gary Becker, Milton Friedman, and George Stigler. During the 1980s, the Chicago school provided the intellectual justification for the policies of U.S. President Ronald Reagan and British Prime Minister Margaret Thatcher, who considered large, intrusive government to be an obstacle to economic growth and human prog-ress. At the time, there were good reasons to cut back many forms of govern-ment ownership and regulation. But the arguments hardened into a libertarian religion, embedding hostility to state action[28] in a generation of conservative intellectuals, particularly in the United States.

Given the importance of strong state action to slow the pandemic, it will be hard to argue, as Reagan did in his first inaugural address, that "government is not the solution to our problem; government is the problem"[29]. Nor will any-body be able to make a plausible case that the private sector and philanthropy can substitute for a competent state during a national emergency. In April, Jack Dorsey, the CEO of Twitter, announced that he would contribute $1 billion to COVID-19 relief, an extraordinary act of charity. That same month, the U.S. Congress appropriated $2.3 trillion[30] to sustain businesses and individuals hurt by the pandemic. Anti-statism may linger among the lockdown protes-tors[31], but polls suggest[32] that a large majority of Americans trust the advice of government medical experts in dealing with the crisis. This could increase support for government interventions to address other major social problems.

And the crisis may ultimately spur renewed international cooperation. While national leaders play the blame game, scientists and public health of-ficials around the world are deepening their networks and connections. If the breakdown of international cooperation leads to disaster and is judged a fail-ure, the era after that could see a renewed commitment to working multilater-ally to advance common interests.

Don't Get Your Hopes Up

The pandemic has been a global political stress test. Countries with capable, legitimate governments will come through relatively well and may embrace reforms that make them even stronger and more resilient, thus facilitating their future outperformance. Countries with weak state capacity or poor leadership will be in trouble, set for stagnation, if not impoverishment and instability. The problem is that the second group greatly outnumbers the first.

Unfortunately, the stress test has been so hard that very few are likely to pass. To handle the initial stages of the crisis successfully, countries needed not only capable states and adequate resources but also a great deal of social consensus and competent leaders who inspired trust. This need was met by South Korea, which delegated management of the epidemic to a professional health bureaucracy, and by Angela Merkel's Germany. Far more common have been governments that have fallen short in one way or another. And since the rest of the crisis will also be hard to manage, these national trends are likely to continue, making broader optimism difficult.

Another reason for pessimism is that the positive scenarios assume some sort of rational public discourse and social learning. Yet, the link between technocratic expertise and public policy is weaker today than in the past when elites held more power. The democratization of authority[33] spurred by the digital revolution has flattened cognitive hierarchies along with other hierarchies, and political decision-making is now driven by often weaponized babble. That is hardly an ideal environment for constructive, collective self-examination, and some polities may remain irrational longer than they can remain solvent.

The biggest variable is the United States. It was the country's singular misfortune to have the most incompetent and divisive leader in its modern history at the helm when the crisis hit, and his mode of governance did not change under pressure. Having spent his term at war with the state he heads, he was unable to deploy it effectively when the situation demanded. Having judged that his political fortunes were best served by confrontation and rancor rather than national unity, he has used the crisis to pick fights and increase social cleavages. American underperformance during the pandemic has several causes, but the most significant has been a national leader who has failed to lead.

If the president is given a second term in November, the chances for a broader resurgence of democracy or of the liberal international order will drop. Whatever the election result, however, the United States' deep polarization is likely to remain. Holding an election during a pandemic will be tough, and there will be incentives for the disgruntled losers to challenge its legitimacy. Even should the Democrats take the White House and both houses of Congress, they would inherit a country on its knees. Demands for action will meet mountains of debt and die-hard resistance from a Trump opposition. National and international institutions will be weak and reeling after years of abuse, and it will take years to rebuild them—if it is still possible at all.

With the most urgent and tragic phase of the crisis past, the world is moving into a long, depressing slog. It will come out of it eventually, some parts faster than others. Violent global convulsions are unlikely, and democracy, capitalism, and the United States have all proved capable of transformation and adaptation before. But they will need to pull a rabbit out of the hat once again.

7.3

Europe Said It Was Pandemic-Ready. Pride Was Its Downfall.

by David D. Kirkpatrick, Matt Apuzzo & Selam Gebrekidan

Originally published in *The New York Times*, JULY 20, 2020

The coronavirus exposed European countries' misplaced confidence in faulty models, bureaucratic busywork, and their own wealth.

LONDON—Prof. Chris Whitty, Britain's chief medical adviser, stood before an auditorium in a London museum two years ago cataloging deadly epidemics[34].

From the Black Death of the 14th century to cholera in war-torn Yemen, it was a baleful history. But Professor Whitty, who had spent most of his career fighting infectious diseases in Africa, was reassuring. Britain, he said, had a special protection.

"Being rich," he explained.

Wealth "massively hardens a society against epidemics," he argued, and quality of life—food, housing, water and health care—was more effective than any medicine at stopping the diseases that ravaged the developing world.

Professor Whitty's confidence was hardly unique. As recently as February, when European health ministers met in Brussels to discuss the novel coronavirus emerging in China, they commended their own health systems and promised to send aid to poor and developing countries.

"Responsibility is incumbent on us, not only for Italy and Europe, but also for the African continent," said Roberto Speranza, Italy's health minister.

"The European Union should be ready for support," agreed Maggie De Block, Belgium's then health minister.

Barely a month later, the continent was overwhelmed. Instead of serving primarily as a donor, providing aid to former colonies, Western Europe became an epicenter of the pandemic. Officials once boastful about their preparedness were frantically trying to secure protective gear and materials for tests as death rates soared in Britain, France, Spain, Italy and Belgium.

This was not supposed to happen. The expertise and resources of Western Europe were expected to provide the antidote to viral outbreaks flowing out of poorer regions. Many European leaders felt so secure after the last pandemic—the 2009 swine flu—that they scaled back stockpiles of equipment and faulted medical experts for overreacting.

But that confidence would prove their undoing. Their pandemic plans were built on a litany of miscalculations and false assumptions. European leaders boasted of the superiority of their world-class health systems but had weakened them with a decade of cutbacks. When COVID-19 arrived, those systems were unable to test widely enough to see the peak coming—or to guarantee the safety of health care workers after it hit.

Accountability mechanisms proved toothless. Thousands of pages of national pandemic planning turned out to be little more than exercises in bureaucratic busywork. Officials in some countries barely consulted their plans; in other countries, leaders ignored warnings about how quickly a virus could spread.

European Union checks of each country's readiness had become rituals of self-congratulation. Mathematical models used to predict pandemic spreads—and to shape government policy—fed a false sense of security.

National stockpiles of medical supplies were revealed to exist mostly on paper, consisting in large part of "just in time" contracts with manufacturers in China. European planners overlooked the risk that a pandemic, by its global nature, could disrupt those supply chains. National wealth was powerless against worldwide shortages.

Held in high esteem for its scientific expertise, Europe, especially Britain, has long educated many of the best medical students from Asia, Africa and Latin America. On a visit to South Korea after a 2015 outbreak of the coronavirus MERS, Dame Sally Davies, then England's chief medical officer, was revered as an expert. Upon her return home, she assured colleagues that such an outbreak could not happen in Britain's public health system.

Now South Korea, with a death toll below 300, is a paragon of success against the pandemic. Many epidemiologists there are dumbfounded at the mess made by their mentors.

"It has come as a bit of a shock to a number of Koreans," said Prof. Seo Yong-seok of Seoul National University, suggesting that perhaps British policymakers "thought that an epidemic is a disease that only occurs in developing countries."

Not every Western democracy stumbled. Germany, with a chancellor trained in physics and a sizable domestic biotech sector, managed it better than most. Greece, with fewer resources, has reported fewer than 200 deaths. But with several countries expected to conduct public inquests into what went wrong, Europe is grappling with how a continent considered among the most advanced failed so miserably.

Its downfall presaged the chaos now unfolding in the United States, where President Trump initially responded to the pandemic by blaming continental Europe and cutting off travel. "No nation is more prepared or more resilient than the United States," he declared on March 11, assuring Americans that "the risk is very, very low."

"The virus will not have a chance against us," Mr. Trump said.

Today, the United States has the highest number of cases in the world and a death rate that is again rising, closing in on the European nations already humbled by the virus.

Belgium, by some measures, has the world's highest death rate. Italy's wealthiest region was shattered. France's much-praised health system was reduced to relying on military helicopters to rescue patients from overcrowded hospitals. Britain, though, most embodies Europe's miscalculations because of the country's great pride in its expertise and readiness.

Prime Minister Boris Johnson was so confident that Britain's modelers could forecast the epidemic with precision, records and testimony show, that he delayed locking down the country for days or weeks after most of Europe. He waited until two weeks after British emergency rooms began to buckle under the strain.

With the number of infections doubling every three days at the time, some scientists now say that locking down a week sooner might have saved 30,000 lives. Dr. Whitty, 54, initially praised in British newspapers as the reassuring "geek-in-chief," has declined to speak publicly about his role in those decisions. His friends say the government has set him up to take the blame.

"The politicians say they are 'following the science' and then if they make the wrong decisions it is on him," said Prof. David Mabey of the London School of Hygiene and Tropical Medicine, a friend and colleague. "I am not sure the politicians listen to him."

Critics, though, say it is impossible to absolve the government's scientific advisers of shared responsibility.

"They thought they could be more clever than other countries," said Prof. Devi Sridhar, an epidemiologist at the University of Edinburgh. "They thought they could outsmart the virus."

Sir David King, a former British chief science officer, said, "The word 'arrogance' comes to mind, I am afraid." He added: "What hubris."

False Alarm

Fear swept the continent. It was spring of 2009 and a new virus that became known as swine flu had infected hundreds and killed dozens in Mexico. European vacationers swarmed airports to get home. Experts recalled the flu pandemic of 1918, which killed as many as 50 million people around the world.

European governments sprang into action. France asked the European Union to cut off travel to Mexico and began buying doses of vaccine for everyone in the country. British hospitals enlisted retired health workers and distributed stockpiled masks, gloves, and aprons.

Every country in Europe had drawn up and rehearsed its own detailed pandemic plan, often running into the hundreds of pages. Britain's plans[35] read like the script of a horror movie, if written in the language of a bureaucrat. More than 1.3 million people could be hospitalized and 800,000 could die. Trying to contain the pandemic "would be a waste of public health resources."

These doomsday scenarios drew on a new subspecialty of epidemiology pioneered by British scientists: using abstruse mathematical models to project the path of a contagious disease.

One early disciple, Neil Ferguson of Imperial College London, had assumed a pre-eminence in British health policy. Professor Ferguson was an Oxford-trained physicist who shifted to mathematical epidemiology in the 1990s after watching a close friend's brother die of AIDS.

Other scientific advisers say Professor Ferguson, now 52, stands out for his self-assured style in delivering easy-to-understand answers under enormous time pressure.

"He is able to answer questions succinctly and clearly and with a very measured conclusion, and it is exactly the sort of information that politicians need," said Peter Openshaw, a professor of medicine at Imperial College London who sits with Professor Ferguson on a panel that advises the government on respiratory viruses.

Traditional public health experts, emphasizing clinical experience and field observations, were skeptical. They warned that the projections were only as good as their data and assumptions and that policymakers without a background in math might treat models as dependable predictions.

An epidemic of foot-and-mouth disease among livestock in Britain in 2001 was the first time policymakers relied on such modeling while addressing an outbreak. Over the objections of veterinarians, Professor Ferguson's work guided policymakers to preventively slaughter more than six million pigs, sheep and cattle.

Later studies concluded most of the killing was needless. A review commissioned by the government[36] urged that policymakers "must not rely on the model to make a decision for them."

"'Muddlers,' we call them," said Alex Donaldson, then head of Britain's Pirbright Laboratory of the Institute for Animal Health. "In future epidemics the first thing that should be done is to lock up the predictive modelers."

Yet when swine flu emerged, British leaders again turned to Professor Ferguson and the large modeling department he had built at Imperial College. He projected that swine flu, in a reasonable worst case, could kill nearly 70,000.

Elected officials were horrified. Boris Johnson, then mayor of London, presided over frantic meetings bracing for the absence from work of nearly half the city's police officers and subway drivers.

"It is impossible to say how bad it will be," Mr. Johnson warned soberly.

But the modelers' "reasonable worst case" was wildly off. Swine flu ended up killing fewer than 500 people in Britain, less than in a seasonal flu. Dr. Catherine Snelson, then completing her training in critical care at a hospital in Birmingham, had been assigned to help transfer out excess patients.

"We actually sat there doing nothing," she recalled.

For Mr. Johnson, the swine flu episode reinforced instincts not to impose restrictions in the name of public health.

"He believes people will make the right decisions on their own," said Victoria Borwick, a former deputy mayor.

An official review[37] cautioned: "Modelers are not 'court astrologers.'"

Hollowing Out

Some experts now say Europe learned the wrong lesson from the swine flu.

"It created some kind of complacency," said Prof. Steven Van Gucht, a virologist involved in the Belgian response. "Oh, a pandemic again? We have a good health system. We can cope with this."

It also coincided with Europe's worst economic slump in decades. French legislators were furious at the cost of buying millions of doses of vaccines and faulted the government for needlessly stockpiling more than 1.7 billion protective masks.

To cut costs, France, Britain and other governments shifted more of their stockpiles to "just in time" contracts. Health officials assumed that even in a crisis they could buy what they needed on the international market, typically from China, which manufactures more than half the world's masks.

By the start of 2020, France's supply of masks had fallen by more than 90 percent, to just 150 million.

"The idea of a government warehousing medical supplies came to seem outdated," said Francis Delattre, a French senator who raised alarms about dependence on China. "Our fate was put into the hands of a foreign dictatorship."

"France has a superiority complex," Mr. Delattre added, "especially when it comes to the health sector."

Two years after swine flu, Britain scattered three-quarters of its spending for public health to local governments, where it was harder to track and more easily diverted. Four hundred health experts warned in an open letter[38] that decentralization would "disrupt, fragment and weaken the country's public health capabilities," and in the following years per capita, spending on public health steadily declined. A national network that had once included 52 laboratories was eventually reduced to two national facilities and a handful of regional centers primarily serving the internal needs of regional hospitals.

Health officials also chose to limit stockpiles of protective equipment to deal with an influenza outbreak: enough for use during certain procedures[39] in hospitals, but not for more general use, emergency rooms, doctors' offices, or nursing homes.

Scientists knew a coronavirus like SARS or MERS could require more equipment.

"It's pretty difficult to build a stockpile for something you've not seen before," said Dr. Ben Killingley, an infectious disease expert who advises the government on what to stockpile. "It depends how much you want to spend on your insurance."

On the surface, Europe's defenses still looked robust. European Union reviews of each country's pandemic readiness seemed to provide oversight, but the process was misleading.

National governments barred the European Centre for Disease Prevention and Control from setting benchmarks or pointing out deficiencies. So the agency's public remarks were almost unfailingly positive. Britain, Spain and Greece were lauded[40] for their "highly motivated experts," "trusted expert organizations," and "confidence in the system."

"We couldn't say, 'You should have this,'" said Arthur Bosman, a former agency trainer. "The advice and the assessment had to be phrased in an observation."

European health officials recognized the vulnerability of national stockpiles. In response, the European Union in 2016 solicited bids to build a continent-wide repository. But the initiative fizzled because Britain, France, and other large countries thought they had the situation covered. Belgium later destroyed tens of millions of expired masks from its own stockpile and never replaced them.

In 2016, Britain tested its readiness in a drill called Exercise Cygnus. Nine hundred officials across the country participated in a make-believe response to a "swan flu" that had emerged in Thailand and killed more than 200,000 people in Britain.

The planners evidently never imagined that acquiring protective gear from abroad could present a problem. "Ordering arrangements in place" was assumed as part of the background.

Overall, the drill revealed that many British officials were unfamiliar with the country's pandemic plans and unsure of their roles, according to participants and a final report.

"It showed a hollowing out of the government, inside the infrastructure," said Prof. Robert Dingwall, a sociologist who advises the government on respiratory viruses and helped draft the plans. "And that was never corrected."

Two years later, in the real world, health industry journals reported a Chinese government crackdown on pollution shuttered a factory that was providing 1.75 million protective aprons each week to British hospitals. Shortages rippled through the system. Newspapers declared an "apron crisis"[41].

No one apparently imagined what would happen to Europe if all Chinese supplies were choked off at once.

Collapse

On Jan. 28, British scientists raised an alarm.

The expanding epidemic was setting off a global run on personal protective equipment, specifically on the face-covering mechanical hoods that provide the gold standard of safety.

A decision to stock up any later "could pose a risk in terms of availability," warned the government's respiratory virus advisory panel.

It is unclear when Britain began in earnest to try to augment its supplies of protective equipment.

The health ministry has said only that it began unspecified "discussions and orders" during the week beginning Jan. 27. But Matt Hancock, the health secretary, later acknowledged[42] that by the time Britain began buying, the spike in global demand had made protective equipment "precious" and procurement "a huge challenge."

The Doctors' Association UK, an advocacy group, later said it received more than 1,300 complaints from doctors at more than 260 hospitals about inadequate protective equipment. At least 300 British health workers eventually died after contracting COVID-19.

"We worry that some died because of a lack of personal protective equipment," said Dr. Rinesh Parmar, the group's chairman. "It was very shortsighted to think that supply lines would continue to China."

On the continent, governments that had resisted benchmarks from the European center for disease control now flooded the agency with desperate questions, including about what equipment to stock. The agency published a list of what was needed on Feb. 7, but by then, global supplies had all but run out.

"It was already way more than what they could get their hands on," said Dr. Agoritsa Baka, a senior doctor at the European center.

In Belgium, a shortage of masks became so desperate that King Philippe personally brokered a donation from the Chinese tech company Alibaba.

European and global health officials had thoroughly reviewed Belgium's pandemic plan over the years. But when COVID-19 hit, Belgian officials did not even consult it.

"It has never been used," said Dr. Emmanuel André, who was drafted to help lead the country's coronavirus response.

In France, President Emmanuel Macron tacitly acknowledged the depletion of the government's stockpile at the beginning of March by requisitioning all the masks in the country.

But he still insisted France was ready. "We are not going to stop life in France," his spokeswoman assured radio[43] listeners.

Ten days later, Mr. Macron declared a state of war and ordered a strict lockdown.

"I don't understand why we were not prepared," said Dr. Matthieu Lafaurie, of the Saint-Louis hospital in Paris. "It was very surprising that every country had to realize itself what was going on, as if they didn't have the examples of other countries. "

In Britain, Mr. Johnson told the public to stay "confident and calm"[44]. But, the same day, Feb. 11, the government's Scientific Advisory Group for Emergencies, or SAGE, privately concluded that the country's diminished public health system was incapable of widespread COVID-19 testing, even by the end of the year.

"It is not possible," the group's minutes note.

The British scientists and officials nonetheless thought they knew better than other countries like China and South Korea. Those countries were driving down the infection rate by imposing lockdowns. The British science advisers thought such restrictions were shortsighted. Unless the restrictions were permanent, any reduction of the epidemic would be lost to a "second peak," SAGE concluded, according to its minutes and three participants.

Britain reported its first death from the virus on March 5. Across Europe, the number of confirmed cases was doubling every three days. Much of northern Italy was already locked down.

Testifying that day before a parliamentary committee, Professor Whitty, the chief medical adviser, was steady and comforting. Slightly hunched over a table in a small hearing room, he told lawmakers to place their trust in Britain's modelers[45].

They were "the best in the world," he said. "We will be able to model this out, as it starts to accelerate, with a fair degree of confidence."

Despite alarming reports from Italy, he said, there was no way yet to predict the virus's ultimate punch.

But he emphasized that Britain had "quite a long period" before the outbreak would peak and said modeling would allow the government to wait until the latest possible moment before imposing social restrictions.

"We are keen not to intervene," he said, "until the point when we absolutely have to."

Mr. Johnson was even more sanguine. "It should be business as usual for the overwhelming majority of people," he said that day in a television interview.

But doctors in British hospitals were already feeling rising pressure. Intensive care wards were pushed to more than double their capacity in Birmingham, London and elsewhere.

"It became clear that the pandemic plan wasn't going to cut it," said Jonathan Brotherton, chief operating officer of University Hospitals Birmingham, England's largest health system.

At an increasingly agitated SAGE meeting on March 10, the scientists concluded from the number of cases in intensive care units that there were at least 5,000 to 10,000 infections around the country.

"There will be thousands of deaths a day," Professor Ferguson remembers warning surprised cabinet officials sitting in on a meeting.

Six days later, Professor Ferguson reported that SAGE's modeling par had moved up its projections. The peak was now almost at hand—within t weeks, at the beginning of April, not over the summer, as previously projec

Professor Ferguson released a public study that day that for the first time projected a potential British death toll in the hundreds of thousands.

Switching course, the committee urged sweeping social distancing measures, including school closures. "It would be better to act early," the group advised, according to minutes of the meeting.

Much of Europe, including France, had already shut down. Mr. Johnson waited another week, until March 23, to order a mandatory lockdown.

Reckoning

Britain, Spain, Belgium, France and Italy have now reported some of the highest per capita death tolls in the world. More than 30,000 people have died in France, and Mr. Macron has admitted his government was unprepared.

"This moment, let's be honest, has revealed cracks, shortages," he said.

After 44,000 coronavirus deaths in Britain, officials continue to defend their actions. The government's response "allowed us to protect the vulnerable and ensured that the National Health Service was not overwhelmed even at the virus' peak," a health department spokesman said.

But Mr. Johnson has admitted that his government had responded "sluggishly," like in "that recurring bad dream when you are telling your feet to run and your feet won't move."

Several scientific advisers have sought to distance themselves from his policies.

Professor Ferguson said in an interview that the decision not to intervene earlier was made by the government and health officials—not the modelers.

"They came back to us and say, 'Can you model this? Can you model that?'" he said. "And we did."

He insisted that he had warned privately in early March that Britain's insufficient testing meant the scientists did not have enough information to track the epidemic.

Across Europe, he said, more testing "would have been the single thing which would have made the biggest difference."

Other scientists say the intensive care reports in early March should have been reason enough to lock down without waiting for more testing or models. But there is another lesson to learn, said Dr. André, who spent years fighting epidemics in Africa before advising Belgium on the coronavirus.

"They keep on telling countries what they should do, very clearly. But all these experts, when it happens in your own countries? There's nothing," he said. "One lesson to learn is humility."

Monika Pronczuk contributed reporting from Brussels.

7.4

How 'Vaccine Nationalism' Could Block Vulnerable Populations' Access to COVID-19 Vaccines

by Ana Santos Rutschman

Originally published in *The Conversation*, JUNE 17, 2020

Hundreds of COVID-19 vaccine candidates[46] are currently being developed. The way emerging vaccines will be distributed to those who need them is not yet clear. The United States has now twice[47] indicated that it would like to secure priority access to doses of COVID-19 vaccine. Other countries[48], including India and Russia, have taken similar stances. This prioritization of domestic markets has become known as vaccine nationalism[49].

As a researcher[50] at Saint Louis University's Center for Health Law Studies[51], I have been following the COVID-19 vaccine race. Vaccine nationalism is harmful for equitable access to vaccines—and, paradoxically, I've concluded it is detrimental even for the U.S. itself.

Vaccine Nationalism During COVID-19

Vaccine nationalism occurs when a country manages to secure doses of vaccine for its own citizens or residents before they are made available in other countries. This is done through pre-purchase agreements between a government and a vaccine manufacturer.

In March, the White House met[52] with representatives from CureVac, a German biotech company[53] developing a COVID-19 vaccine. The U.S. government is reported[54] to have inquired about the possibility of securing exclusive rights over the vaccine. This prompted the German government to comment[55] that "Germany is not for sale." Angela Merkel's chief of staff promptly stated[56] that a vaccine developed in Germany had to be made available in "Germany and the world."

On June 15, the German government announced[57] it would be investing[58] 300 million euros (nearly US$340 million) in CureVac for a 23% stake in the company.

In April, the CEO of Sanofi, a French company whose COVID-19 vaccine work has received partial funding from the U.S Biomedical Advanced Research and Development Authority, announced that the U.S.[59] had the "right to the largest pre-order" of the vaccine.

Following public outcry and pressure[60] from the French government, Sanofi altered its stance[61] and said that it would not negotiate priority rights with any country.

In India, the privately[62] held Serum Institute[63] is developing one of the leading[64] COVID-19 vaccine candidates. The Serum Institute signaled that, if development of the vaccine succeeds, most of the initial batches of the vaccine[65] will be distributed within India.

At the same time, India, alongside the U.S. and Russia, chose not to join[66] the Access to COVID-19 Tools Accelerator, which was launched[67] by the World Health Organization to promote collaboration among countries in the development and distribution of COVID-19 vaccines and treatments.

Vaccine Nationalism is Not New

Vaccine nationalism is not new. During the early stages of the 2009 H1N1 flu pandemic[68], some of the wealthiest countries entered into pre-purchase agreements[69] with several pharmaceutical companies working on H1N1 vaccines. At that time, it was estimated that in the best-case scenario, the maximum number of vaccine doses[70] that could be produced globally was 2 billion. The U.S. alone negotiated and obtained the right to buy 600,000 doses. All the countries that negotiated pre-purchase orders were developed[71] economies.

Only when the 2009 pandemic began to unwind and demand for a vaccine dropped did developed countries offer to donate[72] vaccine doses to poorer economies.

The Problems Posed by Nationalism

The most immediate effect of vaccine nationalism is that it further disadvantages countries with fewer resources and bargaining power. It deprives populations in the Global South from timely access to vital public health goods. Taken to its extreme, it allocates vaccines to moderately at-risk populations in wealthy countries over populations at higher risk in developing economies.

Vaccine nationalism also runs against the fundamental principles of vaccine development and global public health. Most vaccine development projects involve several parties[73] from multiple countries[74].

With modern vaccines, there are very few instances in which a single country can claim to be the sole developer[75] of a vaccine. And even if that were possible, global public health is borderless. As COVID-19 is illustrating, pathogens can travel the globe. Public health responses to outbreaks, which include the deployment of vaccines, have to acknowledge that reality.

How Nationalism Can Backfire in the US

The U.S. is notorious for its high drug prices[76]. Does the U.S. government deserve to obtain exclusive rights for a vaccine that may be priced too high? Such a price may mean that fewer U.S. citizens and residents—especially those who are uninsured or underinsured—would have access to the vaccine. This phenomenon is a form of what economists call deadweight loss[77], as populations in need of a welfare-enhancing product are priced out. In public health, deadweight loss costs lives.

This is not a hypothetical scenario. U.S. Secretary of Health and Human Services Alex Azar has told[78] Congress that the government will not intervene to guarantee affordability of COVID-19 vaccines in the U.S.

Secretary Azar has said the U.S. government wants the private sector to invest in vaccine development and manufacturing; if the U.S. sets prices, companies may not make that investment because the vaccines won't be profitable. This view has been widely criticized. A commentator has called it "bad public health policy,"[79] further pointing out that American taxpayers already fund a substantial amount of vaccine research and development in the U.S. Moreover, as legal scholars have pointed out, there are many regulatory perks[80] and other incentives[81] available exclusively to pharmaceutical companies.

If COVID-19 vaccines are not made available affordably to those who need them, the consequences will likely be disproportionately severe for poorer or otherwise vulnerable and marginalized[82] populations. COVID-19 has already taken a higher toll on Black and Latino[83] populations. Without broad access to a vaccine, these populations will likely continue to suffer more than others, leading to unnecessary disease burden, continued economic problems, and potential loss of life.

What Needs to Be Done

Nationalism is at odds with global public health principles. Yet, there are no provisions in international laws that prevent pre-purchase agreements like the ones described above. There is nothing inherently wrong with pre-purchase agreements of pharmaceutical products. Vaccines typically do not generate[84] as much in sales as other medical products. If used correctly, pre-purchase agreements can even be an incentive for companies to manufacture vaccines that otherwise would not be commercialized. Institutions like Gavi[85], an international nonprofit based in Geneva, use similar mechanisms to guarantee vaccines for developing countries.

But I see vaccine nationalism as a misuse of these agreements.

Contracts should not trump equitable access to global public health goods. I believe that developed countries should pledge to refrain from reserving vaccines for their populations during public health crises. The WHO's Access to COVID-19 Tools Accelerator[86] is a starting point for countries to test collaborative approaches during the current pandemic.

But more needs to be done. International institutions—including the WHO—should coordinate negotiations ahead of the next pandemic to produce a framework for equitable access to vaccines during public health crises. Equity entails both affordability of vaccines and access opportunities for populations across the world, irrespective of geography and geopolitics.

Insofar as the U.S. can be considered a leader in the global health arena, I believe it should stop engaging in overly nationalistic behaviors. Failure to do so harms patient populations across the globe. Ultimately, it may harm its own citizens and residents, and perpetuate structural inequalities in our health care system.

Notes

1   https://www.nytimes.com/2020/04/10/opinion/sunday/coronavirus-america.html
2   https://obamawhitehouse.archives.gov/the-press-office/2014/05/28/
remarks-president-united-states-military-academy-commencement-ceremony
3   https://www.nytimes.com/2020/04/23/world/europe/coronavirus-american-exceptionalism.html
4   https://www.washingtonpost.com/news/made-by-history/wp/2017/08/20/
early-america-had-school-choice-the-founders-rejected-it/
5   https://www.washingtonpost.com/opinions/want-a-leaner-federal-government-hire-more-federal-
workers/2016/04/21/a11cf98c-fd8b-11e5-886f-a037dba38301_story.html?itid=lk_inline_manual_10
6   https://www.economist.com/graphic-detail/2018/02/14/
americans-overestimate-social-mobility-in-their-country
7   https://plato.stanford.edu/entries/identity-politics/
8   https://www.theatlantic.com/magazine/archive/2019/12/how-america-ends/600757/
9   https://www.nytimes.com/interactive/2019/08/08/opinion/sunday/party-polarization-quiz.
html?mtrref=undefined&gwh=014B458A2DD07F34BF497A1097927631&gwt=pay&asset
Type=REGIWALL
10   https://nymag.com/intelligencer/2017/09/can-democracy-survive-tribalism.html
11   https://www.jstor.org/stable/24027184?seq=1
12   https://www.washingtonpost.com/opinions/democracy-in-retreat/2016/03/13/dd2e5eba-e798-11e5-
a6f3-21ccdbc5f74e_story.html?itid=lk_inline_manual_18
13   https://www.theatlantic.com/ideas/archive/2020/01/
confidence-democracy-lowest-point-record/605686/
14   https://www.nybooks.com/daily/2020/03/23/
in-brazil-bolsonaro-gambles-on-a-coronavirus-culture-war/
15   https://www.washingtonpost.com/world/asia_pacific/as-world-looks-for-coronavirus-scapegoats-
india-pins-blame-on-muslims/2020/04/22/3cb43430-7f3f-11ea-84c2-0792d8591911_story.
html?itid=lk_inline_manual_23
16   https://www.npr.org/2020/01/30/800922222/
when-institutions-are-used-as-stages-people-lose-trust-book-argues
17   https://wwwnc.cdc.gov/eid/article/26/7/20-1595_article
18   https://www.who.int/mediacentre/news/ebola/06-october-2014/en/
19   https://www.wsj.com/articles/the-coronavirus-economic-reopening-will-be-fragile-partial-and-
slow-11586800447
20   https://www.wsj.com/articles/the-coronavirus-economic-reopening-will-be-fragile-partial-and-
slow-11586800447

21   https://www.washingtonpost.com/world/hungarian-parliament-hands-orban-power-to-rule-unchecked/2020/03/30/cc5135f6-7293-11ea-ad9b-254ec99993bc_story.html
22   https://www.npr.org/sections/coronavirus-live-updates/2020/03/24/820906636/concerns-in-philippines-after-duterte-given-emergency-powers-to-fight-covid-19-s%20https://www.ohchr.org/EN/NewsEvents/Pages/DisplayNews.aspx?NewsID=25832&LangID=E
23   https://www.nytimes.com/2020/03/17/world/europe/EU-closes-borders-virus.html
24   https://www.npr.org/sections/goatsandsoda/2020/03/30/819151076/how-do-you-wash-your-hands-to-fend-off-coronavirus-if-water-is-scarce
25   https://www.nytimes.com/2020/03/29/world/asia/coronavirus-india-migrants.html
26   https://www.washingtonpost.com/world/the_americas/for-brazils-bolsonaro-isolated-by-corruption-probe-and-virus-denial-the-troubles-mount/2020/04/28/de7de790-8951-11ea-8ac1-bfb250876b7a_story.html
27   https://www.forbes.com/sites/frantisekmarkovic/2019/09/06/vladimir-putins-regime-is-battling-to-survive/#10dca2f32c2e
28   https://www.dissentmagazine.org/article/uses-and-abuses-neoliberalism-debate
29   https://www.reaganfoundation.org/media/128614/inaguration.pdf
30   https://www.govexec.com/oversight/2020/04/wheres-money-keep-eye-cares-act/164334/
31   https://www.bbc.com/news/world-us-canada-52359100
32   https://fivethirtyeight.com/features/americans-trust-the-cdc-on-covid-19-trump-not-so-much/
33   https://www.weforum.org/agenda/2017/02/the-digital-revolution-is-destroying-our-democracies-it-doesn-t-have-to-be-that-way/
34   https://www.youtube.com/watch?v=rn55z95L1h8
35   https://assets.publishing.service.gov.uk/government/uploads/system/uploads/attachment_data/file/213717/dh_131040.pdf
36   http://www.mathsinindustry.co.nz/massey/fms/Colleges/College%20of%20Sciences/Epicenter/docs/ASVCS/Taylor_2003.pdf
37   https://www.gov.uk/government/publications/independent-review-into-the-response-to-the-2009-swine-flu-pandemic
38   https://www.theguardian.com/society/2011/oct/03/nhs-bill-doctors-lords
39   https://www.rdash.nhs.uk/wp-content/uploads/2017/08/Appendix-46-Aerosol-Generating-Procedures.pdf
40   https://www.ecdc.europa.eu/sites/default/files/media/en/publications/Publications/Preparedness%20planning%20against%20respiratory%20viruses%20-%20final.pdf
41   https://www.hsj.co.uk/patient-safety/trusts-hit-by-serious-apron-shortage-following-chinese-pollution-crackdown/7021483.article
42   https://www.bbc.co.uk/news/business-52319576
43   https://www.franceinter.fr/emissions/l-invite-de-8h20-le-grand-entretien/l-invite-de-8h20-le-grand-entretien-04-mars-2020
44   https://www.itv.com/news/2020-02-11/coronavirus-uk-boris-johnson-nhs-covid-19/
45   https://www.youtube.com/watch?v=IfJcwDaZrsA
46   https://milken-institute-covid-19-tracker.webflow.io/
47   https://www.independent.co.uk/news/world/europe/coronavirus-vaccine-trump-germany-us-dietmar-hopp-carevac-a9404646.html
48   https://hbr.org/2020/05/the-danger-of-vaccine-nationalism
49   https://www.theguardian.com/world/2020/may/18/former-who-board-member-warns-world-against-coronavirus-vaccine-nationalism
50   https://www.slu.edu/law/faculty/ana-santos-rutschman.php
51   https://www.slu.edu/law/health/index.php
52   https://www.independent.co.uk/news/world/europe/coronavirus-vaccine-trump-germany-us-dietmar-hopp-carevac-a9404646.html
53   https://www.curevac.com/
54   https://www.biopharmadive.com/news/coronavirus-curevac-trump-access-research-us/574181/
55   https://www.politico.eu/article/eu-weighs-into-german-american-spat-over-vaccine-company/
56   https://www.independent.co.uk/news/world/europe/coronavirus-vaccine-trump-germany-us-dietmar-hopp-carevac-a9404646.html
57   https://www.marketwatch.com/story/germany-investing-in-coronavirus-vaccine-maker-that-it-accused-the-trump-administration-of-trying-to-poach-2020-06-15
58   https://www.curevac.com/en/2020/06/15/bundesregierung-beteiligt-sich-mit-300-millionen-euro-an-curevac/
59   https://www.bloomberg.com/news/articles/2020-05-13/u-s-to-get-sanofi-covid-vaccine-first-if-it-succeeds-ceo-says

60 https://www.france24.com/en/20200514-france-says-unacceptable-for-sanofi-to-give-coronavirus-vaccine-to-us-first
61 https://www.france24.com/en/20200514-france-says-unacceptable-for-sanofi-to-give-coronavirus-vaccine-to-us-first
62 https://qz.com/india/506247/how-an-indian-horse-breeder-built-asias-largest-vaccine-company/
63 https://www.seruminstitute.com/
64 https://www.reuters.com/article/us-health-coronavirus-india-serum-insigh/how-one-indian-company-could-be-worlds-door-to-a-covid-19-vaccine-idUSKBN22Y2BI
65 https://www.reuters.com/article/us-health-coronavirus-india-vaccine/indias-serum-institute-to-make-millions-of-potential-coronavirus-vaccine-doses-idUSKCN22A2YY
66 https://hbr.org/2020/05/the-danger-of-vaccine-nationalism
67 https://www.europeanpharmaceuticalreview.com/news/118549/who-launches-access-to-covid-19-tools-accelerator/
68 https://www.livescience.com/covid-19-pandemic-vs-swine-flu.html
69 https://www.washingtonpost.com/wp-dyn/content/article/2009/05/06/AR2009050603760.html
70 https://www.washingtonpost.com/wp-dyn/content/article/2009/05/06/AR2009050603760.html
71 https://www.wsj.com/articles/SB124243015022925551
72 https://www.kff.org/news-summary/nine-countries-pledge-h1n1-vaccine-donations-to-developing-countries/
73 https://papers.ssrn.com/sol3/papers.cfm?abstract_id=3040974
74 https://www.nytimes.com/interactive/2020/science/coronavirus-vaccine-tracker.html
75 https://papers.ssrn.com/sol3/papers.cfm?abstract_id=3040974
76 https://www.ft.com/content/e92dbf94-d9a2-11e9-8f9b-77216ebe1f17
77 https://www.intelligenteconomist.com/deadweight-loss/
78 https://www.theverge.com/2020/2/27/21155879/alex-azar-coronavirus-vaccine-affordable-insurance
79 https://www.statnews.com/2020/03/05/coronavirus-vaccine-affordable-for-everyone/
80 https://pdfs.semanticscholar.org/d383/484a3a5c88ea853596e8bdebd00cca057e6c.pdf
81 https://www.yalelawjournal.org/article/innovation-policy-pluralism
82 https://www.heartlandalliance.org/covid-19-disproportionately-threatens-marginalized-and-vulnerable-populations/
83 https://www.npr.org/sections/health-shots/2020/05/30/865413079/what-do-coronavirus-racial-disparities-look-like-state-by-state
84 https://repository.law.umich.edu/mlr_online/vol118/iss1/5/
85 https://www.gavi.org/
86 https://www.who.int/publications/m/item/access-to-covid-19-tools-(act)-accelerator

Part Eight

Narratives of Resilience

8.1

A Call from Mothers of Color for True Family Engagement

by Carrie Sampson, Claudia Cervantes-Soon, Dawn M. Demps, Alexandria Estrella, & Lok-Sze Wong

Originally published in *Medium*, MAY 13, 2020

We are mothers of school-aged children and a collective group of education scholars—clinical, assistant, and associate professors; research associates, and doctoral students.

We are educators and researchers in one of the top-ranked education colleges in the U.S. Our scholarship focuses largely on improving educational equity. And our lived experiences as women of color and mothers with young children reflect the harsh realities of the social injustices that occur in schools and beyond.

Over the last few weeks, we struggled to write this collective piece because we are exhausted. We are working beyond our capacity to attend to our full-time jobs and our families' needs, including the loss of loved ones to COVID-19. And we are feeling a mix of emotions toward both our children's schools and the broader education system. We have felt anger, disappointment, fear, and hope. We have pushed through our exhaustion and emotions because we want to ensure that the voices of Black and brown mothers and othermothers are centered in the conversations that will move us forward as we—educators, families, communities—navigate our children's learning through this pandemic and beyond.

Our children attend traditional and charter schools in urban and suburban neighborhoods across the Phoenix metropolitan area. Arizona schools shut their doors eight weeks ago. Educators quickly developed plans for offering daily meals, technology, and online instruction that could happen in homes rather than classrooms. We applaud these efforts. And still, something major was missing. Aside from asking families if they have access to Wi-Fi and computers, no one from our children's schools asked how we, as families, are managing our children's learning at home. Nor have they asked what our most pressing concerns are during this pandemic, and then reflect on what that means for the content our kids need to learn right *now*.

In this major crisis, schools have literally moved into our living rooms, kitchens, and cars. And yet, we believe that many schools throughout the U.S. have missed this prime opportunity to meaningfully engage families. This is not surprising. Along with our personal experiences, plenty of research, including that recently published by Ann Ishimaru[1], reminds us that most schools fail to engage families as real partners in the formal education of our children, especially families of color and low-income families. Many educators assume we have nothing valuable to offer schools, seeing us as barriers to overcome or another cumbersome task on their already onerous to-do list.

The paradox of all this is that schooling can be NOTHING without families. This was true before the pandemic and is especially true now. So how do we move forward differently?

It is time for schools to put families at the center and develop, with families, particularly families of color, a curriculum that is humanizing, culturally-responsive, and revitalizing. This curriculum must be grounded in support, empathy, and love—one that views all families and children as embodying valuable knowledges, interests, and experiences.

Below we include a few recommendations on how educators might get started.

1. Meaningfully connect with students and families. We recognize that many teachers and school leaders are overwhelmed, juggling their personal and professional responsibilities in the midst of this pandemic. So throw out two weeks of assignments, and instead, like some teachers have done[2], focus on building relationships that matter and that can help craft a meaningful curriculum. One of our children had a virtual lunch with her former teacher and that was the highlight of her week; not the daily Google classroom meetings and assignments. Connect with your students and their families in whichever way is easiest for them whether that be video meetings, Facebook, phone calls, or text messages. When this is over, families should remember the ways you reached out and showed you cared rather than the stress of helping their children connect to their online class meetings and complete assignments that feel like busywork.

2. Take advantage of this time to honor teachers as professionals by leveraging their expertise. Sadly, the obsession with standardized tests and high-stakes account-ability in schools has limited our teachers' autonomy and creative potential, boxing their teaching into prepackaged drill-and-kill, decontextualized lessons. Most of the curriculum we received includes pre-packaged worksheets, videos, and activities; none of which are (or have been prior to this pandemic) cultur-ally responsive to our Black and brown children. How significant is learning about long division or the war of 1812 for the child who has to ride with his dad in the delivery truck all day, while he distributes groceries to our stores? With state and federal testing on pause this year, teachers have the opportu-nity to be creative and responsive. Three of us have benefited from creative options offered outside of our children's schools, including a Black-centered social studies course[3] taught by a mother in California and an environmental science class taught by an Oakland-based activist. What if we didn't have to go beyond our children's schools to find these options? What if our schools were responsive to our kids' current interests?

3. Recognize that much of children's most critical learning happens at home. The cultural strengths of families and their surrounding communities can offer important curriculum insights to educators. Solicit and take seriously families' collective ideas, concerns, and feedback. Perhaps school and district leaders can host school and district-wide meetings with families to build community. At the very least, schools can survey their families. And while surveying is a start, educators must go beyond this to develop lasting relationships that build trust between schools and communities.

It is time for educators to radically shift their mentality about family en-gagement. Nobody can predict what next week will look like. But when schools and families are intimately connected, the opportunity to collectively love and support our children is ever more present.

Will we remain unchanged, insisting on detached, top-down learning in the face of human tragedy? Or will we seize this time as a unique opportunity to truly pause and reflect, to reach out to families and really get to know them, and to rethink the meaning of education so that we can co-create a new way?

8.2

Resilience is the Goal of Governments and Employers Who Expect People to Endure Crisis

by John Patrick Leary

Originally published in *Teen Vogue*, JULY 1, 2020

This op-ed argues that the modern emphasis on "resilience" means we're expected to endure hardship and make the best of it.

John F. Kennedy once told[4] an Indiana audience that "when written in Chinese," the word "crisis" contains the characters for "emergency" and "opportunity." It doesn't[5]. But ever since that 1959 speech, politicians and motivational speakers have invoked[6] Kennedy's mistaken language tutorial to talk about the importance of persistence, creativity, and, these days, that favorite buzzword, *resilience*. Resilience is everywhere, its popularity cresting with the setbacks that afflict us: climate change[7], unemployment[8], broken public infrastructure[9], and more recently, COVID-19. Resilience is designed for a world in constant crisis, where instead of benefiting from the repair or prevention of disasters, we are asked to make the best of these circumstances. As Andrew Zolli, author of a book[10] on the topic, put it[11] in a 2012 *New York Times* op-ed, "Where sustainability aims to put the world back into balance, resilience looks for ways to manage in an imbalanced world."

The most literal meaning of the word is "elasticity," or an object's ability to retain its original shape after being bent or compressed, like a trampoline bouncing back after a child jumps on it. This isn't how you usually encounter the word, though; instead, resilience is invoked metaphorically to describe an elusive quality of cities, nations, age cohorts, and individual psyches—in short, anything that can experience a trauma. Local governments and foundations often deploy[12] it as a synonym for disaster-preparedness. Schools[13] and[14] universities[15] teach it to students. A widely quoted definition[16] by psychologists from the American Psychological Association calls it "the process of adapting well in the face of adversity, trauma, tragedy, threats or significant sources of stress—such as family and relationship problems, serious health problems, or workplace and financial stressors." A San Francisco psychotherapist and "executive coach," whose website[17] features the old saw about "crisis" in Chinese, offers advice[18] on building resilience during the pandemic. Self-help and parenting books offer lessons in boosting it in yourself and your kids. Google "resilience" and you'll have more listicles and books offering you three[19], five[20], or seven[21] steps to make yourself more resilient than you could ever muster the resilience to read.

No one doubts that determination and toughness are worthwhile character traits, but a problem arises when we build our political system around the need to endure hardship. Resilience can be an idea well-suited to an era of budget cuts and inequality, according to sociologist William Davies, author[22] of *The Happiness Industry: How the Government and Big Business Sold Us Well-Being*. "It is founded on an ideology that the political and economic world is never going to change, so people have to change themselves so as to cope with it better," he tells *Teen Vogue*. "Therefore people need to have certain character traits so as to be capable of living in a world that ultimately won't look after them."

The idea of resilience as a policy tool and character trait to be cultivated raises some uncomfortable questions: Why are some people asked to be more resilient than others? How much should people be expected to "bend" before they break? And why don't we just stop bending people?

Creating Resilient Citizens

Viewing resilience as a quality of societies and organizations, rather than of objects, was pioneered by C. S. Holling, an environmental scientist who defined it in 1973 as "a measure of the persistence of systems and of their ability to absorb change and disturbance and still maintain the same relationships between populations or state variables"[23]. The field Holling promoted, "ecological economics," applied this concept to the management of natural resources[24]. Holling was trying to describe the ways in which disturbed ecosystems recover—or don't.

Over the past two decades or so, the concept has been taken up in self-help and business journalism, without the caution that often accompanies environmental and psychological discussions of the concept. Recall the American Psychological Association article's measured definition: "adapting well" to trauma or stress. For some of us, adapting well might mean a whole lot of things; sometimes simply getting through the day counts. But too often, resilience is now used to mean "bouncing back"[25], or coming back stronger than ever.

For self-help writers and other professional advice-givers, resilience is predicated less on persistence — critical in Holling's discussion of damaged ecologies — and more on success. "Resilience: The Key Ingredient of Success," announced[26] the headline of an article by a *Forbes* contributor. "Resilience: The Secret to Success," crowed[27] the American Management Association. "Why do some people and some companies buckle under pressure?" asked a 2002 article published in *Harvard Business Review*, the journal of the famous business school[28]. "And what makes others bend and ultimately bounce back?" The unstated implication of much resilience advice is that some people have it, and others don't: Don't be one of the weaklings.

The resilience industry acknowledges that we all go through rough patches, but it insists that our setbacks will only make us stronger. Resilience resources, like this one[29] from Stanford University, aim to destigmatize failure by treating it as an inevitable part of taking on a worthy challenge. But these resources also tend to assume that success will invariably come later. With resilience, a university website puts it, failure can be the "revenue" we invest[30] in later success; a video testimonial[31] from a cofounder of Pandora, a Stanford grad, recalls his early struggles in this way. But while most business ventures fail, student debt skyrockets[32] and college tuition spirals out of control, it's unfair to preach resilience as a prelude to business triumph. What if it's just a willingness to endure what you shouldn't have to?

This may be the biggest problem with the concept: the way it scripts failure, and therefore also success, as an individual achievement, shorn of context. It may be nice to imagine otherwise, but individuals are not islands, much less ecosystems. We are always and everywhere subject to pressures we cannot control—some of us more than others, of course. All the resilience in the world cannot protect you from a pathogen; conversely, it's much easier to bounce back from a hardship when you are already healthy, supported, and comfortably housed.

When we honor Flint residents as Michigan's "most resilient"[33], as the University of Michigan's College of Entrepreneurship recently did, or celebrate Haitians as "the most resilient people on earth"[34], as the U.S. Agency for International Development did in 2017, after the country's devastating 2010 earthquake, we need to ask a question: Why are the people of Flint and Haiti being given so many opportunities to demonstrate their resilience to catastrophe? This is the point of a much-circulated poster[35] in New Orleans after Hurricane Katrina, when a local lawyer, Tracie Washington, conveyed this angry assessment[36] of outsider praise for the Crescent City's resilience: "Every time you say, 'Oh, they're so resilient,' that means you can do something else to me." Celebrating resilience asks us to accept that hardship is inevitable, and we'd better get used to it.

Resilience at Work

A similar dynamic can apply in the workplace, where resilience is pitched by many employers as a strategy for managing everyday stress. Redesigning

Wellness[37], a consultancy that sells what it calls "Employee Resilience Training" for employers, advertises its product as a means to reduce absenteeism, turnover, and workplace accidents.

Margaret, a nurse in suburban Detroit working during the COVID-19 pandemic (who agreed to speak with *Teen Vogue* anonymously to avoid offending her employer), has encountered resilience training at her hospital. Being "resilient," she says with some sarcasm, means "the ability to cope with any amount of stress while still being able to perform our job." Nurses have demanding jobs that certainly require emotional and physical strength. The problem, as Margaret suggests, is that recovering her strength should not be solely her responsibility[38]. Rather than address what she describes as chronic staffing shortages in her unit, Margaret says hospital management has recently offered resilience and mindfulness workshops to its overworked staff. Before the pandemic, Margaret says, she just rolled her eyes at this sort of break-room encouragement. "I am more bitter about it post-COVID," she explains, "because the situation so catastrophically exceeds what any individual's resilience can do."

Given its slippery usage, it is perhaps appropriate that the word's probable origin is from the Latin root *resilientia,* or "fact of avoiding." No hardship emerges from a vacuum, and it is this context that resilience allows us to overlook. As another New Orleans resident put it[39], "When we celebrate resilience, we focus the spotlight on the people who got screwed over. The institutions that did the screwing-over take the opportunity to slink off into the shadows."

8.3

Hawaii Considers an Explicitly Feminist Plan for COVID-Era Economic Recovery

by Mara Dolan

Originally published in *Truthout,* MAY 26, 2020

"The road to economic recovery should not be across women's backs," reads the first sentence of Hawaii's Feminist Economic Recovery Plan[40].

As states put forth dozens of recovery plans that all aim to redress the economic devastation caused by the COVID-19 pandemic, Hawaii's remains the first and only that is explicitly "feminist."

The plan—which was released on April 14 by the Hawaii Department of Human Services' State Commission on the Status of Women—does not seek to reinstate a status quo riddled with inequality. Instead, it recognizes the current crisis as the "moment to build a system that is capable of delivering gender equality."

It calls for a universal basic income, countering the systemic wage and wealth gender gap. It calls for free, publicly provided child care for essential workers, a nearly $25/hour minimum wage for single mothers, and the creation of public emergency funds available for high-risk groups, like undocumented women who are ineligible for the federal cash refund, domestic workers who are experiencing financial hardship, and people classified as "sex trafficking survivors who have recently exited the commercial sex industry."

The plan calls for a reinvestment in midwifery services to provide maternal health care as hospitals become strained with pandemic response. It calls for a 20 percent pro-rata share of the state's COVID-19-response funds to go immediately, no strings attached, to Native Hawaiian communities. The 23-page document is a vision for a new kind of economy while also conveying concrete policy recommendations, delivered directly to Hawaii legislators as they begin to apportion state funds toward recovery.

Khara Jabola-Carolus saw the writing on the wall early. Jabola-Carolus works as the executive director of the State Commission on the Status of Women, and by early March, had seen enough to know that this would be a severely gendered crisis. Women, burdened with the vast amount of unpaid care work, were most impacted by stay-at-home orders, child care and school closures. Women quarantined in abusive homes with their perpetrators had little to no access to financial and social support systems. Women were performing the majority of essential, high-risk health care positions and other essential care work positions like teaching, but weren't even receiving enough protective equipment or livable wages. Any policy response that ignored these gendered realities would only reinforce them.

Jabola-Carolus recalls the exact moment she knew she needed to push for a feminist response. As the head of the Commission on the Status of Women, she was asked by legislators working on the state budget to provide a pro-woman plan to restructure and stimulate the economy—in less than half a day. "I was given only a few hours to answer these enormous questions and it made me damn angry. How could executives and bureaucrats, so far removed from the edge and illiterate in the struggles of women, define their future in a few hours?"

She wanted to draft the recommendations in a very different way, one that modeled a community-based consultative process that prioritized Native, immigrant, and working-class women and LGBTQIA+ peoples. "We were careful to go beyond the elite, White-dominated 'advocates' circles," she told *Truthout*. The contributors in this circle were organizers, academics, activists, midwives and mothers, representing grassroots organizations, large nonprofits, unions and government agencies.

"This is how we should be doing all of our policymaking and planning," said Kathleen Algire, director of the Hawaii Children's Action Network, who was a member of the task force. "We can no longer say that 'we can't wait for the time community collaboration takes.' We did it fast and we didn't sacrifice the community to get it done."

Mykie Ozoa, an organizer with AF3IRM Hawaii, the state's largest grassroots feminist network, saw this collaboration as key to producing pragmatic recommendations. "The Commission was adamant that the voices of women organizing to address issues on the ground in our communities were included, and I believe it is one reason this plan is so unique and offers urgent but easily attainable recommendations."

Within the plan itself, the attention given to care work, such as childcare and eldercare, is substantial. "You cannot separate women from caregiving, unpaid or paid," said Algire, who helped draft the childcare recommendations. They include universal free childcare for all emergency and essential workers, paid family and sick leave, and mandated pay parity for child care workers to educators and nurses. "What we keep repeating is 'there is no economic recovery without child care.' For parents to go back to work, their children need to be cared for."

Algire pointed out the stark shortage of childcare spaces available in Hawaii, even before the pandemic, with space for only 1 in 37 toddlers in the state. For many, childcare costs are already their second-highest expense, after rent. "When families don't have access to safe, affordable, quality child care, they are put in an impossible situation," Algire told *Truthout*. "If it's a two-parent household, one parent will likely leave the workforce. Because women are paid less, they are typically who we see staying home."

This often costs two-parent households a second income and many single mothers their *only* income, and it also impacts the employment side of the childcare industry, too, where the workforce is mostly women. "Like many other professions, you may see men owning or serving as directors of large centers, but the primary workforce is women," Algire said. "Child care is a low-paying job and [that fact] is a disgrace. These are the people we are entrusting our children's lives to and they should be paid more than minimum wage."

The plan emphasizes that the industry cannot return to this unsustainable "normal"—state economic policies must help it change. "If a community, state or country wants to see workforce participation like we had [pre-pandemic], child care as an industry will need support. It will need to be subsidized," Algire said. "The folks that are supporting, teaching, guiding, caring and loving our kids deserve better. Caring for children is hard, draining work. It is undervalued because it is seen as 'women's work.' We've got to change that."

Health care for women and LGBTQIA+ people is also centered in the plan, with significant attention paid to supporting maternal health services in the state. Tanya Smith-Johnson, who worked at an organization called The Big Push for Midwives, told *Truthout* that maternal care policy must include deep and consistent consultation with pregnant and birthing people in order to fully address their needs, especially Black and Native people, who face additional marginalization within the maternal health care system.

In fact, one of the five key recommendations made in diversifying and reshaping the economy is "to harness the role of midwifery to improve deficits in maternal and neonatal health care in Hawaii, especially in rural areas." The plan's recommendations include ensuring that insurance companies and Medicaid cover midwifery services fully, and matching hospital-based midwives with community midwives to meet the increasing demand for out-of-hospital birth options, as many who are pregnant wish to give birth out of hospitals to reduce COVID-19 transmission risk.

The writers of the plan wanted the word "feminism" front and center—in the report itself and in the conversations it will spur. "If the plan isn't feminist, it's patriarchal and will fail to deliver a resilient, strong economy," Jabola-Carolus said, and urged that the individual policy recommendations put forth cannot be removed from the systemic critique that "feminism" actually articulates. "Feminism, in terms of policy, is mostly stuff that has broad public support, but we need to *say* 'feminist' in order to actually talk about the culture surrounding those policies. It has to be about root causes," Jabola-Carolus said.

Take paid family leave, for example. It's an incredibly popular policy and would decrease one form of gender inequality in the workplace, where women are often forced out of careers in order to perform unpaid care work for family members. But if paid family leave is not introduced as an explicitly feminist policy, it can erase the broader structures of inequality that allow other forms of workplace discrimination to persist. It just seems like one problem with one policy fix, and not part of anything systemic. For Jabola-Carolus, "this was a call to the left to be explicitly feminist in the same way that it's finally, explicitly naming systemic racism." She says naming feminism is critical for progressive movements' policy platforms to adequately address institutionalized oppression.

The word "feminism" might be used in popular culture more than ever before, but this is not reflected in policy. Only one federal bill has ever been proposed that uses it: a 2017 piece of legislation to commemorate women's rights leader Bella Abzug for her "feminist presence" in Congress.

Jabola-Carolus said she wasn't aware of any other state-level economic plan that put feminism in its title. All of the advocates *Truthout* spoke to also viewed this first-time inclusion of "feminist" as hugely significant. Sarah Michal Hamid, a youth organizer who also sat on the committee, said it was "groundbreaking," as "it means that finally a government agency is recognizing that women and non-men are unevenly burdened under our current economy and that this needs to change."

But the goal is for its usage in policy to be eventually commonplace, a consequence of serious gender consideration in all planning. "It shouldn't be unique that a state plan centers women and girls. When the most marginalized are centered, everyone else's needs will also be met," Ozoa said. "I hope that other states use this opportunity to take stock and reprioritize."

The women who put together the Hawaii plan do believe that their work can provide a pathway for feminists' engagement in other states.

"I hope other states adapt it to their needs, keeping the essence of the document because it really is a plan that is universal and necessary," Smith-Johnson told *Truthout*. This might look different based on each state's demographic, employment and industry needs but could share common commitments to tackling economic realities that marginalize women.

For other states embarking on their own drafting processes, Hawaii's advocates are the first to admit that there is room for these recommendations to grow. In future iterations, both Jabola-Carolus and Ozoa noted they would like to see a stronger integration of transformative justice frameworks that pursue gender-based violence prevention without relying on mass incarceration. Smith-Johnson would like to see how these recommendations could influence federal-level feminist economic policy: "Can you imagine the impact that would have?"

For now, the report lives in the halls of Hawaii's House and Senate, as legislators review proposals and apportion COVID-19 recovery funds in the weeks that follow. "I know this plan will have a ripple effect on how we move forward," said Algire. "Unlike other plans that will sit on a shelf and be forgotten, this will be a guiding document for years to come."

Hamid said she hopes that the questions raised in this report reverberate all around the country. "As other governments begin this 'road to recovery,' they should carefully consider who is allowed on that road, and whose backs it is being built on."

8.4

Naomi Klein: 'We Must Not Return to the Pre-COVID Status Quo, Only Worse'

by Katharine Viner

Originally published in *The Guardian*, JULY 13, 2020

What kind of world will the coronavirus leave us with? Interviewed for a Guardian Live event, the activist and author insists that the climate, equality, and fairness must be at the heart of the post-pandemic recovery.

Katharine Viner: Hello, Naomi. How are you finding lockdown?

Naomi Klein: For those of us who were teaching our students by Zoom, as I was—homeschooling, doing that juggle and figuring out how to bake—we had it really cushy. Now I am back in Canada for the summer with my family, in quarantine because in Canada, if you come from the US, you have to be in very strict quarantine. I have not left the house in almost two weeks. I am actually developing some phobias about leaving lockdown.

Katharine Viner: There is a great quote in one of your recent essays from a tech CEO, who says: "Humans are biohazards, machines are not." It chilled me to the bone and made me fearful for the future. And you have written interestingly about the "Screen New Deal"[41].

Naomi Klein: Silicon Valley had this pre-existing agenda before COVID that imagined replacing so many of our personal bodily experiences by inserting technology in the middle of them.

So for the few spaces where tech is not already mediating our relationships, there was a plan—to replace in-person teaching with virtual learning, for instance, and in-person medicine with telehealth and in-person delivery with robots. All of this has been rebranded, post-COVID, as a touchless technology, as a way of replacing what has been diagnosed as the problem, which is the problem of touch.

And yet, on a personal level, what we miss most is touch. And so we need to expand the menu of options about how we live with COVID, because we do not have a vaccine; it is not about to arrive. Even if there is a breakthrough, it's going to be many, many months, possibly years before it can be rolled out at the scale we would need it.

So how are we going to live with this thing? Are we going to accept pre-COVID "normal", only much diminished, without the relationships that sustain us? Are we going to allow our kids to have all of their learning mediated by technology? Or are we going to invest in people?

Instead of pouring all of our money into a Screen New Deal and trying to solve problems in a way that diminishes our quality of life, why do we not go on a teacher-hiring spree? Why do we not have twice as many teachers with half-the-size classrooms and figure out a way to do outdoor education?

There are so many ways we can think about responding to this crisis that do not accept this idea that we have to return to the pre-COVID status quo, only worse, only with more surveillance, more screens, and less human contact.

Katharine Viner: Do you see any governments talking like that?

Naomi Klein: I was heartened to hear Jacinda Ardern talk about a four-day working week as a solution[42] to the fact that New Zealand is very dependent on tourism dollars, and yet New Zealand is probably the country that has dealt with the pandemic better than any others in terms of its fatality rates. It can't fling its doors open to tourists in the way that it has in the past, so there's this idea that maybe New Zealanders should work less, be paid the same, and have more leisure time to be able to enjoy their own country safely.

How do we slow down? This is what I am thinking a lot about. It feels like every time we slam our foot on the accelerator marked "business as usual" or "back to normal", the virus surges back and says: "Slow down."

Katharine Viner: We all love those moments of slowing down, but the UK government is hell-bent on getting back to normal, come what may. Everything opening, pubs opening, it is desperate to get us to go on holiday. There is an urgency not to change anything about how we live, just get back to how it was before.

Naomi Klein: And it is madness. It is a very small percentage of the population that wants to just fling the doors open. It is a majority that actually is much more concerned about returning to work before it is safe, sending their kids to school before it is safe. It's sometimes framed as giving people what they want, but this is not what the polling shows.

There are similarities between the way Donald Trump has handled it and the way Boris Johnson has handled it. They are turning it into some test of masculinity, even in Johnson's case after having the virus. Jair Bolsonaro was talking about how he was an athlete so he knows he will handle it [the Brazilian president revealed he has coronavirus shortly after this interview took place]; Trump was talking about his good genes.

Katharine Viner: I was interested in your views on why you think the civil rights protests, in light of George Floyd's death, have happened now? It seems intriguing, in the midst of one crisis, that, around the world, there are these huge demonstrations against racism.

Naomi Klein: This is not the first uprising of its kind. But I think there were certain aspects of it that were unique because of COVID and the outsized impact of the pandemic for African Americans in cities like Chicago where, by some counts, 70% of the fatalities from COVID were African Americans.

Whether it's because they are the ones performing those at-risk jobs, without protections, or because of the legacies of environmental pollution in their communities, stress, trauma, unsafe workplaces and discriminatory healthcare. Black communities are bearing a disproportionate burden of the fatalities from the virus, defying this idea that we were all in this together.

In the midst of this moment of profound trauma, those killings—of Ahmaud Arbery, of George Floyd, of Breonna Taylor—slice through that.

But then there is a question that a lot of people are asking, which is what are all these non-Black people doing at the protests? That is what is new, certainly at this scale. Many of these demonstrations are truly multiracial; Black-led multi-racial demonstrations. Why is this time different?

I have a few ideas. One has to do with the softness that the pandemic has introduced into our culture. When you slow down, you can feel things; when you're in that constant rat race, it doesn't leave much time for empathy. From its very beginning, the virus has forced us to think about interdependencies and relationships. The first thing you are thinking about is: everything I touch, what has somebody else touched? The food I am eating, the package that was just delivered, the food on the shelves. These are connections that capitalism teaches us not to think about.

I think that being forced to think in more interconnected ways may have softened more of us up to think about these racist atrocities, and not say they are somebody else's issue.

Katharine Viner: There's a great line in the new introduction to *On Fire*, your latest book[43], when you say: "whatever was bad before the disaster downgraded to unbearable"—it's an unbearable situation the way Black men are treated by the police.

Naomi Klein: There is always this discourse whenever disasters hit: "Climate change doesn't discriminate, the pandemic doesn't discriminate. We are all in this together." But that is not true. That is not how disasters act. They act as magnifiers and they act as intensifiers. If you had a job in an Amazon warehouse that was making you sick before, or if you were in a long-term care facility that was already treating you as if your life was of no value, that was bad before—but all of that gets magnified to unbearable now. And if you were disposable before, you're sacrificial now.

And we are only talking about the violence that we can see. What we have to talk more about is the violence that's hidden, and that's domestic violence. To put it bluntly, when men are stressed, women get it in the face and so do kids. These lockdowns are so stressful because families don't have any reprieve from each other and even the best family needs a little bit of space. Then you add layoffs, economic stress. It's a very bad situation for women right now.

Katharine Viner: I know you spent a lot of the last year working on the Green New Deal and the Bernie Sanders campaign. How does it all look now? Do you feel more or less positive about the potential?

Naomi Klein: On some level, it is harder. You mentioned Bernie and certainly, my preferred outcome would be a presidential candidate who is running a campaign with the Green New Deal at its center. I do believe we will only win this with an interplay of mass-movement pressure from the outside, but also a receptivity from the inside. I think that we had that chance with Bernie.

It is harder with Joe Biden, but not impossible. At the end of *On Fire*, I gave 10 reasons in favor of a Green New Deal and why it is good climate policy. One of those reasons is that it is recession-proof. We have this really bad track record in the climate movement of winning gains when the economy is doing relatively well because the kind of climate solutions we get from governments tend to be these neoliberal, market-based solutions, like climate taxes or renewable energy policies that are perceived to make energy costs more expensive, or carbon taxing that makes the price of petrol more expensive. As soon as you have an economic downturn, the support for these policies reliably evaporates. We saw that after the 2008 financial crisis. Climate has got a reputation as being a bourgeois thing—the issue that you care about if you don't have to worry about putting food on the table.

What is important about a Green New Deal is that it is modelled after one of the greatest economic stimulus programs of all time, during the greatest economic crisis of all time, and that is FDR's New Deal during the Great Depression. Because of this, the biggest pushback that I got when I released *On Fire* a little less than a year ago was: "But we don't do things like this when the economy is doing well."

The only times that we can point to—and this is a hard truth—when our societies have moved fast and changed big and catalytically are moments of great depression or war. Yet we now know we can change quickly. We have seen it. We have dramatically changed our lives. And we found out that our governments have trillions of dollars that they could have marshalled this whole time.

All of that is potentially radicalizing. I do feel we have a chance. I would not describe myself as optimistic because this is a future we have to fight for. But if we just look at moments in history when we have won big changes, they are moments like this.

8.5

How the Fight Against AIDS Can Inform the Fight Against COVID-19

by Clyde Haberman

Originally published in *The New York Times*, JULY 2, 2020

Dr. Anthony S. Fauci grappled with another health crisis decades ago. What he told Retro Report about the effort against AIDS could apply to the battle against the coronavirus.

Dr. Anthony S. Fauci saw early on how the virus was killing people whose ability to fight disease had weakened disastrously. "I said, 'Whoa, we really have an issue here,'" he said. "It seems to be spreading and spreading."

Dr. Deborah L. Birx, his colleague in the current struggle to tame the novel coronavirus[44], recalled moments "when you not only couldn't make a diagnosis, you didn't know what the problem was, and you didn't know how to treat it."

"It was," she said, "devastating."

Neither of them had the coronavirus pandemic in mind when they made those comments. Instead, they were reflecting on a much earlier time in their public health careers—the 1980s and '90s—when another plague raised discomfiting questions about how vigorously the United States dealt with ruinous infection. For both doctors, the enemy then was H.I.V., the human immuno-deficiency virus, which at its direst led to the life-threatening acquired immune deficiency syndrome, best known as AIDS.

As shown in this latest offering from Retro Report[45], which uses video to cast a spotlight on past events and help illuminate the present, the AIDS epidemic of the '80s resembled the coronavirus pandemic in a notable respect: It caught this country napping.

"The flags were going up, and the warning bells were rung," said Allan M. Brandt, a historian of medicine in a remote interview with Retro Report. But "the United States was extremely poorly prepared to deal with H.I.V.," Mr. Brandt said. "We didn't have a recent history of massive infectious epidemic diseases. We didn't have a preparedness apparatus."

"One of the things about epidemics is that the clock is always moving, and that was really true with H.I.V.," he continued. "Many people died because of the very slow and resistant and inadequate and inconsistent responses."

Sounds familiar in the age of COVID-19, some would say.

AIDS has yet to be conquered, but medications have greatly subdued it in this country, to such an extent that Americans routinely forget the panic and pain of three decades ago as the virus's spread reached crisis dimensions. In those years, the toll fell most heavily on gay men and on drug addicts using dirty needles. That made it easy for many people to shrug off AIDS as not their concern, just a disease confined to those living on society's margins.

Government officials showed scant sense of urgency, and the same might be said about many news organizations. The intense media coverage in late May when the number of United States coronavirus deaths surpassed 100,000[46] contrasts sharply with what happened when the AIDS epidemic reached that same milestone in 1991. *The New York Times*, for example, took note of it with an Associated Press article at the bottom of Page A18.

Even Dr. Fauci came under withering attack back then from AIDS activists who accused him of moving too hesitantly to find a remedy. One of them, Larry

Kramer[47], who died in May at 84, went so far as to call the doctor an "incompetent idiot" and "a murderer." While he may not have appreciated the venom, Dr. Fauci came to agree that the federal bureaucracy had been overly cautious and needed to up its game. Over time, the two men bonded; in later years Mr. Kramer described Dr. Fauci as a "true and great hero" in the AIDS crisis.

Part of the problem in the 1980s was that the country had let its guard down. So many killer diseases had been vanquished—smallpox, polio, typhoid fever, diphtheria and more—that quarantines and other once-automatic protective measures faded into the dim recesses of collective memory. "By the early '80s, when AIDS emerged," Mr. Brandt said, "we had let our public health infrastructure deteriorate, and it was poorly funded—really poorly structured."

Smugness had become a formidable enemy of its own. In a 1992 report, the nonprofit organization Institute of Medicine, now called the National Academy of Medicine, concluded that "complacency (i.e., the assumption that we have conquered a disease and can thus shift our concern to other pressing problems) can also constitute a major threat to health."

Since then there have been plenty of warnings that health crises could descend like sudden rain on a clear day. Five years ago, Bill Gates cautioned that if millions were to die, the cause would most likely be "a highly infectious virus rather than a war." Both Presidents George W. Bush and Barack Obama spoke of the need for clear policies and procedures to be firmly in place well ahead of disaster. "If we wait for a pandemic to appear," Mr. Bush said in 2005, "it will be too late to prepare."

Trump's attitude could not have been more different. As recently as late February, with the coronavirus whirling around the globe, he argued against the need for elaborate public-health systems to be kept on standby, ready to roll whenever disaster struck. "Rather than spending the money, and I am a businessperson, I don't like having thousands of people around when you don't need them," he said. "When we need them, we can get them back very quickly." That proved not to be the case. Stephen K. Bannon, Mr. Trump's onetime chief strategist, has told *The Times* that the administration never took seriously the possibility of a calamity like this coronavirus.

Comparisons to the most catastrophic years of the AIDS crisis go further. Then as now, testing and contact tracing were essential, but many in the most vulnerable groups resisted. It was partly because they feared leaving themselves open to anti-gay discrimination; partly it reflected a mistrust of the government and the medical establishment. A similar lack of faith in authority is evident these days among Americans who refuse to wear masks or be tested for the coronavirus, and who insist they want nothing to do with any vaccine that may come along.

And then as now, there was Dr. Fauci in the eye of the storm. As director of the National Institute of Allergy and Infectious Diseases, he has been an adviser to six presidents, with a sense of mission that remains unchanged. What he told Retro Report about the effort against AIDS could readily apply now to the battle against COVID-19: "I took very seriously to make sure that what I said was never sugarcoating," he said. "Because when you're dealing with any public health challenge, particularly a disease of the nature of H.I.V., communication with the public is as important as the science that we do."

The 12-minute video[48] with this article (entitled "Footage of Dr. Fauci Dealing with the AIDS Epidemic Offers Lessons") is part of a documentary series presented by The New York Times. The video project was started with a grant from Christopher Buck. Retro Report, led by Kyra Darnton, is a nonprofit media organization examining the history and context behind today's news. To watch more, subscribe to the Retro Report newsletter[49], and follow Retro Report on YouTube[50] and Twitter[51].

8.6

What Mutual Aid Can Do During a Pandemic

by Jia Tolentino

Originally published in *The New Yorker*, MAY 11, 2020

A radical practice is suddenly getting mainstream attention. Will it change how we help one another?

We are not accustomed to destruction looking, at first, like emptiness. The coronavirus pandemic is disorienting in part because it defies our normal cause-and-effect shortcuts to understand the world. The source of danger is invisible; the most effective solution involves willing paralysis; we won't know the consequences of today's actions until two weeks have passed. Everything circles a bewildering paradox: other people are both a threat and a lifeline. Physical connection could kill us, but civic connection is the only way to survive.

In March, even before widespread workplace closures and self-isolation, people throughout the country began establishing informal networks to meet the new needs of those around them. In Aurora, Colorado, a group of librarians[52] started assembling kits of essentials for the elderly and for children who wouldn't be getting their usual meals at school. Disabled people in the Bay Area organized assistance for one another[53]; a large collective in Seattle[54] set out explicitly to help "Undocumented, LGBTQI, Black, Indigenous, people of color, elderly, and disabled, folxs who are bearing the brunt of this social crisis." Undergrads helped other undergrads who had been barred from dorms and cut off from meal plans. Prison abolitionists raised money so that incarcerated people[55] could purchase commissary soap. And, in New York City, dozens of groups[56] across all five boroughs signed up volunteers to provide child care and pet care, deliver medicine and groceries, and raise money for food and rent. Relief funds were organized for movie-theatre employees[57], sex workers[58], and street vendors[59]. Shortly before the city's restaurants closed, on March 16th, leaving nearly a quarter of a million people out of work, three restaurant employees started the Service Workers Coalition[60], quickly raising more than twenty-five thousand dollars to distribute as weekly stipends. Similar groups, some of which were organized by restaurant owners, are now active nationwide.

As the press reported on this immediate outpouring of self-organized voluntarism, the term applied to these efforts, again and again, was "mutual aid," which has entered the lexicon of the coronavirus era alongside "social distancing" and "flatten the curve." It's not a new term, or a new idea, but it has generally existed outside the mainstream. Informal child-care collectives, transgender support groups, and other ad-hoc organizations operate without the top-down leadership or philanthropic funding that most charities depend on. There is no comprehensive directory of such groups, most of which do not seek or receive much attention. But, suddenly, they seemed to be everywhere.

On March 17th, I signed up for a new mutual-aid network in my neighborhood, in Brooklyn, and used a platform called Leveler to make micropayments to out-of-work freelancers. Then I trekked to the thirty-five-thousand-square-foot Fairway in Harlem to meet Liam Elkind, a founder of Invisible Hands, which was providing free grocery delivery to the elderly, the ill, and the immunocompromised in New York. Elkind, a junior at Yale, had been at his family's place, in Morningside Heights, for spring break when the crisis began. Working with his friends Simone Policano, an artist, and Healy Chait, a business major at NYU, he built the group's sleek Web site in a day. During the next ninety-six hours, twelve hundred people volunteered; some of them helped to translate the organization's flyer into more than a dozen languages and distributed copies of it to buildings around the city. By the time I met him, Elkind and his co-founders had spoken to people hoping to create Invisible Hands chapters in San Francisco, Los Angeles, Boston, and Chicago. The group was featured on "Fox & Friends," in a segment about young people stepping up in the pandemic; the co-host Brian Kilmeade encouraged viewers to send in more "inspirational stories and photos of people doing great things."

At the Fairway, Elkind, who has dark hair and a chipper student-body-president demeanor, put on a pair of latex gloves and grabbed a shopping basket, which he sanitized with a wipe. He was getting groceries for an immunocompromised woman in Harlem. "Scallions are the onion things, right?" he said, as we wound through the still robust produce section. At the time, those who signed up to volunteer for Invisible Hands joined a group text; when requests for help came in, texts went out, and volunteers claimed them on a first-come-first-served basis. They called the recipients to ask what they needed, then dropped the grocery bags at their doorsteps; the recipients left money under their mats or in mailboxes. The group was planning to raise funds to buy groceries for those who couldn't afford them, Elkind told me. While we stood in the dairy section trying to decide between low-fat Greek yogurt and nonfat regular—the store was out of nonfat Greek—a reporter from "Inside Edition" materialized and began snapping photographs. Elkind apologized; he hadn't meant to double-book media engagements. "Not to be trite, but I feel like this is spreading faster than the virus," he said.

The next day, Representative Alexandria Ocasio-Cortez held a public conference call with the organizer Mariame Kaba about how to build a mutual-aid network. Kaba is the founder of Project Nia, a prison-abolitionist organization that successfully campaigned for the right of Illinois minors to have their arrest records expunged when they turn eighteen. "There are two ways that this can go for us," Ocasio-Cortez said on the call. "We can buy into the old frameworks of, when a disaster hits, it's every person for themselves. Or we can affirmatively choose a different path. And we can build a different world, even if it's just on our building floor, even if it's just in our neighborhood, even if it's just on our block." She pointed out that those in a position to help didn't have to wait "for Congress to pass a bill, or the President to do something." The following week, the *Times* ran a column[61] headlined "Feeling Powerless About Coronavirus? Join a Mutual-Aid Network." *Vox*, *Teen Vogue*, and other outlets also ran explainers and how-tos.

Mutual-aid work thrives on sustained personal relationships, but the coronavirus has necessitated that relationships be built online. After meeting Elkind, I joined a Zoom call with thirteen students at the University of Minnesota Medical School, who had been pulled from their classes or clinical rotations. Their mentors and teachers were putting in fifteen-hour hospital shifts, then waiting in long lines to buy diapers before going home to their kids. The students had rapidly assembled a group called the Minnesota COVIDSitters, which matched nearly three hundred volunteers with a hundred and fifty or so hospital workers—including custodians, cooks, and other essential employees. The students insured that volunteers had immunizations and background checks; they established closed rotations of three to five volunteers for each family in need. On the Zoom call, everyone was focused and eager, crisis adrenaline masking their fatigue. One student held a mellow, pink-cheeked infant on his shoulder.

Just a few days before, on Twitter, I had seen a photograph of a handwritten flyer[62] that a thirty-three-year-old woman named Maggie Connolly had posted in the Brooklyn neighborhood of Carroll Gardens, asking elderly neighbors to get in touch if they needed groceries or other help. Connolly, a hair-and-make-up artist, was newly out of work, and figured that many older people might not see aid efforts that were organized online. The picture of the sign got attention on the Internet, and Connolly ended up on the "Today" show; soon afterward, she began arranging pharmacy runs and wellness checks for her neighbors and getting e-mails from people around the world who'd been inspired to put up flyers of their own. "My mom's always told me that if I feel anxious and depressed I should think of how I can be of service to somebody," she told me. "Hopefully, when we control the virus a little bit more and get back to regular life, this will have been a wake-up call. I think people aren't used to being able to ask for help, and people aren't used to offering."

There's a certain kind of news story that is presented as heartwarming but actually evinces the ravages of American inequality under capitalism: the account of an eighth-grader who raised money to eliminate his classmates' lunch debt, or the report on a FedEx employee who walked twelve miles to and from work each day until her co-workers took up a collection to buy her a car. We can be so moved by the way people come together to overcome hardship that we lose sight of the fact that many of these hardships should not exist at all. In a recent article[63] for the journal *Social Text*, the lawyer and activist Dean Spade cites news reports about volunteer boat rescues during Hurricane Harvey which did not mention the mismanagement of government relief efforts, or identify the possible climatological causes of worsening hurricanes, or point out who suffers most in the wake of brutal storms. Conservative politicians can point to such stories, which ignore the social forces that determine the shape of our disasters, and insist that voluntarism is preferable to government programs.

A decade ago, the writer Rebecca Solnit published the book *A Paradise Built in Hell*[64], which argues that during collective disasters, the "suspension of the usual order and the failure of most systems" spur widespread acts of altruism—and these improvisations, Solnit suggests, can lead to lasting civic change. Among the examples Solnit cites are tenant groups that formed in Mexico City after a devastating earthquake, in 1985, and later played a role in the city's transition to a democratic government. Radicalizing moments accumulate; organizing and activism beget more organizing and activism. As I called individuals around the country who were setting up coronavirus-relief efforts, I kept encountering people who had participated in anti-globalization protests in the early two-thousands, or joined the Occupy movement, or organized grassroots campaigns in the aftermath of the 2016 Presidential election. In 2017, as wildfires ravaged Northern California, a collective of primarily disabled queer and trans people, who called themselves Mask Oakland, began giving out N95 masks to the homeless; in March and April, they donated thousands of masks that they had in reserve to local emergency rooms and clinics.

Radicalism has been at the heart of mutual aid since it was introduced as a political idea. In 1902, the Russian naturalist and anarcho-communist Peter Kropotkin—who was born a prince in 1842, got sent to prison in his early thirties for belonging to a banned intellectual society and spent the next forty years as a writer in Europe—published the book *Mutual Aid: A Factor of Evolution*[65]. Kropotkin identifies solidarity as an essential practice in the lives of swallows and marmots and primitive hunter-gatherers; cooperation, he argues, was what allowed people in medieval villages and nineteenth-century farming syndicates to survive. That inborn solidarity has been undermined, in his view, by the principle of private property and the work of state institutions. Even so, he maintains, mutual aid is "the necessary foundation of everyday life" in downtrodden communities and "the best guarantee of a still loftier evolution of our race."

Charitable organizations are typically governed hierarchically, with decisions informed by donors and board members. Mutual-aid projects tend to be shaped by volunteers and the recipients of services. Both mutual aid and charity address the effects of inequality, but mutual aid is aimed at root causes[66]—at the structures that created inequality in the first place. A few days after her conference call with Ocasio-Cortez, Mariame Kaba told me that mutual aid couldn't be divorced from political education and activism. "It's not community service—you're not doing service for service's sake," she said. "You're trying to address real material needs." If you fail to meet those needs, she added, you also fail to "build the relationships that are needed to push back on the state."

Kaba, a longtime Chicago activist who now lives in New York and runs the blog Prison Culture, describes herself as an abolitionist, not as an anarchist. She wants to create a world without prisons and policing, and that requires imagining other structures of accountability—and also of assistance. "I want us to act as if the state is not a protector and to be keenly aware of the damage it can do," she told me. People who are deeply committed to mutual aid think of it as a crucial, everyday practice, she said, not as a "program to pull off the shelf when shit gets bad."

Historically, in the United States, mutual-aid networks have proliferated mostly in communities that the state has chosen not to help. The peak of such organizing may have come in the late sixties and early seventies, when Street Transvestite Action Revolutionaries opened a shelter for homeless trans youth in New York, and the Black Panther Party started a free-breakfast program, which within its first year was feeding twenty thousand children in nineteen cities across the country. J. Edgar Hoover worried that the program would threaten "efforts by authorities to neutralize the BPP and destroy what it stands for"; a few years later, the federal government formalized its own breakfast program for public schools.

Crises can intensify the antagonism between the government and mutual-aid workers. Dozens of cities restrict community efforts to feed the homeless; in 2019, activists with No More Deaths, a group that leaves water and supplies in border-crossing corridors, were tried on federal charges, including driving in a wilderness area and "abandoning property." But disasters can also force otherwise opposing sides to work together. During Hurricane Sandy, the National Guard, in the face of government failure, relied on the help of an Occupy Wall Street offshoot, Occupy Sandy, to distribute supplies.

"Anarchists are not absolutist," Spade, the lawyer and activist, told me. "We can believe in a diversity of tactics. I spend my life fighting for people to get welfare benefits, for trans people to get health-care coverage." Kaba isn't doctrinaire, either; she had, after all, partnered with Ocasio-Cortez, a member of the federal government, to help people learn how to help one another. (Ocasio-Cortez, for her part, insisted, on Twitter, that organizers and activists, not politicians, are often the ones who "push society forward.") Still, there is a real tension between statist and anarchist theories of political change, Kaba pointed out. In trying to help a community meet its needs, one group of organizers might suggest canvassing for political candidates who support Medicare for All. Another might argue that electoral politics, with its top-down structures and its uncertain results, is the wrong place to direct most of one's energy—that we should focus instead on building community co-ops that can secure health care and opportunities for work. But sorting out the conflict between these visions is part of the larger project, Kaba suggested, and a task for multiple generations. The day-to-day practice of mutual aid is simpler. It is a matter, she said, of "prefiguring the world in which you want to live."

By April, as the death toll rose in New York City, many people I knew in Brooklyn had begun working with a mutual-aid group called Bed-Stuy Strong[67], which serves the neighborhood of Bedford-Stuyvesant. Once predominantly Black, the neighborhood has, in the past few decades, seen an influx of White residents. Bed-Stuy Strong was started by the writer Sarah Thankam Mathews, whose family moved to the United States from Oman when she was seventeen. Mathews organized the group on Slack, and it initially consisted of the Slack demographic: relatively privileged youngish people familiar with the digital workflows of white-collar offices. But volunteers plastered the neighborhood with flyers, and word of the group started to spread through phone calls and text messages. Hundreds of people began joining every day.

James Lipscomb, a former computer programmer in his sixties, who moved to Bed-Stuy from South Carolina when he was a teenager, learned about the group on Facebook—an acquaintance had called the organization's Google Voice number, then written a post wondering if the whole thing was a scam. Lipscomb, who survived polio at age four, after spending months in an iron lung, has limited mobility, and lives alone. He had friends who were already sick with the coronavirus, and he knew that he should stay inside. Not long after he saw the Facebook post, a friend phoned him and said, "James, call this number. They'll get your food." He left Bed-Stuy Strong a voice mail, and someone called him back a few hours later. The next day, a volunteer arrived in his lobby with three bags of groceries. "I looked at everything and was like a kid at Christmas," he told me. (He described himself as a "halfway decent cook," with special skills in the chili arena.) Lipscomb is a longtime member of the Bed-Stuy chapter of Lions Club International, the first Black chapter in New York State. He told the club members about his experience, and the club donated two hundred dollars to Bed-Stuy Strong. He also went back to the person who had written the skeptical Facebook post, he told me. "And I said, 'Look, this group is the best-kept secret going now!' "

When I first spoke with Mathews, she quickly pointed out that other local groups—such as Equality for Flatbush, which organizes against unjust policing and housing displacement—had been "doing the work for much longer." She told me that she didn't want to raise her hand and say, "Look, we're new, we're so shiny, we're on Slack!" The organization's strictly local focus reflects a principle of many mutual-aid groups: that neighbors are best situated to help neighbors. Ocasio-Cortez's team, after the conference call, distributed a guide[68] hashtagged #WeGotOurBlock, with instructions for building a neighborhood "pod" by starting with groups of five to twenty people, drawing on ideas popularized by the Bay Area Transformative Justice Collective. The idea of "pod-mapping," according to one of the group's founders, Mia Mingus, is to build lasting networks of support, rather than indulge in "fantasies of a giant, magical community response, filled with people we only had surface relationships with."

Mingus, a disability activist who was born in Korea and brought up by a White couple in the U.S. Virgin Islands, told me that she'd been spending her days checking in on her pod, dropping off food and supplies for people, and her nights reading articles about layoffs and hospitalizations and new mutual-aid groups. She felt, she said, like the earth was moving beneath her feet. More people were recognizing that the problems Americans were facing weren't caused just by the virus but by a health-care system that ties insurance to employment and a minimum wage so low that essential workers can't save for the emergencies through which they will be asked to sustain the rest of the country. She'd learned, after years of organizing, that, in some ways, people are attracted to crisis—to letting problems escalate until they're forced to spring into action. "Pods give us the structure to deal with smaller harms," she said. "And we have to deal with smaller harms, or this is where we end up."

Mathews told me that Bed-Stuy Strong was trying to plan for coming hardships that the government would also probably fail to adequately address. Unemployment would skyrocket in the neighborhood, and community needs would evolve. She is committed to the chaos of collective decision-making; the group's discussions about operations and priorities happen publicly, with input from anyone who wants to contribute. There are no eligibility criteria for grocery recipients, other than Bed-Stuy residency. (A distinctive quality of mutual aid, in general contrast with charity and state services, is the absence of conditions for those who wish to receive help.)

Jackson Fratesi, a friend of mine in the neighborhood who used to oversee last-mile delivery operations for Walmart stores in New York and now helps run logistics for Bed-Stuy Strong, said, "We have guesses about what community needs will be in the future, but we also know that some of these needs will blindside us, and we're trying to prepare for that." He added, "And—who knows?—maybe one of the things we'll be blindsided by is the government actually doing a good job."

In her book *Good Neighbors: The Democracy of Everyday Life in America*[69], the Harvard political scientist Nancy L. Rosenblum considers the American fondness for acts of neighborly aid and cooperation, both in ordinary times, as with the pioneer practice of barn raising, and in periods of crisis. In Rosenblum's view, "there is little evidence that disaster generates an appetite for permanent, energetic civic engagement." On the contrary, "when government and politics disappear from view as they do, we are left with the not-so-innocuous fantasy of ungoverned reciprocity as the best and fully adequate society." She cites the daughter of Laura Ingalls Wilder, Rose Wilder Lane, who helped her mother craft classic narratives of neighborly kindness and became a libertarian[70] who opposed the New Deal and viewed Social Security as a Ponzi scheme.

I called Rosenblum to ask what she made of the current wave of ungoverned reciprocity. Disasters like this one, she said, have less to teach us about solidarity among neighbors than about our "need for a kind of nationwide solidarity—in other words, a social safety net." She went on, "If you look at these really big, all-enveloping things—climate change, a pandemic—and think they will be solved by citizen mobilization, it may be necessary to consider the possibility that these problems are actually going to be solved technocratically and politically, from the top down, that what you need are experts in government who are going to say, 'You just have to do this.' My own opinion is that you need both top-down and bottom-up." She continued, "But, still, the idea that what we need most, or only, is social solidarity, civic mobilization, neighborly virtue—it's not so."

Rosenblum, though, told me that she had noticed a difference between the mutual-aid groups that were forming in the wake of the coronavirus and the sorts of disaster-relief work that she had studied in the past. Because it had been clear from the beginning that the pandemic would last indefinitely, many groups had immediately begun thinking about long-term self-management, building volunteer infrastructures in order to get ahead of the worst of the crisis, and thinking about what could work for months rather than for days. "That's interesting," she said. "And I think it's new."

On Day Twelve of my self-isolation, I checked in with the Minnesota COVIDSitters. The governor there, Tim Walz, a Democrat, had mandated that health-care workers have access to free child care at school facilities, and I wanted to see how the government's efforts were changing the group's work. The COVIDSitters, like Bed-Stuy Strong, had been careful to coordinate with more established organizations, hoping to reduce redundancy and share resources. The group had funneled donations—many from health-care workers who wanted to pay their volunteer babysitters—toward homeless shelters and food banks.

There were some things that the group could do more easily than the state. Families "need a child-care center that operates in traditional M-F fashion, like school would," Londyn Robinson, one of the group's organizers, told me in an

e-mail, "and they also need a COVIDSitter-like option to fill in the cracks."
I had heard as much from Emily Fitzgerald, a nurse-midwife in Minnesota
who, when the coronavirus first hit the region, had been frantically running
child-care calculations, anticipating her team's change from twelve-hour shifts
to twenty-four-hour shifts. When she learned about COVIDSitters, she told
me, she became emotional. "You're just not expecting to be taken care of in that
way," she said. The Sitters were seeking at least three hundred and fifty new volunteers to support nearly a hundred unmatched families. At the end of March,
the group became a nonprofit corporation so that it could apply for state grants.
The Sitters had also shared their blueprint with more than a hundred and thirty
other med schools, thirty of which had set up operational sister groups.

Invisible Hands had also registered as a nonprofit, Liam Elkind told me
when we spoke again, in mid-April. Lawyers helped the group establish by-
laws, official titles, and oversight practices. The group had signed up twelve
thousand volunteers and taken about four thousand requests. It had also raised
fifty-seven thousand dollars for a subsidy program—whereby needy households could receive free weekly food baskets with staples such as milk, bread,
and eggs—but it had suspended the program after demand increased, making
it unsustainable. Money in reserve is going to administrative costs, such as
software, insurance, and legal fees. Elkind was still in Morningside Heights,
finishing the semester online. ("I have not prepared very well for my presen-
tation tomorrow on comm law," he told me.) Maggie Connolly, who put up
the handwritten sign in Carroll Gardens, had started working with Invisible
Hands, making grocery deliveries in her neighborhood. "I still love what I do
as a hair-and-makeup artist, and I can't wait to get back to work," she said. "But
this has really made me realize that I would like to shift more time into doing
work that serves others." She had raised money from people she knew who
were also out of work—photographers, stylists, models—to buy food boxes for
New York hospital staff.

On day twenty-two of self-isolation, I called Fratesi and Mathews, from
Bed-Stuy Strong, on Zoom. The group, they said, had signed up twenty-five
hundred volunteers, a third of whom were active in the group's Slack channel on a daily or near-daily basis, and a fifth of whom had signed up to shop
and make deliveries. Mathews hoped to sustain the network with the small
donations it was getting, most of which seemed to be coming from Bed-Stuy
residents and people who knew them. The group's tech and operations teams
had revamped the online system so that the most urgent requests—from people who'd been waiting the longest or who had explicitly said that their cup-
boards were bare—were continually resurfaced for delivery volunteers. "Oh,

Sarah, what do you think—should we have a second Google Voice number where we just give people a phone tree of other resources?" Fratesi asked at one point, thinking through logistics as I interviewed them. New York City had announced a daily free meal program, and other nonprofits were turning to coronavirus relief. We talked about whether mutual-aid work represented what the state ought to be doing, or what the state could never do properly, or maybe both. Three minutes after we finished our Zoom call, Bernie Sanders announced that he was suspending his Presidential campaign. "Our best-case scenario is that Biden wins????" Fratesi texted me. "DIRECT ACTION IT IS THEN, I GUESS." By the beginning of May, Bed-Stuy Strong had provided at least a week's worth of groceries to more than thirty-five hundred people in the neighborhood. The group had raised a hundred and forty thousand dollars and spent a hundred and twenty-seven thousand dollars on food and supplies, such as medicine. What was left would keep the group operating for another week.

All the organizers I spoke to expressed a version of the hope that, after we emerge from isolation, much more will seem possible, that we will expect more of ourselves and of one another, that we will be permanently struck by the way our actions depend on and affect people we may never see or know. But the differences among the many volunteer groups that had suddenly sprouted were already sharpening. Some crisis volunteers find their work encouragingly apolitical: neighbors helping neighbors. Some are growing even more committed to socialist or anarchist ideals. "Community itself is not a panacea for oppression," Kaba told me. "And if you think that this work is like programming a microwave, where an input leads to immediate output, that's capitalism speaking." It will be a loss, Spade told me, if mutual aid becomes vacated of political meaning at the moment that it begins to enter the mainstream—if we lose sight of the fundamental premise that, within its framework, we meet one another's needs not just to fix things in the moment but to identify and push back on the structures that make those needs so dire. "What happens when people get together to support one another is that people realize that there's more of us than there is of them," he said. "This moment is a powder keg."

The difficulty of sustaining this more radical vision was also becoming clear. Bed-Stuy Strong has one week of runway at a time. When I asked Rebecca Solnit about the evidence that disasters have prompted lasting civic changes, she pointed me to a number of specific organizations, and described their histories, but she also emphasized something less tangible, something she "heard over and over again from people," she said. "They discovered a sense of self and a sense of connection to the people and place around them that did not go away, and, though they went back to their jobs in a market economy and their homes, that changed perspective stayed with them and maybe manifested in subtler ways than a project." She added, "If we think of mutual aid as both a series of networks of resource and labor distribution and as an orientation, the former may become less necessary as 'normal' returns, but the latter may last."

The coronavirus has already ushered in changes that would have been called impossible in January: evictions have been suspended, undocumented farmworkers have been classified as essential, the Centers for Disease Control has proclaimed that coronavirus testing and treatment will be covered by insurance. There are those who will want to return to normal after this crisis, and there are those who will decide that what was regarded as normal before was itself the crisis. Among the activists I talked to in the past several weeks was a thirty-year-old named Jeff Sorensen, who was working with the Washtenaw County Mutual Aid group[71], which was first created to help students affected by the closure of the University of Michigan. Some activists in the group had been involved with an existing mutual-aid network in Ypsilanti, that was founded last year with long-term goals and radical principles in mind. Sorensen said that he was determined to be hopeful. "These things that are treated as ridiculous ideas," he told me, "we'll be able to say, 'It's not a ridiculous idea—it's what we did during that time.'"

Notes

1   https://www.tcpress.com/just-schools-9780807763193
2   https://www.kut.org/post/austin-teachers-ditch-syllabus-and-ask-students-do-what-they-can-when-they-can
3   https://www.facebook.com/sonia.lewis1/posts/10220917048571348?__tn__=K-R
4   https://www.jfklibrary.org/archives/other-resources/john-f-kennedy-speeches/indianapolis-in-19590412
5   http://www.pinyin.info/chinese/crisis.html
6   http://itre.cis.upenn.edu/~myl/languagelog/archives/004343.html
7   http://www.gaiafoundation.org/climate-change-resilience
8   https://www.huffpost.com/entry/how-to-boost-your-resilie_b_11017716
9   https://www.nytimes.com/2020/05/12/opinion/sunday/flint-inequality-race-coronavirus.html
10   http://resiliencethebook.com/
11   https://www.nytimes.com/2012/11/03/opinion/forget-sustainability-its-about-resilience.html
12   http://www.100resilientcities.org/resources/
13   https://www.centerforresilience.org/where-we-work/classroom
14   https://qz.com/656900/schools-are-finally-teaching-what-kids-need-to-be-successful-in-life/
15   https://news.fsu.edu/announcements/covid-19/2020/04/27/new-tools-for-building-student-resilience/
16   https://www.apa.org/topics/resilience
17   https://yaelmelamed.com/
18   https://hbr.org/podcast/2020/04/cultivating-resilience-in-a-pandemic
19   https://greatergood.berkeley.edu/article/item/three_ways_to_boost_your_resilience_as_a_parent
20   https://www.bouncebackproject.org/resilience/
21   https://www.publishersweekly.com/978-0-7679-1190-0
22   https://www.versobooks.com/books/2162-the-happiness-industry
23   https://canvas.upenn.edu/files/50415002/
     download?download_frd=1&verifier=WSxKBP22pPgBB1jOohFCpWIm3WQCAEqJknZuv6NT
24   http://www.ecologyandsociety.org/vol9/iss1/art1/

25   https://www.google.com/books/edition/Resilience/n90b-I0hgU8C?hl=en&gbpv=1&dq=resilience+bounce+back&printsec=frontcover
26   https://www.forbes.com/sites/jillgriffin/2019/03/27/resilience-the-key-ingredient-of-success/#38d0ccbb22c4
27   https://www.amanet.org/articles/resilience-the-secret-to-success/
28   https://hbr.org/2002/05/how-resilience-works
29   https://learningconnection.stanford.edu/resilience-project
30   https://www.youtube.com/watch?v=aAsGp4wz4yQ&feature=emb_title
31   https://www.youtube.com/watch?v=AzLeK7fe-OI&list=PLEnKK2QoIn5OiJXmv-SBY4dxv4i4T4mGd&index=36&t=0s
32   https://www.teenvogue.com/story/student-loan-strike-debt-collective
33   https://cfe.umich.edu/three-reasons-that-flint-is-michigans-most-resilient-city/
34   https://2012-2017.usaid.gov/news-information/frontlines/haitiwomen-development/most-resilient-people-earth-haiti-still-standing
35   https://frenchquarterbxb.com/2015/08/29/2-protests-on-levee-break-life/
36   https://themigrationist.net/2018/03/02/i-have-a-right-not-to-be-resilient-new-orleanians-of-color-remember-hurricane-katrina/
37   https://redesigningwellness.com/employee-resilience-training/
38   https://www.teenvogue.com/story/nurses-dont-want-to-be-called-heroes
39   https://catfishforlunch.wordpress.com/2012/08/31/the-next-person-who-talks-about-resilience-ill-gonna-stab-in-the-neck/
40   https://humanservices.hawaii.gov/wp-content/uploads/2020/04/4.13.20-Final-Cover-D2-Feminist-Economic-Recovery-D1.pdf
41   https://theintercept.com/2020/05/08/andrew-cuomo-eric-schmidt-coronavirus-tech-shock-doctrine/
42   https://www.theguardian.com/world/2020/may/20/jacinda-ardern-flags-four-day-working-week-as-way-to-rebuild-new-zealand-after-covid-19
43   https://www.theguardian.com/books/2019/dec/19/case-green-new-deal-ann-pettifor-on-fire-naomi-klein-review
44   https://www.nytimes.com/news-event/coronavirus
45   https://www.retroreport.org/
46   https://www.nytimes.com/interactive/2020/05/24/us/us-coronavirus-deaths-100000.html
47   https://www.nytimes.com/2020/05/27/us/larry-kramer-dead.html
48   https://www.nytimes.com/video/us/100000007215009/hiv-aids-coronavirus-video.html
49   https://www.retroreport.org/newsletters/
50   https://www.youtube.com/retroreport
51   https://twitter.com/RetroReport
52   https://itsgoingdown.org/c19-mutual-aid/
53   https://docs.google.com/forms/d/e/1FAIpQLSc7LLhYN243k6xFlmQH26lAN9EoRXgEQGrghbqL8Ttc1K8YNA/viewform
54   https://www.facebook.com/covid19mutualaid/
55   https://www.paypal.com/pools/c/8npG1wcuiJ
56   https://docs.google.com/document/d/18WYGoVlJuXYc3QFN1RABnARZlwDG3aLQsnNokl1KhZQ/mobilebasic?usp=gmail
57   https://www.gofundme.com/f/cinema-worker-solidarity-fund
58   https://www.gofundme.com/f/z6w8v5
59   https://charity.gofundme.com/o/en/campaign/nyc-street-vendor-covid-19-emergency-fund
60   https://www.instagram.com/serviceworkerscoalition/
61   https://www.nytimes.com/2020/03/23/opinion/coronavirus-aid-group.html
62   https://twitter.com/JessicaValenti/status/1238891511888183298
63   http://www.deanspade.net/wp-content/uploads/2020/03/Mutual-Aid-Article-Social-Text-Final.pdf
64   https://www.amazon.com/Paradise-Built-Hell-Extraordinary-Communities-ebook/dp/B003XQEVLM/?ots=1&tag=thneyo0f-20&linkCode=w50
65   https://theanarchistlibrary.org/library/petr-kropotkin-mutual-aid-a-factor-of-evolution
66   https://bigdoorbrigade.com/what-is-mutual-aid/
67   https://bedstuystrong.com/
68   https://www.ocasiocortez.com/we-got-our-block
69   https://www.newyorker.com/magazine/2016/11/07/red-neighbor-blue-neighbor
70   https://www.newyorker.com/books/page-turner/a-libertarian-house-on-the-prairie
71   https://www.facebook.com/groups/2424471741198383/about/

Part Nine

Making Connections: Understanding the Impacts of COVID-19

9.1

Instructional Resources

by Amber Acosta-Green & David Jonathon Jaulus

In an attempt to bridge the gap between aspiring academics, students, and the community at large, this chapter presents instructional materials to deepen the teaching and learning experience. The reflection questions and activities we present below are meant to serve as guideposts to foster a more robust understanding of the multiplicity of experiences during the pandemic.

PART 1: Grammars of Negation: Who Counts? Who is Erased?

1. Identify the various ways marginalized and vulnerable communities are at a higher risk of COVID-19 exposure and contraction.

2. Evaluate what it means to have underlying conditions that exacerbate the negative effects of COVID-19. What are the reforms or abolition tactics (wholesale institutional change) necessary to create equity across communities affected by COVID-19?

3. What are some potential strategies to better protect those most at risk, including underserved communities and frontline, essential healthcare workers?

4. How does the American experience compare with the experience of the pandemic in other parts of the world? Bal Sokhi-Bulley (1.5) describes how the colonial gaze has shaped the representation of immigrants who work in Leicester's garment district as 'dirty'. How has this colonial gaze

affected immigrants who have been disproportionately policed, surveilled, and blamed during the COVID-19 pandemic?

Activity: In small groups, discuss how the disparate racial, gender and socioeconomic class impacts of COVID-19 are tied to longer histories of systemic oppression (e.g., trans-Atlantic slave trade, settler colonialism, Jim Crow segregation). Make a clear connection to the current political landscape surrounding COVID-19.

PART 2: The Pandemic of Racism: Exposing the Racial Contract

1. Many of the chapters in this volume describe 'multiple pandemics' occurring simultaneously with the COVID-19 pandemic. How, for example, are the Black Lives Matter movement and racial uprisings connected to racist healthcare systems? How have the pandemics of structural racism and White supremacy shaped racial disparities in both experiences of and outcomes of COVID-19?

2. In 2.3, Adam Serwer argues that the coronavirus "was an emergency until Trump found out who was dying." Further reflecting on what Elise A. Mitchell (1.1) describes as "American grammars of negation", whose experiences and lives have "counted" in this pandemic, and whose were erased?

3. Describe how anti-Asian xenophobia during the pandemic relates to the historical recurrence of "yellow peril."

4. What are the ways that tribal communities are responding to the pandemic, specific to the conditions of life in Indian country?

Activity: Several of the chapters in this section use the concept and experience of 'breath' to illuminate racialized experiences of COVID-19. What other metaphors or concepts could be used to reveal various experiences of COVID-19? What metaphors or concepts best describe your own experiences?

PART 3: Investments In Coronavirus Capitalism

1. Define disaster capitalism and the shock doctrine. How have pandemics and other forms of crisis, historically and currently, been used to forward policies that deepen inequalities and enrich elites? How has this played out in the current pandemic, and how have these new policies negatively impacted those who are most marginalized?

2. What does Will Bunch (3.2) mean by the term "disaster socialism"? How are forms of community organizing such as mutual aid helping respond to the pandemic?

3. In 3.6, Ian Liujia Tian uses the metaphor of "blood-soaked steam buns" to point to the vampiric effect of capitalism, and to remind us of how "the cost of feeling good is soaked in the corporeal sacrifices of the front-liners, those who cannot not work." How are the consumption practices of Americans during the COVID-19 pandemic linked to the health and safety of consumers and the workers who create goods and services?

Activity: Anne Helen Peterson, in 3.3, states that she "doesn't feel like buying stuff anymore." Take 5 minutes to reflect on your own consumption practices during the pandemic by responding to the following questions:

1. What did you spend more and/or less money on?

2. What has become less important to buy?

3. How has the pandemic changed your willingness to shop in-person?

4. How has the pandemic shaped your desire to consume?

5. Do you consider shopping as a form of patriotism or a civic duty?

PART 4: The Politics of Exposure and Protection

1. Discuss the attempts by governments and health authorities to protect essential workers. How did these attempts succeed or fail? What more could have been done?

2. Describe how the decision to wear a mask (or PPE) has become a political issue.

3. Consider the function of gender roles in a given society and how they inform individual experience and access to group opportunities. From a policy perspective, examine how to fundamentally alter the way we think about gender roles in ways that promote gender equity in the United States.

Activity: Feminist legal scholar Kimberlé Crenshaw coined the term "intersectionality" to describe how people's social identities—gender, class, race, ability, etc.—overlap. Analyze the pandemic from an intersectional perspective. What are the factors that complicate an individual's experience living through the pandemic? How has COVID-19 impacted individuals and communities in different ways?

PART 5: The Politics of Space

1. As Zuleyka Zevallos points out in 5.1, the public health response across nations has resurrected long-standing racial tensions around public housing and criminalizing particular communities. What are examples of how racial segregation has been historically perpetuated through space and place (e.g., racial residential segregation, redlining, discriminatory housing policies)? Assess the policies that were implemented (i.e., local, regional, national, global) to address the needs of "at-risk" individuals and communities during the pandemic.

2. How has COVID-19 impacted rates of domestic violence, and how have social service agencies and advocacy organizations responded? Consider the greater impacts on more vulnerable populations, such as the deaf and hard of hearing community.

3. Explain how the pandemic has further marginalized at-risk communities and individuals, especially those who cannot "shelter in place" or work from home.

Activity: Identify a video and/or TED talk that discusses unemployment, domestic violence, food insecurity, and/or housing instability due to COVID-19. Discuss what it means to be "safe" and/or "get back to normal." What stories and experiences are left out of this conversation?

PART 6: Ecologies of Justice

1. In 6.1, Sidney Fussell argues that "air is political." Define "environmental racism" and consider how residents of "sacrifice zones" are at greater risk for COVID-19 related health disparities.

2. As Beth Gardiner's interview with Elizabeth Yeampierre suggests in 6.3, environmental racism reflects a "long, long history that is centered on capitalism and the extraction" of Black and Indigenous land and labor. How has the downturn in global economic production and consumption created both positive and negative environmental impacts? How are these impacts connected to this legacy of exploitative extraction?

3. Casey Berkovitz in 6.5 argues that, "Environmental racism is inseparable from racial segregation." What are the factors that link communities negatively impacted by racial residential segregation with greater environmental harms?

Activity: In small groups, identify the largest city that is geographically closest to you. Create a map of the city's neighborhoods and list the racial/ethnic make-up of the communities in those neighborhoods. Locate news stories and public health reports (if available) that describe how specific neighborhoods are more impacted by COVID-19. What is the connection between the environmental health of this neighborhood, its racial/ethnic makeup, and the rates and outcomes of coronavirus infections and deaths?

PART 7: Crises in Leadership: (Confronting) Nationalism and Populism

1. Describe the United States' response to COVID-19. Do you consider this response to be successful? If so, in what ways? If not, why not?

2. Define "American exceptionalism." How does Johann N. Neem (7.1) deploy this concept to critique the U.S. response to COVID-19?

3. Identify various strategies implemented by global leaders to combat COVID-19.

Activity: Choose two heads of state, one male and one female. Diagram each leader's response to COVID-19. Compare and contract these responses. What fundamental differences in responses might be attributed to perceived norms and values associated with gender differences?

PART 8: Narratives of Resilience

1. Describe ways that you have engaged in individual and/or collective self-care during the pandemic.

2. In 8.1 Carrie Sampson, Claudia Cervantes-Soon, Dawn M. Demps, Alexandria Estrella, and Lok-Sze Wong center BIPOC mothers' grief as unique in its expression of both personal loss and historical trauma. What are the lessons that all communities can glean from these experiences to create pathways for coping and healing?

3. Mara Dolan describes Hawaii's feminist plan in 8.3. What makes this plan explicitly "feminist"? How does it benefit communities that have been

typically marginalized? What other policies may be compatible with this form of sustainable economic recovery?

Activity: Consider the links between the COVID-19 pandemic of 2020 and the HIV/AIDS epidemic over 30 years ago, particularly since Dr. Anthony Fauci served as the public health leader during both crises. Discuss the similarities and differences between those most affected by HIV/AIDS and those impacted by COVID-19? Why is early response so important in dealing with pandemics? What are the lessons to be learned from the social movement responses to the HIV/AIDS crisis (e.g., ACT UP) in solidifying communities of care to support individuals most deeply impacted?

About the Contributors

Amber Acosta-Green, a graduate student in the school of Social Transformation at Arizona State University, earned her Bachelor's and Master's degree in Human Communication. Ten years of teaching at the Community College level contributes to her pedagogical experience. Her research interests include radical mothering and other mothering utilizing a feminist and intersectional lens.

Olugbenga Ajilore is a senior economist at Center for American Progress. His expertise includes regional economic development, macroeconomic policy, and diversity and inclusion. He has testified in front of Congress and has been featured in *The New York Times* and *The Washington Post*.

Lisa M. Anderson is an Associate Professor of Women and Gender Studies and African and African American Studies in the School of Social Transformation at Arizona State University. Her research focuses on issues of representation of race and gender in literature and popular culture.

Matt Apuzzo is a two-time Pulitzer Prize-winning reporter based in Brussels. He joined *The New York Times* in 2014 after 11 years with The Associated Press. Before joining the international staff, he spent more than a decade in Washington covering law enforcement and security matters. He co-authored *Enemies Within* and teaches journalism at Georgetown University.

Casey Berkovitz is Senior Communications Associate at The Century Foundation. He previously worked in local political organizing focusing on issues including affordable housing, education, and racial and environmental justice. Casey holds a Bachelor's degree in History and Media Studies from the University of California, Berkeley.

Scheherazade Bloul is Director at the Australian Middle East Journalism Exchange, and received a PhD scholarship for the UNESCO Chair in comparative research on Cultural Diversity and Social Justice at Deakin University. Her work explores the intersections of social media, news media, and political participation among youth in post-2011 North Africa.

Rhea W. Boyd is an American pediatrician and child and community health advocate. Boyd is a popular science communicator, making use of social media to amplify a diverse range of voices in an effort to improve the health of communities of color.

Will Bunch is the national opinion columnist for the *Philadelphia Inquirer*, with some strong opinions about what's happening in America around social injustice, income inequality, and especially, Donald Trump. He is author of *Tear Down this Myth*, *The Backlash*, and *The Bern Identity*.

Chelsey Carter is an MPH/PhD candidate in Anthropology at Washington University, St. Louis. Her research examines the intersections of race, class, gender, and chronic illness in the United States. Her work also considers how anti-Black racism stifles health and promotes health inequities for Black people.

Claudia Cervantes-Soon is an Associate Professor in the Mary Lou Fulton Teachers College at Arizona State University. Situated at the intersections of educational anthropology, critical pedagogy, bilingual education, and Chicana/Latina feminisms, her work examines the interplay of sociocultural factors including race, class, gender, language, and citizenship/immigrant constructs in educational contexts.

Dawn M. Demps is a PhD student in the Mary Lou Fulton Teachers College at Arizona State University. A lifelong long community advocate, she uses her own lived experiences to understand how youth can feel disconnected from their elders and the community, and to conceptualize the devices needed to keep them anchored to success.

Mara Dolan works on climate and gender justice research and advocacy at the Women's Environment and Development Organization, focusing on policy change envisioned by the Feminist Agenda for a Green New Deal. Her work has been published in *The Nation*, *Teen Vogue*, *Bitch Media*, and other outlets.

Alexandria T. Estrella is a Clinical Assistant Professor in the Mary Lou Fulton Teachers College at Arizona State University. Her research interests involve literacy development among students from non-dominant communities and

English learners. She focuses on aspects of policy and classroom practices that impact the experiences of culturally and linguistically diverse learners.

Francis Fukuyama is Olivier Nomellini Senior Fellow at Stanford University's Freeman Spogli Institute for International Studies, Mosbacher Director of FSI's Center on Democracy, Development, and the Rule of Law, and Director of Stanford's Master's in International Policy Program. He has written widely on issues in development and international politics.

Sidney Fussell is a senior staff writer at *WIRED* covering surveillance, ad tech, and Silicon Valley's social and political impact. He was formerly a staff writer at *The Atlantic*. He is based in San Francisco.

Beth Gardiner is a journalist and the author of *Choked: Life and Breath in the Age of Air Pollution*. Her work has appeared in publications including *The New York Times*, *The Guardian*, *National Geographic*, and *Smithsonian*, and she is a former longtime Associated Press reporter.

Robert Gebeloff has worked as a data projects reporter for *The New York Times* since 2008 and has taught data journalism for many years in newsrooms and at conferences. He works on in-depth stories where numbers help augment traditional reporting.

Selam Gebrekidan is an investigative reporter for *The New York Times* based in London. She previously was a data and enterprise reporter for Reuters where she wrote about migration to Europe and the war in Yemen, among other stories. She has also covered U.S. oil markets.

Sujatha Gidla is an Indian-American author best known for her book *Ants Among Elephants: An Untouchable Family and the Making of Modern India*. Born in Andhra Pradesh, India, she now lives in New York where she is a Metropolitan Transportation Authority conductor.

Kadia Goba is a political reporter for *BuzzFeed News* and is based in Washington, DC, whre she covers the US Congress and national politics. In 2018 she was awarded the Pulitzer Center's Crisis Reporting Fellowship, which sponsored her travels to Sierra Leone, West Africa to report on environmental strategies.

Clyde Haberman is an American journalist who has contributed to *The New York Times* in various capacities since 1977. He spent nearly 13 years as a foreign correspondent based in Tokyo, Rome and Jerusalem. His stories included everything from pro-democracy uprisings in South Korea to the overthrow of Ferdinand Marcos in the Philippines.

Robert Hamwey is an Economic Affairs Officer with the United Nations Conference on Trade and Development (UNCTAD). His current research centers on ways to ensure trade resilience in the presence of near- and long-term climate change impacts affecting small island states.

Rachel R. Hardeman is an Associate Professor in the Division of Health Policy and Management at the University of Minnesota. She leverages the frameworks of critical race theory and reproductive justice to inform her equity-centered work, which aims to build the empirical evidence of racism's impact on health, particulary for Black birthing people and their babies.

Christine L. Holman, Senior Lecturer in Justice and Social Inquiry (JSI), teaches diverse courses both in-person/online throughout ASU's School of Social Transformation. She also designed/facilitated the School's Graduate Teaching Development Program, and serves as the faculty advisor for ASU's Amnesty International student group as well as JSI's Barrett Honors students.

Shakira Hussein is a research fellow at the University of Melbourne's Asia Institute. She is a regular commentator on issues of gender, Islam, and multiculturalism, and is the author of *From Victims to Suspects: Muslim Women Since 9/11*. She lives in Victoria, Australia.

David Jonathon Jaulus is a second year Justice Studies Doctoral student at ASU. He earned his BA from UC Berkeley in American Studies and his MA in Political Science From San Francisco State University. His research interests revolve around ending the carceral state in America from an intersectional perspective that has its roots from below and to the left.

Akilah Johnson is a narrative health care reporter at *ProPublica*, covering the intersection of people, politics, and policy in health care. She shared a Pulitzer Prize for coverage of the 2013 Boston Marathon bombing and was a Pulitzer finalist as a member of *The Boston Globe*'s Spotlight Team investigation into racism in Boston.

Peter Lawrence Kane is a freelance writer based in San Francisco who writes for *The Guardian*, *SF Gate* and the *Daily Mirror*. His work has also appeared in *SF Weekly*, *Salon*, *VICE*, *MSN*, and *The Bold Italic*.

Sarah Katz is a disability rights journalist and writer whose work has appeared in *The Guardian, The New York Times, Slate,* and *The Washington Post.* She has worked as editor at The Deaf Poets Society, which she co-founded in 2016, Poet Lore, and The Writer's Chronicle.

Ibram X. Kendi is a contributing writer at *The Atlantic* and the Andrew W. Mellon Professor in the Humanities and the Director of the Boston University Center for Antiracist Research. He is the author of several books, including the National Book Award-winning *Stamped from the Beginning: The Definitive History of Racist Ideas in America* and the *New York Times* bestseller *How to Be an Anti-Racist.*

David D. Kirkpatrick is an international correspondent for *The New York Times* and author of *Into the Hands of the Soldiers: Freedom and Chaos in Egypt and the Middle East.* He was part of a team that won a Pulitzer Prize in 2020 for international reporting for coverage of covert Russian interference in the politics of other governments.

Samantha Klein is a Master's student in the School of Marine and Environmental Affairs, University of Washington. She is passionate about studying the impacts of coastal development on near-shore marine ecosystems and the communities that depend on them. She is deeply inspired by grassroots land justice and environmental justice movements in Hong Kong.

Kai Kline is currently a PhD student in Counseling Psychology at Arizona State University and a graduate research assistant at the Center for Gender Equity in Science and Technology. His research and clinical work focus on addressing and fighting oppression, increasing equity, and active advocacy work with various marginalized communities.

John Patrick Leary is a columnist at *The New Republic* and author of *Keywords: The New Language of Capitalism.* His writing has also appeared in *Guernica, The New Inquiry,* and *The Baffler.*

Karen J. Leong is an Associate Professor of Women and Gender Studies and Asian Pacific American Studies in the School of Social Transformation at Arizona State University. She is committed to interdisciplinary research that explores how inequalities of power are reproduced and resisted in our institutions, communities, and every day interactions.

Julia Marcus is an infectious disease epidemiologist and Assistant Professor in the Department of Population Medicine at Harvard Medical School. Her research focuses on improving the implementation of preexposure prophylaxis to prevent new HIV infections and promote sexual health. She also contributes op-eds on current events, including articles in *The Atlantic* on public health communication during the coronavirus pandemic.

Connor Maxwell is a Senior Policy Analyst for Race and Ethnicity Policy at the Center for American Progress in Washington, DC. His work focuses on criminal justice, racial justice, diversity, and inclusion issues.

Lydia McInnes (she/her/hers) is a second-year Gender Studies PhD student and graduate research assistant at Arizona State University's Center for Gender Equity in Science and Technology with research interests in feminist media/ game studies and the potential intersections between video games and social justice initiatives.

Eduardo M. Medina is a family physician in Minneapolis, MN and is affiliated with Park Nicollet Methodist Hospital. He received his medical degree from University of Minnesota Medical School and specializes in public health, health equity, social determinants of health, community health and empowerment, and chronic disease management.

Alessandra Mezzadri is Senior Lecturer in Development Studies, SOAS, University of London. She writes and teaches on issues related to inequality and trade; global commodity chains and production networks; labour informality, informalisation and labour regimes; global labour standards, CSR and Modern Slavery; and feminisms in development.

Elise A. Mitchell is a fellow at the McNeil Center for Early American Studies and a doctoral candidate in the Department of History at New York University, specializing in Atlantic World and Caribbean and Latin American History. Her writing has appeared in *Black Perspectives*, *The Atlantic*, and the forthcoming volume, *Medicine and Healing in the Age of Slavery*.

Amber Jamilla Musser is an Associate Professor in the Department of American Studies at The George Washington University. She has published widely on race and critical theory, queer femininities and race, race and sexuality, and queer of color critique. She recently published *Sensual Excess: Queer Femininity and Brown Jouissance*.

Johann N. Neem is author, most recently, of *What's the Point of College? Seeking Purpose in an Age of Reform* and co-editor of *Jeffersonians in Power: The Rhetoric* *of Opposition Meets the Realities of Governing*. He teaches history at Western Washington University.

Gabriella Onikoro-Arkell is a Ph.D. student at Arizona State University in Gender Studies in the School of Social Transformation. Her research focuses on affect and emotional labor in Black women's media.

Eduardo Ortiz-Juarez is a Ph.D. candidate in Development Studies King's College, London and a non-resident research associate at the Commitment to Equity Institute (CEQ) at Tulane University. He is a Mexican economist with particular interests in poverty, inequalities, human development, and fiscal and social policies in developing countries.

Anne Helen Peterson is an American writer and journalist based in Missoula, Montana. She works as a Senior Culture Writer for *BuzzFeed News*. She earned a PhD in media studies from the University of Texas, where she studied the industrial history of the gossip industry.

Campbell Robertson, based in New Orleans, is a national correspondent for *The New York Times*.

Ana Santos Rutschman is an Assistant Professor at Saint Louis University School of Law. She has published and presented widely on topics related to health law, intellectual property, innovation in the life sciences, and law and technology. Her book, *Vaccines as Technology: Innovation, Barriers and the Public Interest*, is under contract with Cambridge University Press.

Kanchana N. Ruwanpura is Reader in Development Geography at the Institute of Geography, University of Edinburgh. She held leadership roles within the University of Edinburgh as Co-Director of the Centre for South Asian Studies (2015-2018) and Director of the MSc programme in Environment and Development (2013-2019).

Carrie Sampson is a mother-scholar and an Assistant Professor in the Mary Lou Fulton Teachers College, Arizona State University. Her research focuses on educational leadership, policy, and equity from three interrelated perspectives—democracy, community advocacy, and politics, as she explores school boards, school desegregation, English learners, and community organizing in education.

Jennifer A. Sandlin is a Professor in the School of Social Transformation at Arizona State University. Her research focuses on the intersections of education, learning, and consumption, and on understanding and theorizing public pedagogy. She currently seeks to understand public pedagogies in the context of the pandemic, including how conspiracy pedagogies operate.

Ezelle Sanford, III is a Postdoctoral Research Associate in the Program on Race, Science, and Society in the Center for Africana Studies at The University of Pennsylvania. He specializes in the history of modern medicine and public health, African American history, and twentieth-century United States history.

Christine Schwobel-Patel is an Associate Professor at the University of Warwick's School of law. Her research focuses on international law, global constitutionalism, global governance, and critical pedagogy. She adopts a critical approach to the dominant framing of mass atrocity, humanitarianism, and legal institutions through the lens of political economy and aesthetics.

Yasmeen Serhan is a London-based staff writer at *The Atlantic*, where she covers populism and nationalism. She's appeared on many news shows and podcasts, including BBC News, CTV News Channel, KQED Forum, *Ring of Fire*, and *Power Corrupts*. She is a committee member of the Foreign Press Association, and serves as Honorary Secretary.

Adam Serwer is a staff writer at *The Atlantic*, where he covers politics. He has received awards from the National Association of Black Journalists, *The Root*, and the Society of Professional Journalists. He was named a Spring 2019 Shorenstein Center fellow.

Katherine Shonk is a fiction writer and editor based in Evanston, Illinois. She is the author of *Happy Now?* and *The Red Passport*. Her writing has appeared in *Tin House*, *The Georgia Review*, *The Chicago Tribune*, and elsewhere. She has worked long-distance for many years as a writer and editor for Harvard University.

Sharon Henderson Singer is a member of the Diné (Navajo Nation) and a Postdoctoral Research Fellow at the Center for Gender Equity in Science and Technology at Arizona State University. Her research and expertise include Indigenous feminism in education, curriculum and instruction, and Indigenous Knowledge Systems in STEM.

Mary L. Smith is an Assistant Professor of Computer Science at Hawaii Pacific University (HPU). She has been an information systems professional for more than twenty-three years and has taught in Information Systems graduate courses for twelve years. Prior to HPU, she taught at St. Edwards University and Concordia University where she served as Computer Science Chair.

Bal Sokhi-Bulley is Senior Lecturer in Law and Critical Theory, School of Law, Politics, and Sociology, University of Sussex, where she teaches and writes about human rights, critical legal theory, and critical methodologies. She uses poststructural, postcolonial, and feminist approaches to explore alternative narratives to rights discourses.

Marie Solis is a New York City-based writer and reporter. She is staff writer at *VICE*, with a focus on abortion pills (used in a clinic or on one's own). Her writing has also appeared in *Newsweek, Teen Vogue, Glamour, The Awl,* and other publications.

Jessica Solyom is an Assistant Research Professor in the School of Social Transformation and the former Associate Director of the Center for Gender Equity in Science and Technology at Arizona State University. She is the co-creator of CGEST's *CompuGirls Hawaii: Cybersecurity* program and has published on culturally responsive teaching and education justice.

David Omotoso Stovall is Professor of Black Studies and Criminology, Law, & Justice at the University of Illinois at Chicago. His scholarship investigates: 1) Critical Race Theory, 2) the relationship between housing and education, and 3) the intersection of race, place, and school. Bringing theory to action, he works with community members to address issues of equity, justice, and abolishing the school/prison nexus.

Luciana Téllez-Chávez is an Environment and Human Rights researcher for Human Rights Watch. Her research and advocacy have dealt with violent repression of dissent, judicial harassment and violence against environmental defenders, workers' exposure to toxics, water contamination and labor rights violations in the context of oil exploration, mining, illegal logging and industrial agriculture.

Claire Elise Thompson is an editorial intern at *Grist*. She has a master's degree in Environmental Communication and has published stories in *Stanford Magazine, Peninsula Press,* and KQED's *Bay Curious*. Food and farming are two of her favorite subjects in writing, photography, and film.

Ian Liujia Tian is a PhD Candidate in Women and Gender Studies at the University of Toronto. He studies social movements and the pedagogies emerging through activist sensibilities. He engages with themes of socialist and transnational feminism, post-socialism, queer Asian studies and queer

Marxism, paying particular attention to affect, desire, and resistance of the everyday.

Jia Tolentino is a staff writer at *The New Yorker* whose recent work includes an exploration of youth vaping and essays on the ongoing cultural reckoning about sexual assault. Her criticism has appeared in *Grantland*, *The Awl*, *Pitchfork*, *Time*, and *Slate*. Her first book, the essay collection *Trick Mirror*, was published in 2019.

Katharine Viner is a British journalist and playwright. She became the first female editor-in-chief of *The Guardian* in June 2015. She joined *The Guardian* as a writer in 1997; was appointed deputy editor of *The Guardian* in 2008; launched the award-winning *Guardian Australia* in 2013; and was also editor of *Guardian US*, based in New York.

Michelle McGibbney Vlahoulis is a Senior Lecturer and faculty head of Women and Gender Studies at Arizona State University. Her research and teaching interests include online teaching and pedagogy, and gender and popular culture through a feminist lens. She is a contributing editor for *Ms.* Magazine's *Ms. In the Classroom* and serves on the *Ms.* Committee of Scholars.

Mako Fitts Ward is Assistant Professor in the School of Social Transformation at Arizona State University. Her work explores hip hop cultural production and its impacts on social movements. She has published in a range of academic journals, edited volumes, and news blogs.

Jennifer Weiss-Wolf is vice president and women and democracy fellow of the Brennan Center for Justice at NYU Law. Her 2017 book *Periods Gone Public: Taking a Stand for Menstrual Equity* was lauded by Gloria Steinem as "the beginning of liberation for us all." A regular contributor to *Ms.* and *Newsweek*, Weiss-Wolf's writing has appeared in *The New York Times*, *Los Angeles Times*, *Cosmopolitan*, *Harper's Bazaar*, and *Teen Vogue*, among others.

Daniel Wilkinson is Acting Director, Environment and Human Rights, at Human Rights Watch. He has conducted fieldwork and advocacy throughout Latin America, and authored reports on human rights issues—including the persecution of environmental defenders—in Brazil, Colombia, Cuba, Ecuador, Guatemala, Mexico, the United States, and Venezuela.

Lok-Sze Wong is a Postdoctoral Research Scholar in the Mary Lou Fulton Teachers College at Arizona State University. She is a policy scholar who draws upon educational, sociocultural, and organizational theories and mixed methods to unpack how systems (re)produce inequities and how to humanely reform schools and districts as complex social systems.

Erika T. Wurth's publications include two novels, *Crazy Horse's Girlfriend* and *You Who Enter Here*, two collections of poetry and a collection of short stories, *Buckskin Cocaine*. A writer of fiction, nonfiction, and poetry, she teaches creative writing at Western Illinois University.

Aggie J. Yellow Horse is a Korean American social demographer and a faculty in Asian Pacific American Studies and Justice and Social Inquiry at Arizona State University. Dr. Yellow Horse is committed to generating empirical "evidence" to eliminate the racial and ethnic reproductive and sexual health inequalities.

Zuleyka Zevallos holds a PhD in Sociology and has 20 years' experience in research, policy and consultancy. She works as a senior policy researcher and began her career as an academic before working in government, business and not-for-profits leading interdisciplinary research teams.

PERMISSIONS

The cover art was created by Jorge Lucero, https://www.jorgelucero.com, copyright, 2020. Printed by permission of the artist.

1.1, Elise A. Mitchell, 'If Bitterness Were a Whetstone': On Grief, History, and COVID-19. https://www.aaihs.org/if-bitterness-were-a-whetstone-on-grief-history-and-covid-19/, African American Intellectual History Association, copyright, 2020. Reprinted by permission of the publisher.

1.2, Eduardo Ortiz-Juarez, Coronavirus is Pushing People into Poverty—But Temporary Basic Income Can Stop This. https://theconversation.com/coronavirus-is-pushing-people-into-poverty-but-temporary-basic-income-can-stop-this-143545, *The Conversation*, copyright 2020. Reprinted by permission of the publisher.

1.3, Yasmeen Serhan, What the Coronavirus Proved About Homelessness. https://www.theatlantic.com/international/archive/2020/07/what-coronavirus-proved-about-homelessness/614266/, *The Atlantic*, copyright, 2020. Reprinted by permission of the publisher.

1.5, Bal Sokhi-Bulley, From Exotic to 'Dirty': How the Pandemic has Re-Colonised Leicester. https://discoversociety.org/2020/07/16/from-exotic-to-dirty-how-the-pandemic-has-re-colonised-leicester/, *Discover Society*, copyright, 2020. Reprinted by permission of the author.

1.6, Chelsey Carter & Ezelle Sanford, III, The Myth of Black Immunity: Racialized Disease During the COVID-19 Pandemic. https://www.aaihs.org/racializeddiseaseandpandemic/, African American Intellectual History Association, copyright, 2020. Reprinted by permission of the publisher.

1.7, Akilah Johnson, On the Minds of Black Lives Matter Protestors: A Racist Health System. https://www.propublica.org/article/on-the-minds-of-black-lives-matters-protestors-a-racist-health-system, *ProPublica*, copyright, 2020. Reprinted by permission of the publisher.

2.1, Amber Jamilla Muser, Sweat. https://socialtextjournal.org/periscope_article/sweat/, *Social Text Online*, copyright, 2020. Reprinted by permission of the author.

2.3, Adam Serwer, The Coronavirus Was an Emergency Until Trump Found Out Who Was Dying. https://www.theatlantic.com/ideas/archive/2020/05/americas-racial-contract-showing/611389/, *The Atlantic*, copyright, 2020. Reprinted by permission of the publisher.

2.4, Conner Maxwell, The Coronavirus is Worsening Racial Inequality. https://www.americanprogress.org/issues/race/news/2020/06/10/486095/coronavirus-crisis-worsening-racial-inequality/, Center for American Progress (online), copyright, 2020. Reprinted by permission of the publisher.

2.5, Aggie J. Yellow Horse & Karen J. Leong, Xenophobia, Anti-Asian Racism, and COVID-19. https://www.kzoo.edu/praxis/racism-and-covid/, *Praxis Center*, copyright, 2020. Reprinted by permission of the publisher.

2.6, Erika T. Wurth, Coronavirus is Triggering Historical Trauma—and Real Life Consequences—for Native Americans. https://www.bitchmedia.org/article/coronavirus-harming-native-american-communities, *Bitch Media*, copyright, 2020. Reprinted by permission of the publisher.

2.7, Ibram X. Kendi, Stop Blaming Black People for Dying of the Coronavirus. https://www.theatlantic.com/ideas/archive/2020/04/race-and-blame/609946/, *The Atlantic*, copyright, 2020. Reprinted by permission of the publisher.

2.8, Rachel R. Hardeman, Eduardo M. Medina, & Rhea W. Boyd, Stolen Breaths. https://www.nejm.org/doi/full/10.1056/NEJMp2021072, *The New England Journal of Medicine*, copyright, 2020. Reprinted by permission of the publisher.

3.1, Marie Solis, Coronavirus is the Perfect Disaster for 'Disaster Capitalism'. https://www.vice.com/en/article/5dmqyk/naomi-klein-interview-on-coronavirus-and-disaster-capitalism-shock-doctrine, VICE, copyright, 2020. Reprinted by permission of the publisher.

3.2, Will Bunch, 'Disaster Socialism': Will Coronavirus Crisis Finally Change How Americans See the Safety Net? https://www.inquirer.com/health/coronavirus/coronavirus-response-paid-sick-leave-safety-net-inequality-20200312.html, *The Philadelphia Inquirer*, copyright, 2020. Reprinted by permission of the publisher.

3.3, Anne Helen Peterson, I Don't Feel Like Buying Stuff Anymore. https://www.buzzfeednews.com/article/annehelenpetersen/recession-unemployment-covid-19-economy-consumer-spending, BuzzFeed, copyright, 2020. Reprinted by permission of the publisher.

3.4, Christine Schwobel-Patel, Compassionate Consumption: What Is It and Why It Won't Solve Society's Problems. https://www.teenvogue.com/story/what-is-compassionate-consumption, *Teen Vogue*, copyright, 2020. Reprinted by permission of the publisher.

3.5, Samantha Klein, Disaster Capitalism in the Wake of Coronavirus. https://smea.uw.edu/currents/disaster-capitalism-in-the-wake-of-coronavirus/, *Currents: A Student Blog*, copyright, 2020. Reprinted by permission of the author.

3.6, Ian Liujia Tian, Vampiric Affect: The Afterlife of a Metaphor in a Global Pandemic. https://socialtextjournal.org/periscope_article/vampiric-affect-the-afterlife-of-a-metaphor-in-a-global-pandemic/, *Social Text Online*, copyright, 2020. Reprinted by permission of the author.

4.1, Alessandra Mezzadri & Kanchana N. Ruwanpura, How Asia's Clothing Factories Switched to Making PPE—But Sweatshop Problems Live On. https://theconversation.com/how-asias-clothing-factories-switched-to-making-ppe-but-sweatshop-problems-live-on-141396, *The Conversation*, copyright, 2020. Reprinted by permission of the publisher.

4.2, Shakira Hussein & Scheherazade Bloul, What Lies Beneath? COVID-19 and the Racial Politics of Face Masks. https://www.abc.net.au/religion/coronavirus-and-the-racial-politics-of-face-masks/12454308, ABC (Australian Broadcasting Corporation), copyright, 2020. Reprinted by permission of the publisher.

8.1, Carrie Sampson, Claudia Cervantes-Soon, Dawn M. Demps, Alexandria Estrella, & Lok-Sze Wong. A Call from Mothers of Color for True Family Engagement. https://medium.com/a-call-from-black-and-brown-mothers-for-true/a-call-from-black-and-brown-mothers-for-true-family-engagement-bbfda3e7f72d, *Medium*, copyright, 2020. Reprinted by permission of the authors.

8.2, John Patrick Leary, Resilience is the Goal of Governments and Employers Who Expect People to Endure Crisis. https://www.teenvogue.com/story/whats-wrong-with-focus-on-resilience, *Teen Vogue*, copyright, 2020. Reprinted by permission of the publisher.

8.3, Mara Dolan, Hawaii Considers an Explicitly Feminist Plan for COVID-Era Economic Recovery. https://truthout.org/articles/hawaii-considers-an-explicitly-feminist-plan-for-covid-era-economic-recovery/, *Truthout*, copyright, 2020. Reprinted by permission of the publisher.

8.4, Katharine Viner, Naomi Klein: 'We Must Not Return to the Pre-Covid Status Quo, Only Worse'. https://www.theguardian.com/books/2020/jul/13/naomi-klein-we-must-not-return-to-the-pre-covid-status-quo-only-worse, *The Guardian*, copyright, 2020. Reprinted by permission of the publisher.

8.5, Clyde Haberman, How the Fight Against AIDS Can Inform the Fight Against Covid-19. https://www.nytimes.com/2020/07/02/us/coronavirus-fauci-aids-hiv.html, *The New York Times*, copyright, 2020. Reprinted by permission of the publisher.

8.6, Jia Tolentino, What Mutual Aid Can Do During a Pandemic. https://www.newyorker.com/magazine/2020/05/18/what-mutual-aid-can-do-during-a-pandemic, *The New Yorker*, copyright, 2020. Reprinted by permission of the publisher.

CPSIA information can be obtained
at www.ICGtesting.com
Printed in the USA
LVHW011556160821
695405LV00005B/561